Ronald Reagan

ALSO BY JOHN PATRICK DIGGINS

The Lost Soul of American Politics: Virtue, Self-Interest, and the Foundations of Liberalism

On Hallowed Ground: Abraham Lincoln and the Foundations of American History

Max Weber: Politics and the Spirit of Tragedy

Mussolini and Fascism: The View from America

The Bard of Savagery: Thorstein Veblen and Modern Social Theory

The Problem of Authority in America (editor)

The Liberal Persuasion: Arthur Schlesinger, Jr., and the Challenge of the American Past (editor)

Up from Communism: Conservative Odysseys in American Intellectual History

The Proud Decades: America in War and in Peace, 1941–1960

The Rise and Fall of the American Left

John Adams

The Portable John Adams (editor)

The Promise of Pragmatism: Modernism and the Crisis of Knowledge and Authority

Ronald Reagan

FATE, FREEDOM,

AND THE

MAKING OF HISTORY

John Patrick Diggins

W. W. Norton & Company
New York London

For information about permission to reproduce selections from this book,
write to Permissions, W. W. Norton & Company, Inc., 500 Fifth Avenue,
New York, NY 10110

Manufacturing by RR Donnelley, Harrisonburg, VA
Book design by Anna Oler

Library of Congress Cataloging-in-Publication Data

Diggins, John P.
Ronald Reagan : fate, freedom, and the making of history / John Patrick Diggins.—
1st ed.
p. cm.
Includes bibliographical references and index
ISBN-13: 978-0-393-06022-5 (hardcover)
ISBN-10: 0-393-06022-5 (hardcover)
1. Reagan, Ronald. 2. Reagan, Ronald—Political and social views. 3. Presidents—
United States—Biography. 4. United States—Politics and government—1981–1989.
5. Conservatism—United States—History—20th century. I. Title.
E877.D54 2007
973.927092—dc22
[B]   2006033974

W. W. Norton & Company, Inc.
500 Fifth Avenue, New York, N.Y. 10110
www.wwnorton.com

W. W. Norton & Company Ltd.
Castle House, 75/76 Wells Street, London W1T 3QT

1 2 3 4 5 6 7 8 9 0

To the Memory of

Raymond Aron, Theodore Draper, François Furet, Sidney Hook,
and the Honorable Senator Daniel Patrick Moynihan

Wise statesmanship, a ruling star
Made peace itself subserve the war.
—Herman Melville, 1888

The rarest thing of all in men who
have made history is greatness of soul.
—Jacob Burckhardt, 1852

———

Contents

Preface

MANY AMERICANS remember the death and funeral of Ronald Reagan more than his presidency (1981–1989). During early June 2004, the country mourned his passing and praised his character, and people were reminded that Reagan had been ailing with Alzheimer's for almost a dozen years. Ten years earlier, in November 1994, he had announced the disease in a handwritten letter to "My Fellow Americans" that was reprinted upon his death. Reagan sought to make the public aware of the need for research on Alzheimer's as well as other diseases. He wished he could spare his wife the "painful experience" of taking care of him. "When the time comes, I am confident that with your help she will face it with faith and courage." With death approaching, Reagan could only think that the America he loved would never die. "I now begin the journey that will lead me into the sunset of my life. I know for America there will always be a bright dawn ahead."

The recollection of Reagan's slow deterioration also raised a painful awareness of former first lady Nancy Reagan. In her seclusion in southern California, Mrs. Reagan remained heroically reticent. But eldest daughter Maureen, who succumbed to cancer in 2001, once told CNN's Judy Woodruff of home life during those trying years. Her father "makes it very easy for us," she noted, describing how Reagan, who could barely talk and remember what happened five minutes ago, went on walks and did what he was encouraged to do. "But the disease just gets worse every day. It never gets better." He rarely recognized Maureen, but she delighted when she saw her father smile and chuckle. "There's nothing nicer than the sound of his laughter." At the end of the funeral service, another daughter and two sons came together to support Nancy Reagan, who had awakened every morning to face another long day's journey of sorrow and pity.

A former president, a world leader, a person who valued autonomy and self-reliance, Reagan suffered from degenerative cognitive dementia that left him utterly dependent. The brain that once sought to bring "the path of love and peace" to the world was itself under attack, invaded by rogue genes and toxic nerve cells. The first lady bore it nobly, and the country sensed the meaning of tragedy and majesty. "Death and love are the two wings that bear the good man to heaven," wrote Michelangelo.

The late afternoon following the funeral ceremony, on June 11, 2004, provided the elegiac finale in Simi Valley, California, with the stately presidential library in the background, the sun going down over the blue Pacific, the band playing "America the Beautiful" and hailing a nation free "from sea to shining sea." The event was reminiscent of Walt Whitman bidding farewell to the "fallen star" Abraham Lincoln—"When lilacs last in the dooryard bloom'd." The death of Franklin D. Roosevelt, on April 12, 1945, had filled the nation with similar grief, and when some watched the funeral train slowly moving from Warm Springs, Georgia, to Washington, D.C., they thought of Lincoln's train making its way from the capital to Springfield, Illinois, and the poet crying, "Captain, my Captain!" Both Lincoln and Roosevelt had seen the country through five years of war. Reagan, in contrast, did everything to avoid a direct military confrontation, and he succeeded in settling the long, hazardous cold war through diplomatic means—the only modern American president to prevent a major war through patient dialogue and mutual trust. At the tense summit conferences of the 1980s, hope overcame fear under Reagan's confident leadership. Hope even burned brightly at the funeral. Those in attendance, and the millions watching on national television, heard Reagan's children speak poignantly of their father, and as Nancy Reagan leaned over to kiss the casket, a stillness came over the hillside and the tip of the orange sun spread and blazed, a last farewell

before sinking below the horizon. For many Americans, it was a death in
the family.

———

BUT NOT FOR all Americans. Some would never accept Reagan the
Republican conservative, and many more only wanted to hear about his
film career. During the week of his funeral, the media obliged with photos, reports, and reruns of his many movies. Reagan was likened to the
hero of *Mr. Smith Goes to Washington*, the story of a virtuous citizen who
arrives in the nation's corrupt capital to set things right. The film, starring Jimmy Stewart, did have a certain relevance for a president who in
his first inaugural address, in 1981, told us that government itself was
the problem of American political life. For many Americans, however,
Reagan the president would never escape from the portraits of his familiar movie roles: the handsome, trusting nice guy, a tilted head radiating
boyish charm, a smile beaming old-time values, and, in one film, spot-
lighting Reagan with a chimpanzee, an actor a little too silly for his own
good. Reagan's friends John Wayne and Humphrey Bogart gave the audience true grit and wily intelligence. Reagan's image was less clear, in print
and on film.

The books published during and shortly after his presidency were
generally negative, written in a derogatory tone aimed at diminishing his
stature. One was called *Sleepwalking Through History*, another *Our
Long National Daydream*, and a third *Ronald Reagan, the Movie*. Reagan
did have the author he deserved in Lou Cannon, the discerning journalist who treated his subject respectfully and with scrupulous fairness in
several editions of a comprehensive and definitive biography. A recent
major biography, Edmund Morris's long-awaited *Dutch*, aroused, however, more criticism of the author than of his subject, for Morris, a very
engaging writer, wove himself into the story and avoided addressing seriously the many issues confronting Reagan.

The most recent book is Richard Reeves's *President Reagan: The Triumph of Imagination*, an admirable study of the White House years.
Reagan had the imagination to envision a country without high taxes and
the bureaucratic state and a world without the threat of communism.
The author tackled a question that had intrigued Henry Adams. Does

the occupant of the White House make a difference in the political history of the country? Thus Reeves approached Reagan the way he dealt with John F. Kennedy and Richard M. Nixon in previous biographies, where the focus is on policy goals that the presidents have set for themselves and the challenge of implementing them.

My concern is not so much with implementation as conceptualization, the genesis of policy positions, where the ideas came from in the first place before they faded into the fog of politics and, in some cases, failed to be realized. Reagan's political philosophy was fully formed before he entered the White House, shaped by the emotions of his youth, the liberal religious outlook he inherited from his mother, the conservative economic philosophy he studied in college, the experiences of battling the Hollywood Reds, the influence of Whittaker Chambers, his horror at the thought of nuclear war, and, above all, his reaction to the most explosive decade of American history, the radical sixties generation. "It was like a flying saucer landed," recalled the bard Bob Dylan. "That's what the sixties were like." Dylan was, of course, referring to the wild and free counterculture, a saturnalia of subversion when everything was possible and it was forbidden to forbid. Amid the clamoring chaos, no one saw Reagan's landing on the political scene, not even the Republican Party, which had witnessed the devastating defeat of its presidential candidate Barry Goldwater in 1964.

To this day Ronald Reagan remains an image more visual than real, reportedly a screen star who paraded as president. A former actor given to role-playing and make-believe, he was, we are told, shallow, elusive, opaque, too blithely ignorant of his own ignorance to be an important president. The complainers complain too much. Reading Reagan's critics, one would think that the experienced politician is in possession of truth and enjoys a deeper sense of reality than the actor who supposedly lives in a world of illusion and distortion. But why should the actor be dismissed and the politician respected when both perform before an audience? The stage and screen deal not with truth but effect, and reality is little more than reputation; the very essence of democratic politics in servitude to public opinion and popularity. The politician no less than the actor can only succeed by mastering the art of persuasion in striving after ratings. Consistency may be the first casualty of politics, but the actor must behave in character with unwavering consistency to be convincing. Reagan's political character was entirely consistent, from the early moment when he fought communism in the 1940s to the climactic moment when he helped bring it to an end in the late 1980s. Those who complain that Reagan was vague and impossible to pin down were looking for his persona when they should have been looking at his politics.

The reputation of Ronald Reagan improved considerably after the recent publication of his letters, speeches, and radio transcripts, all revealing an intelligent, sensitive mind with passionate convictions. His reflective thoughts came as a surprise to me, however. When I was living in Berkeley in the 1960s, Governor Reagan stood for, at least on the campus, tear gas and police, and his presidency in the 1980s seemed little more than the age of avarice and its savings and loan scandals. My belated respect for the man grew from appreciating his boldness in dealing with the three miseries of the modern era—one terrifying, the other crippling, the third inhibiting.

The first abomination was a suicidal nuclear arms race of such potential massive destruction that it threatened the world with extinction; the second, an expanding welfare state that had made the poor helplessly dependent, reduced them to debilitating objects of pity, and destroyed any hope for self-esteem; the third, a joyless religious inheritance that told people their kingdom was not of this world and they needed to be careful about pursuing happiness in case they came to enjoy it. Reagan, it is now clear, delivered America from fear and loathing. He stood for freedom, peace, disarmament, self-reliance, earthly happiness, the dreams of the imagination and the desires of the heart. With the 1980s came America's "Emersonian moment," when people were told to trust not the state but the self and to pursue wealth and power without sin or shame. Far from being a conservative, Reagan was the great liberating spirit of modern American history, a political romantic impatient with the status quo.

Yet liberals and writers on the Left have always regarded Reagan as a lightweight. They viewed his spiritualization of capitalism as rank hypocrisy and his anticommunism as Hollywood machismo. Convinced that only politics could produce public-minded citizens, the Left dismissed economics as merely pecuniary. The Left blamed the economy with the same zeal as the Right blamed the government. No one dared to consider that the people might bear some responsibility for whatever was troubling America. Thus to the Left Reagan's policies concerning communism, the cold war, government, and the welfare state could only be propounded by one who had neither an intelligent mind nor a giving heart. Conservative writers, on the other hand, tended to concentrate on Reagan's speeches, savoring the words to find the key to his political philosophy and convinced that the capitalist can only be guiltless since private vices result in public benefits. In a curious way that is still not accepted by skeptics, the presidency of Ronald Reagan revived the study of intellectual history, for the historical era of the eighties so overflowed with think tanks and ideas it seemed there could be no policy without a set of beliefs or doctrines, no politics without a political theory. One obvious idea of the Reagan era was the idea of the free market. Conservatives, however, are also said to believe in authority, truth, virtue, order, religion, and the hallowed institutions of the past. One might think, then, that Reagan would honor conservatism and return America to its roots in religion and to the conservative ideas of the founding.

Reagan's orientation, however, was always toward the foreground, not the background, rather to what lay ahead and not what had gone before. He did read some of America's founding political and religious leaders, and he shared their conviction that the basis of a free government is liberty; but he would have grimaced on hearing their thoughts about the human condition. The Puritans and the framers of the Constitution maintained that we must see our errant selves as the problem, whereas Reagan inevitably saw government as the problem. Although many conservatives see religion, especially Christianity, as the bedrock of morality, Reagan's thoughts reveal no suggestion of the doctrines of Calvinism and original sin and the ideas of the framers and their sense of evil. James Madison told Americans that government is essential because not all men are "angels." Reagan told Americans that each and every one of them was a "hero." His own hero was Thomas Paine, the blasphemous rebel (Theodore Roosevelt called him a "filthy atheist") and popular writer of the revolutionary era. In 1789, after the framers completed the draft of the U.S. Constitution, stipulating the mechanisms of control to structure a government so it would have no need to go through another revolution, Paine was rushing off to Paris to plunge into another revolution. An irrepressible, permanent revolutionist, Paine saw freedom as the birth of the new and the death of the old. Valuing authority less, Paine loved liberty more. And Reagan never stopped admiring him for it.

When preparing for the Geneva summit conference in 1985, Reagan and his aides had composed a speech to deliver to Soviet leader Mikhail Gorbachev. "One of the early leaders of the revolution that gave birth to our country—Tom Paine—said, 'We have it in our power to begin the world over again.'" Gorbachev could well have thought the quasi anarchist Paine sounded a tad like Vladimir Ilyich Lenin. In *The State and Revolution*, the Bolshevik leader promised that the realization of freedom will bring forth the "withering away of the state." Reagan accepted completely the libertarian argument that the state poses a threat to liberty. Yet his hero Paine would languish in a Paris prison during the Reign of Terror, a victim not of a strong state but of a failed state. Throughout his presidency, Reagan wrote letters to private citizens telling them that people do not start wars, only governments do. But the bloody wars in eastern Europe broke out after the fall of communism, when there were no effective governments. Today wars erupt all over the world wherever there is no rule of law or a viable political regime. In the war against terrorism in the Mideast, the idea of "state building" had been dismissed by those who, like Paine, deluded themselves into thinking that freedom need not depend upon government, or, like Lenin, deceived others into thinking that freedom arises spontaneously and requires no conscious planning.

As the cold war was winding down, Gorbachev remarked that until he dealt with Reagan he had had no idea how much "the personal" mattered in world politics. Inculcated in the Marxist tradition, he believed that history happens "behind the backs of people," made by changes in the structure of society and driven by historical necessity rather than moral activity. Some American conservative thinkers also downplayed the role of the personal in history. Henry A. Kissinger, for example, thought Reagan was naïve to assume that it would take only "conversation" between the leaders of countries espousing two rival ideologies to reduce tensions and even alter the course of history. To many conservatives, history is determined by the struggle for power by forces aiming to dominate and prevail. Reagan, however, persisted in defying fate and taking control of events, in forcing history to fulfill its promise of freedom without going to war. "History is not predetermined," he told reporters when leaving for Geneva. "It is in our hands." His new diplomacy aimed to challenge a cold war stuck in endless stalemate. He felt the same way about domestic policy as he did about foreign policy. In his first inaugural address, he declared: "We are not, as some would have us believe, doomed to an inevitable decline. I do not believe in a fate that will fall on us no matter what we do. I do believe in a fate that will fall on us if we do nothing." In an age darkened by the shadow of fate, Reagan gave history a bright new birth of freedom.

One of the most inspiring political leaders in the second half of the twentieth century, Reagan was also one of the three great liberators in American history. Abraham Lincoln helped emancipate African Americans from slavery; Franklin D. Roosevelt helped wrest Western Europe from fascism; Ronald Reagan helped liberate Eastern Europe from communism. Each realized that the goal of freeing others jeopardized domestic priorities. Lincoln had to keep in mind the preservation of the Union, Roosevelt the reform legacy of the New Deal, and Reagan the conservative aim of reducing the national government and reaffirming state sovereignty. In the pursuit of victory, Lincoln was forced to wage "total war" in an effort not only to defeat armies and devastate economies but also to undermine the popular will in the South. Roosevelt similarly had to allow the aerial destruction of Berlin and Dresden; and Harry S. Truman approved the atomic bombing of Hiroshima and Nagasaki. Reagan alone succeeded in liberating people from tyranny without going to war, and he did so through conversation and dialogue. Hence the title of this volume's last chapter, "The Homeric Conclusion."

Yet with his Paineite passion for liberty, Reagan rarely appreciated that political life required authority as much as liberty and needed the state as an instrument of power and justice. While Reagan employed the statecraft of *realpolitik* to bring the cold war to a close, big government remained the bugaboo of his lifetime even as he did as much as any president to make it bigger. Under Reagan, the original sin of liberalism and the Democratic Party, a gargantuan government and a huge national debt, became the perpetual curse of conservatism and the Republican Party.

In historical memory, the uses and misuses of the Reagan presidency constitute a chapter in American mythology. The legend involves five claims. The first depicts Reagan as a religious moralist who asked Americans to do their duty by making sacrifices in the name of God and country and to submit to Christianity as the national religion. The second assumes that the Reagan presidency solved the problems it set out to address and thereby "remade" America. The third implies that the words Reagan uttered sounded the horns of Jericho, starting an emotional earthquake that so shook the world that the Berlin Wall came tumbling down. The fourth would have us believe that America "won" the cold war through armed might and that Reagan himself was at heart a militarist. And the fifth clings to the conviction that America was right to have supported the Afghan *mujahideen* as "freedom fighters" in the war against communism.

These claims call for clarification. Reagan subscribed to a Jeffersonian belief in religion because it enabled the mind to resist political tyranny—and not, as some Christian fundamentalists wish, because he wanted to impose it as a pledge of allegiance. The impression that Reagan "remade" America is true in the sense that he restored the people's confidence in themselves and in their country, but the claim would have greater validity had he reduced liberal big government instead of perpetuating it. Some Reagan admirers, in particular neoconservatives, are in the administration of George W. Bush, the president whose attitude toward war is to "bring 'em on." The neocons who see themselves as followers of Reagan have, in fact, left a trail of blunders. In the late 1970s and 1980s, they misinterpreted the nature of the Islamic rebellion in Iran and Afghanistan, confusing a wide-open Muslim coup for a hidden Marxist plot. The neocons also decided to supply arms to terrorists, supported Sadam Hussein with cluster bombs and chemical components for manufacturing poison gas, consistently mistrusted Gorbachev's intentions, spied the Kremlin behind every tree in the jungles of the third world (the Soviets, bogged down in Afghanistan in Reagan's era, had second thoughts about Africa and Central America and rebuffed Fidel Castro), claimed the Soviet Union was permanently unalterable, and then took credit for its collapse while hailing America's triumph in the cold war. In recent years, the same neocon hawks who denied that Russia could change have persuaded Americans that their country has the means to go almost anywhere in the world and bring about "regime change."

The prudence with which Ronald Reagan approached the cold war has little bearing on those who speak in his name. Becoming involved in an all-out war, Reagan realized, risks surrendering freedom to fate and having no control over the unintended consequences of events. In contrast to World War II, which the Nazis instigated and meant to fight, the cold war had yet to exhaust the possibilities of diplomacy, and Reagan, appreciating the differences between the two wars, and reminding Russia that the United States had once been its ally against a common enemy, seized the opportunity for dialogue and negotiation. "The essence of the art of politics," observed Raymond Aron, "is discrimination." Reagan embodied that essence. While others were determined to stockpile weapons to face the possibility of nuclear war, he sought to start the dialogue to defang that horrid prospect. To rescue Reagan from many of today's so-called Reaganites may help rescue America from the pride of its present follies.

Acknowledgments

I wish to express my appreciation for the conversations I had with Martin Anderson, William F. Buckley Jr., Ambassador Jack F. Matlock, Martin Mayer, Martin Skousen, and the Honorable George P. Shultz.

I am also indebted to the keen editorial guidance of Robert Weil, the comprehensive and constructive criticisms of Robert Huberty, and the steadfast support of Elizabeth Harlan.

The book is dedicated to five wise men who taught us how to think about communism and the cold war.

Ronald Reagan

Introduction

RONALD REAGAN'S political consciousness developed during the cold war. In many respects, it was defined by the political positions others took, which he viewed not only as a possible betrayal of America but also as a threat to its well-being. Inspired by the libertarian views of Paine, Reagan saw himself as the lifeguard of American liberalism, rescuing it from drowning in the raging currents of radicalism that inundated three generations of twentieth-century history. In Hollywood in the forties, Reagan the actor saw the Old Left's support of Stalin taint the New Deal; in Sacramento in the sixties, Reagan the governor heard the New Left's paeans to Castro and Mao; in Washington, D.C., in the eighties, Reagan the president watched the antiwar Left's support for Nicaragua's Sandinistas sweep the academy. By then the lifeguard had long given up on liberalism, which he concluded would always be swept away by the siren song of the Left.

Yet Reagan's goal to end the cold war was closer to the hopes of liberals, who thought it feasible, than to the fears of conservatives, who thought it impossible. He stood closer to liberalism on other matters as well. Reagan would quote Ralph Waldo Emerson, who championed the radical spirit of independence in "Self-Reliance" and ridiculed sin as a childhood superstition. Economic conservatives identified with Reagan, but few appreciated his universalistic and radical will to autonomy. Conservative literary intellectuals and legal scholars, following Edmund

Burke, believed in history, precedent, and order; Reagan, following
Paine, believed in hope, experiment, and freedom. Religious conservatives regarded evil as real; for Reagan it was rhetorical.

Allan Bloom's *The Closing of the American Mind* appeared toward the
end of the Reagan presidency and surprised the publishing world by
becoming a huge best-seller. Its author appeared successful in convincing readers that the president was a moral absolutist opposed to every
aspect of liberalism.

Describing the reaction to Reagan's famous 1983 denunciation of the
Soviet Union as an "evil empire," Bloom wrote:

> What was offensive to contemporary ears in President Rea-
> gan's use of the word "evil" was its cultural arrogance, the
> presumption that he, and America, know what is good; its
> closedness to the dignity of other ways of life; its implicit
> contempt for those who do not share our ways. The political
> corollary is that he is not open to negotiation. The opposition
> between good and evil is not negotiable and is a cause of war.
> Those who are interested in "conflict resolution" find it much
> easier to reduce the tension between values than the tension
> between good and evil. Values are insubstantial stuff, existing
> primarily in the imagination, while death is real. The term
> "value," meaning the radical subjectivity of all belief about
> good and evil, serves the easygoing quest for comfortable
> self-preservation.[1]

Bloom was writing in 1985 and 1986, in the midst of the Reagan presidency. Like other conservatives, he argued that America was corroded
by "cultural relativism," the substitution of subjective values for objective virtues, liberalism's tendency to tolerate everything and be committed to almost nothing. Rather than stand firm, the relativist reduces the
tension between values by identifying their moral equivalents and
refuses to face the substantial existence of good and evil and the
inescapable reality of death.

There was only one thing conditionally wrong with Bloom's account.
Reagan did not stand firm as an absolutist.

As Bloom wrote his book, Reagan was negotiating with Soviet leader

Mikhail Gorbachev at the 1985 Geneva summit. Contrary to Bloom, the language of good and evil did not mean that the world was fated to remain as it was. Fully realizing that Armageddon would be real should the world fall into what Reagan called "the nightmare of nuclear annihilation," he committed himself to the preservation of peace as his "highest priority." He even told Americans that he had no contempt for the Soviet Union and that the Russian people indeed "share our values." When later asked by reporters what had happened to the "evil empire," to the dreadful Soviet Union as the sole "focus" of all that was diabolical in the world, Reagan shrugged and replied, "that was then" and said that "all things change."[2]

To admit that an attitude once held may have been wrong, that arms escalation needs to cease and government turn to negotiation, and that, as Reagan told the press before leaving for Geneva, diplomacy was "not an impossible dream"—such sentiments are the pulse of liberalism and the passion of the romantic. Reagan's passion was to open up the American mind, to see the country—as he said, referring to Emerson—never as completed but "always in a state of becoming." Reagan's Emersonian outlook had no place for evil. The much-quoted "evil empire" expression Reagan used only once, relying on an ill-advised speechwriter. Reagan was wise to refrain from misusing the phrase, which could only mean that communism springs from metaphysical rather than historical causes and that God, not man, is answerable for the Gulag, while the Soviets are absolved of it. Convinced that Soviet leaders were free agents, Reagan held them responsible for their conduct in Eastern Europe and the third world.

—

WHAT RONALD REAGAN liked to deride as "the 'L' word" had long been seen as the kiss of death in modern politics. In the latter part of the twentieth century, the liberalism of the Democratic Party took on some of the attitudes of the turbulent 1960s generation, and Reagan, who became governor of California in 1967, knew very well that the politics of student activists had no resonance beyond the campus. A few years earlier, the year of the Berkeley Free Speech Movement (FSM)—1964—celebrated the victory of Democrat Lyndon Johnson over Republican Barry Goldwater and set the stage for LBJ's Great Society domes-

tic programs, most famously the "war on poverty." The high tide of liberalism marked the beginning of its end, as the South began to move
away from the Democratic Party in reaction to civil rights legislation,
and middle-class workers started to vote Republican—partly in reaction
to the counterculture but also in response to Democratic legislation that
provided increasing assistance to minorities and the disadvantaged.

With the radicalization of politics, "the center cannot hold," the poet
Yeats once reminded us, and "liberalism has passed away without receiving a proper obituary," commented Ortega y Gasset. An obituary for
American liberalism might observe that the lost causes of the 1960s
found a mausoleum in the Democratic Party. Many years earlier, Reagan
had indeed been a Democrat and had regarded himself as a dedicated
liberal. But while the party veered Left, he moved Right. What Reagan
said of the trajectory of his politics could have been said by many Americans. "I didn't leave the Democratic Party; it left me."[3]

Reagan's relation to liberalism may illuminate modern America more
than his relation to conservatism. What Reagan sought to do for America has been the goal of liberalism since the eighteenth-century Enlightenment: to get rid of authority, the meddlesome intrusions of controlling
institutions, whether of church or state. Reagan quoted Emerson to
remind America that it is "the land of tomorrow" unburdened by the
authority of the past.

In his determination to break free of the past and start afresh, Reagan
meant to get rid of the notion not just of big government at home but of
a cold war abroad that fueled government's excesses. He would challenge communism rather than simply contain it. Reagan and the generation of conservatives who came of age with him believed the old anticommunist Left of liberals and socialists had turned soft. They had
witnessed the Left's failure of nerve during the Vietnam War, followed
by its complete collapse in 1972, when the Democrats chose the antiwar Senator George McGovern, who pleaded, in his campaign against
Richard Nixon, "come home, America."

Vietnam, the longest war in American history, cost the lives of 58,226
American soldiers and more than a million Vietnamese. The internecine
struggle in southeast Asia turns out to have been a war for national liberation and not for international communism. Some American liberals
predicted the nationalist sentiment, as did Charles de Gaulle. But no

one predicted that in our era Vietnam would be rushing toward the free market. The post–cold war world has had even greater surprises. Today the United States finds itself in the deepest financial debt in its history, and we witness the spectacle of capitalist America completely dependent on borrowing from communist China. "Forgive us our debts," says the Bible's Matthew. ". . . And lead us not into temptation." It almost seems that America lost the cold war as an economic rivalry. Reagan led America into temptation, and since then, with one exception, the country has been unable to start saving and stop spending.[4]

In the 1980s, Reagan and the conservatives opposed communism anywhere in the world as part of what *National Review* writer James Burnham once called "the struggle for the world."[5] Even as communists in underdeveloped countries futilely tried to defy Karl Marx by skipping the capitalist stage of history, Reagan's advisors insisted that communists had to be resisted every step of the way in every part of the globe. Once a country goes communist, it was held, there was no turning back and no going forward. Where communism prevails, liberalism cannot be conceived and capitalism cannot be born.

When Reagan became president in 1981, American conservatives' great fear was that communism would overrun what was then called the third world. The State Department and the CIA responded by undertaking clandestine and often brutal counterinsurgency initiatives in Angola, Afghanistan, El Salvador, Iraq, and elsewhere. One Reagan advisor, Pat Buchanan, warned that we must fight communism on the streets of San Salvador or we would be fighting it on the sidewalks of San Diego. Senator Daniel Patrick Moynihan, on the other hand, insisted that communism was going nowhere in the impoverished third world and that it had lost all credibility in the Soviet Union, where every man and woman in Red Square knew that the "workers' state" was not working.

Reagan's cold war has been depicted as a morality tale, simply the stance of righteousness against the stealth of wickedness. Admirers point to the president's political language on the assumption that words are the equivalent of deeds and the rhetoric of the "evil empire" was meant to bring about the fall of communism and did indeed do so. But if Reagan's actions are a truer expression of his thoughts, this is not always recognized to be the case. The president was eager to help the Contras fight communism in Nicaragua but reluctant to help Solidarity

fight communism in Poland.[6] He was willing to negotiate with Russia's
Mikhail Gorbachev but not with Nicaragua's Daniel Ortega. He supported Jewish "refuseniks" in flight from communism in Russia but not
students who rose up against it in China's Tiananmen Square. After
leaving office in 1989, he went along with President George H. W. Bush,
Richard Nixon, and Henry Kissinger, who, failing to speak out openly
against it, sided with Red China and its brutal crackdown.

The optimistic Reagan could never accept communism as history's
fate. However, here we face a disjunction between Reagan's religion and
his politics. Early in his career, when Reagan survived a disappointment,
he assured his followers that his mother had told him that setbacks in
life should be accepted as part of Providence, that "God has a plan for
each of us."[7] If religion required the acceptance of Providence, though,
politics defied it. In diplomacy communism could not possibly be part
of God's plan for the world. Religious resignation represented the fatalism that had no place in Reagan's passion for freedom.

Yet in the 1980s two philosophies of history existed, one on radical
college campuses, the other in the White House and in conservative
think tanks. Both philosophies were deterministic, almost fatalistic, and
Reagan refused to subscribe to either of them. Obviously he could
hardly agree with the Marxist Left that the rise of communism is
inevitable, but neither could he agree with the Machiavellian Right that
the existence of communism is irrevocable. Both extremes on the political spectrum assumed that to understand communism is to see that it
is inexorable in moving toward power and irreplaceable once in power,
whether it be a force of liberation or a force of domination. If it could be
said that Reagan had a philosophy of history, however, it was a philosophy of choice that promised a self-willed destiny. Reagan might leave the
judgment of history to God, but he was determined to make history by
taking control of it. Hence he identified freedom with the ability to
choose, convinced that nothing is foreordained, and when he gave that
message at Moscow State University in 1988, the audience leaped to its
feet with a thunderous ovation.

It must be said that neither Reagan nor anyone in his administration
foresaw the sudden collapse of the Soviet Union in 1989.[8] Lack of prescience, however, did little to prevent Reagan's neoconservative advisors
from taking credit for what they once considered inconceivable. All

along the advisors insisted that the United States not negotiate arms reduction and urged that defenses be strengthened. However, Reagan, his wife, Nancy, Secretary of State George P. Shultz, and Deputy Chief of Staff Michael Deaver believed important changes were taking place inside the USSR and that negotiations could expedite them. When, to everyone's surprise, Soviet power collapsed beginning in 1989, the entire doctrine of irreversibility held by key Reagan advisors, the conviction that Marxist regimes cannot change except by force, was refuted.

———

REAGAN WAS NOT the first president to unnerve America with words and ideas. Liberals criticized the president for his righteous rhetoric, but so had nineteenth-century conservatives criticized Abraham Lincoln for declaring the "sin" of slavery the cause of an eternal conflict between "right and wrong," paralyzing an America that "cannot endure, permanently half slave and half free." Lincoln's reputation suffered as the biases of Southern conservatives influenced the writing of American history in the late nineteenth century, just as Reagan's reputation has suffered from northern liberal biases that dominate the teaching and writing of American history today. The older conservatives, convinced that the Civil War was unnecessary, saw slavery on its way to extinction without Northern intervention. Today's liberals, convinced that the cold war was unnecessary, believed communism was contained and dying without the meddling of anticommunist conservatives.

In confronting the Soviet Union, Reagan invoked the principles of freedom, human rights, democratic elections, and self-determination, liberal ideas derived from the natural rights legacy of John Locke and the foreign policy of Woodrow Wilson. Yet if Reagan carried forward the message of liberalism, why did he become the emblem of conservatism? The beginning of his distrust of liberalism went back more than thirty years before his presidency, to his struggles with procommunist groups in the film industry. Ironically, at the same time that Reagan battled the Hollywood Reds, New York intellectuals, liberals and socialists, battled the communists who had defended Stalin's Russia. Some of Reagan's early allies in the screen world were liberals like himself. Reagan, however, appears to have undergone a profound shift when he was given a copy of Whittaker Chambers's *Witness* (1952). Indeed, the work of a former communist spy convinced Reagan that liberalism was even more of an enemy of the West than communism itself. The book also reinforced the convictions of William F. Buckley Jr., author of *Up from Liberalism*, a play on Booker T. Washington's *Up from Slavery*. And it turned into a disciple Anthony Dolan, the Reagan aide who wrote the "evil empire" speech.

Whittaker Chambers was the Captain Ahab of the cold war. So demonic was Ahab that he projected the guilt-driven evil within himself onto the white whale as he pursued it to the ends of the earth. The struggle against communism, declared Chambers, came down to "Faith in God or Faith in Man," and he was sure that liberalism's indifference to religion misled him into forsaking his country. Ahab was incapable of blaming himself for his zealous drives, and he set out to wreak vengeance on a harmless beast. The traumatized Chambers traced evil to an allegedly godless liberalism in order to be absolved of past sins. "Communism is what happens when, in the name of Mind, men free themselves from God," scolded Chambers.[9] Curiously, the six ex-communist authors who contributed to *The God That Failed* arrived at a different conclusion. Communism is what happens when, in the name of history, men assume they are free from responsibility to think for themselves and fail to "consider that they were in any way answerable for the actions of the Cause which they supported."[10] At one time Chambers's soul hung suspended between God and Satan, and, choosing Stalin, he would lead a life of sin and repentance. The betrayer must suffer. His dark emotions had no resonance with Reagan's bright optimism, nor could the president see the West on the losing side of history. Chambers was a fatalist.

Yet Chambers had grounds for his anger toward liberalism. When he reported that Alger Hiss had been a secret communist agent, many liberals rushed to the defense of their fellow Ivy League liberal and started a smear campaign against Chambers, hinting that he was a drunkard, a homosexual, mentally impaired. His coworkers at *Time* magazine shunned him. In *Witness*, Chambers recalled an encounter with a young woman Ph.D. " 'How dare you,' she asked with the voice of Bryn Mawr but the snarl of a fishwife, 'how dare you call us Communists?' It was no use to explain to her that what I had said was not that she and others like her were Communists, but that they were non-Communists who were letting the Communists lead them by the nose."[11]

The Hiss-Chambers controversy was one of those episodes in history that tore a nation apart, much like the Dreyfus affair in late nineteenth-century France. It was a political awakening in Reagan's life, final evidence that liberals could not face the truth and communists would never tell it. The recently opened Russian archives reveal that every single person Chambers named as a communist turned out, in fact, to be a party member.[12] Such facts have yet to be part of the curriculum in the teaching of American history, as revealed in the scandal over "The National History Standards" in the 1990s. The document on the standards was drafted by reputable scholars and had the endorsement of the American Historical Association. It depicted the anticommunism of Chambers and Reagan as paranoid "McCarthyism." Even some families, especially those on the Left, denied the truth to their children, as indicated in a childhood memoir by an author brought up in an ideologically charged household:

> Mama, why did Stalin have Trotsky assassinated?
> Who says he was assassinated, darling? Some deranged person killed him. . . .
> Mama, are the Rosenbergs Communists?
> They're progressives, darling. They're being persecuted because they believe in justice for all people, and because they're Jews.
> Is Alger Hiss a Communist?
> Of course not. He's a liberal person who's opposed to the warmongers.
> What about Whittaker Chambers? He says *he* was a Communist?
> He's a very sick man.[13]

Reagan's hostility toward liberalism had its origins in the Hiss-Chambers affair. Those who rushed to Hiss's defense besmirched liberalism, and those who thought they had to support Stalin and turn a blind eye to his regime in order to defeat Hitler succumbed to self-deceit. "The sin of nearly all left-wingers from 1933 onwards," wrote George Orwell, "is that they wanted to be anti-Fascist without being anti-totalitarian."[14]

It is understandable that in the eyes of conservatives, Chambers emerged as a martyr who told the truth and was crucified in the left-wing press. Chambers's influence on what became the conservative movement was profound. Reagan would cite *Witness* as the book that had shaped his political outlook. If Chambers worried that modern man had turned away from God, Reagan worried that he had turned toward the state. New Deal liberals, warned Chambers, thought of themselves as reformers, but the "concealed inner drift" of Franklin Roosevelt's experiment, the move toward a planned economy, could be as dangerous as revolutionary communism. Chambers claimed that he never knew a New Dealer who was not a "communist or a near-communist"; hardly surprising for an underground agent. But the reasoning is maddening. "For men who could not see that what they firmly believed was liberalism added to socialism could scarcely be expected to see what added up to Communism." Why could liberals not see who they actually were?

> Any charge of Communism enraged them [the liberals] precisely because they could not grasp the differences between themselves and those against whom it was made. Conscious of their own political innocence, they suspected that it was merely mischievous, and was aimed, from motives of political malice, at themselves. But as the struggle was really for revolutionary power, which in our age is always a struggle for control of the masses, that was the point at which they always betrayed their real character, for they reacted not like liberals, but with the fierceness of the revolutionists whenever that power was at issue.[15]

Chambers took the character of Alger Hiss, a liberal who denied his communist affilliations, and projected such conduct onto liberalism in general. In his Hollywood days battling the Reds, Reagan began to share Chambers's conviction that liberals allowed communists to lead them by the nose, and the Reagan presidency would promise to save America from liberalism. In the 1930s and 1940s the cause of antifascism did lead some liberals to makes excuses for the Soviet Union, but certain conservative thinkers believed that liberalism represented the first step on the road to the servile state of Soviet totalitarianism.

What is communism? To understand a political phenomenon requires
knowing how it happened and discovering its purpose. As an effort to
redeem humanity from its fallen condition simply by eliminating private
property, communism was the most fallacious idea of modern history,
not unlike fascism, which would claim to regenerate civilization by eliminating ethnic diversity. Communism would purge the world of class differences, fascism would cleanse it of racial impurity. However, Reagan
saw the phenomenon of communism acting through infiltration rather
than revolution, what he called "losing freedom by installment," as
though the Leninist would rather creep toward power than simply seize
it. Yet in post–World War II Eastern Europe, the defeat of fascism meant
the advance of communism and the Red Army. Communism imposed
itself not by installment but by brute force, either through military occupation and a blockade followed by a wall (East Germany), denying free
elections (Poland), arranging a party coup (Czechoslovakia), or arresting
and executing non-Stalinist political leaders (Hungary).[16] Influenced by
Chambers, Reagan seemed less interested in knowing how communism
came to power in Europe than in worrying about its rise in America—
hence his misplaced fears that it could happen here. In that sense alone,
his role in helping Russia free itself from totalitarian power—a phenomenon some saw as being as permanent and as unchangeable as the law
of gravity—was remarkable. Yet in the end what brought down communism was liberalism itself, specifically Gorbachev's introduction of *glasnost* and *perestroika*. The first expression signified "openness," the
attempt to free up the political mind; the second, "restructuring," the
attempt to reorganize the economy closer to a free market system.
Chambers, however, had convinced himself that liberalism combines
with socialism to culminate in communism. He and his followers completely misinterpreted history. Far from evolving from liberalism, communism bypassed it, moving from czarism to Leninism almost overnight.
The Soviet Union skipped the liberal stage of history, and when Gorbachev tried to return to it by reforming its institutions, he brought
about communism's own demise and his own defeat in his own country.
Contrary to Chambers and Reagan, liberalism is the death of communism. Today Cuba, China, and North Korea dare not flirt with it; America dare not forsake it.

Liberalism is neither the moral sickness depicted by Chambers nor

the monstrous fraud of American politics denounced by the hosts of
today's right-wing cable television shows. Actually, Reagan had more in
common with liberals than he cared to admit, especially a dread of
nuclear war and a desire for disarmament.[17] John F. Kennedy even anticipated the conservative president in putting the Soviet Union under
stress by increasing America's military budget, as Reagan would do.
Kennedy's arms buildup took place in 1962, after the harrowing Cuban
missile crisis, a thirteen-day nightmare from which America struggled to
awake. Kennedy feared that war, even a victory, would be "ashes in our
mouth," and Nikita Khrushchev said of nuclear war, "the survivors
would envy the dead." With visions of a nuclear holocaust in mind, Kennedy supplemented his strategy of strength by simultaneously proposing
to negotiate disarmament and a nuclear test ban with the Soviet Union.
The following year, on November 22, 1963, Kennedy fell victim to an
assassin. Two decades later, on March 30, 1981, Reagan was shot and
critically wounded, far more seriously than the public was aware. He
recovered from the assassination attempt and went on to see those very
liberal hopes for peace realized.

A president who seemed to start out a hawk and ended a dove was
indeed a riddle. Secretary of State Shultz confessed he found the president to be a bundle of contradictions, nothing less than a "mystery," the
political Sphinx of the Oval Office. "Even some of his close aides were
puzzled," writes Shultz, recalling advisor Robert McFarlane saying of
Reagan: "He knows so little, and accomplishes so much."[18]

Reagan did indeed accomplish a great deal, so much so that he may
be, after Lincoln, one of the two or three truly great presidents in American history. All earlier presidents believed that the cold war could be
stabilized and communism at best contained—the position of Harry S.
Truman, Dwight D. Eisenhower, and Lyndon B. Johnson. Some recent
evidence indicates that Kennedy was planning to withdraw troops from
Vietnam and seek better relations with the Soviet Union. After his
death, the war in Asia escalated and relations between the United States
and Soviet Union continued to deteriorate. The startling breakthrough
came with Reagan in the mid-eighties, which forecast the beginning
of the end of the superpower rivalry. Two momentous urgencies—
Gorbachev's desperate need to initiate domestic reform, and Reagan's
growing fear of nuclear escalation veering out of control—converged to
change the course of history.

To use the two categories in Sidney Hook's *The Hero in History*, Reagan was both the *"eventful man* in history," a leader "whose actions influence subsequent developments along a quite different course than would have been followed if these actions had not been taken"; and also the *"event-making man,"* a leader "whose actions are the consequences of outstanding capacities of intelligence, will, and character rather than of accidents of position."[19] Reagan may be admired not only for what he did but also for who he was, a thoughtful, determined man of character and vision. No doubt some Americans, especially intellectuals, would laugh at such a description. Such skeptics share a widespread assumption that the cold war was inevitably coming to an end and that Reagan happened to be in the right place at the right time. Reagan, however, was not simply receptive to a historical situation; on the contrary, he helped to create it. In taking action that would force events, Reagan led rather than followed, often going against the counsel of his national security advisors and secretary of defense. Some advisors insist that Reagan's military budget caused the Soviet Union to capitulate, a thesis Peter Schweizer and other conservative writers have argued.[20] To be sure, Reagan supported the arms buildup, actually begun under President Jimmy Carter, but he soon came to see that the only answer to the cold war was to call it off. If he sought to convince the Soviets that they could not afford an arms race, it was because he was even more convinced that "a nuclear war cannot be won and must never be fought."[21] In addressing the cold war on his own terms, Reagan made a difference and helped undo what both neoconservatives and Marxists had claimed to be the everlasting fate of communist countries. *Commentary* magazine warned its readers that the Soviet Union had no capacity to change or even to collapse; the Iron Curtain and the Berlin Wall were permanent monuments of the cold war. Khrushchev was reported to have said: "When shrimps learn to whistle, the cold war will end." But by putting an end to the suicidal madness of the arms race, Reagan made history. Even if Reagan, like so many others, did not fully envision exactly how communism would fall, he ended the cold war by creating what Prime Minister Margaret Thatcher insisted was the "essential trust" that would be necessary to allow the peaceful exit of the Soviet Union from history.[22]

American history has seen nothing like Reagan's achievement over two centuries of unrelenting military conflict. Only George Washington and John Adams, who faced the Napoleonic lust for battle in revolutionary France in the late 1790s, wisely resisted the call to arms urged upon them by their own Federalist party. Since the era of Washington and Adams, Reagan was the only president in American history to have resolved a sustained, deadly international confrontation without going to war.

—

BEFORE TAKING UP a narrative on Reagan's early life and political career, the book first considers his convictions about religion and government. The nature of Reagan's religious beliefs is baffling. He seemed to offer a Christianity without Christ and the crucifixion, a religion without reference to sin, evil, suffering, or sacrifice. Reagan's sense of religion was opposite that of Whittaker Chambers, who condemned America to purgatory. Chambers spoke to our fears, Reagan to our desires.

Reagan's political philosophy is also problematic because his theory of government has little reference to the principles of the American founding. Tom Paine, Reagan's hero, is anathema to most conservative intellectuals, who prefer *The Federalist Papers* as the foundation of political wisdom.[23] In many respects, Reagan departed from the message of both the Bible and *The Federalist Papers*. Each text was restrictive, consisting of commandments or regulations, and each required obedience to doctrine and submission to authority, whether the sufferings of the Cross or the sovereignty of the State.

Reagan, the scourge of big government, made it inevitable. The true conservatives, the founders, framed a specific system of authority in government to check the demands of the people. Reagan's rejection of authority and his celebration of the people thwarted efforts to limit their will. As always, people were free to curse government while looking to it for generous checks. Under Reagan, Americans could live off of government and hate it at the same time. Americans blamed government for their dependence upon it, and then easily denied that the national debt had anything to do with their own demands that government provide more services with less taxes.

Although Reagan aimed to bring history under control by shaping the course of events, the economy was in the hands of the "invisible hand," the laws of supply and demand, what Reagan liked to call the "magic of the market." Reagan's policy of supply-side economics promised to reduce federal expenditures by cutting taxes and leaving government with less revenue. The logic, it turned out, proved illusory. Whether taxes decreased or increased, spending went up along with a soaring national debt. No one has yet to face squarely this problem of lower taxes and higher deficits. Perhaps the problem was too obvious to be noticed. While America was confronting communism abroad, its enduring problem at home was, paradoxically, Emersonianism.

In his college years, Reagan majored in economics and read Frédéric Bastiat, the French social philosopher who denounced *dirigisme*, a state-controlled economy. Reagan also took a course in the literature of British romanticism and wrote essays on William Wordsworth, the poet who rebelled against the rules of classicism to make freedom and pleasure the emotions that move the world.[24] In the nineteenth century, liberals like Bastiat and Wordsworth valued spontaneity, the natural impulses of the self, whether in the economy or in the emotions. Karl Marx called Bastiat the "modern bagman of Free Trade," an economist who believed in the natural harmony of interests between labor and capital.[25] What Marx meant as a criticism, Emerson would have accepted as a compliment. Like Bastiat and Wordsworth, Emerson also saw the spontaneous as a life force, the realm of freedom that defies fate and resists the state. Americans would, the poet advised, seek freedom, power, and wealth had not religion so repressed what the conscience found too sinful to admit. Reagan, our Emersonian president, was carrying out the poet's wish when he aimed to rid us not only of government but of guilt itself, not realizing that without a bad conscience we can only have big government. Reagan liked to quote Paine to prove that government had become alienated from the people. But Paine was writing about the era of monarchy, not democracy. As Alexis de Tocqueville demonstrated, people in a democracy see the state as their servant. "It is a waste of time to prove to these people that extreme centralization can be harmful to the state, since they are centralizing it for their own benefit."[26] Was all of Reagan's inveighing against government a waste of time? He berated it without acknowledging that in a democracy people consent to government precisely because they hope to command it. As long as Reagan continued to blame government for the faults of the people, America's political culture had no means of self-knowledge, no shock of recognition of who we are.

One wishes Reagan had read Whittaker Chambers less and James Madison more. Yet it is difficult to imagine him returning to the wisdom of the *Federalist* authors. They were realists; he was a romantic. Ronald Reagan was the young man who drove his Nash convertible, open top and without stopping, from Des Moines to Hollywood in the thirties, and ended up in the eighties arriving at the White House in a stretch limousine. But far from presiding over the closing of the American mind, he opened it. Reagan offered three of the most radical thoughts ever held by an American president: We have no history at our back; the people know no evil because our God-given desires are good; and only the state knows how to sin. In the Christian tradition, to make life an end in itself is to turn away from God. But the genius of Reagan was, like that of Emerson, to persuade us that we please God by pleasing ourselves and that to believe in the self is to live within the divine soul. Reagan opened the American mind to optimism and innocence, leaving it closed to sin and experience.

President Reagan was quite willing to take responsibility for the misdeeds of government. He had no hesitation accepting blame for the Iran-Contra scandal. But rarely did he ask the American people to take responsibility for their own lives and discipline their desires. Government and its deeds might do wrong, the people and their wants and wishes never. In the Reagan era, a proud celebration would rule out self-examination, and the American mind would never know itself as long as the people could do no wrong. No subsequent political figure would ever dare to ask the American mind to take a look at itself in the mirror and gaze upon its own shortcomings. Not Bill Clinton, not George W. Bush. Reagan remedied America of all self-doubt. Thus to run against the Reagan legacy is to lose the race before it has begun.

Ronald Reagan changed the course of American politics in ways that would be enormously difficult to turn around. Traditionally it was the Left that put its trust in popular sovereignty and called for all power to the people in the name of participatory democracy. Traditionally it was the Right that put its trust in God and natural law and called for some source of authority that would come down from above to guide the people and rescue them from relativism. Reagan remained convinced that people had no need of compulsory authority and that if left to themselves they could run their own lives. What Reagan stood for had once been the great fear of the conservative imagination. In the eighteenth century, the *Federalist* authors believed that if the democratic people were left free to act on their own without external restraints, nothing would be safe—property, social order, women's virtue, or the bottles of madeira behind the tavern bar. The confident Reagan felt no need to listen to either the somber warnings of the founders or the sermons of sin-struck fundamentalists. Instead he convinced Americans to believe in themselves.

In doing so, Reagan brought to a head a paradox of American democracy. America's political culture is both liberal and conservative, with one steadily waning and the other seeming to be gaining in recent years. America is liberal in its means and confident in its ends. People enjoy the liberal premise of opportunity and labor and use it as a means to pursue the conservative ends of property and leisure. A rights-based liberalism is more about opportunity than duty—claims and entitlements made upon the government by a people Reagan regarded as "heroes." The paradox of liberalism is that it begets conservatism. Rights trump responsibilities and make it possible for people to pursue what Tocqueville called "materialism" and its "petty pleasures." In the 1930s, Franklin Roosevelt's New Deal put millions of people to work; after World War II and the return of prosperity, many voted Republican and were later called "Reagan Democrats." To a certain extent, the same pattern repeated itself with affirmative action, a liberal program that brought excluded minorities into the economy and the professions. Once in the upper income brackets, a number of arrivistes moved to suburbia and voted Republican. Reagan avoided taking a firm stand against affirmative action, a program that benefits the few at the expense of the many. Perhaps Reagan realized that liberalism spawns its own defeat by breeding defectors.

Reagan believed in work and wealth, and he had no trouble whatsoever with the thought that an excessive pursuit of material pleasure might jeopardize the political principle of civic virtue or the religious principles of charity and benevolence. As long as the state stayed out of the way, Reagan had no imagination for sin and corruption. An admirer of Calvin Coolidge, the president who told the public that "the business of America is business," Reagan would have had a good laugh at the anxious thoughts of political philosophers, their dread that the "uneasiness of desire" (John Locke) leads to the busy life of business and its "joyless quest for joy" (Leo Strauss). In always looking ahead, Reagan left behind both the worry of liberals and the wisdom of conservatives.

Few other presidents had so passionate a faith in the future, or were so sure that the country could shape the "bright dawn ahead," so certain that the "city upon a hill" would hold fast to the good. Reagan was no populist demagogue catering to our worst instincts, no warmonger in search of dragons to destroy, no McCarthyite preying upon the innocent. To get American history right is to see Paine suspicious of the state, Emerson sanctifying the self, and Reagan defying fate and the paralysis of the will and affirming freedom and the hope of the future. If government is the call of duty, democracy is the theater of desire as well as freedom, and the actor, more than the politician or the preacher, knew that the heart vibrates to dreams born of desire. The question the Reagan legacy leaves us with is whether America can live by desire alone.[27]

In the following chapter, Reagan's religious and political philosophy provides an answer to that question.

ONE

The Political Romantic

The Radicalization of Religion
and the "Evil Empire"

CHRISTIAN FUNDAMENTALISM made its move into twentieth-century American politics at just about the same time as Reagan left the governorship of California in 1975. The Reverend Jerry Falwell, warning the country that "Satan had mobilized his forces to destroy America," mobilized older conservatives called the Moral Majority to rescue the country from spiritual jeopardy. In 1988, the Reverend Pat Robertson set up the Christian Coalition. The followers of these groups all worked strenuously to assure Reagan's election in 1980, and when he gave his famous "evil empire" speech to the National Association of Evangelicals, on March 8, 1983, blaming liberalism on the secular drift in America, the religious Right must have felt portents of the Second Coming.[1]

But what exactly was the nature of Reagan's religious beliefs? The striking thing about his sense of religion is how much it enables us to forget religion. On this subject the radical Left has had it all wrong.

In the 1960s, when Reagan was governor of California, activist students assumed he was a reactionary conservative who would find himself in thrall to the fundamentalist Right that was sprouting in Orange County. But those who advocated "participatory democracy" in the expectation it would lead to socialism faced a Reaganite conservatism advocating popular democracy to bring capitalism to fruition. It was tempting for the New Left to dismiss the religion of the American Right as the "opium of the people," a set of beliefs that promised to relieve what Marx called the "sigh of the oppressed." In Reagan's America, the Left saw religion as repressive, distorting the people's deepest yearning for freedom and the fulfillment of humanity's every need and wish. The

guru of the era was Herbert Marcuse, the German émigré and author of
One-Dimensional Man, a text that taught the students of Reagan's sunny
California that not only the mind but the body itself had been crippled
by Christianity, denying its desires for the "polymorphous perverse," sex
any which way. No one seemed to notice how Reagan transformed religion from the governor's podium and later from the president's pulpit.
Redefining the nature of desire, Reagan's religion would deny nothing
because life offered everything. Our beliefs about God no longer repress
but liberate, as though Christ died on the Cross so that we might better
pursue happiness, not the salvation of our souls.

Reagan's carefree attitude toward religion reminds one of America's
great master of mockery, H. L. Mencken, who, in *Treatise on the Gods*,
contrasted the nation's civil religion to the first Christian sects:

> Observing a Roman cardinal dashing down Fifth avenue in
> his Rolls-Royce, with bands braying, drums rolling, and cops
> clearing his regal way, one forgets the rule of St. Benedict,
> and the sisters in the hospitals. One forgets, too, the Stylites
> on their pillars, the Dendrites roosting in trees, the Boskoi
> who ate only grass, the Euchites who prayed incessantly, the
> Trappists who never speak.[2]

As Mencken noted, it is not what one believes about religion but what
one forgets about it—the saints and the sinners.

President Reagan almost never left the White House to go to church,
and he seldom invited a chaplain in to give services (though he attended
church occasionally upon leaving office). Reagan defended religion
against those who sought to purge it from public life, but he hardly
wished to see Americans submit themselves to an ecclesiastical establishment. Conservatives who hold up the family as a source of authority
hearken back to the seventeenth-century monarchist Robert Filmer,
whether they know it or not. Filmer had justified the "divine right" of
kings with such reasoning. Reagan's relations toward his own children
reveal a man who would not see the young suffer from patriarchal or
churchly repression, or from any inhibitions alien to their own being. As
his family letters indicate, he tried to advise his children based on his

own experiences with life, but he did not preach or pontificate. He advised his son Michael that infidelity is a natural impulse but perilous to genuine love; he did not browbeat young Ron when he told his father that he had lost his faith; he taught his daughter Patti how to improve her essay on *Bonnie and Clyde* without seeming to mind the film's erotic content.[3]

In his campaign speeches, Reagan asked Americans whether or not they were "better off," and he assured his followers that his economic programs intended to "let the people flourish," establishing a criterion for American politics that was as far from conventional religion as was imaginable.[4] He made comfort and pleasure, not conviction and piety, the measure of all things. Two centuries earlier, when the historian Edward Gibbon asked whether Christianity did anything to contribute to the happiness of Roman civilization, he had to be reminded that Jesus' message offered a way to rise above the longing for material possessions, and it had nothing to do with being "better off." Like Thomas Jefferson, Ronald Reagan revered Jesus of Nazarus as an oracle of moral wisdom. While Jefferson denied the divinity of Christ and Reagan upheld it, however, neither political leader believed that the meek shall inherit the earth or that the self was the seed of sin. One president could not stay away from Sally Hemings, the other would not chase the money changers from the temple.

Conservatives who are convinced that America is fundamentally a religious country like to quote Tocqueville to the effect that the "tie" of religion is what binds America together, and if that tie is broken, all is lost. Tocqueville indeed says as much in *Democracy in America*, calling religion "the first of American political institutions." He also advised, however, that neither the Christian principle of sacrifice nor the political ideal of classical virtue dares stand in the way of modernity. What, then, binds America together?

"What serves as a tie to these diverse elements?" Tocqueville wrote to a friend of the riddle of America's fragmented social order. "What makes of them a people? *Interest*. That's the secret. Individual interest which sticks through at each instant, *interest* which, moreover, comes out in the open and calls itself a social theory." Tocqueville, an anguished Catholic, assumed that there existed a dualism between virtue and interest, idealism and materialism, God and Mammon. Thus he worried that both classical and Christian ideals would be unable to withstand the material reality of the coming commercial society. Americans believe in religion not because it is "true" but because it is simply "useful," and thus a democratic people "will not easily believe in messages from a divine source," as they "choose the main arbiter for their beliefs within, and not beyond, the bounds of human understanding." Equality compels people "to have concern only for themselves. It exposes their souls to an excessive love of material enjoyment." Religion and democracy, Tocqueville worried, are at odds. "The main purpose of religions is to purify, govern, and restrain the overly fervent and exclusive taste for comfort which men experiences in times of equality," where their only concern is to leave the public square behind and retreat to the private sphere to "ameliorate their fate, increase their well-being, their riches."

Tocqueville saw in America what Max Weber, the German philosopher and author of *The Protestant Ethic and the Spirit of Capitalism* (1904–1905), later called "a war of the Gods," a struggle to the death between two antithetical value systems. Egalitarian democracy, observed Tocqueville, "tends to isolate men from each other so that each thinks only for himself. It lays the soul open to an inordinate love of material pleasure." Thus the great advantage of religion "is to inspire diametrically contrary urges" by placing "man's desires outside and beyond worldly goods and naturally lift[ing] the soul into the regions far beyond the realm of the senses." However, the "passion for well-being" in America "is the most lively of all the emotions aroused or inflamed by equality," and "should any religion attempt to destroy this mother of all desires, it would itself be destroyed thereby."

Reagan's religious background was such that he could readily preserve the "mother of all desires" and still adhere to a religious outlook. Tocqueville would regard such a resolution as a "false" religion that left no place for the theology of God or the threat of Hell. Both Tocqueville and Weber saw Americans leaving a soul-searching religion behind as they accepted the coming of commerce and later embraced the material pleasures of capitalism. This *immanentization* of religion, in which belief dwells within the mind and not in any external authority or doctrine, may not be peculiar to America, but those televangelists who supported Reagan while selling religion suffered from no "cognitive dissonance," at least not until they were caught in the company of prostitutes or in trouble with the Internal Revenue Service.[5]

American democracy, Tocqueville observed, was too bustling an environment to allow its people to have "fixed ideas about God and human nature." The American, free of established institutions of authority, cannot defend his opinions, and "he despairs of ever resolving by himself the greatest problems presented by human diversity," and hence in liberal society "he beats a cowardly retreat into not thinking at all." The only thing the American truly thinks about and understands is "self-interest rightly understood."

Tocqueville presaged Reagan in sensing that the American people, instead of seeking to be right with Jesus, or putting the public good ahead of all other concerns, only loved "material enjoyment." If a life devoted excessively to an evanescent materialism and its "petty pleasures" filled Tocqueville with "religious dread," it delighted Reagan. As a Catholic, what Tocqueville admired about Christianity was the commandment "to love God with all your heart and to next love yourself." Reagan's sense of religion, however, placed God within the self. Thus Tocqueville's angst about the loss of genuine religion to the *egoisme* of modernity troubled Reagan not at all. Reagan's ancestral Protestant religion turned inward to the "oversoul" the better to find God. America's fortieth president recognized no Tocquevillian dualism between matter and spirit, no distinction between worldly success and spiritual salvation. "Let me add my own deeply held belief," Reagan wrote to a young man in search of a happy life, "that true success and happiness—especially happiness—can only come from letting God be part of your life." Reagan was expressing a peculiarly American way of religion that called upon the self to open itself up to a God already residing within the human soul, a religion he learned in Dixon, Illinois, in the 1920s.[6]

To understand how Reagan viewed religion, one must first know about his upbringing. In his hometown, Reagan derived the lessons of religion from his mother, Nelle Clyde Wilson Reagan. Unburdened by creedal dogma, she taught young Ronald the tenets of the Church of the Disciples, an offshoot of nineteenth-century Unitarianism that had relieved America of Calvinism and all the gloomy doctrines of depravity and predestination. Nelle Reagan was a devout Christian who engaged in good works and acts of charity, helping the sick and feeding the poor.

However, it was scarcely a piety of compassion that Reagan carried away from the religion of his youth. Once he was in political office, the religious duty of benevolence was no part of his public policy.

Yet in the Reagan 1980s and for decades after, religion grew powerfully in American "civil society," in evangelical church organizations existing independently of government. Although Reagan succeeded in stigmatizing taxes in the realm of politics, churchgoers came increasingly to donate time and money to causes for which government once assumed responsibility, especially poverty, disease, famine in Africa, and the resettlement of refugees. Some pastors even recognized that the New Testament is close to socialism and the welfare state in its preachings. "Give us this day our daily bread." Yet most of Reagan's supporters, like George Gilder and Michael Novak, insisted that Christianity had its true economic expression in modern capitalism.

The 1980s provided a field day for neoconservative intellectuals and their think tanks. Many looked to the Reagan administration as a reaffirmation of their own values, even some famous thinkers who should have known better. In Allan Bloom's *The Closing of the American Mind*, for example, readers across the nation were told that the curse of America was "value relativism," an openness to all experience that allows people to "do their own thing." Such a secular attitude, said Bloom scornfully, offers "a great release from the perpetual tyranny of good and evil, with their cargo of guilt and shame." During the Reagan years, Bloom saw intellectual history reaching the climax of "nihilism," and the only thing holding it back was the conservative presidency of Ronald Reagan and the conservative campus of the University of Chicago, where Bloom taught and where the classics were still pondered.[7] Not only did a teacher of classical wisdom look to Reagan as a bastion of resistance to liberal relativism; so too did many Christian fundamentalists, especially those who grasped at the president's every mention of God as evidence of his profound religiosity. Yet one wonders what to make of Reagan's habit of dropping God's name. In 1984, Reagan was about to make a public address in which he referred to the United States as "the greatest nation God ever created." An aide immediately rushed to correct the president with all the tact he could muster. The aide was John Roberts Jr., then in the soliciter general's office and presently Chief Justice of the Supreme Court. "According to Genesis," Roberts advised Reagan, "God creates things like heavens and the earth and the birds and the fishes, but not nations."[8]

Reagan's first instinct is perhaps more telling than Roberts's instructions. Reagan would have to defer to the Genesis account of creation only if truth is literal, simply a matter of words, and if God and man were as separate as soul and body. Yet Reagan recognized no such dualisms, no dichotomy between matter and spirit, the natural and supernatural. Religion for Reagan rested on faith and vision, not knowledge and doctrine. He had an Emersonian sense of the becoming and unfolding of all things, a cosmic assurance that Americans could always count on a "bright dawn ahead," that time is boundless and the world endless. What Reagan sought to do with the idea of God, to make the Supreme Being endow America with a special creation, is straight out of Friedrich Nietzsche, the German philosopher who discerned how easy it would be to reconceive the religion of the Bible. In the late nineteenth century, the philosopher saw modern history turning away from the severe teachings of Christianity and reformulating religion in flattering terms that gave men and women faith in themselves so that they would feel "not merely better but also 'better off.' "[9] Thus Reagan had his own religion to offer America, just what Nietzsche predicted and Bloom deplored—a religion that would get rid of all "the cargo of guilt and shame," the condition of the "last man" who could no longer shoulder the burden of the Cross. No more would Christianity be a matter of moral laws that leave the conscience filled with angst and responsibility because they emanate from the will of God. On the contrary, the genius of Reagan was to keep God and get rid of guilt.

Such was the case in domestic politics. In foreign affairs, however, the presence of nuclear weapons filled President Reagan with the burden of unavoidable guilt, a sinking sense of helplessness unless he could do something to avoid a nuclear holocaust. But faced with the Soviet Union, he never had to question his optimistic outlook and consider, as did Lincoln during the Civil War, that humankind is morally wrong no matter what it does. That the cold war could be identified with the actions of the state, and not its people, rendered humanity innocent, at least in the eyes of a libertarian president.

Nietzsche is cited as the originator of a contemporary school of thought called deconstruction, the notion that truth is not "out there" to be found but instead has been constructed out of human need and arti-fice; presumably what has been constructed has no basis in nature, rea-son, or religion, and hence it can very well be deconstructed. This logic cuts both ways, as seen in Reagan's reconstruction of the meaning of God in America.

The Puritans recognized that if God is sovereign humanity cannot be; they recognized further that free will does not exist. The will cannot be a self-determining agency, free to act on its own. Only God is. That is what John Winthrop taught the first settlers of Massachusetts. Reagan, however, was determined to think otherwise. "God meant America to be free because God intended each man to have the dignity of freedom," he wrote in a 1969 letter. Lincoln was considerably less sure, and wrote a "Meditation on the Divine Will," in which he wondered how one could possibly know God's intent in creating the world. In letter after letter, Reagan never hesitated to identify God's will and purposes with his own political ambitions and even defeats. After being denied the Republican presidential nomination in 1976, he assured a supporter that the loss must be part of God's plan.[10] Reagan appropriated religion and freed it from what Nietzsche called "the bite of conscience." In turning religion inside out, in removing every vestige of threat and damnation, Reagan radicalized it, even before devout fundamentalist conservatives.

Reagan's use of the word "evil" to describe the Soviet Union should be seen in its political context. After all, Reinhold Niebuhr, Arthur Schlesinger, Will Herberg, and many others used the term earlier in his-tory, and Hannah Arendt's idea of the "banalty of evil" would be reiter-ated in Reagan's famous speech before the gathering of evangelicals in 1983, when he described how diabolical deeds can be carried out by the most normal of people. The idea of *l'empire du mal* pervaded the writ-ings of Aleksandr Solzhenitsyn, and Whittaker Chambers convinced many conservatives that the only way to escape evil was to embrace God. Yet the idea of evil could be invoked even by those who did not believe in God, those liberals who were called Atheists for Niebuhr. The liberal Niebuhrians took to the idea of evil as a concept that might help explain why their fellow liberals had been taken in by Stalin's Russia and assumed that communism had resolved the problem of power and human sinfulness. The pro-Soviet liberals who did so, and who drove Reagan to conclude that the Hollywood communists had no patriotism, may have been worse and even more dangerous. In assuming that communism was overcoming the evils of capitalism, they saw themselves on the side of good and could maintain their innocence and all along condone oppression and tyranny. The phenomenon of totalitarianism, and the intellectuals' complicity with it, compelled the liberal mind to return to the idea of "original sin" as the fount of political wisdom.

The rhetoric of the notorious "evil empire" speech presented the cold war with three ironies. The first is that the controversial speech was meant for one audience and had an even greater impact on another. After a couple of years of Reagan's presidency, the Christian Right remained unsure about an administration that had yet to do anything to get God into the classroom. Thus the speech in Florida was meant to solidify the fundamentalists by striking out at an atheist political regime behind the Iron Curtain. But the speech had even more of an impact on the secular socialist Left in Europe, as anticommunist dissidents took heart that an American leader was, at last, describing the legacy of Leninism as the work of Lucifer.

The second irony lies in the way that its author, Anthony Dolan, formulated the speech. "Now and forever," Dolan emphasized in his draft, "the Soviet Empire is an evil empire."[11] Fortunately, Reagan deleted the first two words, "now and forever." Yet the idea of evil could hardly be made compatible with the other conviction of the Reagan administration, the die-hard belief that the Soviet Union as a communist state remains a permanent fixture of totalitarianism, an ironclad system that could only tighten its grip on power but could never reverse itself. The idea of totalitarianism implied that there was no way a communist system could be altered; thus, in theory at least, one cannot condemn that which cannot have been otherwise. There is, after all, no sin without free will. But Reagan dubbed the Soviet Union "the focus of evil" of the entire world without specifying how evil emanated from the actions of men and women whose human nature he never doubted was essentially good, as he found the Russian people to be when he visited Moscow in 1988.

The third irony of the "evil empire" speech is what philosophers call the theodicy problem. Why did an all-benevolent and all-knowing God bring evil into the world? The traditional answer was that God had inflicted evil upon mankind as a punishment for disobedience and the banishment of Adam and Eve from the Garden of Eden. If God intended an evil adversary to challenge America, then Americans must be in a state of sin. Such was the reasoning used by Lincoln during the Civil War when he told Americans they were suffering because of the offense of slavery. In contrast, Reagan never accepted that America was anything but innocent. Unlike Lincoln, Reagan never suggested that America had any moral deficiency. God smiles on America. Whittaker Chambers, however, did see America, and the liberal West in general, as deserving the calamity of communism because modern man had lost sight of God. Reagan considered Americans to be as pious as they were patriotic, and yet evil exists—or does it?

"My personal belief is that God couldn't have created evil so the desires he planted in us are good," Reagan wrote to Florence Yerly, a close friend, in 1951. Yerly's husband had died, and Reagan was encouraging her to stop worrying about sin, consider the children, and start dating men.[12] The letter was written long before Reagan was president, but private correspondence or conversation may be more telling than public speech. Reagan wrote the letter a year before he read *Witness*. If Chambers convinced Reagan that evil did indeed exist and that it inhered solely in communism, how could it be that atheism succeeded in creating a power stronger than the Supreme Being? Chambers's book scarcely dealt with such theological riddles, and Reagan's outlook was too sublime to be worried about them.

What is striking about Reagan's 1951 letter to Yerly is his reference to "desires." In the eighteenth century "desire" replaced "evil" among the thinkers of the Enlightenment. When the framers of the Constitution constructed a government to control the unruly "passions and interests" stemming from desire, they were addressing the problem of evil. Reagan, however, saw the people as so full of the "dignity of freedom" as to be capable of self-government. Like Paine, he would dismiss the necessity of heavy constitutional controls because no evil lurked in the heart of humanity.

Reagan's denial of the existence of evil and his affirmation of the essential goodness of desire indicate how far he was from conservatism and how close he was to liberalism. Walter Lippmann captured this distinction when he described thinkers of the past pondering the human condition:

If they thought their natural impulses were by way of being lecherous, greedy, and cruel, they have accepted some form of the classical and Christian doctrine that man must subdue his native impulses, and by reason, grace, or renunciation, transform his will. If they thought that man was naturally innocent and good, they have accepted some one of the many variants of liberalism, and concerned themselves not with the reform of desire but with the provision of opportunities for its fulfillment.[13]

Both liberals and conservatives may find disturbing the philosophy implict in this unphilosophical president. When Nietzsche describes the "masters of alchemy," he refers to those leaders capable of transforming Christianity so that we feel no shame about our possessive desires and we stop regarding morality as "something forbidden." Contrary to Bloom, the American president delivered us from angst and doubt. "I ask God to rid me of God," implored Nietzsche. Without quite knowing it, our fortieth president did pretty much the same thing in ridding America of a God of judgment and punishment. "The gods we stand by," wrote William James, a philosopher who well knew what America had done with religious belief, "are the gods we need and can use."[14]

Reagan's most biting critique of Jimmy Carter was that the president tried to make the people feel contrite. Carter asked them to think small, to face an era of limits. Reagan proposed to save America from such sickness of will. He would sublimate the commandments of the deity so that politics could be about what he called our "God-given rights"—rights to property, liberty, and the self-preservation of life. Reagan's is a liberal political philosophy. It is not about our duties and obligations or about any source of authority beyond ourselves. It is not about what we should do for our country, but what we should do for our own satisfaction. Reagan's political philosophy had no relation to what the Puritans called "obedience to the Covenant" with God. Reagan did not mean to "restrain and subdue" man's natural rights, but would leave man free to do as he pleases.

Reagan often called for returning God to the classroom, and he favored school prayer; he treasured the unadulterated expressions of the Bible, spoke fervently before religious groups, and consulted with his pastor, Donn Moomaw (a former UCLA All-American linebacker turned Beverly Hills Presbyterian). He saw to it that Camp David would have a chapel; cheered on Athletes in Action, the Campus Crusaders for Christ's winning college basketball team; cited Lincoln, and rightly so, to justify mixing politics and religion; and had his own moments of religious mysticism. However, the content of religion was of less interest to him than the freedom to believe. Reagan trusted what came from within and resisted what was imposed from without. He was reluctant to lodge authority in a religious morality extrinsic to human desire or in a political system that risked becoming alienated from the people. Again and again he wrote to his critics to make the point that he did not espouse a particular mandatory school prayer, as though the state should tell students what to believe. "I simply ask that they be allowed to pray if they so desire—and that prayer can be to the God of Moses, the man of Galilee, Allah, Buddha, or any others."[15]

At a conference on religious liberty in 1985, President Reagan spoke of the distinction between the "City of God" and the "City of Man," and one might have expected him to refer to the author of those concepts. St. Augustine would surely have muddied things by making us aware that since God is good, the "evil empire" behind the Iron Curtain would not exist unless it were good that it did exist. However, a political speech is no time for Christianity's enigmas. The point Reagan sought to make is more revealing. In the speech he cited Nicaragua and Russia as evidence that the "machinery of the state is being used as never before against religious freedom." Reagan looked to religion less as a source of divine guidance than as a bulwark against the power of the state.[16]

In the struggle against communism, Reagan looked to some early American leaders for spiritual as well as political inspiration. Convinced that "freedom prospers only where the blessings of God are avidly sought and humbly accepted," he insisted that this "discovery was the great triumph of our Founding Fathers, voiced by William Penn when he said: 'If we will not be governed by God, we must be governed by tyrants.'" Reagan was also happy to report that Jefferson said: "The God who gave us life, gave us liberty at the same time." The conclusion is all-comprehensive. "The evidence of this permeates our history and our government. The Declaration of Independence mentions the Supreme Being no less than four times."[17]

Reagan convinced himself that a political leader who believed in God could not do other than be dedicated to freedom. The conviction hardly describes Jefferson, who sided with Napoleon in putting down mercilessly the Haitian revolution of 1801. Actually, it was the anti-Jeffersonians, namely John Adams and Alexander Hamilton, who were more consistent in promoting liberty than the slave-holding Virginians, and the Federalists did so without invoking God. The real founding is not the Declaration but the Constitution, where there is no mention of a deity or a Supreme Being. In the Declaration, Jefferson "wanted to use only his strongest guns," observed the philosopher Morton White, and hence "God" could be invoked along with "Reason" and "Virtue" to justify the right to rebel.[18] Whereas the Declaration is about liberty, the Constitution is about authority, and the explanation why the classical principle of virtue and the Christian idea of love disappear in the document is that America could not count upon such concepts. Today, fundamentalists may jump with joy when they see the word "God" in the Declaration and other documents. Adams, Hamilton, and Madison doubted, however, that older religious ideas had sufficient authority any longer to command people's obedience. The doubt scarcely troubled Reagan, who believed that God created human beings to be free to obey themselves. Such self-direction was the story of Reagan's life.

—

AS A TEENAGER Reagan followed his mother into the church of the Disciples of Christ. In his memoirs he briefly mentions that he "invited Christ into his life," without bothering to say what religion itself meant to him. During the following decades, in his Hollywood days, he certainly lived out his desires: he dated starlets, enjoyed hearing about Errrol Flynn's sexual escapades, and made ribald jokes about Howard Hughes's controversial, erotic film *The Outlaw*, starring the voluptuous Jane Russell. Still, Reagan's life in Hollywood was hardly libertine. Apparently having no carnal knowledge, he had no need of religious absolution. The same insouciance continued a decade later when Reagan was governor of California. While he talked of the importance of religion in the classroom, he made no political effort to see it happen. Indeed, he told students at the University of California that their professors should teach them not "what" to think but "how" to think, and in this advice he sounded more like the dreaded secular humanist than a Christian moralist, convinced that the young should be taught not the truth but the ways of knowing. The political act that had perhaps the greatest religious significance for Reagan was his reversal on the right to abortion. As governor, he had signed a bill in 1967 granting the right, but soon he had second thoughts and, convinced of the sacredness of life, called for its repeal.

When he became president, Reagan had a religious awakening, the result of a near-deadly encounter. On March 30, 1981, an assassin attempted to kill him. Reagan's profound religious epiphany came about during his recovery, and it elevated his sense of the vocation of politics. On leaving the hospital he wrote in his diary: "Whatever happens now I owe my life to God and will try to serve him in every way I can." One way was working for peace, an initiative that had roots deep in his life, even though he was often regarded as a warmonger. While still in his college years in the twenties, he wrote a short story, "Killed in Action," which reflects the Lost Generation and its protests against the human waste of war. Reagan's words echo those of Ernest Hemingway, who lamented that "abstract words such as glory, honor, courage, or hallow were obscene." Young Reagan thought the words "sacrifice and glory and heroism" had turned sour due to the First World War. Not for a moment did Reagan harbor unpatriotic thoughts, but his antiwar convictions led him to join the Left in the Ban the Bomb movement that started after the atomic obliteration of Hiroshima and Nagasaki in 1945. Four decades later, Reagan's antiwar sentiments reemerged in full passion, kindled by his new thoughts about religion and his moral revulsion at the thought of retaliation.[19]

A reluctant cold warrior, Reagan was actually an abolitionist who sought to rid the world of nuclear weapons, as Paul Lettow has demonstrated.[20] Yet Reagan's hopes, while morally understandable, are politically puzzling. If total disarmament had taken place before the cold war had come to an end, America and the West would have been vulnerable to the Eastern bloc's vastly superior land forces, a possibility that concerned Margaret Thatcher and others. It was not disarmament itself but the emotional trust that had been established between Reagan and Gorbachev that turned history in a new direction. Reagan's lifelong inner conviction about the dread of nuclear weapons was little known to the

public, however, and even to this day many of his admirers still think he
was the John Wayne of the cold war, itching for a duel. He was just the
opposite.

At a National Prayer Breakfast, on February 2, 1984, Reagan delivered an approximation of Jesus' Sermon on the Mount, with its message
of turn thy cheek and love thine enemy. Reagan told the parable of
Roman gladiators ready to fight until they heard the message of Jesus.
Then they laid their swords down and walked from the Coliseum with
heads bowed. The gladiator games scarcely ended with the arrival of
Christianity. But Reagan saw a relation between religion and pacifism.
In a speech before the U.N. General Assembly, on September 24, 1984,
the president cited St. Ignatius of Loyola, the Jesuit and "Spanish solider
who gave up the ways of war for that of love and peace." Although Reagan liked to read religion, some parts of the Bible seemed oppressive to
him; he cringed at the story of Calvary, and certain scriptural passages
haunted him. When thinking about nuclear weapons, he couldn't help
but think about Armageddon. In Reagan's presidential years, politics and
religion were never far apart, as emotions, not as doctrinal convictions.
The religious imagination is shadowed by the thought of catastrophe,
and the tragic explosion of the space shuttle *Challenger* as it ascended
could only leave the president with the hope that the astronauts had left
the earth to "touch the face of God." The *Challenger* disaster shook Reagan in much the same way that the nuclear explosion at Chernobyl shattered Gorbachev's confidence in continuing the arms race. When Reagan heard the atheist Gorbachev say, "God help us," he knew there were
grounds to begin negotiation, to follow the biblical injunction and turn
swords into ploughshares.[21]

———

THUS WE NEED to clear up a confusion. When Reagan invoked the
expression "evil empire," he was not, as his critics feared, about to
embark upon an aggressive war with the Soviet Union. Instead, he
wanted to deal with the power of evil by bringing its effects under control. However, Christianity, as Abraham Lincoln acknowledged, has
nothing to say about the handling of power. Both the North and the
South, observed the president during the Civil War, pray to the same
God, and each side hears no answer. "The Almighty has His own pur-

poses," reflected Lincoln, who knew America was on its own. Political leaders can scarcely consult scripture to know how to deal with the enemy. Reagan was aware that the United States had to continue to develop a nuclear arsenal, but to ever use it would be complicit in the very evil America must oppose. The cold war confronted America with a moral dilemma. Can democratic ends be realized by diabolical means?

In 1982, Reagan had no answer to the question as he stood firmly opposed to the nuclear freeze movement, headed by those who sought to end the arms race. At that time his position aroused the delight of neoconservatives and drew the despair of Protestant ministers and Catholic bishops. Three years later, by 1985, something of a conversion experience occurred. Reagan himself began to call for a freeze, indeed the elimination of all nuclear weapons within a period of years. What explains the turn of mind?

Some scholars claimed that it had to do with America's having achieved "nuclear superiority." That was, however, hardly Reagan's view. He would not have America fighting a nuclear war, no matter how overwhelming the Pentagon's weapons. He knew he was not about to launch a preemptive strike, and in the event America suffered an attack, he had no option but nuclear retaliation. Ambassador Jack F. Matlock paraphrased Reagan's horror at the thought. "How can you tell me, the president of the United States, that the only way I can defend my people is by threatening other people and maybe civilization itself? That is unacceptable."[22] Without in the least acknowledging it, Reagan's sensibility partook of the tragic vision of liberalism, the conviction that the cold war presented the world with no possibility of a morally good choice. Had Reagan been a true religious fundamentalist, he would have had no cause to agonize about such a situation, since his diplomatic decisions would have been guided by divine grace. That he did so agonize puts Ronald Reagan in the company of Abraham Lincoln.

Nuclear warfare was like the introduction of original sin into diplomatic thought. Although Reagan rejected such an idea, he seemed to have intuited what Reinhold Niebuhr taught liberals: that the use of atomic military power, even in defense, meant the loss of innocence and the burden of guilt. Niebuhr also cautioned against "our effort to establish the righteousness of our cause by a monotonous reiteration of the virtues of freedom compared with the evils of tyranny."[23] In dealing with

Gorbachev, Reagan realized that the time for righteous rhetoric was over, even if he had to write private correspondence to reassure his worriers, like his friend William F. Buckley Jr., that he knew the Soviet Union still remained the "evil empire." The deeper point was that America could do nothing about it militarily. Realizing that evil provokes evil, that the moral conscience is lost when employing the enemy's weapons of mutual annihilation, that freedom may perish in the act of defending it, Reagan had no choice but to renounce retaliation and to seek an end to the cold war by means other than war. Ironically, the presence of nuclear weapons saved the world from nuclear war. No matter how much the Reaganites may have spoken of evil, Reagan himself dared not smite it. Although some of his diplomatic and military advisors may have thought of victory, Reagan's religious conscience guided him on the path to peace.

The Emersonian President

RONALD REAGAN was no "born-again" Christian. Although he used the expression, he was not one who had to be saved from a dissolute life by divine grace, embracing the Bible to rid himself of inner demons. His religion resided calmly in a mind that had been serene almost throughout his life. The relaxed nature of his religion probably came from the faith of his mother. Her church of the Disciples of Christ derived from a nineteenth-century set of attitudes, creeds, and sects that looked to the democratization of religion and the turning away from external authority to trust the inner self as a source of guidance. Liberal Unitarianism partook of this outlook, which replaced predestination and depravity with voluntarism and agency. The rejection of old-fashioned religion, however, had its most profound expression in the writings of Ralph Waldo Emerson. Reagan was an Emersonian, not only in temperament but sometimes even in thought. He quoted Emerson on several occasions, cherishing his optimism and his antinomian politics. The president could agree with Emerson on a number of convictions, especially the need to overcome the doubts and worries that plague a troubled conscience. Emerson held that we are born free and good but

that everywhere we are regulated and corrupted, that "organization tyr-
annize[s] over character," and "all public ends look vague and quixotic
beside private ones."[24] Reagan followed Emerson in turning his back on
what both saw as forces inhibiting America.

Turning away from Christianity's idea of the Fall and the doctrine
of original sin, Reagan also turned away from the doctrine of the
republic's political foundation, from the lessons and teachings of the
Federalist authors, who insisted that the republic could not survive
without a strong government. Lincoln worried that evil might be here
in our own soul, but Reagan ignored Lincoln's legacy and told Americans that evil existed only behind the Iron Curtain. Economics also
turned away from traditional religion. For the temptation of political
economy was to forget God so that capitalism could live solely for itself
with its own criterion of success. According to Max Weber, capitalism
arose in a seventeenth-century Calvinist environment where wealth
was seen as a sign not of enjoyment but of abstinence, the product of
savings, frugality, hard work, self-denial, all necessary for investment.
"You may labor to be rich for God," exhorted the Puritan Richard Baxter, "though not for the flesh and sin." In America in the 1980s, it was
the other way around.[25]

Perhaps the last modern political figure to try to sustain the idea of
true Christian piety in American life was President Jimmy Carter, Reagan's opponent in the election of 1980. The devout Baptist president
thought he could scold Americans for their indulgent ways, for succumbing to an all-devouring greed and a soul-deadening malaise. After
1980, though, the ideas of sin, suffering, and sacrifice were fast disap-
pearing from American politics and culture. Like Emerson, Reagan was
determined to rid America of the fear of selfishness, since the self itself
was sacred. Both the poet and the president believed in the strength and
success of self-reliance. Nietzsche happened to be an admirer of Emerson, and he regarded self-reliance as the will to power that would overcome the crippling emotions of guilt, a liberation that represented nothing less than "greatness" itself. To deny the ego, said both the American
poet and the German philosopher, is to be "castrated."

The idea that liberal guilt emasculated America in its capacity to fight
the cold war was a central complaint of conservatism, nowhere better
expressed than in James Burnham's *Suicide of the West*. Reagan thought

liberals suffered from too much guilt on many subjects. Of those environmentalists who lamented the disappearance of species, Reagan asked, "How much do you miss Dinosaurs? Would your life be richer if those giant prehistoric flying lizards occasionally settled on your front lawn?" But contemplating what he called "the horrors of war" would rarely leave Reagan without a pang of guilt.[26]

Neither so-called Reaganomics in domestic policy nor what came to be known as the Reagan doctrine in foreign affairs concerned itself with suffering, humility, pity, remorse, mercy, or charity. The Reagan administration did not promote anything akin to "compassionate conservatism" to counter liberals or attract Christians. In its domestic doctrine, people would be empowered by wealth; in the diplomatic, made safe by weapons ("peace through strength"). Yet Reagan seldom relied exclusively on the language of money and power. Instead, he firmly believed that the spiritual could overcome any material force and that ideas rule the world. Radicals assume that ideas are simply hot air, epiphenomena, existing only in the mind. As Marx put it in *The German Ideology*, they are "the illusions of the epoch." Reagan thought ideas were real and could move mountains. "The time has come," he told an audience at Notre Dame in 1981, "to dare to show to the world that our civilized ideas, our traditions, our values, are not—like the ideology and war machine of totalitarian societies—just a façade of strength. It is time for the world to know our intellectual and spiritual values are rooted in the source of all strength, a belief in a Supreme Being, and a law higher than our own."[27]

It was a cold war speech, and Reagan was preaching to the choir of Catholics, who believed that the worst offense of communism was its atheism. Perhaps Reagan and all Catholics should have thanked God that Russia was largely a nation of nonbelievers. One wonders how else the Soviets could have been persuaded to disarm and bring the cold war to an end. If there is no afterlife, why risk nuclear warfare? Or if there is, why fear it? Reagan may have invoked God with the implication that heaven awaits his chosen Americans, but the theory of deterrence and retaliation, with its mutually assured destruction, was based on the fear of death and the right to life—neither of which obtain in America's war against suicidal Islamic terrorists.

To see God invoked for the purposes of the cold war reminds us of the Catholic Charles Péguy's dictum that what begins in mystery ends in politics. But the key to Reagan's speech is the equation of spiritual values with political strength. Wealth, force, will, and spirit move together toward freedom, and they represent power itself. Here Reagan was in the company of Emerson:

> The pulpit and the press have many commonplaces denouncing the thirst for wealth; but if men should take these moralists at their word, and leave off aiming to be rich, the moralists would rush to rekindle at all hazards this love for power in the people, lest civilization should be undone.[28]

To put people in charge, to rekindle their love for power, to make America strong so it would prevail—such a vision might well be the definition of Reaganism. However, does love for power imply liberation or domination? Emerson's contemporary Herman Melville worried that America had "law on her brow" and "empire in her eyes" and that "power unanointed" would take possession of the soul of the republic. Of that prospect, Emerson and Reagan remained sublimely untroubled. And while the poet, like the later president, would make evil disappear from America, the novelist wrote *Billy Budd* to make us feel its presence and the helplessness of innocence to combat it. Yet Ronald Reagan was truly our most Emersonian president, a leader who assumed, as did the poet, that as power enters the fiber of the people, the state will wither away and never be missed, and the burdens of sin will turn out to be, through the alchemy of the marketplace, the benefits to society. In a speech on the curse of taxes, Reagan delighted in quoting the poet: "In a free and just commonwealth, property rushes from the idle and imbecile, to the industrious, brave & persevering."[29]

Emerson said other things that resonated with Reagan. From his earliest teenage years as a lifeguard, when he pulled ashore drowning swimmers, to his last presidential days in office, when he sought to obtain the release of hostages in Lebanon, Reagan saw himself as a rescuer, the romantic hero who saves life from the treacherous currents of nature and politics. He saw himself doing so as an individual—a head of state who, in the spirit of Emerson, headed history in the right direction. It is revealing that in his last public address, delivered to the Republican National Convention in 1992, a few years after leaving office, Reagan

invoked Emerson as if to give the country a statement of his own philosophy of life. "Emerson was right. We are the country of tomorrow. Our
revolution did not end at Yorktown. More than two centuries later, America remains on a voyage of discovery, a land that has never become, but
is always in the act of becoming."[30]

Whether or not Reagan was interpreting Emerson correctly, he could
hardly resist seeing America as an "act of becoming," sharing the poet's
conviction that America grows not old but young, that freedom annuls
fate, and that weakness is want of willpower. When Reagan insisted that
the best was yet to come, he contrasted himself to Jimmy Carter. During the last years of his presidency, Carter invited various officials, academics, and public figures to Camp David to talk over the state of the
world. After these meetings, Carter delivered a televised address, on July
15, 1979—his notorious "malaise" speech. The word was used by
reporters, not Carter, but it encapsulated a description of America's
decadence and decline that he said he had taken from the Camp David
meetings.

Allan Bloom offered the same description of America lacking confidence and conviction in *The Closing of the American Mind*. The ironies
are staggering. What Bloom meant by "closing" was actually its opposite:
a mind as open as a sponge, tolerating anything and everything, optimistic, delighted, without worry—exactly what Reagan promised America in 1980. Reagan had no time for the doom and gloom of the Carter
years. Rather than face an environment of exhaustion, America could
find itself through hope and by following the example of the founders,
the pioneers, and the immigrants. Life could be renewed and revitalized.
Long before his presidency, Reagan spoke of "America as a place in the
divine scheme of things that was set aside as a promised land." Reagan
sacralized the meaning of America, and during his presidency, one of his
speechwriters, Peggy Noonan, provided the theme of his two administrations. "America is back," she wrote upon Reagan's victory in 1984; it's
"morning again." The sense of spiritual rebirth came to be called "morning in America."[31]

Reagan's critics dismissed all this as the politics of puffery, with the
president more a salesman than a statesman; they said that this was
more theater than theology. Few discerned what was going on. Again and
again in his speeches Ronald Reagan told the American people that the

era of liberalism was over for good. Yet his definition of America as the "land of tomorrow" reflected a liberal and Emersonian outlook. Reagan did not rescue America from liberalism, he reaffirmed it, in all its materialistic possessiveness, in the name of higher purposes. Americans, George Santayana once observed, see themselves as "idealist[s] working upon matter" and thus the sense of sin evaporates in the conceits of self-justification.[32] With Reagan, Americans had no need to realize the ideal, they idealized the real; they need not pursue the public good, which Virgil called "the noblest motive," but simply their own private interest.

Toward Reagan's intellectual gymnastics, the mind stands aghast and not a little awed. Reagan turned the history of political and social thought on its head. For centuries philosophers worried themselves sick about the dualism of matter and spirit. Even Adam Smith, who recognized that the fate of morality in a market economy rested on moral sentiments, honestly acknowledged that he had no success in resolving the dualism and that ethics may be at odds with the pursuit of self-interest. Today Reaganite conservatives draw upon Smith to reconcile capitalism and Christianity. In the eighteenth century, Smith had hoped that pride and the "love of praiseworthiness" would be the distinctly moral motive compelling people to do good and act benevolently rather than selfishly. The craving to win the respect of others would force people to behave respectfully and their capacity for sympathy would enable them to feel the pain of others. But Smith recognized that all his hopes depended upon religion and that his theory was identified with the conception of God. Without a deity, there would be no reason for people to feel guilt and fear punishment for their self-serving acts. Today those acts command respect as the public comes to honor wealth without work, just as the public did in the days of pagan Rome and would in the days of affluent America. Waiting at the end of the line of Adam Smith's thinking was Thorstein Veblen, the late nineteenth-century American economist who demonstrated that the working classes suffer the stigma of labor and the wealthy classes enjoy the status of leisure.[33]

What troubled moralists like Smith and cynics like Veblen troubled Reagan not at all. The "desires" God "planted in us are good," Reagan was convinced, seemingly unaware that in Christianity desires hover like an ominous transgression. Reagan had no need to explain how the temptation of desire contradicts the passion for freedom; for most past thinkers, when the will is driven by the objects of its desire, it is compelled by something alien to itself, and not free to act on its own. Insofar as our desires choose us, a human condition imbued with desire required some means of control and regulation. Reagan, however, hated any thought of control and regulation. Believing that the meaning of life is to find God's purposes in our own needs, Reagan embraced a religion that expressed not the truths of the Cross but the hungers of the heart. What Reagan did was nothing less than a political miracle. Consider how he brought the language of Emerson to the land of Lenin to present his romantic sense of religion, the metaphysical illusion that spirit dwells in matter.

In a lecture hall of students and professors at Moscow State University in 1988, a year before communism began to collapse, Reagan, standing before a statue of Lenin, delivered a message so bizarre that it did more to upset Christianity than Marxism. "In the beginning was the spirit," Reagan told the audience, "and it was from this spirit that the material abundance of creation issued forth." God created the world to bring forth the affluent society of sheer abundance. Religious faith depends upon the fecundity of plenty.[34]

Every major modern thinker, from John Locke to Adam Smith, from Darwin to Marx, believed that history moved in the opposite direction, from the bottom up, with humanity's moral nature evolving from below out of the material struggles of existence. Even the Christian evolutionist tells us that the miracle of life is the birth of mind out of matter, from inanimate things to living self-conscious creatures, the eternal climb from the lower to the higher that finally reaches some mystical or metaphysical level that promises reunion with God. Reagan brought mysticism to Marxist atheists and reversed the scheme. Spirit was at the beginning and it gave rise to the "material abundance" of the world. Our purpose in life is to enjoy that abundance and give thanks to the spirit that created it. By a bold inversion, the religious conception of creation as a ladder of ascent, by which humanity mounts its way to beatitude, sublimely disappears, and in the mind of the alchemist beatitude becomes abundance itself.

In the nineteenth century, Karl Marx noticed that material abundance had little to do with the religious idea of the sacred, what was "worthy" of the spirit. Plenitude was simply what was valuable to life, nothing more, he wrote, quoting an economist; it was an "appetite of mind . . . as natural as hunger to the body."[35] Reagan, however, was certain that what was desirable was valuable and spiritual, and while Marx promised that socialism would overcome scarcity, Reagan knew that only capitalism could deliver on that promise. Where all this left Christianity is puzzling, particularly in respect to a religion that warned: "For what shall it profit a man, if he shall gain the whole world, and lose his own soul . . . ?" Whatever Jesus may have preached, America's "Great Communicator" believed in earthly happiness and told the Russians that the treasures of life were theirs to be had in this world. The message was a stunning success; the audience jumped to its feet. Communists wanted neither the crown of thorns nor the agony of the Cross; they simply wanted what Marxism had failed to deliver—prosperity. A nation largely of atheists knew that it was man, not God, who bestowed value upon things. Centuries ago, however, Jesus opposed the pleasures and vices of a decaying and declining Roman civilization, and Christianity was born, becoming the greatest mass movement in history. America offered Russia not the longings of the soul but the comforts of consumption. Remarking on Reagan's speech at Moscow State University, Aleksandr Solzhenitsyn was pleased that the American president would restrain the power of government so that the "essential values" of family and faith might come to life, though he wished he had heard less Emersonian gush and gusto and more the imperative of "self-limitation" and the authority of "Christian self-discipline."[36]

Solzhenitsyn, one of the truly courageous figures of the cold war, won his war against communism, but he was fighting a hopeless battle against what Walter Lippmann once called, in A Preface to Morals (1929), "the acids of modernity." Nietzsche foresaw this secularization of spirit that would overtake America: The future of the world would be up to the actor, he observed, not the philosopher. It was the performer who had the power to convince and create a new god subordinate to humanity's needs. A sea change in the history of modern thought, however, does not necessarily imply manipulation on the part of an insincere actor. Reagan believed in what he beheld, and with good reason.

The possibility that the essence of spirit could actualize itself in the sphere of matter had been put forth by Max Weber. In Weber's outlook, it is spirit that determines matter, the agony of consciousness bringing forth the fruits of capitalism, even if the poor chap, the sin-struck Calvinist, was striving for the salvation of his soul. We need not concern ourselves with the irony. The more telling detail is that Weber's mother raised him on the teachings of the American William Ellery Channing, Emerson's close friend, who also shared the conviction that spirit compels matter. Since God delights "to diffuse himself everywhere," Channing insisted, and since His "nature is unfolded within us," our desires are divine. Channing and Emerson fascinated Weber and Nietzsche because the American thinkers could do what the brooding Germans could not—stop worrying about the soul, forget sin, and start smiling. The famous American preacher, however, scarcely fascinated Tocqueville, who interviewed Channing in Boston in 1831, and asked the high priest of Unitarianism whether his dismissal of all the mysteries of Christiantity, including sin, evil, and the doctrine of atonement, subverted the whole meaning of religion by substituting reason for authority. Channing replied that it was easier to understand theological matters than the "tariff question."[37]

Reagan's belief that God could not possibly have been the author of evil and that therefore the "desires he implanted in us are good" is a marvelous reversal of Christian theology, an irony anticipated by Weber and previously affirmed by Emerson and Channing. Historically, religious philosophers such as St. Augustine believed that God had implanted the emotion of desire to create a sense of emptiness in the heart, a restless searching for some object beyond the self, the need to be reunified with God. Unfulfilled desire ought to turn the mind to a spiritual yearning far more meaningful than any earthly satisfaction. For Reagan, however, desire finds its fulfillment in the here and now, and the wonderful romantic seemed to have no doubt that he could drive his Cadillac convertible through the eye of a needle.

He would also drive America into the promised land without going through the valley of woe. According to Max Weber, all the enduring religions in history were attempts to make sense of the meaningless suffering in the world. In doubting that God could have created evil, however, Reagan relieved America of the thought of sin and suffering and enabled the people to see God as an idealized conception of their own goodness. Reagan's sense of religion conveyed no sense of the tragic, no reason why the world had to remain in a state of perilous conflict. As a political romantic, he wanted us to see not the sorrow of death but the joy of life.

—

RONALD REAGAN'S presidency was so belittled by his intellectual critics that this excursion into intellectual history becomes necessary. Reagan was accused of being close to a Hollywood huckster. "The mixture of self-indulgence and sanctimony yields that well-known condition, hypocrisy," wrote Joseph Kraft, in a column titled "Reaganism and the Politics of Piety." Reagan would use the language of idealism to rationalize the schemes of materialism, forgetting altogether Jesus and poverty and humility in order to reconceive Christianity to make it serve the interests and power of the rich classes. "Frank Sinatra is a dear friend, and California millionaires comprise the Kitchen Cabinet," complained Kraft. The libertarian Murray N. Rothbard called the politics of the self "The Reagan Fraud."[38] Was what Reagan had to offer a fraudulent hypocrisy? Or was it what Nietzsche called a necessary "alchemy"? The German philosopher would not have minded seeing Reagan returning to the sensibility of his hero Emerson in order to liberate the world from the "corpse-cold" body of religion.

It should be remembered that in the nineteenth century, the Transcendentalists, who influenced the religion of Reagan's mother, also anticipated her son in taking American thought away from the framers. The authors of the Constitution had seen the country seething with sin, conflict, and suspicion. The Transcendentalists purged the idea of sin as the Puritan baggage of depravity, and they reconceived America as a healthy, harmonious whole. Reagan loved to quote Winthrop on how "we shall be a city upon a hill," and he emphasized the Puritan's warning that "if we deal falsely with God in this work we have undertaken," He will "withdraw His present help from us." But Winthrop's imperative to give absolute fidelity and devotion to God above oneself was simply reversed by the Transcendentalists to locate God within the self. The Puritan sermon was a jeremiad lamenting an America about to fall into temptation. Reagan would have no patience with a religion of perdition. Be true to thy self in politics as well as religion, Reagan urged, as did Henry David Thoreau, who took Jefferson's dictum "That government is best which governs least" and changed it to "which governs not at all." Emerson insisted that "the appearance of character makes the state unnecessary."[39] Reagan was perfectly Emersonian in believing that we should beware of submitting to external authority lest we fail to perfect our own potential. When one listens to Reagan talk about finding common heroes in every walk of American life, one thinks of Walt Whitman redeeming the country by poetizing each and every occupation, a lyrical rapture that departs from Emerson in extolling the masses over the individual. But this is how Reagan put it in his 1981 inaugural address:

> Those who say that we're in a time when there are no heroes, they just don't know where to look. You can see heroes every day going in and out of factory gates. Others, a handful in number, produce enough food to feed all of us and then the world beyond. You meet heroes across a counter—and they're on both sides of that counter. There are entrepreneurs—with faith in themselves and faith in an idea—who create new jobs, new wealth and opportunity. They're individuals and families whose taxes support the government and whose voluntary gifts support church, charity, culture, art, and education. Their patriotism is quiet, but deep. Their values sustain our national life.[40]

In "Wealth," Emerson called upon Americans, especially intellectuals, to reconsider their animosity toward profit and avarice and regard gain and productive activity as a romantic, even spiritual, adventure that simply reflected the human command over matter. "Wealth has its source in applications of the mind to nature, from the rudest strokes of spade and axe up to the last secrets of art." Emerson even presaged the *zeitgeist* of the Reagan era in a poem. "The inevitable morning" that arrives with a leader who "forbids to despair; / His cheeks mantle with mirth; / And the unimagined good of men / Is yearning at the birth." Reagan was the alchemist of American political and religious history, a leader who would deny the dualism between matter and spirit and so sublimate sin that he could convince us that evil is nowhere and God everywhere and that abundance need only be made abundantly abundant. His political language is full of dawns and sunsets, of life springing eternal without a trouble in the world, where every man and woman is a hero and every day is "morning in America."[41]

"We see God around us because he dwells within us," instructed

Channing, whom Emerson called "our bishop." The message was passed down to the church of Reagan's mother. Even young Patti Davis, Reagan's daughter, could provoke the response of the Transcendentalist. "If," she asked her father, "I reach up high enough, can I touch God?" Reagan replied gently: "You don't have to reach up. God is everywhere, all the time, all around us." Perfect Emersonianism.[42]

The State as Menace:
The Secret of Reagan's Success

I F GOD IS EVERYWHERE, why have government? Edmund Burke, a true conservative, believed that government expressed the character of a nation and that the state would bind together the lives of those who came before, those living, and those still to come. Reagan, however, took his stand with Tom Paine, Burke's antagonist. Paine was the Pied Piper of eighteenth-century revolutions, seemingly rushing everywhere once he heard they were about to break out. It may seem odd that Reagan would side with a permanent revolutionary. Yet during the cold war Reagan's counterrevolutionary causes carried on the spirit of Paine, who had declared that his mission in life was to be where liberty was not. Paine also declared that the state was "the badge of lost innocence," like clothing necessary to cover our guilt after the fall from grace enjoyed in the Garden of Eden.[43] Reagan, like Paine, could neither bring himself to believe in the fall nor convince himself of any need for meaningful government.

It might appear that Reagan's antistatist sentiments derived from Emerson. Consider these positions taken by Reagan and Emerson, respectively:

> Those who preach the supremacy of the state will be remembered for the sufferings their delusions cause their people.

> Every actual State is corrupt. Good men must not obey the laws too well. What satire on government can equal the severity of censure conveyed in the word *politic*, which now

for ages has signified *cunning*, intimating that the State is a trick?[44]

Both the president and the poet convinced themselves that to get rid of the state was to get rid of damnation. Emerson's statement occurs in his essay "Politics," and he disdained the state not because it was strong and threatening but because it was weak and cowardly. Reagan felt the opposite, seeing the state always and everywhere an omnipresent menace to liberty. "The French philosopher De. Tocqueville," Reagan told a radio audience, "spoke of gov't covering the face of society with a network of small, complicated rules until the Nat[ion] is reduced to a flock of timid and industrious animals of which gov't is the shepherd."[45] Actually Tocqueville saw just the opposite in America in the 1830s, the impotence of government in the face of "democratic despotism." It is difficult to accuse government of "covering the face of society" with stifling rules and regulations when it is society itself, "the tyranny of the majority," that determines what government does or does not do. Reagan blamed government for the intractableness of its institutions that the people themselves spawned as they beseeched government to do what they wanted. The democratization of society, Tocqueville anticipated, meant that the state and its people would be locked in a relationship of mutual dependency, each needing the support of the other—as today, senior citizens rely on Social Security, and government counts upon their vote.

Tocqueville, however, also warned that the democratic politician in America runs for office by running against the state, winning the right to control government by promising to weaken it. Reagan would do just that, and the hidden secret of his popular success was his blaming government for problems that are inherent in democracy itself. He could, with a straight face, tell the public that the American farmer wants more than anything to be free of government, at the same time that the Iowan farmer is writing to his senator demanding that price supports, acreage allotments, and other subsidies be continued.[46] Tocqueville would not be surprised, and perhaps Thomas Paine would say to Reagan that when he was inveighing against eighteenth-century government as parasitical, it was monarchy and the aristocratic nobility (which he mocked as "noability") and not the modern democracy he wished to see rise in America. The *Federalist* authors could also remind Reagan that the people are the problem and government the solution, that irrational desires require rational control. Reagan not only insisted that people's desires were good; he flipped the formulation around and had the American people believing how virtuous they were and how vicious their government was. It worked. Reagan never lost an election. Was he sincere? Reagan's deeply felt position on this issue was far less hypocritical than historical.

Reagan's animus toward government echoes back to Thomas Jefferson, who ran against John Adams in the election of 1800, claiming the Federalist leader was augmenting the power of the state and destroying liberty. The lesson seems to be never blame the people for anything and blame government for everything. You'll win every time. It hardly matters that when Jefferson was elected, he increased the power of the centralized federalist government, just as Reagan would increase the power of liberal big government.

Today Americans are told that it is good to live with big government conservatism, leaving behind both Jefferson and Reagan, embarrassments to the conservative conscience. How did conservatism come to negate its own identity?

The answer was provided by the great-grandson of John Adams, our supreme historian Henry Adams. In a dialogue in his novel *Democracy*, the Honourable Silas P. Ratcliffe, senator from Illinois, is being questioned by Madeline Lee, a widow who came to Washington, D.C., to observe the operations of government out of a fascination with power. She finds that power corrupts, that money is the "grease of government" and party politics little more than the "systematic organization of hatreds." Disgusted, she asks: "Is a respectable government impossible in a democracy?" A crowd gathers around Mrs. Lee, wondering what she is demanding. "I am asking Senator Ratcliffe," she informs the room, "what is to become of us if corruption is allowed to go unchecked." "My reply," says Ratcliffe, "is that no representative government can long be much better or much worse than the society it represents. Purify society and you purify government. But try to purify the government artificially and you only aggravate failure."[47]

Ronald Reagan would set Ratcliffe on his ear. He agreed with Tom Paine that "society is produced by our wants, and government by our wickedness." Reagan's aim was to reduce the scope of government on the assumption that he did not have to address the character of society, particularly a society where everyone is a hero. But Adams's point was that society makes government what it is, and today government caters to the will of society and its insatiable demands. The unmentionable irony is that today big government conservatism, a phenomenon that seems a paradox because big government was understood to be precisely the wickedness of liberalism alone, actually derives from Reaganism itself. An American people encouraged by Reagan to pursue their desires would also make demands upon government. A political leader who told America that he had extirpated liberalism had in reality exacerbated it.

How can government cease growing if all people are heroes and their desires good? Surely Nietzsche must have the last laugh and Christ the last tear. The president rid America of what the philosopher knew was the last threat of religion—"a bad conscience." The president "alters the direction of ressentiment," removing the people's religiously driven repressive feelings about themselves. Then, like an alchemist, he takes society's guilt for its selfishness and turns it against government itself, to be blamed as the source of all of America's problems, the very institution that grows out of the people's own egoistic desires. Christ preached that sin lies in the soul; Reagan convinced America that it lies in the state. Christianity never had a chance.[48]

At times it seemed that Reagan believed we could enjoy a free and full life without any significant role for government—"an awful spectacle," a proposition as useless as "a nation, without a national government," complained Alexander Hamilton, in making a case for strong government. Reagan the romantic dreams of a state of almost happy statelessness, a vision, Burke warned, that would be "the wild gas" of the liberal imagination.[49]

———

MY PERSONAL RESERVATION about Ronald Reagan is not that he was a conservative; on the contrary, he was a liberal romantic who opened up the American mind to the full blaze of Emersonian optimism. Like the poet, the president left the American mind innocent, without knowledge of power and evil and the sins of human nature. The Reaganite ethos of morning in America, of the country as always in a state of becoming, as the land of tomorrow, is old New England Transcendentalism somehow finding a home in Illinois, Hollywood, Sacramento, and then the White House. As Santayana said of Emerson: "If there was anything which he valued more than the power to push on to what might lie before, it was the power to escape what lay behind. A sense of potentiality and a sense of riddance are, as he might have said, the two poles of liberty." Ronald Reagan might have said it too. However, an Emersonian president who tells us our desires are good still leaves much to be desired.[50]

In "Self-Reliance," Emerson taught Americans that if only they would spurn politics and government, "power ceases in the instant of repose." So did Reagan, who saw power, domination, and corruption emanating from government and government alone. But does power really cease with the cessation of the state? And can the ideals of democracy be realized without the state? To raise such questions may well suggest how Reagan brings America face-to-face with what might be called the Paine Problem.

As would Emerson and Reagan, Paine believed that liberty lies in minimizing the state, since freedom is, by definition, the absence of restriction. In the study of the American past, many American historians regard themselves as radical, some even Marxist, and they cite Paine as a predecessor in championing democracy. Yet historians are reluctant to see that the causes they have espoused—abolition of slavery, rights of labor, civil rights, women's liberation—have all required the power of the state for their realization. Historically, democracy stood in the way of such causes. In Reagan's era, causes like the right to abortion and gay rights also came to depend upon the courts and the protections of the Constitution, not upon democracy and the will of the people. While scholars on the Left continue to teach their students how radical is participatory democracy, conservative followers of Reagan have well understood that throughout American history democracy has been less than liberal and in many instances downright conservative. Hence today conservatives believe in states' rights and local sovereignty, while the Left continues to call for "all power to the people," only to cringe when the people go to the polls. In American scholarship, some radical historians have written glowing books on Thomas Paine with the aim of taking Paine away from Reagan and redeeming America from capitalism. But here we arrive at one of the oddest moments in modern intellectual history.

Ronald Reagan was governor of California in 1968, the year the world shook to its foundations with student rebellions almost everywhere. In Paris especially, the generation of '68 that took to the streets would be influenced by a poststructuralist school of thought based on three quasi-anarchist convictions: language functions as an instrument of manipulation (Jacques Derrida); the state and its regulations dominate the citizen and exercise surveillance and punishment (Michel Foucault); all forces inhibiting the full flower of human desire must be exposed and eliminated (Félix Guattari and Giles Deleuze). The aim of *"pensant '68"* was to escape the restricting codes and the organizational structure of the bureaucratic state. The shibboleth was *dégagement*—extrication, releasing, clearing, freeing up, hands-off, what in American parlance is called decentralization and deregulation. Today some astute scholars argue that what the '68 rebels were emotionally striving for was not the tired old schemes of socialism but "a new spirit of capitalism." If the Right couldn't recognize it, the Left refused to admit it.[51]

For the intellectual historian, Reagan presents other problems. Not only did the president so optimistically look ahead to a new dawn; he rarely looked back to the profound wisdom of the American framers. Seeing nothing wrong with the American people and almost everything wrong with their government, Reagan was unwilling to see that the two were inextricably related and that the devices of the state are necessary to deal with the divisions of society. Reagan told the people what they wanted to hear, whereas the framers told them what they needed to know—a government that refuses to educate, lead, and guide, to elevate and "refine and enlarge" the "passions and interests" of the people, is a government that cannot control the governed and cannot control itself.[52]

One would like to say to this Emersonian everyman, this prince of a president, stop watching old films, forget Errol Flynn, and read *The Federalist Papers* and Tocqueville's *Democracy in America*, where the claims of commerce are not simply to be celebrated but "properly understood," and the trail of the serpent is to be seen in the heart of society and not only in the halls of government. When Reagan advised Florence Yerly that God could not have possibly created evil, he was encouraging her to return to the life of intimacy and accept that "the physical relationship between a man and a woman is the *highest form of companionship*." It is easy to applaud such advice as one way of getting rid of a nagging bad conscience, and Emerson would agree that evil simply disappears when one feels good about one's self and one's desires. Private life is one thing, however, and public another, and without the wisdom of the eighteenth-century founders, one wonders how Reagan ever thought he could open up the American mind to the fulfillment of desire without leaving America with a government bigger than ever.

Democracy may absolve people of their moral failings, but our founders sought to educate us, to keep the conscience alert to the presence of "ambition, avarice, jealousy, and personal animosity" that tempt human beings to project on to government their own vices so that greed can escape guilt and sin avoid shame. It is difficult to see how government alone can be the problem when its system of checks and restraints was designed to be a direct "reflection" of the problem of human nature itself. Reagan let human nature off the hook, as did Emerson, who told Americans there is nothing to repress but repression itself. Both liberals could benefit from listening to true conservatives. For in society everyone is not a hero, and Madison's warning about "the defect of better motives" reminds us that if democracy is simply left to the dictates of desire, we shall never get to what Reagan promised in his farewell address: the "shining city upon a hill."

———

THE POLITICAL EDUCATION of Ronald Reagan defies a generational explanation since so many people of his era remained liberal and underwent no conversion to conservatism. If not generational, perhaps the explanation is geographical and turns on where Reagan came from: the Illinois that produced Abraham Lincoln and Adlai Stevenson, two statesmen who looked to government, not away from it. Can there be a class explanation of Reagan, the youth who rose from obscurity and poverty to fame and the presidency? His critics claim that he betrayed his roots, while his admirers are more interested in celebration than explanation. We scratch our head here. Whether or not Ronald Reagan is a riddle, he represents "the mysterious gem which must lie hidden somewhere in politics."[53] Those are the words of Henry Adams, who confessed his bafflement in studying the history of the American presidency. The mysterious gem lies somewhere in a remarkable leader who inherited the dark night of malaise and brought forth morning in America.

CHAPTER TWO

From Huck Finn to Film Star

"By the Way I Was Raised in Poverty"

RONALD REAGAN may be less a riddle if we learn about his early life. "All history becomes subjective," advised Emerson. "There is properly no history, only biography. Every mind must know the whole lesson for itself. What it does not see, what it does not live, it will not know."[1]

Only by studying the private experience of the individual, instructed Emerson, can we see the world as he or she saw it. Reagan's biographical background helps us understand how he came to shape history and the values he hoped to see realized in the world. He relished talking about his boyhood, even though some of the details of his formative years were far from happy. Home life came down to getting by from day to day, but life on the playing field young Reagan lived for and would remember the rest of his days. In his memoirs, he recalls seeing people of all kinds, farmers, small merchants, salesmen, striving to get ahead, working hard and long, pushing the limits of their lives. Even during the years of the Great Depression, the realities of hardship did little to deflect the dreams of the romantic. The experience of his youth was preface to Reagan's moral philosophy.

In 1983, two years after Ronald Reagan took office as president, he received a telegram from Leonard Kirk, a black unemployed Vietnam veteran, who wrote to convey his support for Reagan's defense policy but also to call him "a worse president than tricky Dick Nixon" and a "closet racist and friend of the rich." Reagan replied in the politest terms, pointing out to Kirk that he had no way of knowing that the man sitting in the White House was raised by parents who admonished bigotry, that he had campaigned against the prohibition of black players in big league baseball, and that as governor of California he had appointed more blacks to executive and policymaking positions than "*all* the previous governors of California put together." He also mentioned that his father slept in a car during a blizzard rather than stay in a hotel that excluded Jews. Reagan then concluded with an afterthought: "By the way I was raised in poverty."[2]

In another letter Reagan told a correspondent that he and his family endured poverty in the twenties, when there were no government programs that might have provided relief. In his letters and in his two volumes of memoirs, Reagan mentions almost in passing the impoverished circumstances of his early life, but the vivid details of the deprivation are telling. The Reagans, while not dirt poor, nonetheless led a nomadic existence that had young Ronald living in a half-dozen places within a few years, one residence a dreary flat over a bakery with no indoor toilet facilities. The family had to give up chicken on Sunday and turn to liver, considered a pet food by the butcher, who would add a pound to the grocery order without asking questions. "Soup, potatoes, and bread were served daily," biographer Anne Edwards discovered in her valuable research. "On Sundays—since the cats ate the mice they caught in the barn anyway—the Reagans ate the cats' liver dressed up with a slab of bacon and some homegrown onions."[3]

Reagan's father, John Edward Reagan, known as Jack, was of Irish ancestry, with roots in County Tipperary, a peasant land that had been devastated by the potato famine of the 1840s. Rugged and handsome, Jack was brought up in America as a practicing Catholic, and he was fond of sports, pranks, storytelling, dancing, daydreaming, and corn whiskey. Moving from town to town in Illinois, Jack worked as a shoe salesman, spending much of his free time shooting the breeze with the passersby. He was sometimes laid off and once was arrested for public drunkenness. Since many Illinois towns were dry, he occasionally went to Chicago for a spree, returning home with the whiff of whiskey and the spice of women.

While Jack Reagan was restless with dreams and discontent, Nelle Clyde Wilson Reagan possessed a remarkable determination. Unlike her husband, Nelle was of Scottish ancestry. Her father had searched for gold in California and her mother had found God in the Bible. The mother's piety carried over to Nelle, who had a curious mixture of assertiveness and kindness. Her father disapproved of his daughter marrying Jack Reagan, but Nelle was persistent. She forgave Jack's weekend benders while pursuing a life of good works, weekly Bible studies, visits to prisons and state mental institutions to minister to the sick, and experiments in faith healing. While Jack smoked, drank, and laughed at life to ward off depression, Nelle prayed, worked hard, and saw that there was food on the table and the rent was paid. Although Reagan was baptized into his mother's Protestant church, theirs was a relaxed religion, a nineteenth-century frontier faith rooted in scripture and fellowship. The Disciples of Christ preached optimism about progress and disdained doctrinal disputes. Arrogance, fanaticism, and meddlesomeness had no place in the Reagans' church.

Seven years after his parents' marriage, Ronald Wilson Reagan was born, in Tampico, Illinois, on February 6, 1911. Jack Reagan, bending down to get a close look at his son, remarked, "for such a little Dutchman, he makes a hell of a lot of noise, doesn't he?" The reference to Dutchman implied that Jack saw his son as robust and assertive, as though he was meant to be heard. Thereafter Reagan was called "Dutch." In 1920 the Reagans moved to Dixon, a large town of ten thousand with a public library, several churches, and a main street lined with shops. Reagan later recalled life in Dixon as "my Huck Finn years." He went hiking, exploring, fishing, dove into the Rock River, scaled steep cliffs, pored over insects and butterflies, fooled around with firearms, got in playground fistfights—any pleasure beyond the gaze of adult authority.[4]

The young boy acquired lasting traits from both of his parents. From Nelle, a former amateur actress, young Ron learned reading and voice training and practiced dramatic recitals as the first step to the stage and theater. She also taught him that God is essentially benevolent and that all the "twists of fate" are part of "His plan." Ron's older brother, Neil, nicknamed Moon, also liked to consider himself a budding actor, but he was less disciplined and more brassy than the introspective Ron, who had at a very young age the drive to succeed at whatever challenged him.

Reagan's exuberant ambition had its roots in his early environment. In his memoirs he tells us that he never regarded his family as deprived, even though he heard later that, in comparison to other families, townspeople did indeed think the Reagans poor. "But I didn't know that when I was growing up. And I never thought of our family as disadvantaged. Only later did the government decide that it had to tell people they were poor."[5] Reagan made this observation in his 1990 autobiography, *An American Life*. Lyndon Johnson grew up in similar circumstances in Texas and took an entirely different view of the New Deal and the Great Society as rightful "wars on poverty." Reagan was president during the 1980s, when the culture of complaint was everywhere and more and more people saw themselves as victims in need of government support. Liberals believed that Reagan's pinched life in Illinois should have made him sympathetic to the welfare state, as were his mother and father. But Franklin D. Roosevelt's welfare state was a response to the Great Depression of the 1930s, a half-century old by the time Reagan became president.

Was father Jack an inspiring role model? In his memoirs Reagan tells us that his father "believed energy and hard work were the only ingredients for success." During much of the Depression, however, Jack was out of work, until the New Deal employed him in the Works Progress Administration, which distributed food and food stamps to the distressed in Dixon. The townspeople wanted jobs, not handouts, and it was not until the New Deal offered the Civic Works Program that jobs paving streets, trimming trees, and repairing the park became available. Reagan does not record his reaction to his father's work for the WPA. His memoirs leave the impression that the federal government administered a means test and that families were cut off from support if the head of household worked. That government would require an able-bodied man to avoid work before it offered him support became a fixation of Reagan's. Whether or not that was actually the case, to a friend Reagan wrote bitterly: "My father finally got a job during the New Deal in charge of what we call welfare now but it was called 'Relief' then and it wasn't spelled ROLAIDS." Both father and son enthusiastically supported FDR in the 1932 campaign, and Reagan would vote for FDR in three subsequent elections. Yet Reagan seemed to identify government with the Depression itself, and to believe that to survive both meant to survive helplessness and humiliation, as the proud Reagan family had.[6]

Reagan always admired his father for speaking out against bigotry and racial prejudice, yet he also defined himself in opposition to his irresolute father, his memory haunted by a scene that took place when he was eleven years old. "I came home to find my father flat on his back on the front porch, and no one there to lend him a hand but me. He was

drunk, dead to the world. I stood over him for a minute or two. I wanted
to let myself in the house and go to bed and pretend he wasn't there."
The son knew of his father's weakness and knew what his absence from
work had meant, but the youth's emotions boiled over. "I felt myself
filled with grief for my father at the same time I was feeling sorry for
myself. Seeing his arms *spread out as if he were crucified, as indeed he
was*—his hair soaked with the melting snow, snoring as he breathed. I
could feel no resentment against him." Reagan lifted up his father and
carried him into the house. Later he reflected in his memoirs how for
everyone "must come that first moment of accepting responsibility."[7]

The historian Robert Dallek believes that the porch scene in Dixon
remained with Reagan the rest of his life, making him value all the more
freedom, autonomy, and disciplined self-determination. "The needy
reminded him of his dependent father, from whom he had tried to separate himself all his life." Reagan "lived in fear of his father's uncontrolled behavior." And Dallek supposed that such an explanation applied
to Reagan's followers as well. "If it were possible to probe the psychology of the Reaganites, I suggest that one might find a shared problem
with authority stemming from childhood. I speculate that the conservative world view is based on an inner need that is satisfied by fighting
against excessive power and control in government."[8]

The problem with such a psychoanalytic explanation is that other
political leaders, including Reagan's contemporary Daniel Patrick
Moynihan, had alcoholic fathers but had no fear of government. Moynihan remained a liberal who had no problem with authority. Nor did Bill
Clinton, whose memory of his drunken, abusive step father remained
an open wound. Reagan's obsession about the power of government is a
riddle; but an unconscious psychological phobia hardly explains his con-
sciously developed political principles.

The question of freedom and responsibility remained with Reagan
throughout his life. His work as a young lifeguard during the summers
in Dixon, in the late twenties, is legendary, and not only for his many res-
cues, seventy-seven in all, and each rescue carved into a notch on a log
by the river. A tall figure, with broad shoulders and handsome tanned
face gleaming in the sun, young Reagan was the all-American, the
proverbial real thing. Later in Hollywood his exploits were the butt of
jokes: the powerful swimmer who plunged into the Rock River and

saved good-looking girls to strike up a date. But in his memoir Reagan claimed his summer job helped him understand the complexities of human nature. "Lifeguarding provides one of the best vantage points in the world to learn about people," wrote Reagan. "I guarantee you they needed saving—no lifeguard gets wet without reason. . . . Not many thanked me, much less gave me a reward, and being a little money-hungry I'd done a little daydreaming about it. They felt insulted," he reflected. "I got to recognize that people hate to be saved. Almost every one of them later sought me out and angrily denounced me for dragging them to the shore. 'I would have been fine if you'd let me alone,' was their theme. 'You made a fool out of me trying to make a hero out of yourself.'"[9]

The historian Kenneth Walsh believes that Reagan had learned "the lesson in laissez-faire applied just as much to politics and government as it did to recreational swimming. People want to take care of themselves, and it wounds their pride and makes them resentful when someone intervenes to 'save' them."[10] Reagan would in turn be a rescuer in politics and diplomacy, saving people, as he saw it, from the dangerous currents of the liberal welfare state and from the "evil empire." But do the saved really resent their savior? FDR won four straight elections, in large part a hero for rescuing people from the ravages of the Depression. And yet many of the same people who benefited from the New Deal in later years turned against the welfare state. The descendants of the people known as Okies are a prime example. Immortalized in John Steinbeck's *The Grapes of Wrath*, they escaped the Dust Bowl in broken-down jalopies and gratefully approved a government camp and accepted free food, showers, and sleeping barracks upon their arrival in the West. Years later, however, when the sharecroppers became established California landowners, many voted Republican.

The irony was not lost upon California conservatives. Reagan's stalwart Republicans, whose families had been saved by the Democrats from the ravages of the Depression, helped bring an antigovernment platform to power. "A man receiving charity practically always hates his benefactor," observed George Orwell.[11] To take and then to refuse to give is the "unenlightened self-interest" of the American character that troubled Tocqueville, who would recognize the farmers who complain about government and depend upon it for subsidies. Emerson and Niet-

zsche believed that charity breeds dependency and that resentment and
ingratitude go together. Reagan could well agree with Jefferson that
dependency begets servility. But neither president understood the mentality of denial on the part of those who need the state. In the German
language, Nietzsche pointed out, the term *Schuld* means both guilt and
debt. The lifeguard formulation needs to be revised: People in distress
want to be saved, but are too guilty to admit it.

"The Happiest Times of My Life"

I N THE FALL of 1928, Reagan enrolled at Eureka College, working
his way through the school year as a janitor, dishwasher, and laborer
on construction sites. A hundred miles south of Dixon, Eureka
was a small Christian college of about 250 students. Reagan retained
a fondness for the place and would return there as president to give
heartwarming talks. "Everything good that has happened to me—
everything—," exclaimed Reagan to an enthusiastic crowd, "started here
on this campus in those four years that still are so much a part of my
life." Majoring in economics, Reagan was content to be an average
student—though years later he would impress upon his children the
importance of studying hard and getting good grades. In his youth Reagan had an amazing memory, and his acting career taught him how to
learn his lines by heart. Later in his political life, even when his memory
began to falter, he still enjoyed a good sense of language, a feel for narrative, and an attraction to anecdote, either for moral or comic purposes.
In college, he wrote in his memoir, "I loved three things: drama, politics,
and sports."[12]

At college Margaret Cleaver, Reagan's high school sweetheart, drew
him to theater productions, and he landed the lead in several plays. A
Eureka production of Edna St. Vincent Millay's *Aria da Capo*, in which
Reagan played the shepherd Thyrsis, garnered him an honorable mention in a national contest at Northwestern University. "I guess that was
the day the acting bug really bit me," Reagan recalled. He was not altogether sure he could make it as a big-time actor, but in the late twenties
the Hollywood film industry was producing box office blockbusters with

glamorous stars, and it was difficult for Reagan to buckle down and hit the books with such an irresistible lure waiting out West.[13]

During these college years his fellow students looked to Reagan to take charge and try to handle whatever problems were facing them, particularly in the fraternity house he pledged. As early as his freshman year he was chosen to speak for both faculty and students at a strike demonstration opposing the budget cuts of Eureka's president Bert Wilson. Reagan delivered his first political speech late in the evening to an auditorium ringing with applause. The speech "was as exciting as any I ever gave," he recalled years later. "For the first time in my life, I felt my words reach out and grab an audience, and it was exhilarating." The controversy received national attention, and Wilson resigned. Ironically, forty years later it would be Reagan as governor of California who would be making the budget cuts. Government to Reagan always meant cutting costs; politics meant giving speeches, not the grubby task of fundraising but addressing an audience and knowing how to speak well, thoughtfully, and concisely. Once as president, Reagan faced an audience eager to break for lunch. He opened his speech with the reassuring message: "As Henry the Eighth said to each of his six wives, 'I won't keep you long.'"[14]

Football, Reagan's third passion along with acting and politics, may have prepared him for politics even more than acting or politics itself. Historians and biographers of Reagan seem reluctant to take seriously his enthusiasm for the game because he never became a star player. His poor eyesight precluded him from playing quarterback, wide receiver, or running back. All that was left was the line, and at 170 pounds young Reagan seemed like a half-pint. The coach refused to allow him to play early in his freshman year, but an injury to a player opened a position at guard and Reagan finally took to the field at Eureka.

One player Reagan teamed up with was William Franklin Burghardt, a black lineman whose endurance of racial insults Reagan later recalled in correspondence, and in a 1986 speech on Martin Luther King Jr. Reagan also thought fondly of his coach, Ralph McKinzie, even though the coach only played the scrawny kid for lack of reserves. Reagan recalled that playing football was thrilling, the test of courage on a field of friendly ferocity. "I worshipped the wild charge down the field and the final melee—but being underneath it all, once or twice, gave me my first taste of claustrophobia. I got frightened to the point of hysteria in the darkness under the mass of writhing, shouting bodies." Later the claustrophobia would cause Reagan to have some fear of flying. Still, "the lure of sweat and action always pulled me back to the game," and even though he would walk off the field bruised and battered, Reagan could only conclude: "Those were the happiest times of my life."[15]

The thrill of the game remained with Reagan for life. William F. Buckley Jr. recalled a Washington, D.C., banquet in 1985 at which the president spoke. As Reagan was about to depart, he heard New York Representative Jack Kemp, a former quarterback for the AFL's Buffalo Bills, call out, "Hey, Mr. President!" Cocking a football behind his ear, Kemp drilled a bullet pass at blinding speed thirty yards across the room. "Reagan reaches out with one hand, catches it," said Buckley. "The crowd goes berserk."[16]

The curious thing about Reagan's football reminiscences is his seeming indifference to winning or losing. In an essay for his college literary magazine, he described a star player who was reluctant to risk his reputation when his team was behind thirteen to nothing, but then got off the bench to take charge. "He didn't scurry like so many open field runners, neither did he push and fight his way, but sailed, and as he sidestepped a man the rhythm remained unbroken, until, as he hit an inevitable tackler and his bird-like flight changed to a ripping, tearing smash that gained the very last yard." Though the game ended in a tie, the coach attributed the team's success to the great halfback. "It matters not that you win or lose, but how you played the game."[17]

Fortunately for American history, Reagan did not have Vince Lombardi for a coach. "Winning isn't everything," declared the famous head of the "fighting Irish" of Notre Dame and the Green Bay Packers, "it's the only thing." Later, when Reagan negotiated with the Soviet Union, winning the cold war was neither everything nor the only thing. Ending the cold war was Reagan's goal. A tie, and no need for overtime.

Reagan's memoirs devote much more attention to sports and drama than to what he studied in his college courses. As an economics major, he read, as we have seen, Frédéric Bastiat, the advocate of laissez-faire whose ideas were close to those of Jean-Baptiste Say, another Frenchman regarded by some scholars as a forerunner of the supply-side economics that became prominent during the Reagan presidency. Unlike many college students, who were taught by liberal or radical professors that labor alone creates value, Reagan could well have learned from Bastiat and Say that the producer as entrepreneur creates exchange value by generating consumer desire and demand. Of Bastiat's *Harmonies économiques* (1851), Marx fumed: "Nothing is more dry and boring than the fantasies of a commonplace mind."[18] When President Reagan delivered his address at Moscow State University in 1988, the economic message he brought no longer seemed dry and boring to an audience bitterly disenchanted with Marxism.

Another course Reagan took may help explain his instincts, why his earliest emotions were more poetical than political. He wrote essays on Joseph Warton, whose "Enthusiast," published in 1744, is, according to Arthur O. Lovejoy, the seminal statement on the British romantic movement. In one essay Reagan remarked positively on the romantic's "growing disgust with all classical subjects so worn out in Europe."[19] Surely Reagan was impressed with the romantic's revolt against restriction. Curiously, all the elements of romanticism—enthusiasm, imagination, passion—are precisely what the framers of the U.S. Constitution sought to purge from matters of government. The authors of the *Federalist* believed that a politics of "interest" must replace the older politics of "zeal" that tore apart European society. Reagan, however, had little patience with the rules and restraints of the Constitution. He believed in freeing up markets so that individuals could zealously pursue their interests.

Radio Days

GRADUATING FROM Eureka College in 1932, Reagan left Dixon to seek employment at the height of the Depression. The country seemed an economic wasteland, with men loitering on sidewalk corners out of work, street beggars with hands out. Banks had closed down, crops were rotting on farm fields, ragged hoboes were staring out from railroad boxcars, and everywhere people were idle and down and out. The buoyant Reagan would not be depressed; his mother had taught him that any adversities in life were "His plan," and God could only mean well. He remembered the Depression years as a time when people entered movie houses to escape into fantasy from the harsh realities outside. At the same time Americans came together in their common need. Recalling "the human warmth," Reagan wrote that "there was a spirit of helpfulness and yes kindliness abroad in the land."[20]

Reagan knew he wanted to be in the entertainment business. In the Midwest, however, "you didn't say out loud to someone that you wanted to be an actor. So I told him," he said of an older man who took him under wing, "that I thought about radio and being a sports announcer." The man told Reagan to look for work at nearby stations. Accordingly, Reagan hitchhiked to Chicago but found no positions. He then crossed the Mississippi to Davenport, Iowa, checked in at a YMCA, and followed up on a vague job offer at radio station WOC. On the day he showed, Reagan was told that there would be no more interviews for the position. He trudged out of the room and uttered loud enough to be heard, "How in the hell can you get to be a sports announcer if you can't even get a job at a radio station?" The station director followed him and in a raspy voice said, "Hold on, you big bastard. What was that you said about *sports* announcing?" After explaining that he had played college football, the director asked him to go into another room and, when the red light went on, to "describe an imaginary football game to me and make me *see* it." Reagan was asked to imitate life on the gridiron by verbal invention alone. He set the scene with Eureka College behind 6–0 and the teams exchanging possession, the late afternoon shadows settling over the field. On the final play, Reagan dramatized an off-tackle rush to the goal line and a successful conversion. His voice conveyed the thrill of the cheering crowd. "Ye did great, ye big SOB," said the director. "Be here Saturday, you're broadcasting the Iowa-Minnesota Homecoming game. You'll get $5 and bus fare."[21]

By the mid-thirties radio had entered people's lives, and no politician took greater advantage of it than Roosevelt, with his fireside chats. So did Roosevelt's antagonist Father Coughlin, the anti-Semitic "radio priest" who told millions of listeners of the wickedness of Wall Street and the wonders of Benito Mussolini. Thrilling to dramas like H. G. Wells's *The War of the Worlds*, which aired in 1938, Americans followed great sports by the radio: the rematch of the Joe Louis–Max Schmeling heavyweight fight, which the "Brown Bomber" won at Yankee Stadium;

the Rose Bowls in Pasadena, the World Series in New York and Brooklyn. Over the airwaves "Dutch Reagan" became well known throughout the Midwest, covering baseball and football. Admirers thought he should run for political office. Those who worked at the radio station felt his wit and charm. "He was handsome, charismatic, always joking," remembered one colleague.[22]

Actually, Reagan rarely attended the sports events. Instead he dramatically created them as details were reported over the telegraph wire and his assistant, Curly, typed up the bare facts for Reagan to embellish. A few visits to the stadium enabled Reagan to memorize all the visuals: the outfield, diamond, grandstand, bleachers, press box, the gestures of the players and their slang. He also had a turntable that sounded the fans' applause, which he turned on with a foot pedal. When he saw Curly starting to type, Reagan would begin his narrative, describing the windup and the pitch, "and at that moment Curly would slip me the blank. It might contain the information S2C, and without a pause I would translate this into 'It's a called strike breaking over the inside corner.' " But on one occasion he had nothing to go on but his imagination. It was during a scoreless game between the Chicago Cubs and the St. Louis Cardinals, with the famous Dizzy Dean on the mound.

> I saw Curly start to type so I finished the wind-up and had Dean send the ball on its way to the plate, took the slip from Curly, and found myself faced with the terse note: "The wire's gone dead." I had a ball on the way to the plate and there was no way to call it back.

With the game tied in the ninth inning, Reagan could not possibly tell listeners that he had lost contact. "I knew of only one thing that wouldn't get in the score column and betray me—a foul ball."

Reagan had the batter, Billy Jurges, hitting down the left-field foul line, and then he at looked Curly, who just shrugged his shoulders helplessly. Reagan had no choice but to have Jurges hit foul after foul. He colorfully described kids scrambling to retrieve the balls in the upper deck and enhanced the tension by dramatizing some hits that just missed being home runs. Incredibly, he kept the story going for six minutes as he lost count of the number of fouls.

I began to be frightened that maybe I was establishing a new world record for a fellow staying at bat hitting fouls, and this could betray me. Yet I was into it so far I didn't dare reveal that the wire had gone dead.

My voice was rising in pitch and threatening to crack—and then, bless him, Curly started typing. I clutched at the slip. It said: "Billy popped out on the first ball pitched." Not in my game he didn't—he popped out after practically making a career of foul balls.[23]

Mark Twain could not have done better. "Mr. Twain . . . he told the truth, mainly," wrote the author in introducing *Huckleberry Finn*. One reads the passage above with humor and marvels at Reagan as a raconteur. By contrast, the historian Garry Wills reads it with gravity and sees in Reagan's story the beginnings of his career in make-believe. Reagan started out neither as an actor with a guiding script nor as a journalist with a sense of accuracy and objectivity. Rather, he was a sports reporter caught up in the action on the field, whether real or imagined, and reaching for an audience moved more by emotion than fact. "Sportcasters are encouraged to lose their equanimity over a right hook or a forty-yard run," writes Wills, who comes close to depicting Reagan as suffering from prolonged adolescence.[24] For him, Reagan is something of a fabulist, always ready to embellish a story or legend.

Reagan saw his storytelling as the creation of instructive parables. The life and death of the great Notre Dame halfback George Gipp became irresistible to Reagan, who later played the part in the Hollywood film. In what became a famous half-time locker room pep talk, Notre Dame's coach, Knute Rockne, started the story that Gipp, as he lay dying in a hospital, uttered a deathbed request that the team go onto the field and bring home one last victory. Years later the locker room appeal "Win one for the Gipper" became a rallying cry for President Reagan's supporters. "Now, it's only a game," wrote Reagan, reflecting on the making of the film *Knute Rockne—All American*.

And maybe to hear it now afterwards—and this is what we feared might sound maudlin and not the way it was intended—but is there anything wrong with young people having an experience, feeling something so deeply, thinking of someone else to the point that they can give so completely of themselves? There will come times in the lives of all of us when we'll be faced with causes bigger than ourselves, and they won't be on the playing field.[25]

It bothers some people that the Gipper story may have been invented by Rockne and then memorialized by Reagan. Another story Reagan liked to tell was of a World War II pilot who, after ordering his crew to bail out of their crippled B-17 bomber, saw that the belly gunner, terrified and in tears, was too wounded to get out. "Never mind," says the pilot, "we'll ride it down together." That story had its origins in a Hollywood film, but Reagan had no qualms about repeating the apocryphal tale to a military audience gathered to honor recipients of the Medal of Honor.

Another occasion when Reagan told the same story reveals more about the conflict of generations that had divided America, and it may also show us how a romantic knew whereof he spoke. In 1981, President Reagan had invited actors Warren Beatty and Diane Keaton to the White House for a screening of their new movie, *Reds*. The film is about the life of the American journalist John Reed, who died in Russia shortly after going to report on the Bolshevik Revolution. Reed had written the ecstatic *Ten Days That Shook the World*, a text perhaps most remarkable for its exposure of its author's political infatuation. As Bertram D. Wolfe observed, when Reed arrived in St. Petersburg in 1917, he thought he was going to a wedding and only later did he realize he was attending a funeral. Director Beatty takes into account Reed's realization that the situation had changed, and Reagan told Beatty how impressed he was that the young star could act the major part he played in the film and be its director as well. Reagan then added, to Beatty and others in the screening room, "What's really wrong with the Russians in this film," and went on to tell a story of American aviators going down together. In Reagan's estimation Reed, fighting for communism, died in vain, unlike the American flyers, who went down with their plane fighting for freedom. When the film ended, Reagan was reported to have risen from his seat and stepped in front of the director to ask: "Well, Warren, where's the happy ending?" Beatty thought Reagan was being "funny." But a happy ending never came for John Reed, who died of typhus and was buried in the Kremlin Wall next to Lenin's tomb.[26]

Hollywood

IN THE MID-THIRTIES, the Chicago Cubs had spring training camp at Catalina, a beautiful, pristine island off the southern California coast. With a yen to see the West, and especially Hollywood, Reagan as sportscaster accompanied the Cubs to Catalina. In Los Angeles he looked up some contacts in the film industry—he already had an agent—and managed to get a screen test with Warner Brothers. He was told to wait for the results. Unaware that everyone was knocking down doors to break into film, Reagan let the studio know that he had to return to his job in Iowa. No sooner had he returned than he received a telegram offering a seven-year contract starting at $200 a week. Instantly Reagan wired his agent: "Sign Before They Change Their Minds." He then jumped into his Nash convertible, left Des Moines "in a cloud of dust," and drove the seven hundred miles to California in three days, stopping only for roadside naps. He crossed the scorching Mojave desert at night, inhaled the fragrance of orange blossoms as he raced through San Bernardino, and turned into Los Angeles's Biltmore Hotel, his body so stiff he "could hardly wobble." At twenty-five, hitting his prime, he was poised for success.[27]

Reagan arrived in Hollywood in 1937, right after F. Scott Fitzgerald had written his confessional essay "The Crack-Up" and had begun to work on a novel about the film industry, the posthumously published *The Last Tycoon*. The would-be actor and the worn-out author both hailed from the Midwest. However, Hollywood was the end of the line for Fitzgerald. For Reagan, Hollywood was a new beginning, a chance to reinvent himself. He knew Fitzgerald's *The Great Gatsby* and believed in the "green light"; the American dream was not lost to the past, as it was for Fitzgerald.

Reagan, like Fitzgerald, was a romantic who drew from the fountain of life and the ideals of youth, looked up to wealth, fame, and glory, and stood ready to believe in every possibility. The actor, however, did not become, as had the novelist, a moneyed celebrity corrupted by success. Reagan paid no heed to the founders' fear that wealth threatened virtue. He believed all people yearn for happiness, and his idea of God and country freed America from feeling guilty about it. Even during the Depression the budding actor felt no contrition or self-doubt. When Reagan arrived in Hollywood, it was as though American innocence walked into the Polo Lounge.

No setting could have been more nurturing to Reagan's romantic temperament than the film world. In becoming a star, he had no time for tragedy or even the anxiety of stardom. In a culture determined solely by popularity and visibility, there was no time for authority or fixed truth. A conservative takes pride in having a firm grasp on reality, while a romantic is impatient with reality and reaches out to the impossible to make it possible. Reagan was indeed of the romantic persuasion. Even in his college years, knowing the meaning of defeat in the sports arena, he relished the contest and enjoyed the limelight. Like many an Irishman, Reagan would not give up on the dreams of youth. Yet in contrast to Fitzgerald, whose torment over recovering lost ideals was to "beat on, boats against the current, borne back ceaselessly into the past," Reagan realized that history is never over. The novelist said there are "no second acts" in American life. Reagan would act in so many roles that he knew life went on and that history was destined to have a happy ending.

America was still in a depression in the late thirties, but Hollywood was prospering. Reagan thrilled to the city, to the handsome people in white sport clothes, their sun-tanned faces hidden behind dark glasses. Hollywood glistened with pastel colors, bungalows with red tile roofs and rows of poinsettias. On the corner of Hollywood and Vine, walk-on extras stood at hot dog stands in cowboy hats and boots or pirate costumes. In the booths at Schwab's, the legendary drugstore, screenwriters and directors made deals and talked scripts, plots, agents, budgets, studios, and Academy Award prospects. A competitive, challenging environment, Hollywood was about two things: first, success, then, survival. "It's a tough racket," Reagan told the *Des Moines Register* in 1937, "but when you consider the rewards you're shooting at—fame such as couldn't be won in any other profession and wealth that mounts to dizzying heights—it's worth the chances you take."[28]

Altogether, from the late thirties to the sixties, Reagan starred in

about seventy-five productions that included major movies, documen-
taries, war propaganda presentations, and TV serials. While he first
gained recognition with *Knute Rockne—All American*, his most important role was in *King's Row* (1942), a gothic soap opera about a young
man whose legs are amputated by his girlfriend's jealous father, a sadis-
tic doctor. In his memoirs Reagan remarks that he almost forgot his real
legs were hidden in a hollowed-out section of the bed. Opening his eyes,
he looked down too see only his upper thighs and screamed out the
unrehearsed line: "Where's the rest of me?" There was no need for a
retake. The line would become the title of his first autobiography and
the source of satiric jokes.

"Could He Act?" is the title of one of Garry Wills's chapters in *Reagan's America: Innocents at Home*. Wills's verdict is no, and his criterion
is telling: Reagan could only play an all-American good guy and failed
when he tried to act the villain. This is underscored in *The Killers*, based
on a short story by Ernest Hemingway. The role, Reagan's last, called for
him to sneer at and slap Angie Dickinson. Legend has it that the scene
failed to convince moviegoers that Reagan could play a menacing,
scowling thug. Actually, that smack is quite convincing. Reagan is
almost as sinister as Jack Palance, the smirking villain and hired gunman
in the movie *Shane*. "He could never change his nature," Wills observed
of Reagan, "as great actors do." Do actors change their nature or simply
vary their manner? Laurence Olivier worried that his being a "habitual
liar" as a youth turned him into an actor—which suggests he had no
need to change his nature to know that the roles he played could be false
to his true self. Whether or not Reagan was an accomplished actor, he
knew who he was and he followed Emerson's injunction to be nothing
other than who you are.[29]

As it turned out, Reagan was a popular success in films. Fan magazines spoke of his goods looks and engaging personality, his "crinkly eyes
and a wide grin for glamour," the "clear-eyed, clean-thinking young American." Modesty became him. "I'm no Flynn or Boyer," Reagan said of the
top stars, the dashing Errol Flynn and the suave Frenchman Charles
Boyer. To become important he did not have to outshine others. "Average
will do it." You can "get to the top" if you "love what you are doing."[30]

Four years after his Hollywood start, it was estimated that Reagan
earned $52,000 per film in 1941, compared to the country's top box

office draw, Clark Gable, at $210,000, and Errol Flynn, Warner Brothers's leading man, with $157,000. Pollsters found Reagan was a little more attractive to women than to men and favored more in small cities than in large metropolitan areas. Ten percent of moviegoers, asked if they would see a film if Reagan's name was on the marquee, replied yes; after *King's Row*, the number increased to 18 percent. Those who would purchase a ticket to see Flynn ranged between 30 and 40 percent. It bothered Reagan not a whit that other actors commanded the limelight. When his political advisors later worried that he might be overshadowed in a room filled with illustrious figures, Reagan, showing no concern, replied, "I once played next to Errol Flynn."[31]

Reagan had sent for his mother and father and bought them a house in southern California, the first time they owned a home of their own. To give his parents something to do, he asked them to take care of his fan mail; he got Warner Brothers to give his father a pass to go to the studio and pick it up. Jack Reagan was also put in charge of ordering photos and stationery to answer fan letters. The replies, signed "Dutch," "Ron," "Ronnie," or "Ronald Reagan," were actually written by his mother. A number of letters, not surprisingly given his looks, were written to Reagan by gay men.

As much as performance, Hollywood lives off publicity, and Reagan was always fortunate in his friends. The gossip columnist Louella Parsons, who also happened to be from Dixon, Illinois, became a close friend. To take advantage of the coincidence, Warner Brothers helped organized a homecoming for Reagan and Parsons in the summer of 1941. The actor and the columnist boarded the train the *City of Los Angeles* accompanied by Bob Hope and Robert Montgomery. Reagan and Parsons made an odd pair: the actor was polite and gracious, the journalist aggressive and scurrilous. In the long run, however, her gossip may have done as much as his glamour to stir up interest. Fifty thousand midwesterners turned out to greet the returning celebrities. Dixon hosted a ten-block parade with five bands and fifteen floats. The Chicago press heralded the careers of Parsons and Reagan as concrete evidence of rags-to-riches in Depression-era America, a "slice of Americana in the heart of a country where a simple beginning is a stepping-stone to success."[32]

Hollywood proved as well a stepping stone to fame. Reagan enjoyed the company of, among others, James Cagney, William Holden, Edward G. Robinson, Henry Fonda, John Wayne, Lana Turner, Bette Davis, and Katharine Hepburn. He also acted in films with screen gangster Humphrey Bogart. Reagan knew "Bogey" as "an easygoing, extremely friendly fellow who went out of his way to be helpful to a beginner like myself." Bogart only got the part in *Casablanca*, Reagan told a fan, because George Raft was unavailable. "It was one of those magic blessings every actor dreams of. He became a top star and deservedly so but he remained the same unassuming, nice guy he'd always been."[33]

At the height of Reagan's screen popularity, on the Sunday morning of December 7, 1941, the Japanese attacked Pearl Harbor and shocked America out of its isolationist slumber. The aerial assault also disrupted Reagan's movie career. Poor eyesight made Reagan 4-F and ineligible for combat, but even though he was married and had a child, he did serve as a reserve officer in the Army cavalry. Second Lieutenant Reagan went to work on films that advised viewers on how to spot enemy airplanes and co-starred in morale boosters like Irving Berlin's *This Is the Army*, with future California senator George Murphy. Reagan played on the Army basketball team and made appearances at war bond drives, troop departures, and hospitals for the returning wounded. In a January 1941 one-hour radio broadcast, Reagan played the role of an officer while others acted the parts of Dwight D. Eisenhower, naval commander Chester Nimitz, and treasury secretary Henry Morgenthau Jr. When Morgenthau says that the war will be fought to a final, unconditional surrender, Reagan joins in : "That brings up a point, sir. What's going to happen to the apes that started this thing . . . the Nazis and the Fascists and those little . . . yellow . . ." Morgenthau interrupts: "You'll find your answer in Russia. . . . The Russians are removing some of the worst stains from the face of this earth . . . by stringing the ringleaders of hate up and letting them hang there until they are dead. That is the final assurance of the future of free men."[34]

After Pearl Harbor, Reagan and the rest of the country saw the Nazis and the Fascists as the murderous "apes" who started it all, and the character who plays Morgenthau assures American listeners that the Russians would take care of them. Within a few years, with the Soviet Union occupying Eastern Europe, America wondered who would take care of the Russians.

Reagan left the army holding the rank of captain, and after the war his films became bland and commercially unsuccessful. Briefly, he tried to take his career in a new direction as a nightclub host in Las Vegas, but the gambling, glitter, and vulgarity was not his idea of entertainment. More to his liking was television, the new medium of the fifties. Reagan, who had started out in radio, quickly took to television, which promised to bring wholesome programs into the home at a time when cinema was becoming "arty," with the import of French film and the appearance of "method" actors such as Marlon Brando, whose sexual energy was as direct as his diction was garbled. Reagan's simple, clean-cut persona melded naturally to the requirements of television. The gossip columnist Sheila Graham, who was with Scott Fitzgerald the day he died in Holly-wood in 1940, recalled attending a screenwriters' union meeting to hear Reagan taunting its members, "I don't want to see any of you going over to the enemy." He was referring to television. No friend of Reagan's, Graham also recalled actress Ann Sheridan, Reagan's co-star in *King's Row*, turning "on my seven-inch set and there was that son-of-a-bitch on television."[35]

—

BY THE MID-FIFTIES, Reagan became known all over America as the host of *G.E. Theater*, when he presented a weekly drama on Sunday evenings. He traveled throughout the country to speak at General Electric offices and factories. Reagan frequently acted in the program but he is best remembered as the program host and pitchman for G.E., preaching the virtues of free enterprise. He repeated the same lines week after week in speeches at the American Legion, the Elks Club, Veterans of Foreign Wars, the Lions, the Rotary, the Masons, and other serious, civic-minded organizations far removed from the sensuality and frivolity of Hollywood. The same lines never seemed stale, for the fervor of his emotions came across as fresh as ever. Those deeply felt sentiments once got him into trouble when he attacked the Tennessee Valley Authority as an example of government waste. Administering a complex of electrical generators built during the 1930s by the New Deal, TVA bought fifty million dollars' worth of equipment from G.E., whose executives made clear to Reagan that they could not afford to lose such a customer.

After G.E. discontinued its television program in 1962, Reagan was unemployed and without job prospects. The summer was particularly stressful as Reagan testified before Robert Kennedy's committee investigating trade unions in the movie industry. Fortunately Reagan's brother, Neil, an executive with an advertising agency, helped secure him a leading role on *Death Valley Days*, a program his company sponsored. The setting was the Mojave Desert, and scriptwriters were told that western sagas of covered wagon trains had to be historically accurate and realistic. They were, and the romantic Reagan was happy to see the drama of the western movement as proof that the rugged American character would go through hell to get ahead.[36]

"But He Is My Hero"

UNLIKE ERROL FLYNN, Ronald Reagan was no Don Juan in Hollywood. More pursued than in pursuit, he could be politely unresponsive when approached by a young starlet, and he seemed to show no romantic interest in such beauties as his co-stars Ann Sheridan and Susan Hayward. Not that he was chaste; he just wasn't on the make. The studios were full of womanizers more interested in conquests than in facing what Susan Sontag called "the breakfast problem." Reagan was not totally immune to the behavior, but seemed to have a different perspective. He woke up one morning in bed with a woman and, upset not to know her name, decided this would be his last such experience. That's getting ahead of the story, however. It was an experience he had at the end of one marriage and as he hesitated to begin another.[37]

Much of Ronald Reagan's vast correspondence has recently been published, but so far readers have uncovered no love letters. Perhaps they are still too private to see the light of day. Thanks to Anne Edwards's meticulous research, though, we do know what women who knew Reagan thought of him. Some actresses who dated him found him charming but distant. He engaged not so much in conversation as in lengthy discourses on political subjects. One woman who spent a good deal of time with him felt he was playing the room. Virginia Mayo delighted in his wolf calls from across the room. Reagan "contracted leading lady-

itus," writes Edwards, attracting the attention of beautiful up-and-
coming starlets and radiant athletes. The ice-skater Sonja Henie found
him kind, protective, and fair-minded. She recalled, for instance, that he
spoke to waiters without condescension. Female co-stars were impressed
that he never grew bored while waiting endlessly on the set for the camera to roll. He seemed absorbed in the news of the day and in reading
statistics, so absorbed that a woman might well wonder what place in his
life there would be for her. Reagan was not drawn to dominant women
and it was usually he who decided whether the relationship should continue or end—until he met Jane Wyman.

In July 1938, Reagan met Wyman on the set of the film *Brother Rat*,
and eighteen months later they were married, in January 1940. Wyman
struck Reagan as the ideal Hollywood woman. Pert features, fine bones,
pouting lips, wide brown eyes, shapely legs, sculpted figure, Wyman had
arrived in Hollywood a few years before Reagan, and she would become
a recognized actress, nominated for an Academy Award in *The Yearling*
(1946) and winner of the Oscar the following year for her portrayal of a
deaf mute in *Johnny Belinda*. "Ron and Jane" were the talk of the town,
the glamorous lovebirds seen in nightclubs and sunbathing and body
surfing on the beaches of Santa Monica. Wyman gave birth to daughter
Maureen on January 4, 1941, and in March 1945 the Reagans adopted
son Michael, theirs only twelve hours after birth.[38]

A Hollywood marriage is often made in hell more than in heaven.
Jane Wyman, an adopted child, had two short failed marriages before
she met Reagan, and she seemed to walk away from both husbands in
relief. She took to Reagan, however, to rescue her from the void of her
own vague longings. Outwardly the picture of confidence, she was often
anxious and insecure, compulsively busying herself with polishing silver,
rearranging furniture, and indulging in shopping sprees while waiting for
a call from the studio. Reagan, on the other hand, was relaxed, thrifty,
and confident, and he was as concerned about the state of the world as
he was about his own career. If opposites attract, the more impulsive
Wyman should have stayed with the more deliberative Reagan. But after
World War II they began to drift apart. A friend, June Allyson, felt that
the tension set in because Wyman's career took off as Reagan's peaked.
In the late forties, Reagan was increasingly caught up in Hollywood politics and was always off to meetings.

Once while Reagan was in England, Wyman was seen dating the actor Lew Ayres, a pacifist and conscientious objector. Reagan heard through a third party that Wyman was leaving him. Nevertheless, when she started divorce proceedings, Reagan told the press, "It's a very strange girl I'm married to, but I love her. . . . I know we will end our lives together." After the marriage ended, Reagan's emotional life went into limbo. Friends saw a dismal emptiness set in, as though the once cheery actor was no longer a stranger to sorrow.[39]

Nancy Davis first met Ronald Reagan at MGM producer Dore Schary's house in September 1949. Shortly afterward she contacted him over a case of mistaken identities regarding membership in the Screen Actors Guild. Legend has it that there were two people in the guild with the same name, and Nancy sought to make clear she was not the one who had the reputation as a radical, perhaps a communist. As head of the Guild, Reagan agreed to straighten things out. A month after the meeting at Schary's he rang her apartment doorbell, leaning outside in cast and crutches recovering from a broken leg. In Nancy, Reagan saw an attractive, petite woman, modest and prim, more pleasant than provocative, but far more interested in politics and public affairs than Jane Wyman had been, and far more demure than the stylishly dressed Wyman. Perhaps politics brought out a side of her character that lay dormant. Years later, when he was president, members of his cabinet would find Nancy willful and so protective of her husband that she insinuated herself into political decision making, and so frightened after an assassin's attempt upon his life that she began consulting an astrologist. Years earlier, on warm southern California evenings, Reagan encountered a face that seemed delightfully tender, and he could not have been unmoved by her large brown, wide-apart eyes. Bells indeed must have rung when they first met, Reagan recalled years later, only to add that the recent divorce experience had so buried his emotions he couldn't hear them.

Nancy Davis, the stepdaughter of a prominent midwestern surgeon, was born in 1921 in Flushing, Queens. Matriculating at Smith College, she majored in drama and English and then lived in New York City for a few years, taking jobs in advertising and modeling and acting in minor roles in several Broadway plays. In the late forties she went to Hollywood for a screen test. Studio heads found her speech stilted but her pose graceful. She dated Spencer Tracy and Clark Gable and came to the attention of Dore Schary, who cast her in *East Side, West Side* with stars Barbara Stanwyck, Ava Gardner, and James Mason. Once she was asked on a studio biographical questionnaire, "What is your greatest ambition?" Nancy Davis replied, "Sure to have a successful marriage."

In February 1952, almost three years after she met Reagan, they were married. "It's about time," remarked William Holden, the best man. Thereafter, Nancy came to be seen as her husband's totally devoted wife, her eyes fixed like a beam on Reagan whenever he gave a talk. "Nancy," said a friend of her mother's, "people just don't *believe* it when you look at Ronnie that way—as though you're saying, 'He's my hero.' You know what she said to me? 'But he *is* my hero.' "[40]

A legend in Hollywood has Nancy turning Reagan on to politics and pushing him to become a powerhouse out of her own driving ambition. Nancy Davis was no Lady Macbeth, however, and Reagan needed no encouragement. Since his college days Reagan had taken to politics as he had to football, and well before he met Nancy he had been involved in the intense politics of the film industry. Another legend has Reagan going into politics because his film career had dried up. But why politics, an occupation that could be little more than a grinding routine rather than the grand role a romantic needs? Once elected to office, Reagan cared little for committee work, fundraising, maneuvers and manipulations, though doubtless he had to stoop to such activities. To Reagan politics had to be about causes and lively contests, challenges to his own convictions about right and wrong, not backroom deals but high drama.

Delivering his famous essay "Politics as a Vocation" to a lecture audience, Max Weber observed that those whose true calling is politics must have "a passionate commitment to a cause." An elderly poetess, who sat in the first row taking in Weber's lecture, recalled: "I suddenly had this feeling that Max Weber was like an actor." The "fountain of his instincts," she observed, "instead of flowing through him, are channeled by his intellect and consciousness." And so, too, with actor Ronald Reagan.[41]

CHAPTER THREE

To Repent or Not to Repent:
The Communist Controversy in Hollywood

Reagan and HUAC

I F MAX WEBER'S "passionate commitment to a 'cause'" was essential in politics, then Ronald Reagan found his vocation in the cause of anticommunism. That seminal issue carried Reagan from the 1940s, when he was an actor, to the 1980s, when he was president. It was always on his mind, whether he was performing before the camera, dining out with his wife, negotiating labor contracts and writing letters to friends, or, later, preparing to enter American politics and the world's stage. Even during his early years in California, beneath all of Hollywood's glamour and frivolity, politics was extremely serious, and Reagan was passionate about it.

The anticommunist is not born but made, shaped by the political experiences of the age. Reagan arrived in Hollywood just as the Spanish Civil War was beginning to inflict on many writers and cultural figures what Albert Camus called "the wound in the heart." The war first united and then divided Hollywood's radical partisans and its anti-Stalinists. The former followed Moscow's line; the latter saw their loyalties to the Spanish Republic betrayed in Catalonia by communists who followed Moscow's orders and executed anarchists and liberals. Reagan knew about the Abraham Lincoln Brigade, American volunteers who fought in Spain against Franco, some communists, many more progressive liberals shocked to find out how Stalinists violated "the popular front," the call for all disparate political elements to unite against the threat of Hitler. A half-century later, President Reagan would invoke the organization's name to justify America's support of counterrevolutionary insurgencies in the third world. Reagan had even flirted with joining the Communist Party in the United States (CPUSA) for a short time before the contours of the cold war emerged.

By 1946, however, Reagan had turned anticommunist with a vengeance. In this respect, he was no different from many others who went
from Left to Right, including those who would write for William F. Buckley Jr.'s *National Review*. The pattern was predicted in an essay by the
Italian novelist Ignazio Silone in *The God That Failed* (1950): "The final
struggle . . . will be between the communists and the ex-communists."[1]

The struggle exploded in public view in 1947 when politicians in
Washington decided to investigate communist activities in Hollywood.
Until that moment, liberals and communists were weary of one another
but not bitterly hostile. During the war years they were allies in an
united front in the struggle against fascism (even though that front had
been betrayed in Spain). Hollywood's communist controversy, however,
which many considered the first American inquisition since the Puritan
witch hunts, launched Reagan's ideological odyssey. It was a time when
former communists either prepared their confessions or maintained a
defiant oath of silence The American public eagerly awaited the daily
headlines. Hollywood was not only on screen; it was on trial.

In October 1947, the House Un-American Activities Committee
(HUAC) began to conduct hearings quite unlike any that had ever before
been held in the nation's capital. Glamorous movie stars stepped from
the screen and into the gray political world, walking into the House
office buildings and down the corridors past onlookers "oohing and
aahing," according to press reports. Some were so-called friendly witnesses like Ronald Reagan, Gary Cooper, and Robert Montgomery, willing to testify before the committee and answer questions under oath.
The Hollywood Committee for the First Amendment also made the trip
to the capital, with Lauren Bacall, Humphrey Bogart, John Huston, and
other liberals protesting the investigations on constitutional grounds.

Most attention, however, was focused on nineteen subpoenaed witnesses who expressed clear contempt for the proceedings. Their number was soon reduced and they came to be called the Hollywood Ten.
Now made legendary by their supporters, the ten refused to answer the
committee's questions. They often pleaded the Fifth Amendment and
pointedly challenged their interrogators, to the laughter and applause of
the audience. Some, such as Dalton Trumbo and John Howard Lawson,
were important scriptwriters and playwrights. Trumbo, who was banned

from writing for the film industry, submitted scripts under a pseudonym and would win an Academy Award for one of his stories. The Oscar was accepted by a bogus author, a subject made popular in the 1976 film *The Front*, which starred Woody Allen. The Hollywood Ten and other uncooperative witnesses were portrayed as heroes of the hour in that movie and in playwright Lillian Hellman's all-too-fictional memoir, *Scoundrel Time*. Reagan was one of the scoundrels.[2]

The committee's chief investigator was counsel Robert E. Stripling, a soft-spoken Texan who never rose to the bait of the insults of unfriendly witnesses but instead quietly sipped a glass of water to case the anger that his face could scarcely conceal. Reagan became the ideal witness, the picture of civility and responsibility.

> MR. STRIPLING: Mr. Reagan, what is your feeling about what steps should be taken to rid the motion-picture industry of any Communist influence?
>
> MR. REAGAN: Well, sir, ninety-nine percent of us are pretty well aware of what is going on, and I think, within the bounds of our democratic rights and never once stepping over the rights given us by democracy, we have done a pretty good job in our business of keeping those people's activities curtailed.[3]

Reagan's antistatist convictions made him uncomfortable with government investigations, and as head of the Screen Actors Guild he tried to convince the committee that he and his allies could handle the situation. They had successfully opposed the communists, challenging their propaganda and exposing their lies, he emphasized. How, then, did Reagan's name appear on a list for a fund-raising event sponsored by communists, asked Stripling? Reagan replied that he knew that the event had communist backing because Paul Robeson was singing at it, but that cause, a badly needed hospital in a poor section of Los Angeles, seemed worthy of support. Should the CP be outlawed? Reagan answered that the government should decide, especially if it determined that the party was "an agent of power, a foreign power, or in any way not a legitimate party." Reagan's remarks seemed to validate the work of the "fact find-ing" committee. "I believe that, as Thomas Jefferson put it, if all the American people know all of the facts they will never make a mistake."

Reagan exuded confidence and conviction in his appearance before the Committee. Leaning toward the microphone he observed, "I never as a citizen want to see our country become urged, by either fear or resentment, to compromise with any of our democratic principles through that fear or resentment." Reagan saw no reason to panic and argued that communist influence in Hollywood was exaggerated. "I do not believe the Communists have ever at any time been able to use the motion-picture screen as a sounding board for their philosophy or ideology."[4]

Reagan's testimony was admirable but questionable. Both he and Stripling could cite Jefferson and assert that facts would demolish false-hoods. But some witnesses who questioned HUAC's purposes also would invoke the author of the First Amendment and the right of free speech. These latter-day Jeffersonians opposed any attempt to silence opposition and force a conformity of opinion upon Americans. The Holly-wood Ten, by contrast, preferred the Fifth Amendment to the First: They invoked their constitutional right to remain silent and refused to give answers that they said might be self-incriminating. Asked to speak openly, they chose not to reply at all. Why that tactic? Reportedly, some-one testifying earlier, at a California hearing into communism, denied under oath he was a member of the CP and chose to remain silent before Congress to avoid perjury. No one wanted to be caught lying under oath. While in 1947 it was still no crime to belong to the CP, nervous Holly-wood studio executives threatened to fire those who did belong to what was increasingly regarded as a subversive organization, as the party would be so defined in the Smith Act trials of 1949.

Reagan's testimony must be qualified in other respects. Although in his statement he said he "would hesitate to see any political party out-lawed on the basis of its political ideology," a few years later at the onset of the cold war, he fully supported banning the CP, on the grounds that it was an illegitimate party serving as an agency of a foreign power. And although decades later he told *Playboy* magazine publisher and editor Hugh Hefner that Hollywood had no blacklist, in 1950 he was helping to prepare a loyalty oath for actors and filmmakers that studios would administer. Reagan freely criticized liberals for hesitating to "smoke out communists" and took responsibility for showing his "misguided actors and actresses the road back to America." Although at first uneasy with HUAC, he became one of its staunchest supporters in the early 1950s, when critics of McCarthyism were desperately needed to stand up to it. By then the world was in a very different place. Central and Eastern Europe, including democratic Czechoslovakia, were behind the Iron Curtain, Russia had exploded an atomic bomb, communists ruled China, and the United States was at war against communists in Korea. As the cold war intensified, Reagan's position hardened.[5]

What is the difference between an anticommunist and a McCarthy-ite? Essentially the difference is between clarity and conspiracy. The anti-communist saw communism as a threat *to* America and demanded of those who defended it that they clarify why they do so. The McCarthy-ites, in contrast, saw communism as a threat *in* America and demanded confessions of treason, not explanations of convictions. McCarthyism was also a form of demagogy that politicians used to win elections to office by playing upon the fears of the people. Once in office, the polit-ical anticommunist could forget about communism or even make a trip to a communist country and shake hands with its leaders. Whittaker Chambers, a principled anticommunist, repudiated McCarthyism.

Reagan did not go in for "Red baiting," and he recognized that the threat to America came from Soviet strength. In 1950 Reagan was actu-ally still a liberal Democrat, and he initially supported Helen Gahagan Douglas, the wife of actor Melvyn Douglas, over Richard Nixon in their bitterly contested race for U.S. senator from California. Nixon's cam-paign clamed that the "Pink Lady" was on her way to becoming a "Red." While Reagan made speeches on her behalf, by Election Day, according to Anne Edwards, he quietly switched his support to Nixon. Later he would say that he belatedly realized that most of his friends were Repub-licans. FDR was dead and so was Reagan's father, who always voted Democrat. By the early 1950s the Democrats seemed too inept to han-dle the cold war.[6]

In politics Reagan's career pattern followed that of Nixon. While Rea-gan was taking on the Hollywood Reds, Congressman Nixon became famous for coming to the support of Chambers against Hiss. Thirty years later, in 1980, Reagan ran for president claiming the Democrats were losing the cold war against communism, and within a few years he was, as with Nixon and his earlier visit to China, shaking hands with communist leaders, possibly with no intention of winning the war but instead simply settling it.

Unlike Nixon, however, Reagan never insinuated that his political opponents were communists, though he implied that liberals were too innocent to see what communists were up to in posing as American progressives. Yet even during the tumultuous student uprisings on the campuses of the University of California, Governor Reagan refrained from following the McCarthyites and claiming communists were storming the campus. Except for CP member Angela Davis, a marginal figure, the student radicals were democratic socialists, revolutionary Trotskyists, Castroites, Maoists, anarchists, even free enterprise libertarians, not one of whom had any illusions about the Soviet Union. But the Hollywood Ten of the previous generation did have illusions, and unlike the New Left of the sixties, the scriptwriters kept their mouths shut, mutes for the revolution.[7]

There is no evidence that any of the Hollywood Ten had engaged in espionage or were agents of a foreign power. To Reagan that was not the issue. "Sir," he said to Stripling, "I detest, I abhor their philosophy, but I detest more than that their tactics, which are those of the fifth column."[8] Reagan's reference to a fifth column implied that communists could join ranks with liberal groups and at the same time be working for different ends, as they did in American trade unions and in the Spanish Civil War. On orders from Moscow, Spanish communists arrested and executed partisan leaders who stood in their way. Ernest Hemingway had first denied the atrocities but fully included them in his great novel *For Whom the Bell Tolls*. Communists saw the future in Russia and thought Marxism could work in America as well, whereas so-called fellow travelers sympathized with the Soviet Union but thought communism had no place in America. Both groups insisted upon their integrity, claiming that what they stood for had been arrived at freely and independently of the Soviet Union. In the thirties and forties, however, many intellectuals suspected that American communists followed the party line out of Moscow, with directives usually arriving by means of cables sent to New York from the Comintern, the central organization of the international parties. The message would tell the CP what policies to take on the race question, trade unions, and FDR's New Deal. So dependent did some members become on cablegram instructions from Moscow that anti-Stalinists could barely resist a joke:

> What does your CPUSA and the Brooklyn Bridge have in common?
> We're both as strong as steel?
> No, you're both suspended by cables.[9]

Liberals and other critics on the Left dismissed Reagan's anticommunism as mere demagogy, but in Hollywood, Reagan could not help but notice how communists would change their position on war and peace almost overnight, depending upon how Stalin dealt with Hitler. Many of Reagan's critics also denied the mass suffering in the Soviet Union, dismissive not only of the party purges but the twenty million lives lost in a famine in the Ukraine. The critics thought they were defending a great cause in Russia and saw themselves as useful promoters of noble ideals. Lenin, who knew that all was not well just before he died in 1924, was reported to have called Russia's foreign admirers "useful idiots."[10]

Hollywood and World War II Movies

THE HOLLYWOOD TEN and others would spend the rest of their lives insisting that they did not take orders from Moscow, and they may have told the truth. When the Soviet archives were opened, scholars found plenty of evidence indicating that many American communists had accepted directions from the Soviet Union, and a few were on its payroll. But not one of the ten is mentioned.[11]

The more intriguing question about the ten is why they supported communism and the Soviet Union but refused to answer the committee's questions about their political views. Of course, fear for their careers is one obvious answer. Reagan advised a young actress to participate with the investigations and, if asked to name names, to give the committee a name that had already been listed. Reagan seemed to assume that one had only to answer a couple of questions to be cleared and return to work. Those who cooperated with the committee were expected to denounce communism, however, and that posed a dilemma for those who still thought communism worth defending.

Reagan was aware that the Soviet Union had assigned an operative, V. J. Jerome, to persuade sympathetic Hollywood actors, writers, and directors to promote the Stalinist party line. The Polish-born Jerome became an American citizen in 1928 and graduated from New York University. Short, bald, with horn-framed glasses, Jerome was an intellectual who believed that it was not the economic mode of production that would win the day but the cinematic mode of presentation. He directed the CP's culture wars in Hollywood. Having had run-ins with Jerome, Reagan knew that the motion picture camera could be used as a political tool. When he appeared a second time before HUAC in 1951, Reagan boasted that "the extent of Hollywood's victory over the Communist Party is all the more remarkable because Hollywood for many years was a prime target of the Red propagandists and conspirators in this country." Reagan said further that these communist sympathizers were carrying out orders from Stalin, who had said:

> The cinema is not only a vital agitprop [active propaganda] device for the education and political indoctrination of the workers, but also a fluent channel through which to reach the minds and shape the desires of the people everywhere. The Kinofikatsiya [turning propaganda into film] is inevitable. The task is to take this affair into your hands, and vigorously execute it in every field.[12]

The Hollywood communist controversy placed Reagan in a dilemma. Although in his later years he expressed alarm about the dangers of communism in America, he minimized it when testifying before HUAC. No doubt he desired to ward off the intrusion of government authority, but the Hollywood experience suggests a pattern. When Reagan was in charge, as he was when heading the Screen Actors Guild or as governor or president, the situation was under control; when others were in office, they could not be counted upon to handle the threat of communism and its fifth columns. But infiltration was happening under Reagan's watch. In 1995, the United States government revealed the existence of the secret Venona Project, the decoding of thousands of Soviet

messages having to do with espionage activities and cultural tactics carried out in America. The decrypted Venona cables of the Soviet archives
reveal that the KGB, the Kremlin's secret service, tried to infiltrate Hollywood and place American agents in the studios with directors and on
sets with actors.[13] Yet Reagan, even though he believed communism was
a danger to America, testified that it had no significant influence in the
movie industry. Initially Reagan, always suspicious of the power of the
state, had no use for government investigations, and he sought to protect the film community from a witch hunt. However, he seemed over-
protective in his denial that "Communists have ever, at any time, been
able to use the motion picture screen as a sounding board for their philosophy or ideology." The screen showed otherwise.

During the years of World War II, Hollywood produced pro-Soviet
films like *The North Star* (1943) and *Song of Russia* (1944). The first,
written by Lillian Helman, who received an Oscar nomination for her
screenplay, starred Dana Andrews, Anne Baxter, Walter Huston, and
Walter Brennan. Produced by Sam Goldwyn, with a musical score by
Aaron Copland and Ira Gershwin, the film contained no mention of
communism or Soviet Russia. It depicted peasants living happily on a
collective farm until the German army arrives and they fight nobly to the
end. In her review of the film, the anti-Stalinist novelist Mary McCarthy
wrote that the characters were like "feudal Serbian mountaineers, or
Norwegian fisherman, acting naively on their own initiative." But by
1943 Stalin had already executed any Russians acting on their own
initiative.[14]

Song of Russia starred Robert Taylor as a symphony conductor tour-
ing the Soviet Union. He falls in love with a beautiful peasant girl, played
by Susan Peters. They marry on her collective farm. With the Nazis
advancing, the peasants burn their village and crops to leave nothing for
the enemy. The conductor returns to the United States to tell Americans
that "we are soldiers side by side—in the fight for all humanity."

The popular media had to convince the American public that the
United States and the USSR were fighting not only on the same side but
for the same cause. Such treatment contrasted with the late 1930s,
when the American press reported stories coming out of Stalin's Russia
about the purges and mass executions. The *New York Times*, with its
Moscow correspondent Walter Duranty, covered up some of these atroc-

ities. However, no newspaper could deny Stalin's nonaggression pact
with Germany in 1939. The American public could only wonder about
the nature of a regime that formed an alliance with its professed enemy.
Of course, within two years Hitler invaded Russia, Japan attacked Pearl
Harbor, and Germany declared war on the United States. America's capitalist democracy found itself allied with a totalitarian communist state
fighting a common enemy.

The 1943 film *Mission to Moscow* was based on a book by Joseph E.
Davies, former ambassador to Russia. According to George Kennan, a
diplomat stationed in Moscow at the time, Davies's appointment was a
fluke. At the urging of his socialite wife, Marjorie Merriweather Post,
Davies approached Roosevelt about an appointment to the Court of St.
James in England. Instead the president sent him to the frigid climes of
Moscow, and with a grin remarked that he had "fixed him." The film version has the president dispatching an assistant to Davies's lakeside vacation cottage to urge him to accept an appointment to the USSR. No one
expected that an eminent figure of the American establishment, a corporate capitalist no less, would become one of America's greatest apologists for a communist state.[15]

The film's aim was to convince Americans that Stalin could be trusted.
Stalin was no murderer but a noble leader who sought only peace and
freedom for his people. His pact with Hitler was understandable in light
of the Western democracies' refusal to enter into diplomatic alliances
with a communist state and the USSR's legitimate concerns for its
own national security. The real enemy of America was Leon Trotsky, who
still believed in world revolution, whereas Stalin was a great Russian
nationalist.

When the film came out in New York, it created a firestorm of controversy, especially among the city's fractious intellectuals. Democratic
socialists and Trotskyists believed that Stalin's brutal dictatorship had
betrayed the October Revolution of 1917 and violated the democratic
principles of Karl Marx. The film depicts Stalin as a benevolent despot
seeking only security for Russia, an aim that his Trotskyist opponents
jeopardized by their determination to wage "permanent revolutionary
struggle." Even Stalin's infamous purge of his old Bolshevik comrades is
depicted as a defensive response to a plot of Trotskyists allied with Nazi
Germany to bring him down. Many New York intellectuals denounced

the film as sheer propaganda in the service of Soviet totalitarianism, and as a result of the film some Hollywood actors began to organize the Motion Picture Alliance for the Preservation of American Ideals.

Mission to Moscow may be clumsy propaganda, but it has some aesthetic moments that are politically telling, especially in view of Reagan's claim that communists had no opportunity to use the cinema for ideological purposes. The film was a topflight Hollywood feature. Walter Huston plays Ambassador Joseph E. Davies, the score is by Max Steiner, and the director was Michael Curtiz, who had directed Reagan and Errol Flynn in earlier productions and who directed *Casablanca* (1942). The film also deserves attention since communists started the myth that the Roosevelt administration prevailed upon producers to make it.[16] Although there is no evidence for this story, it was commonly understood that the war on the eastern front was vital and that if Russia withdrew from the fray, as it had in the First World War, there could be no possibility of an Allied victory. Hence Hollywood, in treating Stalin as a historical hero, was serving the aims of American foreign policy.

The film's depiction of the 1936–1937 Moscow purge trials is an example of how the screen determines what the viewer sees and how the eyes respond to the political control of culture. The arrest of Nikolai Bukharin takes place in quiet silhouette; the film moves to a ballet stage, as the graceful motions of dancers are shadows cast against a wall. Old Bolsheviks are arrested in a concert hall, a sanctuary of high art, as though only the greatest urgency requires politics to intrude upon culture. In both the actual trial and the film, the accused confessed to crimes that they could not possibly have committed, even though they know they are to be sentenced to death. Bukharin's testimony has remained a riddle, which led Arthur Koestler to write the gripping novel *Darkness at Noon* (1940). What perplexed Koestler was Bukharin's acknowledgment that he had indeed conspired against the Soviet Union, only to realize the enormity of his crimes and sign a confession. The show trials remain one of the great enigmas in modern intellectual history. The intellectual, defined as "a mind devoted to minds" (Paul Valéry), turns the mind over to the totalitarian party. In *The Middle of the Journey* (1947), Lionel Trilling employed a fictional portrayal of Whittaker Chambers to suggest the reasoning of the communist mentality. He described Chambers citing Melville's *Billy Budd* to suggest the "tragedy of Spirit in a world of

Necessity." Budd, the innocent sailor, had no means of confronting his accuser other than to strike him. "Struck dead by an angel of God. Yet the angel must hang." In Moscow in 1938, the innocent are condemned to death to assure the survival of the revolution. Any college freshman would question such a reading of Melville's brilliant parable. But in the thirties the point of the Stalinist Left was not to explain events but to justify them.

The Moscow trials had a hypnotic effect upon the radical American mind that was almost cinematic. Trotsky had been accused in the trials of crimes against Russia, but in a countertrial held in Mexico, and presided over by the eminent American philosopher John Dewey, Trotsky was acquitted. Still, doubts remained. "Trostkyists of long standing," wrote Mary McCarthy, "would wake sweating in the night to ask: 'What if Stalin were right?' " The whole affair had such a "melodramatic and improbable manner" it seemed like "a bad spy picture that you hissed and booed and applauded," and the confessions of the defendants "the invention of a movie writer."[17]

In the film *Mission to Moscow*, the mild-mannered Bukharin, the economic genius of the old Soviet regime who today is admired for attempting to move Russia to a market economy in the 1920s, speaks almost poetically. He is prepared, he says in the film, to face the firing squad convinced that Stalin's enemies needed to be purged to prepare Russia for the showdown with the Third Reich.

It is difficult to tell whether Bukharin is being ironic. To this day one wonders whether he went to his death a rededicated Bolshevik or realized that Bolshevism without democracy was already a living death. To the Hollywood communists, however, there was no riddle to the purges and executions, which they defended. When they themselves were put on trial a decade later they confessed nothing and forgot everything as they pleaded the Fifth Amendment. What rankled Reagan was American communists claiming the protection of laws guaranteed by the U.S. Constitution and at the same time insisting that the Russian people enjoyed greater political freedom than Americans themselves.

Reagan could justify *Mission to Moscow* and other films as part of the war effort that required America to sustain friendly relations with Russia. With Russia's heroic victory at the battle of Stalingrad in early 1943, Stalin was lionized in the American press as "Man of the Year" by none other than *Time* and featured on the cover of *Life*. In Hollywood, people occasionally viewed the newsreels that appeared in movie houses before the film started. They read, and sometimes saw, the siege of Leningrad and the battle of Kursk, the largest tank battle of World War II, with the Russian T-34 outmaneuvering the dreaded German Panzer. The Russians fought magnificently on the eastern front. But those Americans who followed the military news remained unaware of the politics of Stalin's regime. One writer who was keenly aware was Max Eastman. A close friend of John Reed and companion of Charlie Chaplin, Eastman went to Moscow during the Bolshevik revolution, learned Russian, translated Trotsky, and championed Lenin. Years later he heard from émigrés about the purges, the famine in the Ukraine, and the slave labor camps. During World War II, Eastman tried to publish a report on the Gulag Archipelago, later brought to international notoriety by Aleksandr Solzhenitsyn. The FBI intervened to prevent publication on the grounds that the United States could not afford risking a break with Russia. The suppression of such news made sense, but it explains why America was so unprepared for the cold war and why the country succumbed to a Red scare.[18]

Reagan saw Hollywood liberals and communists working together in a common effort to defeat Hitler and the Third Reich. The Stalin question was muted because the Western Allies played down or disputed news of his atrocities. Prime among them was the 1943 massacre in the Katyn Forest, near the Russia city of Smolensk, in which 21,000 Polish military and other prisoners were machine-gunned and buried on Stalin's orders. In September 1944, Stalin cynically ordered the Red Army's drive toward Germany to halt at the outskirts of Warsaw to allow the Germans to put down the Jewish uprising. After the war, Stalin went back on his word to hold free elections in Poland. He intended to see democratic liberalism crushed in Eastern Europe, an ambition that certain members of the Hollywood Left failed to address. Many defended Stalin's Russia, convinced that world peace depended on acquiescence to the Iron Curtain.

All this was too much for Reagan. He, too, wanted to see peace in the world, and he joined the Left in signing petitions to "Ban the Bomb" and protested further development of atomic weapons. Yet he did not join the crowds who stood and wildly applauded Paul Robeson at the Hollywood Bowl in 1949, crowds that included such illustrious stars as Katharine Hepburn. Robeson, a renowned actor and singer, returned from the Soviet Union in that year to claim that the Russian people enjoyed complete political freedom, that Eastern Europe was free of racism, and that Stalin's Russia had overcome poverty—a country in which twenty million people died from a famine. At the Hollywood Bowl Robeson seemed a messenger of truth and hope, to some a messiah. Yet in 1963, he suffered a mental breakdown, and to some it appeared that the finest black actor of the era had wasted his life on a false cause.[19]

Reagan's critics have always accused him of living in a fantasy world. What was more fantastical, however, than the image of the Soviet Union that Hollywood Reds promoted in the 1940s? Even Karl Marx repudiated the idea of communism in historically backward Russia. The czarist Russia that the Bolsheviks took over had yet to develop the "forces of production" that would enable it to pass through the modernizing stages of history: the Enlightenment, Western liberalism, industrial capitalism. This bypassed country, *le mensonge russe* (the "Russian deceit"), was in the eyes of Hollywood radicals a dream of heaven on earth. Such mystical faith in the historically impossible taxed Marx's patience. Backward Russia, he wrote a century earlier, "never ceases being considered as an affair of belief and not of fact."[20]

The Struggle for Power

THE STRANGE CHARACTER of Hollywood "communism" only proved Marx right. If communism were to come to power, Marx had prophesized, it would come by way of the working masses, the proletariat, who would achieve such heightened class consciousness as to "negate" the whole idea of private property and the profit system. In leftist imagery the Bolshevik revolutionary was history from below, a huge fist breaking through the floorboards of a mansion filled with rich quests partying in black tie and glittering gowns and sipping martinis. The proletariat would storm Pacific Palisades.

In Hollywood, however, communists were the ones who were partying, and they had no desire to abolish property or the profit system. One Santa Monica hostess tried to persuade the film director Ernst Lubitsch not to resign from the Anti-Nazi League simply because it was dominated by Reds. They're harmless, she reassured him. "All these people do is sit around their swimming pools, drinking highballs and talking about movies, while the wives complain of their Filipino butlers."[21]

Ronald Reagan's political education began in Hollywood, but it hardly derived from cocktail party chitchat.

For many years Reagan had been a board member of the Screen Actors Guild, a group formed to represent actors in their dealings with the film industry's powerful studios. Elected president in 1947, he tried to practice the politics of cooperation, conciliation, and compromise. He did not believe in an insurmountable difference between labor and capital or think in terms of class conflict. His antagonists in the ranks of labor, however, believed in class warfare, strikes, boycotts, direct action, whatever it took to win. The battles in Hollywood would be a dress rehearsal for the campus conflicts that Reagan would later face as governor.

In his memoirs, Reagan recalls fondly the working conditions of his early days in the film industry. Every hired laborer was then a jack-of-all-trades. "The stagehands, in those days, did everything from swinging and moving props to painting scenery and dismantling it."[22] These workers formed a union called the International Alliance of Theatrical Stage Employees (IATSE). Within a few years stage employees had specialized their occupations; there were carpenters, painters, plumbers, electricians, each with specific duties written into his or her contract. A stagehand was no longer allowed to nail a poster to the stage door, now the job of the carpenter alone. In the late 1930s IATSE went on strike to assure control of the electrical workers' union. Reagan had no patience with these divisions of labor and he began to distrust the union's leaders, who seemed more interested in organizing workers than working.

During this period Reagan was a liberal internationalist who had little in common with either conservative isolationists or union militants. His conversion to conservatism is usually attributed to a later period, perhaps to his work for General Electric in the early 1960s. A few biographers claim that he fell under the influence of Nancy Davis's conservative father after their marriage. He did indeed mainly vote for Democrats until 1950. His conservative skepticism about institutionalized power, however, may have originated with the realities of American labor organizations of the late forties.

Reagan's trajectory parallels that of the novelist John Dos Passos. Like Reagan, Dos Passos strongly supported the cause of workers but became increasingly disturbed by union leaders who made their decisions for them and took the spoils. What always offended Reagan, and impassioned his subsequent critique of the welfare state, was parasitism, the indolent and idle who, he claimed, sought nothing more than to live off the productive and responsible members of society. Later, in his radio broadcasts, he would retell the parable of the little red hen, who saw such laziness around her she concluded that only animals who work should eat. How can union leaders set an example of hard work when they themselves sit at their desk jobs while giving orders and collecting dues? They do not do so, as dramatized in the film *On the Waterfront*, which derived directly from the Hollywood controversies of the forties. It was directed by Elia Kazan, a friendly witness before HUAC. Terry Malloy, played by Marlon Brando, punches a time clock to start his workday, then climbs up to a loft, stretches out on a soft bed of sacks, and takes out a comic book that he'll read until the lunch break. Work was the curse of the working class!

Reagan was nothing if not a hard, dedicated worker at whatever task he took up in his long career. Like the author of the *U.S.A.* trilogy, he esteemed the honest worker but distrusted labor unions, and years later, as governor and then president, his critique of the welfare state was based on his suspicion that government bureaucrats, like labor leaders, were as much interested in perpetuating their position as in helping the needy. He would criticize welfare cheats, but why he said almost nothing about corporate cheats is the subject of a future chapter. To get something for nothing offended Reagan, yet it seemed to depend on who's getting it.

Herbert Sorrell was a scrappy ex-boxer who as a youth had worked twelve hours a day in an Oakland sewer pipe factory. A communist who believed fervently in the rights of labor, he once led a successful strike of cartoonists and technical color workers against Walt Disney. The struggles in Hollywood were as much between different unions as between labor and the studios. The electrical workers' union, for example, tried to take over control of sound-recording operations. Painters organized their own union and chose Sorrell as their leader. As head of the Conference of Studio Unions (CSU), Sorrell had the support of Father George Dunne, a Jesuit who fought for working-class causes. Sorrell was also supported by John Cogley, a Catholic writer who investigated communist activities in California. Dunne and Cogley tried to assure Reagan that the politics of Sorrell's CSU and that of the CP only happened to "coincide" and that once, in 1945, Sorrell had even called for a strike in support of set designers, a move that went against the communist no-strike pledge while America was an ally of the Soviet Union. *The People's World*, a CP paper on the West Coast, even ran an article on Sorrell, entitled "A Good Guy Gone Wrong."[23]

As the key agency in the strike negotiations, the Screen Actors Guild became a source of controversy, and Reagan has been criticized as being less than candid in the positions he took. Garry Wills takes Sorrell's side against Reagan, who tended to dismiss the labor conflicts as unions rivaling one another and regarded SAG as a "noble organization" formed by idealistic actors whose talents required no union. It is difficult, however, to establish clearly what was at stake in the strikes: wages and working conditions; the politics of ideology driven by communism; or a jurisdictional struggle for power. The object of any union is job control, and in the post–World War II era, Hollywood became a battlefield of warring factions.[24]

At first Reagan believed that SAG should try to remain neutral in response to the various strikes, but Sorrel's CSU sought to win over members of IATSE by staging a strike that called upon actors as well as laborers not to show up for work. Had actors decided not to, the film studios would be shut down. Reagan sensed that the strike was part of a communist effort to paralyze the motion picture industry, and he led SAG in taking a stand against it. The morning of October 7, 1946, saw almost a thousand picketers and strikebreakers going at one another with clubs and brass knuckles in an event dubbed the "Battle of Burbank." By the end of the day, the press reported, "about a dozen persons were injured, some by fire hoses which swept them off their feet on the glass littered pavement, some by tear-gas bombs and some by fists of missiles." At an outdoor meeting at the Hollywood boxing stadium, Reagan spoke for SAG in recommending that union members ignore the strike, cross the picket lines, and return to work. Two days earlier, while on a movie set, Reagan was called to a telephone at a nearby gas station. The caller would not identify himself but warned Reagan: "Your face will never be in pictures again." Reagan notified the Burbank police, who showed him how to wear a gun and holster under his arm and provided a twenty-four-hour guard on his house.[25]

Reagan believed Hollywood's labor struggles taught him a lesson in power and deception. "These were the opening years for me," he would write in his memoirs. "Now I knew from firsthand experience how Communists used lies, deceit, violence, or any other tactic that suited them to advance the cause of Soviet expansionism. I knew from the experience of hand-to-hand combat that America faced no more insidious or evil threat than that of Communism."[26]

Reagan's conclusion in his memoirs is a little premature. During this period, 1946 through 1948, Reagan continued to lend his name to committees that included communists, as he still saw himself as a man on the Left and advocated banning the atomic bomb. At this time Reagan even signed a petition protesting America's support for the nationalist Chiang Kai-shek against the communist Mao Zedong. The document was brought to the attention of J. Edgar Hoover, and the FBI actually decided to keep tabs on Reagan. The FBI also approached Reagan's brother, Neil, and talked him into spying. In an oral history interview, Neil recalls proudly following the FBI's advice and hiding in the bushes while taking down license numbers of vehicles arriving for political meetings in fancy Bel Air. Neil said of his brother, "He was in an organization that was as bad as you could get: Hollywood Citizens Committee of Arts, Sciences, and Professions. And I used to beat him over the head. 'Get out of that thing.' There are people there who can cause you real trouble. They're more than suspect on the part of the government, as to their connections that are not exactly American."[27]

The Hollywood Independent Citizens' Committee of the Arts, Sciences, and Professions, or HICCASP (which, joked Reagan, was pronounced as a dying man's coughing), represented a tenuous fusion of liberals and communists. It supported Franklin Roosevelt's reelection in 1944, and while it was known that communists had been part of the executive committee, there was little concern about the group's politics until after the war ended. Reagan had dismissed the allegation that

HICCASP was controlled by communists as "Republican propaganda." Yet at a stormy session of the committee in July 1946 James Roosevelt, the son of FDR, offered a resolution to condemn communism and a raucous dispute broke out, described by Reagan as "a Kilkenny brawl":

> A well-known musician [Artie Shaw] sprang to his feet. He offered to to recite the USSR constitution from memory, yelling that it was a lot more democratic than that of the United States. A prominent movie writer leaped upward. He said that if there was a war between the United States and Russia, he would volunteer for Russia.[28]

Reagan did not follow his brother's advice and "get out of that thing" for good reason. The FBI had asked him, as well as Jane Wyman, to stay in HICCASP to become informants. Reagan's FBI code name was T-10. Later, he testified that agents would drop by his house with tips but that he was told "if I ever got into trouble from using it they would deny they had done so." When Reagan was first approached by government officials seeking his help in outing communists, he strongly objected, stating "I don't go in for Red baiting." The FBI worked hard to convince Reagan that those he was protecting were out to get him. "What did they say about me?" Reagan demanded. "The exact quotation," an official replied, was: " 'What are we going to do about the sonofabitch Reagan?' Will that do for openers?"[29]

Reagan's suspicions about communists took some time to develop. As a talented orator, the head of SAG had been accustomed to giving speeches denouncing fascism, imperialism, and other familiar targets. At one talk, in spring 1946, a minister who was also a friend of Reagan's approached him and remarked, "Don't you think, while you're denouncing Fascism, it would be fair to speak out equally strongly against the tyranny of Communism?" Reagan agreed, and at his next speech he denounced fascism to thunderous applause and then came out against communism, only to wait for applause that never came. "I stumbled off the stage into the clasp of my friend [a fellow actor] whose face reflected my own amazement. 'Did you hear that?' he whispered. 'I didn't hear anything,' I muttered. 'That's what I heard,' he said."[30]

Actors, composers, and scriptwriters each responded to the commu-

nist dilemma differently. For one eminent writer the moment of truth
came not in Hollywood but in Moscow. Budd Schulberg had written one
novel of Hollywood ambition, *What Makes Sammy Run?* (1941) and
another of failure, *The Disenchanted* (1950), and the talented scriptwriter would collaborate with Elia Kazan in producing *On the Waterfront*. Schulberg remarked that in Hollywood during the Depression
years the CP "was the only game in town." In 1951 at HUAC's second
hearing on communist involvement in the film industry, he testified that
he had joined the party because no other political force in America had
taken a stand against Mussolini and Hitler and the threat of fascism. He
also told the committee of being harangued for failing to write proper
social realism. Then he recounted attending a writers' conference in
Moscow in 1934. He was impressed by what appeared to be a tolerant
attitude toward literature in Russia. "I remember Gorky speaking, and a
man named Bukharin spoke, and Isaac Babel spoke, and many of the
great poets, Pasternak and so forth." Schulberg thought he saw what
Gorbachev later called *glasnost*, "openness." It turned out to be a mere
flicker. "I think it is a striking fact that every man who had appeared on
the platform and called for greater leniency—I think it was called a new
silver age of literature—every one of these men by 1938 had either been
shot or been silenced, and after that none of these writers, who were trying to follow their individual line, were able to function anymore. Some
were silenced. Some committed suicide. Some disappeared."[31]

In Hollywood's ideological wars, Schulberg and Kazan sided with
Reagan against Dalton Trumbo and John Howard Lawson. That American writers like the Hollywood Ten had no sympathy for writers in opposition and exile in Russia may have reflected their reaction against anything that would undermine a common front against fascism, yet
fascism was defeated in 1945. Many in the Hollywood Left continued
to defend the Soviet Union even after the death of Stalin in 1953 and
Khrushchev's "Crimes of Stalin" speech in 1956.

In 1973 I had occasion to be in the company of Lester Coles, one of
the Hollywood Ten, while watching the Watergate coverage at a summer
house in Laguna Beach. One evening a news bulletin interrupted the
program to announce that the democratically elected Chilean government had fallen and Salvador Allende had been assassinated. "Of
course," snapped Coles. "Will they ever learn? There's only one way
to go."

"What way is that?" I asked.

He replied with unflappable confidence: "Castro's way."

Coles was half right. Ironically, Allende's fate was indeed a victory for Castro, who denied the democratic route to freedom and claimed his way was the "only way to go." However, it was also an achievement of the CIA, which would "destabilize" a regime that sought to take that parliamentary route to democratic socialism. Allende's murder was a victory for both communism and anticommunism. For liberalism, it was a tragedy.

Marxist in Malibu

IN LATER YEARS Reagan would jest that he had once been "a near-hopeless hemophiliac liberal" who "bled for 'causes,'" and that when he abandoned liberalism it was as though he had recovered from a disease.[32] Reagan spoke not solely of himself but for all "bleeding heart liberals." Reagan's embrace of anticommunism is not as perplexing as his transformation into an impassioned antiliberal. In some respects Reagan is unlike most other American cultural figures who traveled from Left to Right. They began as communists or Trotskyists and moved from one end of the political spectrum to the other, always disdaining liberalism. When first on the Left, figures like Max Eastman and James Burnham criticized liberalism for in its inability to make a revolution; when later on the Right, the same figures criticized liberalism for its inability to prevent one. Whether radical or conservative, they had never allied with liberalism, convinced that it could neither forge communism nor fight it. Reagan, on the other hand, had once allied with liberalism, and thus his turn against it deserves attention.

A supreme symbol of late 1940s liberalism was James Roosevelt. Communist leaders of HICCASP naturally valued his participation in its activities, but Roosevelt complained that they continually deleted all criticisms of the Soviet Union from drafts of his speeches, which he would put back in. On July 11, 1946, the night of what Reagan described as the "Kilkenny brawl," Roosevelt had proposed to refute charges that HICCASP was a communist front by issuing a public statement critical of the Soviet Union. Reagan recalled that Dalton Trumbo denounced the proposal and that John Howard Lawson "persisted in waving a long finger in front of my nose and telling me off. One woman of liberal leanings had a heart attack and had to be taken home, the emotional atmosphere was so stirring."[33]

A few days after the affair at HICCASP, a friend nudged Reagan and told him, "come up to Olivia de Havilland's apartment." The actress, famous for her role in *Gone with the Wind*, also sensed something was wrong. Only recently, in Seattle, Trumbo had given her a speech to read containing communist rhetoric, and she refused to deliver it. In her apartment Reagan caught himself grinning at the actress until she asked him what seemed so funny. "Nothing," Reagan replied, "except that I thought you were one." Smiling right back, "I thought *you* were one," she mumbled softly. "Until tonight, that is."

Roosevelt, Reagan, and Olivia de Haviland were the three outspoken voices of liberalism in the HICCASP, but they were in the minority. They were always being challenged by communists who hoped to gain power by eliminating all diversity. Reagan remembered the screenwriter Lawson shouting in his face. "This organization will never adopt a statement which endorses free enterprise and repudiates Communism. . . . A two-party system is in no way necessary or even desirable for democracy." Lawson refused Reagan's request to allow the membership to vote on the resolution. When a vote was taken, however, de Havilland was the only voting member to voice an "aye" in support of Reagan. At a subsequent meeting the resolution criticizing communism was voted down 60 to 10, and Reagan immediately submitted his resignation from HICCASP by telegram.[34]

Reagan knew what was going on in HICAASP, as did the FBI, but he expressed surprise at the Machiavellian politics of the communists, their ability to disguise their true aims in the language of liberation. At the conclusion of one meeting, Reagan said: "One of us (old liberal me) was so wide-eyed by this time it seemed my eyes could never close again."[35] Reagan would forever wonder how long would it take liberals to realize that American communists were as desirous of power as anyone else. The rites of liberal innocence would be repeated again on the college campuses in the 1960s, when the struggle for power within moderate student organizations reached new heights as extremists took over meetings.

In his memoir, Reagan relishes recounting a phone call from his friend, the actor William Holden. It was mid-summer 1946. Said Holden, "I've found out there is a meeting at Ida Lupino's."

"But Ida isn't one of Them," Reagan replied.

Holden: "I know. They are just borrowing her patio."

When Holden and Reagan arrived at her house, Ida Lupino welcomed them with a big smile, but out on the patio many in the crowd of labor activists seemed "astonished and miffed" by their appearance. The two actors listened while Sorrell's radical CSU was lauded; IATSE, the original stagehands' union, blasted; and SAG faintly complimented for serving as a peacemaker. As the political rhetoric escalated against supporters of moderation, Reagan "writhed" in his seat. He was about to stand up but felt Holden's arm on his shoulder, holding him back "as though a jockey going into the stretch." When the denunciations tapered off, Holden patted Reagan and said, "Now!"

Reagan leaped up and asked for the floor. Sterling Hayden, chairing the meeting, gave it to him. The audience was the most hostile Reagan had ever faced. He talked for forty minutes, explaining how SAG was patiently looking into labor disputes with the hope of solving them. He answered questions to loud boos and "the customary name calling." Then John Garfield, the popular, handsome actor who won recognition in the film *Four Daughters*, spoke up from the rear of the audience. "Why don't you listen to him?" Garfield demanded. "He does have information you don't have." The gesture surprised Reagan, who thought Garfield was in the other camp. Throughout the remainder of the meeting, what he saw was more surprising than what he heard.

As Reagan fielded questions, he watched the actor Howard Da Silva take Garfield to the back of the garden and push him up against a tree. With one arm grabbing Garfield's shirt and the other jabbing a finger in his stomach, Da Silva gave Garfield a verbal lashing. Later that evening, Reagan and Holden talked of calling Garfield to see if he was all right. They never did so, and Reagan regretted it the rest of his life. "What a difference," he lamented, "it might have become for John if we had." A few years later he died of a heart attack, and after his death, the press carried the story of his last forty-eight hours, and Reagan retold it in his memoirs. "He had gone to the FBI and the House Committee and poured out a story of fourteen years in which the Communist party had turned him on and off like a hot-water faucet. He had never been a member because he was more useful to them the other way. He told of trying to break away once and how they talked him back into line: it was that night at the patio meeting."[36]

One talented actor who broke away was Sterling Hayden. A ruggedly handsome man who sailed around the world on a schooner when he was teenager, Hayden fought for the Yugoslavian partisans in World War II, and for him becoming a communist was as natural as becoming an antifascist. Hayden cooperated with HUAC and told its members that one of the reasons he left the CP was that he "was constantly told that if I would read forty pages of [Stalin's] *Dialectical and Historical Materialism* I would understand communism. I never got beyond page 8, and I tried several times."[37] The actor knew whereof he spoke. Max Eastman once remarked that the Hegelian dialectic was "like a mental disease; you don't know what it is until you get it, and then you don't know because you've got it." Communists didn't get it and they never got that they didn't get it.[38]

Reagan was troubled to see Hayden, "a man with a magnificent war record" who parachuted behind enemy lines to fight the Nazis in the Balkans, siding with the communists in Hollywood. Yet Hayden later broke with them, and when asked under oath what had prevented communist maneuvers from taking over Hollywood, he replied: "We ran into a one-man battalion named Ronald Reagan."

In his unpublished memoirs, Hayden acknowledged that the Communist Party turned to him to persuade actors to support strikes and put Reagan in his place. However, he "had laid an egg," Hayden wrote of himself in the third person. "Reagan showed up and took over and ground you into a pulp; they all kept looking to you to hold him down but he dominated the whole thing and when it was over they told you right to your face you were pretty weak and the gathering did more harm than good."[39]

The communist controversy in Hollywood embittered nearly everyone who got involved in it. Reagan, Kazan, and Schulberg were denounced as traitors to the principles of liberalism for cooperating with investigations that supposedly violated the principles of the Constitution. Sorrell, Trumbo, and Lawson were denounced as traitors to the principles of liberalism for supporting trials in Russia that sent the accused to the firing squad, people we now know were innocent of charges against them and had no constitutional protection or legal counsel to plead their case.

Save for a few films made in Eastern Europe, Stalin's victims have no role in the film community's collective memory. What endures from that era in our popular culture is instead the role of the informer. In Kazan's 1954 *On the Waterfront* Marlon Brando is the "stool pigeon," denounced by a neighborhood youth for testifying against corrupt, murderous labor racketeers. The film viewer, however, knows he is the hero Kazan intended him to be. Kazan believed all along, with Reagan, that his act of cooperation with HUAC was courageous, while communists denounced it as snitching, a violation of solidarity. Reagan, Kazan, and Schulberg were also accused of acting out of self-interest, willing to testify before HUAC to save their careers. A more plausible explanation might be that it was easier for them to testify, since they had nothing to hide. Early on they realized what Andre Gide wrote in 1936: "The Soviet Union has deceived our fondest hopes and shown us tragically in what treacherous quicksand an honest revolution can flounder."[40]

Reagan's enemies remain powerful in Hollywood. In 1999, it was announced that director Elia Kazan would be presented with an Academy Award for Lifetime Achievement. Kazan was born in Istanbul in 1909, the son of Greek immigrants, and he financed his education by working as a waiter and a dishwasher. At the award ceremonies, television cameras were trained on Warren Beatty, a star in Kazan's 1961 movie *Splendor in the Grass*. Since Beatty had directed and starred in *Reds*, and Kazan and Reagan had turned against communism, the expectation was that Beatty would go along with others and sit on his hands in protest. Many in the audience did so when Kazan went to the stage to receive the award, but not Beatty, who jumped to his feet with a joyous smile, applauding. The public was unaware that Reed, the protagonist of *Reds*, one of the founders of American communism, buried in Russia next to Lenin's tomb, was on the verge of breaking with Soviet communism just before he died in Russia in 1920, and that the four other major historical figures in the film—Max Eastman, Floyd Dell, Emma Goldman, and Eugene O'Neill—all became anticommunists. Had they been alive in 1999, they too would have applauded Kazan.

One wonders whether Arthur Miller would have applauded. The emotional turmoil of the Hollywood experience stayed with the eminent playwright, and the career of Ronald Reagan lingered in his memory. In the fifties, Miller wrote *A View from the Bridge* and *The Crucible*, plays that were allegories of anticommunism in the McCarthy era. In the first, a dockworker turns an illegal immigrant in to government officials to win the man's girlfriend for himself. In many ways an answer to *On the Waterfront*, the play dramatizes Miller's sense of the selfish motives of the snitch. *The Crucible* conveys the hysteria of the McCarthy era through its depiction of the seventeenth-century Salem witch trials. Miller's other great plays excoriate the achievements of postwar America. In *Death of a Salesman* social recognition and economic success are false and fleeting, while in *The Price* family is held together only by property, as in much of Chekhov. What was sacred for Reagan, family man and G.E. salesman, was for Miller sullied.

Miller testified before HUAC, but while he would answer questions about himself he refused to go along with other friendly witnesses in naming names. "My conscience will not permit me to use the name of another person." Cited for contempt of Congress, Miller was fined five hundred dollars and handed a suspended thirty-day jail sentence. Miller had not belonged to the CP. "I'm not calling him a Communist," a New York City official earlier explained when denying Miller permission to shoot a film in the city. "My objection is [that] he refused to repent." The ever-astute columnist Murray Kempton observed: "As time went on, the Un-American Activities Committee's Hollywood investigation was less a search for the guilty than a confessional for the repentant." The drama critic Eric Bentley noted that it was not clear what one was supposed to repent—"just so long as you repented of it, and it was at least pink."[41]

The Miseducation of Ronald Reagan

LILLIAN HELLMAN, who refused to cooperate with HUAC, not surprisingly praised her own courage in *Scoundrel Time*, claiming she did not know what was going on in Russia. Since so many other intellectuals did know, perhaps she did not want to know. Yet she did know a few things about the mentality of her cohorts. "American Communists accepted Russian theory and practice with the enthusiasm of a lover whose mistress cannot complain because she speaks few words of his language," she wrote, and added, "that may be the mistress many men dream about, but it is for bed and not for politics."[42] Sterling Hayden tried to understand the theory and practice of communism and immediately gave it up; others studied it for years, only to conclude that it had no validity as history, science, or philosophy. The Hollywood Ten may not have taken to communism as a lover to a mistress, but they were all too willing to suspend disbelief. Whether they had any communist affiliation was not the major issue. The disastrous error was their willingness to suspend all doubts about the ethics of means and ends in order to defend communism as the last bastion against fascism, and in ignorance of how much the Soviet Union and the Third Reich had come to emulate each other. Certain Hollywood Reds also refused to value liberalism, which they identified with capitalism. So disdainful of liberalism were communists and some communist sympathizers that they believed Russia could skip over it, moving directly from feudalism to freedom in one single stride, in violation of Marx's theory that history moves in stages, including the stage of bourgeois capitalism. Coles, Lawson, and others believed that democracy had no need of more than one political party, as though liberty was not grounded in the right of opposition.

Reagan himself would come to disdain liberalism for different reasons. In his Hollywood years, his quarrel was with communism, but many of those who later came to admire him seem to forget that it was liberals such as Olivia de Havilland, Elia Kazan, and Budd Schulberg who also fought the Marxists in Malibu. Why did Reagan become so distrustful of liberalism? Not only did he refuse to see that the history of America is the history of liberalism (that is, as Tocqueville described it), he left office having only slightly reformed liberalism and thereby leaving its institutions intact. Later, when he cooperated with Mikhail Gorbachev to bring about the end of the cold war, he was fulfilling the goals of liberalism going back to the containment policies of George Kennan and Harry S. Truman and to the disarmament hopes of JFK.

—

IRVING KRISTOL, the eminent neoconservative writer, once made an observation that has been so endlessly quoted that it enjoys the status of

a truism. A neoconservative, he said, "is a liberal who has been mugged
by reality." He was referring to the predicament of certain college professors in the 1960s and '70s. In New York City, a spate of campus inci-
dents found academics pushed up against the wall, literally and figura-
tively, and graduate students taking over classrooms. Kristol responded
by changing cities and changing political parties. Yet Reagan never lived
in New York, and by the time he had become governor of California he
had already moved to the Right. What is needed is a corollary to Kristol's
explaining why liberals become conservative. It is this: Reagan was not
mugged by reality but by theory, by what he had learned from books that
convinced him that liberalism was the enemy.

The authors of the books were the Austrian economist F. A. Hayek
and the ex-communist Whittaker Chambers. One saw communism as
an institutional phenomenon, the other as psychological. Reagan and
many conservatives accepted Hayek's thesis that liberalism paves the
way for communism by institutionalizing a centralized state. Conservatives also accepted the conventional impression that the liberal mentality is susceptible to the "totalitarian temptation" because of the irresistible urge to transform society in the belief that its processes are
comprehensible and controllable. The fatal conceit is the idea of a
planned economy. Reagan was even more taken by Chambers's conviction that communism derives from an allegedly liberal assumption that
the world is perfectible and the intellectual infallible. Liberalism is dangerous in its assumption that it can redeem a world corrupted by sin.
Behind communism looms liberalism's impulse to invest history with a
revolutionary purpose. As Reagan put it in his first memoir:

> The tragic and lonely Whittaker Chambers wrote that in
> turning his back on Communism, he knew he was leaving
> the winning side, but he preferred to go down with the losers
> rather than continue supporting a cause he knew to be so
> evil. Commenting on the aftermath to his decision, he said,
> "When I took up my little sling and aimed at Communism, I
> also hit at something else. What I hit was the force of that
> great Socialist revolution which in the name of *liberalism*,
> spasmodically, incompletely, somewhat formlessly, but
> always in the same direction, has been itching its ice-cap

over the nation for two decades. I had no adequate idea of its extent, the depths of its penetration, or the fierce vindictiveness of its revolutionary temper."[43]

Whittaker Chambers became the hero of Reagan, William F. Buckley Jr., and many American conservatives. Sam Tanenhaus, author of a discerning biography of Chambers, is rightfully perplexed about Chambers's easy equation of liberalism with communism.[44] Yet when Silone predicted that "the final struggle . . . will be between the communists and the ex-communists," there was seemingly no role for liberalism. Whether in the communist or the ex-communist phase, the true believer is forever haunted, unable to free himself from the zealous emotions of his beliefs, even when he had ceased to believe them. Chambers proclaimed himself an oracle on the subject, though it should be noted that when he decided to become a communist he assumed he was joining the winning side. Even when he broke with the party and became an anticommunist who saw himself on the losing side of history, however, Chambers did not share Reagan's faith in free market economics and was more supportive of the welfare state. Reagan allowed himself to be influenced by Chambers, but one could never imagine the political romantic going through the emotional turmoil that resulted in the writer's conversion experience.

In *Witness*, Chambers tells us that the decision he made to become a communist was not choosing a theory or a party but making "a choice between life and death." To choose to save society was tantamount to choosing to saving oneself. Thus he accepted communism unconditionally, following all orders, enduring all suffering and sacrifice.

> For it offered me what nothing else in the dying world had the power to offer me at the same intensity—faith and vision, something for which to live and something for which to die. It demanded of me those things which have always stirred what is best in men—in courage, poverty, self-sacrifice, discipline, intelligence, my life, and, at need, my death.[45]

"Writers of the world unite," Dos Passos loved to say, "you have nothing to lose but your brains." Reagan and the neoconservatives looked to a man who lost his brains to the Communist Party, and they continued to regard him as the American sage. What Chambers saw in communism was precisely what liberalism was incapable of giving him: faith beyond doubt. Reagan liked to quote Jefferson, but the author of the Bill of Rights believed that the mind was a sacred temple, not a faculty to turn over to others to escape the burden of thinking. Liberalism never promised to ease one's anxieties. Communism did so, and Chambers flew to it, only to flee from it to discover religion and a God who would not fail.

Chambers's weakness for moral angst and self-dramatization was not all that appealed to the Right. When Chambers was a communist, he regarded the New Deal as fascist; when he broke with the CP and became a fervent anticommunist, he warned that the New Deal and liberalism itself was communist. With Chambers, Reagan and the Reaganites could regard themselves as the real force of anticommunism in America. Rarely did they acknowledge that the first outspoken critics of communism were liberals and anarchists, figures such as Bertrand Russell and Emma Goldman. In my dedication of this book to Raymond Aron, Theodore Draper, François Furet, Sidney Hook, and the Honorable Daniel Patrick Moynihan, it should be clear that I regard those men as writers who taught us how to think about communism. Anticommunism has a long, honored history, and for Reagan conservatives to claim it as their own, as they did in the 1980s, represents another great train robbery of American intellectual history.

Ronald Reagan's miseducation led him to believe that in order to fight communism he had also to fight liberalism. Yet such a stance had the sequence of history backwards. It was the communists who believed that in order to realize communism they had to fight liberalism. In Russia, as history revealed, it was the liberals, the Constitutional Democrats, known as the Kadets, who were the first group that the Bolsheviks set out to liquidate. In America, the first to organize against Stalin's Russia were liberals belonging to Americans for Democratic Action (ADA) and the American Committee for Cultural Freedom. Hollywood itself was polarized in July 1946 when *Life* published a fragment from Arthur Schlesinger Jr.'s forthcoming *The Vital Center*. The Paul Revere of liberal anticommunism, Schlesinger warned that communists under direction from Moscow "are hostile to the principles of freedom and democracy on which this republic has grown great." In Hollywood, Schlesinger believed, the communists were trying to take over the actors' union and have it serve as the cultural mouthpiece for the USSR. With prescience, Schlesinger saw that

> the Communist Party is no menace to the right in the U.S. It is a great help to the right because of its success in dividing and neutralizing the left. It is to the American left that the Communists present the most serious danger. On the record, Communists have fought other leftists as viciously as they have fought fascism. Their methods are irreconcilable with honest cooperation, as anyone who has tried to work with them has found out the hard way.[46]

Reagan was indeed aware of Schlesinger's dire forewarning, and he had even joined ADA. In the early days of the cold war, however, American conservatives listened to the ex-communist Chambers, a Dostoevskian underground ghost filled with guilt in search of contrition. Schlesinger predicted that the communists would do more harm to the Left than to the Right, and the author of *The Vital Center* anticipated that the ex-communist would put liberalism on the defensive.

Ever since the cold war, conservatives have distrusted liberals as "soft" on communism. Curiously, though, conservative capitalists have been so tender on the subject that they all but slept with the enemy, as did Ambassador Joseph E. Davies. In our time, "Henry Kissinger & Associates" have done business with communist China as though capitalism and communism have no quarrel whatsoever. They are the rightful heirs to the industrialist Henry Ford, who opened up the Soviet Union to American business, to Wall Street financiers who demanded that the United States bestow diplomatic recognition on Russia in 1933, and to oilman Armand Hammer, who reputedly laundered money for CPUSA in the 1920s, the start of his long career in Soviet influence-peddling. When communism was on the verge of collapsing, Hammer offered unsolicited advice to the Reagan administration on how to get along with high-ranking Soviet officials. The oil magnate J. Paul Getty tells the story of his associate Hammer responding to a question regarding the secret of making millions:

Armand, I am told, furrowed his brow and said: "Actually, there's nothing to it. You merely wait for a revolution in Russia. Then you pick up all your warm clothes and go there. Once you've arrived, you start making the rounds of the government bureaus that are concerned with trade, with buying and selling. There probably won't be more than two or three hundred of them . . ."

At this point, Dr. Hammer's questioner muttered something in anger and disgust and stomped away.[47]

Reagan and the conservatives rightly remembered that liberals had their share of communist sympathizers. They needed only to look at the zigzag record of the *New Republic* magazine as it followed the Soviet line on the Spanish civil war and on the Moscow purges in the 1930s. A series of essays in that magazine by the liberal Edmund Wilson were a literary achievement but a political embarrassment. Wilson dramatized Lenin's return from exile and his arrival at St. Petersburg's Finland Station as the fulfillment of the meaning of history, of reflective thought culminating in the world of political action. However, by the time the author finished the manuscript, in the late thirties, he knew something had gone wrong in Russia, and the last chapters of what became his monumental *To the Finland Station* (1940) quiver with doubt. Compared to the Hollywood Ten and Whittaker Chambers, the mind of the liberal could at least face itself.

If Reagan's hostility to liberalism is understandable from a strictly political standpoint, it is even more immediately and viscerally understandable in terms of human relations—for Reagan perhaps the starting point of all subsequent thought. According to his memoirs, when he encountered his antagonists on a Hollywood street corner, they would hiss in his ear, "Fascist!" The slings and arrows of one generation, however, hardly prove Chambers's conviction that the "Socialist revolution" moves "in the name of liberalism" and "always in the same direction." On the contrary, Lenin gave Trotsky and his Red Army the opposite advice: to eliminate the liberal Kadets, who "have absolutely nothing in common with the Bolsheviks."[48] American liberalism had been cornered by American conservatives and Soviet communists—a bizarre united front.

Ronald Reagan and Whittaker Chambers had entirely different temperaments. One was a romantic optimist, the other a brooding pessimist. Chambers's psyche, as revealed in his own confession, *Witness*,
and in Lionel Trilling's treatment in his novel *The Middle of the Journey*,
represented a curious mix: Christian terror approaching the inexorability of death, communist determinism acknowledging the inevitability of
history. In certain respects, Chambers's political trajectory can even be
said to presage our own contemporary poststructuralist nihilism in its
deconstruction of the human subject. Gifford Maxim, the Chambers
character in Trilling's novel, tells the liberal humanist John Laskell why
what he stands for has no future, why the self and the power of will
are to be overwhelmed by history, why communism will triumph over
liberalism.

> You stand there now, thinking that you know us all, and dis-
> approve of us all, and yet do not hate or despise us. You are
> proud of that flexibility of mind. But it won't last, John, it's
> diminishing now. . . . It is the last time that you will see it.
> . . . The supreme act of the humanistic critical intelligence—
> it perceives the cogency of the argument and acquiesces in
> the fact of its own extinction.[49]

Clearly Reagan was closer to Laskell than to Maxim, closer to the
voice of reason and moderation than to the thunder of rage and apocalypse. Years after his Hollywood period, when Reagan decided it was
imperative to engage Gorbachev in a dialogue as the first step in ending
the arms race, what did he display but the "flexibility of mind" that
Chambers derided as the curse of liberalism?

Reagan had legitimate reasons to hold negative views of liberalism.
Long before most liberals, Reagan saw the value of a laissez faire economy as an instrument of material progress and human freedom. And for
every liberal anticommunist, there were even more who traveled to Russia, China, or Cuba and thought they saw the future. Chambers was too
much the fatalist and defeatist for Reagan, for whom, as we have seen,
Thomas Paine and Ralph Waldo Emerson resonated more clearly.

—

IN HIS ESSAY "Character," Emerson observed that the unique personal
quality of a human being is on display even if its depths cannot be
plumbed. Character is better conveyed than comprehended, better seen
than known. In politics especially it is not clear how and why greatness
emerges out of the squalid scrimmage of smoke-filled rooms. All we can
know, Emerson advised, is that greatness of character "lies in the man;
that is all anybody can tell you about it. See him, and you will know as
easily why he succeeds, as, if you see Napoleon, you would comprehend
his fortune."[50]

The playwright Arthur Miller saw the actor Ronald Reagan become
president of the United States, and he was intrigued to know how and
why he had succeeded. In 2001, long after Reagan left office and three
years before his death, Miller was selected by the National Endowment
for the Humanities to deliver the Jefferson lecture in Washington.
Miller's lecture was entitled "On Politics and the Art of Acting." It was
later expanded and published as a book. What the actor as politician
needs to display, wrote Miller, is "relaxed sincerity." This was a "certain
underlying cool, a self-assurance that suggests the heroic." Ronald Reagan had it, Miller wrote, with a hint of aspersion, but mainly with genuine admiration. He "disarmed his opponents by never showing the
slightest sign of inner conflict about the truth of what he was saying."
His critics may have found him simplistic, but what counted was the
sincerity he summoned, which "implies honesty, an absence of moral
conflict in the mind of its possessor." Reagan loved acting, Miller noted,
and his tendency to confuse events in films with those in real life was "a
Stanislavskian triumph, the very consummation of the actor's ability to
incorporate reality into the fantasy of his role." If indeed the line
between acting and actuality was erased, then the audience was reassured that the president had mastered both, along with his own uncertainties. Miller continued, slightly misquoting T. S. Eliot, "Human
beings, as the poet said, cannot bear very much reality, and the art of politics is our best proof. The trouble is that a leader somehow comes to
symbolize his country, and so the nagging question is whether, when real
trouble comes, we can act ourselves out of it."[51]

First, Reagan had to act himself into it. When elected governor of California, he was asked how he thought he would do in such a daunting
political role. "I don't know," he replied, "I've never played a governor."[52]

CHAPTER FOUR

Governor Reagan: The Golden State

The California Dream

BORN AND RAISED in down-home Illinois, Ronald Reagan became governor of up-and-coming California. Unique in many other ways, Reagan was a typical midwestern transplant to the Golden State. He was part of the mass migration to California that began in desperation with the Dust Bowl exodus of the 1930s and continued in exhilaration after World War II, as returning GIs went in search of blue skies: new jobs and houses, sandy beaches and ski-sloped mountains. Many Americans fled to southern California to find work in the fledgling aircraft industry; still others, like Reagan, came to start a new life, and to reinvent themselves.

Would a state composed largely of newcomers have any interest in preserving the old? The two American presidents of the twentieth century who were emphatically conservative, Herbert Hoover and Ronald Reagan, were born in the Midwest and arrived at the White House by way of California, a state that had historically set out to conserve nothing and change everything. Californians were all too ready to plow up orange groves, and to build freeways, suburban track developments, and shopping centers. In time, they would begin to worry about traffic congestion, and massive immigration and cheap labor from across the Mexican borders. They would eventually fret over air pollution so oppressive that children and the elderly were warned to stay indoors to escape the darkness at noon.

Yet most of those coming to the state did not pause to complain but wanted instead to pursue—in that Reaganesque way—their dreams. The adventurous spirit had begun a century before, with the excitement of the gold rush of 1849. Long before oil or movie stars were discovered, California had seemed an irresistible crapshoot. The 49ers who set out to strike it rich used a pan full of water and gently shook it so that gold dust and nuggets sunk to the bottom. Ralph Waldo Emerson smiled upon the gold rush for what it was, further evidence that the will to wealth will not be thwarted. His contemporary, the poet Henry David Thoreau, saw no difference between shaking sand and shaking dice. "Everyone's a winner," was America's siren song, and years later Reagan himself, in one of his speeches, exclaimed that "nothing is impossible" and that everyone should "dream heroic dreams."[1] He asked only that Californians draw upon their willpower and determination to dispel res-ignation, despair, cynicism, and, the gravest sin of all, dependency upon government.

During Reagan's term as governor (1967–1975), the state of Califor-nia was about to become the seventh largest national economy in the world, and it surpassed New York as the nation's most populous state. All was not well, however. In northern California, San Francisco was a city of waning economic fortunes. It had the finest harbor on the Pacific coast, but just before Reagan became governor city officials decided to turn its shipping over to the port at Oakland, across the bay, in order to reorient the city's waterfront to the tourist industry. Despite its dramatic hills and vistas and the Golden Gate Bridge, the most scenic city in America was soon crowded with tacky souvenir shops and pizza parlors; homeless panhandlers roamed the streets, and strollers and not trawlers made Fisherman's Wharf their destination. The arrival of the gay com-munity and other homeowners restored the city's Victorian neighbor-hoods, making headway against urban blight, but in much of the rest of San Francisco, beauty was a thing of the past.

Four hundred miles to the south was Los Angeles—not so much a city as an urban hydra, spreading out over a hundred square miles, from the Hollywood Hills and Pacific Palisades to the flatlands of San Fer-nando Valley. Unlike most other big cities, L.A. embraced wide streets and detached houses with broad front lawns. Cars were everywhere, public transportation almost nonexistent. The suspicion that southern California was never meant to be inhabited—that its sprawl was an affront to nature—was borne out by earthquakes, floods, Santa Ana winds, sandstorms, and raging fires followed by rain and mudslides. With scant water of its own, southern California had to import Colorado River water, stored behind the massive Hoover Dam and diverted from the snow-capped Sierra Nevada mountains. Northern California came to the rescue, with a 444-mile aqueduct, part open canal, part covered pressure pipe, that ran from north to south under and over the mountains and across deserts to help irrigate arid farmlands, control flooding, and bring water and electricity. The aqueduct, the Hoover Dam, and other constructions that helped California bloom were built with the help of the federal government—the bane of Ronald Reagan.

San Franciscans named their football team the 49ers to capture the daring spirit of the prospectors and the wild freedom of the mining camps. Socially, however, since the 1960s the state seemed, as it does today, a moral curiosity. Its more flamboyant life styles were permissive, its politics unwelcoming, with stiff criminal laws, including the death penalty. Today, a "three strikes and you're out" policy can put felons in jail for life after three convictions for the most petty crimes. When Reagan was governor, San Francisco's Haight Ashbury and Santa Monica's Venice Beach teemed with hippies, and the state's college campuses rumbled with political rage. The eminent British historian Arnold J. Toynbee took a stroll through the Haight and told the press that he had witnessed a "religious revival." Toynbee also had a theory of history which postulated that for every challenge there would be a response. It came when America turned to Reagan to be rescued from the 1960s.

California has always been animated by a drive to take on all challenges, a will to believe that the impossible can be realized, and an assurance that anything goes: that church on Sunday morning should never interfere with a Saturday night on the town. Just south of Los Angeles is Orange County, where Richard Nixon was born and where the airport is named after John Wayne. In Orange County there is a huge drive-in church, whose congregation asks God to come into their lives as they worship from their cars. Orange County, the most conservative region in America, the part of California that went wild about Reagan, was founded in the late nineteenth century by the followers of the utopian socialist John Humphrey Noyes, who advocated open marriage and free love. It was in Orange County that the state's contradictions were best exhibited, and it was here that the Republican Party gained its foothold in the state.

The Three Souls
of the Republican Party

I N MODERN AMERICA, three groups have struggled to claim control over the Republican Party, established in the mid-nineteenth
century by Abraham Lincoln and the unionists and antislavery
northerners who were his followers. The oldest claimants are liberal
nationalists, who believed in using the powers of government to collaborate with the power of wealth as a *noblesse oblige* class, patricians willing to promote an agenda of social reform and the general welfare. The
leader of progressive northeasterners in the 1960s was New York governor Nelson Rockefeller, who, in keeping with Lincoln's legacy, supported civil rights.

A second group, concentrated mainly in the West and Southwest,
were followers of Arizona senator Barry Goldwater. They came together
in the 1960s and proclaimed their libertarian commitment to individualism, free enterprise, states' rights, and personal privacy, and their
opposition to the hated eastern establishment. In June 1964, Goldwater and Rockefeller fought over the soul of the Republican Party in the
California primary election, the last state contest before the party's convention to select a presidential nominee. Goldwater's victory by a narrow margin of less than 3 percent marked the triumph of the party's
conservative wing.

A third force, Christian conservatives, had yet to make their growing
numbers felt in California politics in the sixties. But Protestant fundamentalism had roots in the deep South, the Midwest, and the inland
enclaves of southern California, where devotion to God was as strong
as faith in freeways. The fundamentalists first looked to the Reverend
Jerry Falwell as their leader. However, the rising tide of true believers
who sought to bring religion into public life would not emerge until
the 1970s, when the Republican Party took firm control over a once-
Democratic South.

The liberal nationalist Republicans had shallow roots in California,
and their political influence declined after Governor Earl Warren was
appointed Chief Justice of the U.S. Supreme Court, where he wrote the
landmark 1954 *Brown* decision on school desegregation. Religious con-

servatives would always remain a little uneasy with Reagan, a divorced man who had thrived in hedonistic Hollywood, but they were not yet politically organized over issues of social morality when he first entered California politics. While Christians believed that Americans should fulfill moral obligations, Reagan believed Americans should fulfill their desires. A Goldwater Republican in his loyalties and a libertarian in his proclivities, Reagan was also an Emersonian, who believed deep down that the best thing the state could do was expire and leave us alone.

Yet Reagan's political philosophy was as ambiguous as the state's political identity. In California, culture and politics seemed to be at odds. Usually it was the liberal who encouraged tolerance, openness, and an adventurous life style. The conservative, in contrast, cautioned personal prudence, social respectability, and moral responsibility. In theory, the conservative clings to tradition; the liberal craves change. It remained to be seen whether a state that was open to experience, and found it hard to resist seeing the landscape transformed, would turn out to be liberal or conservative. The course California took could well determine the future of America itself. As the poet Richard Armour phrased it:

> So leap with joy, be blithe and gay
> Or weep, my friends, with sorrow.
> What California is today,
> The rest will be tomorrow.[2]

To Pat Brown, the question of California's future was obvious. Elected governor of the state in 1958, Brown served two terms as a genial, wheeler-dealer, back-slapping politician who had the tax-and-spend habit conservatives detested. In his race for a third term Brown was captured in a television commercial joking to a group of schoolchildren: "You know I'm running against an actor. Remember this, you know who killed Abraham Lincoln, don't you?" A tasteless joke, but that was Brown's problem—he took Reagan as a joke.[3]

Brown had every reason to be cocky. His political career seemed dramatic evidence that liberalism was on the rise and conservatism on the wane. In 1958, the amiable, paunchy Brown, a San Francisco Irish Catholic who earned his way through college and attended law school at night, defeated Senator William Knowland, an antilabor, right-wing

Republican. For the first time since 1878 the Democratic Party would control both houses of the state legislature as well as the governorship. Two years later, in the presidential election of 1960, Richard Nixon, Dwight D. Eisenhower's vice president, lost a close race to the young, glamorous John F. Kennedy. In his inaugural address, JFK exhorted young Americans: "Ask not what your country can do for you; ask what you can do for your country"—a pronouncement that spurred an outburst of idealism. Young Americans joined the civil rights movement and Kennedy's Peace Corps program to help poor people overseas.

Nixon returned to California after a decade's absence and announced he would run against Brown in 1962. A native Californian born in the town of Yorba Linda in a house his father built, Nixon was raised a Quaker and, after law school and navy service in World War II, won a seat in the House and then the Senate before becoming Eisenhower's running mate in 1952. Nixon was a nationalist Republican who believed in strong government. Liberals, however, had always viewed him as a crafty opportunist. In 1947, when Reagan testified before the House Un-American Activities Committee, Nixon was a freshman member of it. Despite his weakness for McCarthy's demagogic tactics, Nixon effectively pursued Chambers's accusation to prosecute Hiss. When he was president thirty years later, members of his administration would break into the Democratic headquarters in the Watergate Hotel in search of evidence.

In 1962, to the surprise of many, Brown defeated the nationally known Nixon and earned the title "the giant killer." His sulking opponent held a press conference and announced to journalists that he had always been hated: "You won't have Nixon to kick around any more." President Kennedy called Brown to congratulate him for driving Nixon "to the nuthouse." That "last farewell speech of his," Kennedy added, "shows that he belongs on the couch." Nixon's great passion was international relations, and when presidential scholar Stephen Hess asked him how he felt about losing, Nixon replied: "Well, at least I won't have to deal with crime, dope addiction and all that other crap."[4]

In the early sixties, Reagan had his work cut out for him. Although Nixon was a moderate, much of the Republican Party did seem like it could use the services of a psychoanalyst. The party was full of extremists overcome by paranoia. The John Birch Society, a national group strong in the state, was started by the Massachusetts candy maker Robert Welch, who declared President Eisenhower a "conscious, dedicated agent of the Communist conspiracy." On his TV program *Firing Line*, William F. Buckley Jr. borrowed a line from the conservative scholar Russell Kirk to educate the Birchers with the advice: "Ike isn't a communist; he's a golfer." The Birch Society was comprised of small businessmen, retired military officers, and little old ladies in tennis shoes who busily compiled files of research on suspected communists. Liberal social scientists had published an anthology of essays, *The Radical Right*, to find out what was wrong with conservatism and why some Republicans felt so threatened. They concluded that the Right was fearful of change and suffering from "status anxiety." Conservatives were deeply suspicious of communist subversion, but liberals preferred to characterize them as living in dread of modernity and permissiveness.

William F. Buckley Jr. and Senator Barry Goldwater replied that the real problem was liberalism itself, its lack of principle and failure of nerve. Conservatives denounced Chief Justice Earl Warren for using social science research to overturn the principle of federalism and state sovereignty in the *Brown* desegregation decision. The stalemate of the war in Vietnam also compelled Goldwater to write *The Conscience of a Conservative* (1960) and *Why Not Victory?* (1962) to protest high taxes, high-handed Washington bureaucracy, and the cold war impasse. Across the state many a fin-tailed sedan rolled down the freeways sporting bumper stickers demanding "Impeach Earl Warren" or "U.S. Out of the U.N." And yet, except in California, the far Right of the Republican Party had relatively few significant successes in winning state and federal offices.

Then came the presidential election of 1964.[5] That Goldwater won the Republican nomination seemed to suggest that conservatism had enjoyed a sudden resurgence. In his acceptance speech, at San Francisco in July, the flippant, dour Goldwater loudly proclaimed: "Extremism in the defense of liberty is no vice. . . . moderation in the pursuit of justice is no virtue." The stark shibboleth brought a standing ovation. Conservatives promised the electorate, as placards waved at San Francisco's Cow Palace read, "A Choice and Not an Echo." The chic radicalism of Hollywood lost its luster as the country heard thunder on the Right for the first time in recent American history.

"The Speech"

THE 1964 PRESIDENTIAL race did offer voters a clear choice: Goldwater stood against a government that imposed high taxes and social welfare programs, enforced laws against racial discrimination, and carried out a cold war with no victory in sight. Lyndon Johnson, who succeeded Kennedy after his assassination in 1963, offered the Great Society program, with its civil rights legislation, war on poverty, and renewed commitment to the continuing struggle in Vietnam. Late in the race, a week before Election Day, on October 27, 1964, Americans heard another voice coming across the TV, that of the familiar actor Ronald Reagan, who insisted that the time had come to choose either the patriotic convictions of America's founding fathers or the craven amorality of a liberalism ready for peaceful coexistence with communism.

"This idea is that government is beholden to the people, that it has no other source of power except the sovereign people, is still the newest and the most unique idea in all the long history of man's relation to man," exhorted Reagan. The issue at hand was whether America had the capacity for self-government or "a little intellectual elite in a far-distant capital" should plan our lives. "You and I are told increasingly that we have to choose between a left or right. . . . there's only an up or down— up to a man's age-old dream, the ultimate in individual freedom consistent with law and order—or down to the ant heap of totalitarianism. . . . You and I have a rendezvous with destiny," he added, taking a line from Franklin D. Roosevelt. Paraphrasing Lincoln, he said, "We will preserve for our children this, the last best hope of man on earth," concluding, with a Reaganesque touch of the dramatic, "or we'll sentence them to take the last step into a thousand years of darkness."[6]

Reagan's famous speech is both radical and not a little unpatriotic. Those who established the political foundations of the American Republic had proclaimed just the opposite of what Reagan was saying. Government is not beholden to the people but to their representatives. Through checks and restraints, representatives will deflect popular democracy and, by "enlarging" and "refining" its views, assure that an elite guides its decisions. What is radical in the speech is that the student New Left was saying exactly the same thing as Reagan. So were professors such as C. Wright Mills, who had convinced a generation that the government had become alienated from the people and run by a power elite. Yet Reagan's claim that politics is not about "left or right" but "up and down" struck a populist chord of truth.

The year 1964 saw radical professors across the country telling students to examine history "from the bottom up" in order to plumb the "class consciousness" of the poor and powerless. Few Americans, however, believed that they could enjoy upward mobility by listening to the Left or turning their thoughts to the down and out. While the radical sixties was on its way to becoming an adversary culture, Reagan stood rhetorically with the mainstream, "the other sixties," the quiet, solid middle-class citizenry, those who wanted to avoid going down and aspired to going up and never looking back. Reagan's references to Roosevelt's " rendezvous with destiny" and Lincoln's "last best hope." were meant to redefine America, to give direction to a country that seemed to be adrift. Curiously, though, the two presidents he invoked saw the authority of the national government as necessary to make up for the inadequacies of state government, whose claims to sovereignty led to the Civil War. Reagan's sentiments were perhaps closer to those of Lincoln than to those of Roosevelt. In the Depression years, Roosevelt realized that what the American people desired most of all was security, whereas with Lincoln it was opportunity. In the more confident mid-nineteenth century, Lincoln saw the people charged with ambition and claiming what he called "the right to rise." Reagan's stirring TV address, widely hailed as "The Speech," became legendary in modern American politics even as it rejected the promises of government.

Reagan knew how to play to his audience, and as his speech began, the camera swooped down from his head to his torso and back up again to his eyes, which fastened onto viewers' eyes, and the contact stayed fixed. The tenor of his message only reinforced the practiced visuals. Unlike the cranky utterances of right-wing extremists, Reagan's talk was positive rather than negative. Unlike Goldwater, he did not snap at this and that but patiently explained what was wrong with having thirty-seven cents of every dollar earned going to the government to feed a welfare system whose costs were soaring and a national debt that soared along with it. To resist the road that would lead to the "ant heap of totalitarianism," Reagan called upon America to uphold the values upon which the nation was founded. The journalist David Broder extolled Reagan's address as the "most successful national political debut since William Jennings Bryan electrified the 1896 Democratic convention with the 'Cross of Gold' speech.' "[7] Never mind that Bryan's speech assaulted the corporate wealth of Wall Street in finance, while Reagan had in mind the bureaucratic power of State Street in government. In the end what mattered was that Bryan the evangelist and Reagan the alarmist were midwesterners striking out against the elites of the eastern seaboard.

However, the incumbent Johnson had attended Southwest Texas State Teachers College and sported boots and a cowboy hat. He was hardly an eastern elitist, and his Great Society program promised to aid blacks and the poor. Reagan's speech did little good for Goldwater. In November, Johnson earned a spectacular victory, with 43,126,218 votes to Goldwater's 27,174,898, and forty-four of the fifty states, losing only five, in the South and Arizona. The results seemed to spell the end of all that Reagan had called for in his famous address. Goldwater "not only lost the presidential election yesterday," announced columnist James Reston in the *New York Times*, "but the conservative cause as well."[8]

Journalists and much of the public misinterpreted the election's results. Johnson's triumph had little to do with the Great Society and its programs to eliminate poverty, bills that had passed through Congress almost as atonement for the assassination of Kennedy. The 1964 election was about foreign policy. Goldwater's frustration with Vietnam and his saber rattling against the communist world led many voters to believe that he could well unleash atomic weapons in a crisis and risk retaliation by the Soviet Union. His militancy and cavalier defense of "extremism" were repudiated by an America that preferred to live for tomorrow rather than die to prevent Reagan's nightmare of a "thousand years of darkness."

The election of 1964 proved prophetic, although this was not widely understood at the time. As California exploded with student protests for free speech and against war, wealthy Orange County rose up in anger against liberalism and the Left. While campus radicals announced demonstrations by Students for a Democratic Society (SDS), conservative students at UCLA and Berkeley organized chapters of Young Americans for Freedom (YAF) and the Intercollegiate Society of Individuals

(ISI). The Left used the language of democracy and socialism, the Right that of freedom and individualism.

In 1966, just as the New Left was beginning to peak, voters in California went to the polls and chose Reagan as governor. Years later he would win the presidency based on the same appeal he had made in The Speech, espousing faith in freedom through democratic means, all in the pursuit of happiness. It would take some time for the meaning of Reaganism to sink in with the Left. SDS had placed all its faith in democracy, but Reagan knew what his constituency wanted, not the theory of socialism but the taste of capitalism. Yet the struggles that began in California during his governorship continued in American politics and remain with us in our era.

Upon taking presidential office in 1981, Reagan appointed to powerful positions in the federal government dozens of California conservative activists who had been galvanized by the events of the 1960s. By contrast, only one SDS member won significant office. Tom Hayden, author of the Port Huron Statement, the Magna Carta of the New Left, was elected to the California State Assembly from liberal Santa Monica. Many members of SDS became Ph.D.s and controlled universities, which left members of YAF and ISI out in the cold. Young conservatives had to find positions in newly created Washington conservative think tanks. Thus the struggle for power that Reagan had seen taking place in the union conflicts of Hollywood recurred during his career. Conservatives overcame their traditional suspicion of popular democracy and appealed to voters. They won the country. Radicals, acting in the name of democracy, resorted to administrative regulations and bureaucratic procedures to secure appointments to positions of influence. They won the campus.

Few foresaw the momentous shift in American politics, which occurred between 1964 and 1966, between Berkeley's student uprisings and Reagan's election as governor. The triumph of conservatism in the nation occurred simultaneously with the radical takeover of the classroom. In California the polarization was felt, but its direction was not recognized. While media attention focused on student activists and radical causes, and liberal officialdom stood proudly by Pat Brown, a governor with a sound record of accomplishment, California was undergoing a sea change that went largely unnoticed. After all, to radical students, the sixties were the springtime of youth, and Reagan seemed on the downward slope of life, muttering the stale thoughts of a senior citizen. How little did they see.

The Unseen Revolution

GOVERNOR BROWN'S record could hardly be denied. He had presided over the development of state highway transportation and the California Water Project, which resulted in the aqueduct that irrigated farmlands and brought water down from the north, so that southern Californians could have their golf courses and swimming pools. Brown also sponsored California's Master Plan for Higher Education, leading to a three-tier system of community colleges, state colleges, and a university system of nine campuses that would be the envy of the country. The low fee, $26 a semester in the fifties, $240 per academic year in the sixties, made education available to the masses. The University of California at Berkeley, with its Cyclotron and Lawrence Radiation Laboratory, became internationally renowned, boasting one of the most eminent physics departments in the world, with many Nobel Prize–winning scientists.

The state, however, was not without its problems of class, culture, and race. In the San Joaquin Valley, Mexican American agricultural workers went on strike against farm growers who refused to recognize their union. Led by Cesar Chavez, the grape pickers asked for wage increases of $1.50 an hour, health insurance, and the right to organize. Many Californians, sympathetic to the cause of marginalized workers, made the supreme sacrifice and stopped sipping wine.

The cause of the grape pickers was also taken up on the Berkeley campus, where students had already been protesting against the Vietnam War. Historically the University of California had a ban on political activism on the campus's premises, and when tables were set up at Sather Gate for students to pass out leaflets, campus police ordered their removal. Inspired by the fiery leadership of Mario Savio, a bright physics major and powerful orator, the students responded by organizing what would become the Free Speech Movement (FSM) in 1964. In one dramatic confrontation, crowds of students surrounded a squad car and rescued a fellow student held in a vehicle by the campus police. The standoff lasted thirty hours, as television conveyed the story across the country, showing Savio standing atop the police car, invoking Thoreau to claim that "we must put our bodies against the gears, against the wheels and machines and make the machine stop until we're free." In December, students took over Sproul Hall, the administration building, and bedded down overnight listening to tapes of Joan Baez singing "We Shall Overcome." Governor Brown, who supported civil rights and opposed the death penalty, at first sympathized with the students and their prolabor, antiracist protests. But FSM threatened a general strike to close down the campus, and the students' continuing disruptive tactics forced Brown to call in the California Highway Patrol. In all, 773 students were arrested, their limp bodies dragged down the stairs of Sproul Hall to shouts of "police brutality." Brown's hesitation to act was criticized as "dithering," and the different ways in which Brown and Reagan handled student radicalism would go far toward explaining the demise of liberalism.[9]

A year later, on August 11, 1965, just outside Watts, south of the Los Angeles city boundary, a black motorist was stopped by a white highway patrolman for reckless driving. The twenty-one-year-old driver flunked the sobriety test, and as the officer arrested him, the driver's older brother, who had been a passenger in the car, sprinted back home to tell their mother what had happened. She rushed to the scene to berate her son for drinking, and he became hysterical, his shouts arousing the neighborhood in the midst of a torrid summer night. Many Watts residents knew nothing about the circumstances leading to the arrest, only that the officer was white. As crowds gathered, the patrolman sent for backup. Police cars arrived with screaming sirens and were hit by rocks. The riot that began that evening lasted for six days, took the lives of thirty-four people, twenty-five of them black, and injured more than a thousand people. Afterwards there was plenty of finger-pointing. Blame was placed on the poverty of Watts, its violent gangs, racial discrimination, the brute force of the Los Angeles Police Department, the passage of Proposition 14 in November 1964, which made it more difficult for blacks to buy houses, and the absence of Governor Brown, who was vacationing in Greece.

As the Watts riot and student disruptions polarized the state, leaders of the Goldwater wing of the Republican Party looked to Reagan as a savior. In preparing his bid for the governorship, Reagan had unenthusiastically accepted the support of members of the John Birch Society and refused to criticize them publicly. They "have the right to be wrong," he wrote in a private letter, and if they listened to his thoughts "they will be buying my philosophy—I'm not buying theirs."[10] Moderate Republicans desperately sought a leader to oppose Reagan to prevent the state from veering to the far Right and the conspiratorial politics of suspicion and accusation. Reagan had the support of Stu Spencer and Bill Roberts, head GOP political consultants, and of Henry Salvatori, the sun-tanned, self-made millionaire and fund-raiser.

Governor Brown believed that Reagan's right-wing supporters would drag him down just as they had Goldwater, and that liberalism in California would be bolstered. So confident was Brown of the state's progressive politics that he championed the Fair Housing Act (FHA), a bill with little statewide support that aimed to prohibit race discrimination in the purchase and rental of houses and apartments. Brown and other liberals expected that the real estate lobby would oppose the bill, which had passed the state senate by a narrow margin, but they had no idea of the hostility it aroused among the millions of homeowners who saw such legislation as a threat to private property and individual rights. White homeowners shuddered to think of the Watts riot. In a ballot initiative, FHA was soundly repealed.[11]

Ronald Reagan was a political phenomenon waiting to happen. California was a liberal state during the Progressive era, when Governor Hiram Johnson (1911–1917) challenged the power of big business, especially the Southern Pacific Railroad and the Standard Oil Company. However, the liberal mechanisms devised by the Progressive movement to return government to the people—the initiative, recall, and referendum—were increasingly used for decidedly conservative purposes. Years after FHA was repealed, California used the initiative to pass Proposition 13 and reduce property taxes to one of the lowest rates in the country. In 2003, voters employed the recall to replace, midterm, one governor for another. He turned out to be another Republican actor, Arnold Schwarzenegger.

The Reagan phenomenon in California, which might have been a passing, provincial episode in history, reveals a good deal about the nature of America's political culture. The New Left shouted "All power to the people!" Reagan declared that "government is beholden to the people." Since the time of the framers of the Constitution, it was believed that if the will of the people prevailed, the institutions of society would be endangered. The masses, it was feared by older conservatives, posed a threat to religion, morality, community, family, and especially private property. Such institutions Tocqueville regarded as the meaning and essence of American liberalism, and he discerned that democracy posed no threat to them. It took the conservative Reagan to teach conservatives that the masses sought not to destroy but to preserve such institutions.

Government without Guilt

ALIFORNIA IS CONSISTENT only in its lack of consistency. After Reagan left the governorship in 1975, voters elected Jerry Brown, Pat Brown's son, a seminarian who had trained to be a Jesuit. If Reagan reminded the people of how good and virtuous they were in their pursuit of freedom and pleasure, Brown reminded them of their sin and guilt. He refused to live in the governor's lavish mansion that Ron and Nancy Reagan had the state build, preferring a small apartment. He drove his own used car and shunned the awaiting limousine. The difference between Reagan and the young Brown goes to the paradox at the heart of American politics. Believing that small is better, Jerry Brown, heir of the rebellious, antiinstitutional sixties generation, fought against big state government institutions and thereby paralyzed them. Running for office by running against government, Reagan, heir of the union battles of the thirties and forties, knew that political success required using government even if it meant strengthening it. A critic of bureaucracy when out of power, Reagan once in office had to wield power, even the power of the dreaded state. With liberalism in retreat, his governorship was a prologue to his presidency.

A state known as liberal in culture and Democratic in registration had gone for a conservative Republican governor. As the polls had predicted, Reagan defeated Pat Brown handily, 3,742,913 to 2,742,174. And, signaling the rise of what would be known as the Reagan Democrats, he carried traditional Democratic white working-class neighborhoods, especially in Los Angeles, as well as suburban and rural areas that had inclined to the Democrats. Voters in these areas had once been avid FDR supporters but now crossed parties in angry reaction to the countercul- ture on the campuses and the riots in the streets. Workers would claim, as did Reagan years earlier, that they did not leave the Democratic Party—it left them.

Reagan's first promise as governor, reducing high taxes, underscored how quickly political rhetoric is undone by reality.[12] Candidate Reagan had promised to lower taxes drastically. His budget adviser, Caspar Weinberger, a San Francisco attorney who later became the president's secretary of defense, informed Reagan that former governor Brown had left the state with a $200 million deficit. The treasury had been "looted and drained," complained the new governor. While announcing dra- matic cutbacks in public expenditures, Governor Reagan called for a stiff tax increase, which raised rates four times higher than under Brown. "An economist who analyzed the tax bill without knowing its political background," wrote Lou Cannon, "might conclude that it had been crafted by a New Deal Democrat."[13] The bill made California's regressive rate structure progressive by doubling corporation and bank taxes and raising personal income taxes from 7 to 11 percent. Inflation further helped state revenues overcome the deficit, and the late sixties would be prosperous years for California. Reagan, to the chagrin of the state assembly, returned part of the surplus to the taxpayer.

Garry Wills maintains that Reagan rushed to obtain his substantial tax increase not only to tie it to the wasteful Brown administration but to put the issue behind him as he allowed his governorship to be "dom- inated by presidential considerations."[14] Perhaps, but the state revenue was already allocated to popular programs—education, water, medicine, law enforcement. Moreover, Reagan had no qualms about his severe tax increase, for he wanted taxpayers to feel the pain. Hence he thought of abolishing the payroll withholding tax so that hapless Californians would have to send a lump sum to the government at the end of the fiscal year. His halfhearted proposal went nowhere, but it suggests how far he would take America away from classical conservatism. In ancient Rome,

Cicero declared: "Taxes are the sinews of the state"; in modern California, Reagan declared: Taxes are the spoils of the state.

Upon taking office Reagan had to deal with Jesse Unruh, the powerful leader of the state assembly. Together they faced such issues as Medicare (a federal-state program of health care for the poor, a version of the nationwide Medicaid), college tuition, a hiring freeze on state employment, the sales tax, and judicial appointments. A child of humble Texas sharecroppers, Unruh worked his way through college, found time to be passionately active in politics, and sustained his loyalty to liberal social causes even as he became an astute and feared powerbroker working with lobbyists and state legislators. Reagan avoided the Sacramento restaurants where Unruh and other politicos drank whiskey and played poker. Called "Big Daddy" for his size and domineering gruffness, Unruh was Reagan's liberal adversary, though he sometimes helped the governor push bills through the legislature, sided with him against student campus uprisings, and endorsed property tax relief.

Voters had repealed Brown's Fair Housing Act, but the California Supreme Court voided the repeal, arguing that it denied people equal protection of the laws guaranteed by the federal Constitution. The state's real estate lobby then sponsored a new bill to revise the proposal, and it anticipated the governor's assistance. Reagan, however, chose to support fair housing legislation as a law with symbolic importance to minorities. Another controversial 1968 bill permitted abortion in case of rape or incest, lethal danger to the mother, or risk of a child being born deformed at birth. Catholics in the legislature, even liberals, opposed the bill, but after much soul searching, Reagan refused to veto it. Two years later, Reagan reversed himself when a new bill on abortion was introduced. "You can't allow an abortion on grounds the child won't be born perfect," he exclaimed. "Where do you stop? What is the degree of deformity?" Of the doctors performing the operation: "Who might they be doing away with? Another Lincoln, or Beethoven, an Einstein or an Edison? Who shall play God?"[15]

State policy on mental illness raised similar questions. When Reagan drastically cut the budget for the Department of Mental Hygiene, many state psychiatric hospitals and clinics closed, releasing former patients onto the streets of Los Angeles, San Francisco, and Oakland. The sad

spectacle of wraithlike figures, walking like zombies, twitching and muttering to themselves, became commonplace. Some intellectuals hailed
the end of institutionalizing the mentally ill. In France, Michel Foucault
asserted that mental institutions made patients worse and represented a
social impulse to incarcerate the strange and different. In America, the
novelist Ken Kesey claimed that doctors and nurses put mental patients
in a state of infantile dependency, a point reinforced in the popular film
based on Kesey's *One Flew over the Cuckoo's Nest*, starring Jack Nichol-
son. Reagan did not agree, and he came to realize his misjudgment and
restored $28 million to the Department of Mental Hygiene. Nancy
showed her husband the many letters she received on the issue from voters. Reagan, in carefully written responses, assured his constituents that
the mentally ill and retarded would continue to receive custodial care.
He said no minors would be removed from a hospital without the parents' consent.[16] But neither California nor any other state has been able
to deal with this issue adequately, and today the mentally ill continue to
walk the streets of our cities, with nowhere to go.

Still, there was much to smile about when Reagan's first term as governor ended in 1970. He successfully confronted the fiscal crisis with a
balanced budget and a progressive tax bill. A scandal was quietly brewing, however, and would explode in the press.

Phil Battaglia—dark, well dressed, good looking, gay—was a member
of Reagan's cabinet. Soon a whisper spread about his "inappropriate conduct." It was still largely an era of closeted homosexuality, and some Reagan advisors worried that the press would reveal Battaglia's sexual orientation and suspect even more going on in the governor's office. Advisors
hired a private detective to follow Battaglia and his lover in search of evidence and presented a report to Reagan, who asked another member of
his cabinet to notify Battaglia that he was being replaced. The story
spread in the California press and reached the national level in a Drew
Pearson column in October 1967. Before long there were rumors of an
orgy at a cabin in Lake Tahoe. Reagan attacked Pearson and wondered
how newspapers could carry a columnist who would stoop "to destroy
human beings."[17]

Reagan expressed no intolerance toward homosexuals, and his Hollywood acting career introduced him to numerous gay people. He helped
defeat a 1968 state ballot initiative prohibiting gays from teaching in

public schools by voicing his opposition, a stance that emboldened gay conservatives to found a political group, the Log Cabin Republicans. (Reagan's response to the AIDS crisis, which exploded in the midst of his presidency in the 1980s, will be addressed in chapter 10.)

—

IN THE TWENTIETH century, more politicians have been elected to the presidency after serving as governor than after having served in any other office. Reagan's ascendancy to the highest office in the land was in the tradition of Theodore Roosevelt, Woodrow Wilson, Franklin D. Roosevelt, and—his favorite president—Calvin Coolidge. But a governorship can be more grind than glory. Reagan found the duties of governing California more tedious than he had expected, and Nancy, finding Sacramento less than exciting, longed to be back in Pacific Palisades with her social circle. Her devoted husband, in his sixties, would come back from the state capitol at the end of the day exhausted. Driven home by a chauffeur, he would do some exercises, take a shower, slump into a couch, and then have a simple dinner while watching television with Nancy, sometimes in his pajamas. He might watch the popular spy show *Mission: Impossible* or a professional football game. Nightly entertainment, however, could do little to relieve his mind of two subjects, his rebellious children, and the wildly raucous students on the state's campuses. Life in the governor's mansion was as personal as it was political.

"Dad, It's Me, Your Son."

THE CHILDREN CONSISTED of four independent spirits. Maureen was born in 1941, when Reagan was married to Jane Wyman, and Michael was adopted four years later. On October 22, 1952, Nancy gave birth to Patricia Ann (Patti) by cesarean section, and then, on May 20, 1958, the Reagans had a second child, Ronald Prescott Reagan. The father was determined that his son not be called "Junior," hence the different middle name, and also a nickname, Skipper. During Reagan's second year in office as governor, Maureen was 27; Michael 23; Patti 16; and Ronald, 10.

The year 1968 saw a cultural rebellion that shook the world, with student uprisings in Paris, Berlin, Rome, Prague, and Mexico City, as well
New York, Berkeley, and Madison, Wisconsin. America had never seen
anything like the sixties, a time when the old refused to listen and the
young refused to hear. The counterculture, the New Left, hippies and
flower children, Haight Ashbury, and the heady expectations of "consciousness raising" made it seem that the country was going to hell on
an acid trip. In Reagan's California, no one over thirty could be trusted
and no one under thirty could be taught.

The oldest of the children, Maureen, would become a courageous
rebel. Although a college dropout, she involved herself in the issues of
the day, becoming a feminist supporter of the Equal Rights Amendment
(ERA), the right to abortion, and, with her own ailment facing her, the
campaign against breast cancer. She had a winning smile, took to
politics with gusto, and had the public speaking talents of her father.
Unlucky in love, she was married several times. She was much admired
by women activists in a period when national electoral politics was dominated by men. In her last years she put aside her own struggle with
melanoma to help with caring for her ailing father.

All the Reagan children felt alienated from their parents. They specifically complained that they never got to know their father. But, then,
every other friend and associate of Reagan's, save Nancy, would say as
much. Reagan's brother, Neil, noting that he had taught Maureen how
to swim, remarked that his brother thought his children should be on
their own. Michael recalled his father showing up at his high school
graduation as guest of honor and featured speaker. After the class had its
picture taken, Reagan introduced himself to each of the students. "Hi,
my name's Ronald Reagan. What's yours?" Michael remembered his
father looking right into his face. "I took my cap off and said, 'Dad, it's
me. Your son. Mike.'"[18]

The Reagans knew they were better as husband and wife than as
father and mother. Of all the children, Michael seemed to feel the most
estranged, taking out his frustration in tantrums: smashing glasses, making hostile telephone calls, and cracking up cars. Later, he settled down,
raced speedboats and became a popular radio talk-host in Los Angeles.
When Michael was about to marry and was on the verge of having an
affair, he wrote his father for advice. Reagan replied with a moving let-

ter, sharing with him the ordeals of marriage and monogamy and then suggesting from experience that locker-room masculinity is not what life is all about. "Michael, you know better than many what an unhappy home is and what it can do to others," Reagan wrote, referring to his marriage to Jane Wyman. "There is no greater happiness for a man than approaching a door at the end of the day knowing someone on the other side of that door is waiting for the sound of his footsteps." Obviously, Reagan had Nancy in mind. At his father's funeral, Michael spoke of the letter as a treasure of moral wisdom.[19]

Ronald Reagan, "Skipper," had the well-proportioned body of his father when he was a young, scrawny football player. Although Ron never took to sports, he had much of the wit and charm of his father. None of the Reagan children finished college. The parents were particularly concerned when Ron dropped out of Yale in the late seventies, moved to New York, and turned into a promising young dancer with the Joffrey Ballet Company. Reagan senior offered to call his friend Gene Kelly to ask him about dancing studios in Los Angeles. The Reagans worried that Ron would be hanging out with the wrong crowd, the fast lane of gay men. One evening Nancy and Ron returned home from a campaign trip to find their son with a woman—"using our room and our bed!" In Greenwich Village, Ron fell in love with a book editor, Doria Palmicri, an older woman of middle-class Italian American background. Ron inherited from his father a zest for political debate, a sardonic humor, and a fierce, tenacious set of political and social convictions, although his were liberal. He moved to Seattle and became a TV talk-show host on *Coast to Coast*. Unlike the conservative Michael, who addressed the 2004 Republican National Convention, Ron spoke before the 2004 Democratic National Convention in support of embryonic stem cell research.[20]

Patti, a willowy, beautiful woman, also has her father's linear features, but not his conservative politics. During the 1960s and 1970s she embraced the youth movement: guitars, bongo drums, rock concerts, Dylan and the Beatles, Hare Khrishna, the Age of Aquarius, antiwar activism, and support for abortion rights. When her father was governor of California, she was so uncomfortable she adopted her mother's name, becoming Patti Davis, and distancing herself from her father's conservative law-and-order policics. In an interview with *Vanity Fair*, she spoke openly of sleeping around, taking pleasure in nudity and autoeroticism, experimenting with drugs and having "a serious six-month bout with cocaine."[21] In her thirties she settled down and learned to enjoy solitude. In time she reconciled herself to her parents, and became especially close to her mother when her father was suffering from Alzheimer's. Her filial affections are expressed in her book *The Long Goodbye* (2004). Few of the millions of Americans who watched Reagan's funeral on national television, on June 11, 2004, will forget Patti's favorite memory of her father. When she was a child her goldfish died, and she and her father took it out to the backyard for a proper burial. After putting a cross atop the little mound, Reagan assured Patti that her pet was going on to a better world, at which point she got up from her knees and started to go back to the house to kill other watery creatures so they too could enjoy that wonderful afterlife. "Not now," said Reagan softly, "everything in its time."

All presidential families have a black sheep or two. In the public's mind, it seemed that the Reagans had four. Patti was interviewed by Mike Wallace on *60 Minutes* just after coming from exercise classes in Jane Fonda's gym. Reagan abhorred Fonda's support of the Vietcong. Wallace told the audience that a New York reporter wrote "a fascinating piece about the Reagan children," all so different and rebellious—"one an ERA organizer and an actress, divorced twice; second, divorced once, sells gasohol and races boats; third, a rock musician and composer and actress; fourth, a ballet dancer, 22 years old. Does this sound like children of Ronald Reagan?" Patti's reply is telling:

> Well, you know, each of us are very individual and we have our own careers and our own interests that we have been working towards—I mean, what would make us normal? If we were bookkeepers or waitresses. . . . I mean what do they want? Not that I would give them what they wanted anyway.[22]

The Emersonian tendency comes out stronger in the daughter than in the father. The poet warned Americans not only to distrust government but to stay away from politics lest the individual be lost to the democratic masses. Reagan would distrust government, but how could he continue in politics and not give the people what they wanted?

The emotional ordeal of the Reagan family seems to support the contention that the political is the personal. No doubt the children were temporarily estranged from their parents for personal reasons, but the generational alienation of the sixties was political. Conservative anti-communism had little appeal for students who opposed the Vietnam War, and the cold war seemed an absurdity to young Americans who knew little about it. Urged on by professors to take politics away from the politicians, radical students in California discovered that they would have to contend with a figure who was more than ready to confront the ambitions of their generation.

Years of Rage

WHEN REAGAN TOOK the office of governor in 1967, many colleges throughout California, as in the rest of the United States, were in a state of rage. The seemingly endless Vietnam War and the growing civil rights protests radicalized students, and campuses became the scene of disruptions, uprisings, and even violent riots. Until he ordered the state police onto the campus, however, the presence of Governor Reagan in Sacramento was scarcely noticed. Todd Gitlin, author of the memoir *The Sixties*, spent a month going through a decade of old copies of the *Berkeley Barb*, the free street paper of the student Left. For an entire ten years the publication mentioned Reagan only once as it devoted its passions to the Black Panthers, Castro's Cuba, Cesar Chavez, Che Guevara, and Mao, and to the beauties of the Chinese Cultural Revolution. Few students, and not many more professors, were aware that the sixties was to give birth to a new brand of conservatism, and that the ideas Reagan symbolized would determine American politics for years to come. In their years of rage, many of California's students and scholars missed seeing one of the greatest ideological transformations in American history.

Part of the reason it went unseen is that the sixties generation convinced itself that history could only move in one direction, toward the Left, toward rebellion, insurrection, revolution. "Professor, may I ask you a question that may be embarrassing but one that is on the minds of all us in your class?" Well, sure, I thought, go ahead. "Are you against the revolution because you do not think it is going to happen, or because you do not want it to happen?" The question was asked of me at San Francisco State (SFS) in 1967.

"The times they are a-changin'," sang Dylan. But in what direction? Listening to the young, it was as though they were carrying out Reagan's own antigovernment animus to its logical extreme. "Two, four, six, eight. Organize and smash the state!"[23] Reagan even agreed with students that a campus run by bureaucrats and punch-card functionaries could stifle learning and the spirit of inquiry. "I understood their sense of alienation," he wrote in his memoir, *An American Life*. Reagan might have even told radical students that if they believed in revolution they should follow his hero Tom Paine and help bring the message of '76 to the rest of the world. Activists, however, regarding American history itself as the problem, looked elsewhere in the world for deliverance from what they perceived to be bourgeois society. Reagan remembered the union struggles of his Hollywood days and saw worthy issues being raised that actually concealed the struggle for power. "But whatever the sources of this alienation," he observed of sixties students, "it was expropriated by articulate agitators—many of whom had never been inside a college classroom— who then turned it into an ugly force that could not be tolerated."[24]

No one who read a newspaper during the time could help but be aware of Berkeley's Free Speech Movement or the student uprising at Columbia University in 1968. In both cities, the American people observed what came close to being urban guerrilla warfare. However, the events that took place at San Franciso State in the early sixties involving academic issues may be closer to Reagan's description of what indeed was happening on the campus.[25]

SFS's History Department had been offering a course on Afro-American history at a time when radical students were demanding a voice over curriculum matters. In fall 1966, activists protested that the history course was not being taught by a black teacher. The department expressed a willingness to cooperate and expected that the activists would suggest the hiring of a black professor with a Ph.D. Instead they came up with a high school graduate whose knowledge of history went little beyond the lessons of street life, and the faculty were told that only people of color were qualified to evaluate the credentials of someone teaching black studies. Before long, activists made fifteen nonnegotiable demands; one stipulated that all black instructors be immediately promoted to the rank of full professor. The faculty refused, and as soon as its position became known, up went the roaring shout, "On Strike! Shut It Down!"

SFS was an outstanding liberal arts college devoted to teacher training and providing education to lower-class students, ethnic minorities, and recent immigrants and their children. Because of its location, it could recruit high-caliber faculty, and it had nationally recognized departments in art, theater, music, and creative writing. Most professors in these fields supported the strike. Those in history and the social sciences were divided, while business and engineering were decidedly against, and majors from the athletic department would square off against radical students before the police arrived to intervene between the jocks and the Jacobins.

The city of San Francisco had a time-honored radical labor history going back to the famous general strike of 1934, in the midst of the Great Depression, and continuing with the longshoremen's union, headed by the communist Harry Bridges. When HUAC tried to hold hearings in San Francciso in 1960, students from SFS and Berkeley showed up at San Francisco's City Hall to demonstrate, and hundreds were arrested and taken away in paddy wagons. For a brief moment student's emotions became hopeful with the election of John F. Kennedy, but his assassination in 1963 seemed to bring an end to the possibility of peace and freedom through conventional political means.

The scene at SFS grew desperate. Leathered-jacketed armed giants from San Francisco's "tactical squad," policemen protected by plastic face shields and armed with nightsticks, waited like linebackers to tackle agitators entering the building to disrupt classes. With SFS an armed camp, several professors had to hold classes off campus. Black Panthers came over from Oakland to give muscle to the strike and denounce the professors as "white oppressors." One black student injured his hand trying to plant a bomb; a few faculty had their tires slashed, some received threatening phone calls, one's office was raided by hooligans in stocking masks, and an administrator narrowly escaped when his house was firebombed.

During this time of troubles, SFS went through two liberal presidents until it appointed Reagan's kind of academic leader. The liberal presidents represented the last remnants of academic civility, urging faculty to meet with students and try to "reason with them." However, when the faculty would agree to one demand, the next day several more would be posted throughout the campus. Liberals hesitated to revert to force and call in the police. Then came the man on horseback, S. I. Hayakawa, known affectionately to Reagan as "My Samurai."[26]

Hayakawa was a Japanese American whose parents had been interned during World War II. Without a trace of bitterness, young Hayakawa went to college and graduate school and became a nationally known Ph.D. in the field of semantics, the study of language expressions and how their meanings change over time. As president of SFS, Hayakawa was more samurai than semanticist, a leader who refused to allow student radicals to change the meaning of the college. Until they encountered Hayakawa, however, students activists had the SFS campus in a funk.

One day the administration locked its doors and a mob stood outside pressed up against the main entranceway, seemingly stymied. "The art of revolutionary leadership in its most critical moment," wrote Leon Trotsky, "consists nine-tenths in knowing how to sense the mood of the masses."[27] It also helps to know how to use your feet. Suddenly arriving at the standoff at SFS was Professor John Gerassi, a Marxist and friend of Jean-Paul Sartre. The bearded, Che-like Gerassi pushed the students aside and put his foot through the glass door, opened the latch from the inside, and, with a cry of class warfare, waved the students in. The Bastille had been stormed. To radical students Gerassi was the ideal professor who would not simply teach power but take it. The Door of History opened with a kick.

When Reagan appointed Hayakawa president, activists assumed they could continue to roam freely as guerrillas. But on his first day in office, as a demonstration was beginning, Hayakawa, sporting a tam-o'-shanter, leaped onto the floorboard of a pickup truck and pulled the plug on the public address system, thereby silencing the revolutionary cries. TV cameras were on hand to capture the incident, and instantly Hayakawa became a national hero. Like a western gunfighter, Hayakawa faced down the villains and told the press that the confrontation was the "most exhilarating day" of his life. He went on to be elected to the U.S. Senate, where life turned out to be less dramatic and he would be seen as a fop, often falling asleep as his colleagues debated the price of soybean subsidies.

The UC Berkeley campus had been headed by Clark Kerr, an eminent academic, former labor negotiator, architect of the idea of a "multiversity" that would meet the demands of the new scientific age, and a witty president who knew he could keep the alumni happy with winning football teams and the faculty with open parking spaces. Kerr's bald dome gave him the "egghead" appearance of Adlai Stevenson, the Democratic candidate who in the 1950s lost two successive presidential races to the military hero Dwight D. Eisenhower. Even before taking office, Reagan sensed Kerr was a loser, and the president hardly helped matters when he announced that the university's various campuses would have to restrict enrollment because of the governor's proposed budget. UC's Board of Regents voted to oust Kerr weeks after Reagan took office, and the announcement hit the news like a funeral notice. A lead editorial in the *New York Times* was entitled "Twilight of a Great University." The impression spread that UC's eminent faculty would be raided by other campuses. Students grew demoralized and the public believed that no distinguished administrator from the outside would take a position that had become so politicized, but the radical Left was delighted. The UC Student Strike Committee released a statement: "Good riddance to bad rubblish. The new Reagan administration has begun auspiciously. The multiversity is dead. Long live the university."[28]

Kerr's place was taken by Charles Hitch, a rather colorless administrator and financial expert with connections to the Defense Department. But the battle over the budget continued, and students and professors protested the proposed increases in tuition, which at one time had been little more than a minimal registration fee. Reagan clashed with Jesse Unruh and some Democratic members of the legislature who saw the coming of the end of free public education in the institutions of higher learning. The clashes involved culture as much as economics. Berkeley had become, as Reagan saw it, a haven for hippies, bearded revolutionaries, and Black Panthers selling Maoist pamphlets, and around Sproul Plaza's fountain the whiff of pot breezed by openly. Reagan referred to the "orgy" at Berkeley as "obscene."

In February 1967, on an overcast Saturday, 7,500 students and professors, led by the American Federation of Teachers, staged a march on the capitol in Sacramento. Reagan had planned to be in Oregon giving a speech, and his advisors urged him to leave town. But like Hayakawa, Reagan loved a confrontation, and he told his aides, "I wouldn't miss this for anything."

No sooner had Reagan made his surprise appearance on the steps of the capitol than he was drowned by a chorus of boos. "Ladies and gentlemen, if there are any," he responded. Over the hostile chants Reagan declared: "As governor, I am going to represent the people of the state," only to be answered by the demonstrators, "We are the people." Reagan kept a plaque over his office door that read: "Observe the rules or get out." It had been his deepest conviction that those who disobeyed and disrupted had no following among the public at large or the student body. Just before departing the capitol rotunda, he told reporters, "If they represent the majority of the student body of California, then God help the university and the college system." The confrontation went on evening television, and Reagan was hailed across the country as the man of the hour. Journalists chided Reagan aides, suggesting that the angry crowd scenes had been called up from Central Casting. Even if far from the case, the Left could not have done more to give Reagan a public relations victory; and the governor never lost his sense of humor. He told the press that the protesters carried placards declaring "Make Love, Not War," and he doubted they knew how to do either. Of the scruffy flower children of the counterculture, he noted in speeches throughout the country: "We have some hippies in California. For those of you who don't know what a hippie is, he's a fellow who dresses like Tarzan, has hair like Jane, and smells like Cheetah."[29]

Liberal academics, anguishing about the Vietnam War, tended to support the sentiments of the striking students, if not their tactics. Students on the Left blamed the war on liberalism itself, especially an anticommunist liberalism that started in the early days of the cold war and led, it was held, to the quagmire of the Mekong Delta. As governor, Reagan seldom mentioned the war and avoided specifically defending it. Clearly the war had few supporters on campus. In a survey on the war conducted by *Time* magazine, 11,280 Berkeley students cast mock election votes for 1968, showing 19 percent favoring withdrawal and 43 percent for reducing America's war effort. No other policy had any support.[30]

Berkeley was not the only campus in turmoil. At the Irvine campus a Bank of America building was bombed, and at Santa Barbara, the coastal town of Isla Vista, also a student housing ghetto, exploded into days of street rioting. Crowds overturned a police car and set it ablaze. As the outnumbered police withdrew, demonstrators burned down the Bank of America. A student who was trying to douse the fires was killed by a stray bullet. "Burn, baby burn," shouted the incendiaries, whose targets were not so much the university as nearby businesses and corporations, the "running dogs of capitalism." The property destruction at Santa Barbara surpassed anything that happened at Berkeley or SFS, and it caught the public somewhat by surprise, since the bucolic campus overlooking the Pacific had been known to be an island of tranquillity in a sea of raging protest.

The San Francisco Bay area remained the most dramatic scene: demonstrations against the draft and the movement of troop trains (efforts also supported by some conservative libertarians); marches, with protesters carrying banners that read "Fair Play for Cuba"; a "Human Be-In" in Golden Gate Park featuring Allen Ginsberg blowing on a conch shell and humming "Ommmm"; the psychedelic sounds of the Jefferson Airplane and the Grateful Dead; nude bodies frolicking in the grass like puppies; and the young echoing Timothy Leary's advice to "Tune in, turn on, and drop out." Reagan felt the repercussions of the counterculture within his own family. Conservative Republicans blamed it on a liberalism too permissive to have controlled the children in the household; liberal Democrats blamed it on a conservativism too permissive to discipline the desires of a market-driven consumer society. Wherever the blame lay, the counterculture was not so far removed from Reaganism in its conviction that desires are meant to be fulfilled and that private life is fulfilling and public authority inhibiting. At Golden Gate Park even the police were amused by the sight of pleasure seekers listening to Dylan's "Blowin' in the Wind."

Golden Gate Park proved child's play compared to what would happen at Berkeley's People's Park in 1969. UC Berkeley had torn down old wooden houses, leaving open and vacant a city block intended for the construction of new university buildings. Street activists claimed the space as People's Park and, after seeding their own lawn, agreed among themselves that the space would never be relinquished to the city or the university. His patience exhausted, Reagan first requested the California Highway Patrol and the Oakland Tactical Squad. Overhead helicopters dropped tear gas, and police guns fired and wounded bystanders. As the melee raged, Reagan summoned the National Guard, and Berkeley became a military battlefield. The city was occupied for seventeen days, with the Guard bivouacked on the streets. Everywhere rose barricades corralling crowds at once enraged and terrified. Students wretched from inhaling gas. One rooftop observer, a teenager, was shot dead. Berkeley residents at one time had little sympathy for the riotous students, but they began to turn against the governor, who had to explain to his admirers how he handled "the Berkeley war" now that the occupation had escalated the violence it had set out to control. "I'll agree, bayonets are not pretty," he wrote to a friend, "but they brought an immediate end to the hand-to-hand conflict that had prevailed."[31] Reagan was later to regret using the expression "bloodbath" to describe Berkeley, but he had no regrets about ordering in the power of the state. "I'm convinced we win when we defy the little monsters." In a state government report on People's Park, the activist Arthur Goldberg was quoted as saying that the confrontation was not "merely a spontaneous, joyous outpouring by revolutionaries, idealists, flower children, and do-gooders. For most participants it was a calculated political act designed to put the expansionist and repressive university up against the wall."[32]

People's Park was the Thermidor of the sixties, the point at which the emotions of a rebellious upheaval moved so far to the Left that it led to a counterreaction from the Right, leaving the center discredited and defeated. The radical Ronald Dellums would be elected to Congress from the district of Berkeley after defeating an incumbent liberal Democrat, and the conservative Ronald Reagan would eventually be elected to the presidency. As for the future of American liberalism, it died at People's Park.

Conservation and Welfare Reform

"IF YOU'VE SEEN ONE, you've seen them all." Such was the dismissive statement Reagan was said to have uttered in reference to California's beloved redwood trees. Actually, before a conference of lumber producers, he said: "A tree is a tree—how many more do you need to look at?" During a cabinet meeting, discussing the possibility of a national redwood park, Reagan stated in opposition to the proposal: "People seem to think that all redwoods that are not protected through a national park will disappear." Lumber companies had always opposed such a park, and the impression grew that Reagan catered to their wishes simply to obtain their financial contributions. As Lou Cannon has pointed out, the reality was even worse. Reagan believed what he said![33]

Reagan's attitude toward the environment would prove disastrous when he became president. His appointment of James Watt as secretary of the interior was an act that was tantamount to asking someone to guard what he hates. The smiling Watt boasted of how much he intended to turn over public lands to private interests that would mine, drill, and cut everything in sight. As governor, Reagan had proved more prudent and had made better appointments and listened to sounder advice.

Under the governor's director of Parks and Recreation, William Penn Mott, California embarked upon a vast program of parkland acquisition and beach shore preservation. Reagan also appointed, as director of resources, Norman B. Livermore Jr., an outdoorsman and ardent conservationist. Livermore was a close friend of David Brower, president of the influential Sierra Club. Together they worked to preserve the Eel River and its steelhead trout from dam development, restrict offshore oil drilling, and create a 112,597-acre Redwood National Park. Another person Reagan listened to was Peter Behr, a Republican from Marin County whose efforts with the federal government led to establishing the beautiful Point Reyes National Seashore. The environmentalists Behr and Livermore prevailed upon Reagan to prevent the building of a giant dam at Dos Rios that would have flooded the surrounding area, particularly lands belonging to Indians that had been given to them by treaties. Opposing the dam, Reagan remarked—it was said with tears in his eyes—that "agreements are made to be kept." Later, he added, "We've broken too many damn treaties"—"his finest environmental moment," added biographer Lou Cannon.[34]

Reagan's attitude toward the environment seems puzzling. An outdoorsman who loved to ride his horse, cut wood for hours, and relax amid the tall trees of his Santa Barbara ranch, Reagan expressed indifference to the landscape. Cannon observes that "Reagan thought like a rancher," a cowboy for whom the vastness of West left little sense of the earth's fragility. Certain Texas ranchers would also give up their herds for a couple of oil wells at the drop of a Stetson. Perhaps Reagan's reluctance to take up conservation also derived from his suspicion of the role of the federal government. In his essay "A Guide to Reagan Country," the political scientist James Q. Wilson makes a relevant distinction. "A conservative is usually thought of as a person who favors limited government, minimal administrative involvement in private affairs, maximum free choice. A conserver, however, needs *more* government to protect present stakes from change, from threats posed by other groups, and from competition."[35] In the eighteenth century, the *Federalist* authors were conservers, believing that the Constitution was necessary and the national government imperative so that people would not be able to "vex and oppress" one another at the local level. Thomas Jefferson had no use for such sentiments, and Reagan was a Jeffersonian who also believed in local government and states' rights. Reagan and Jefferson had little regard for either the Constitution or the federal government as the ultimate source of sovereignty; instead they believed that people should be free to do what they wished, whether they wanted to cut, mine, dam, pave, pollute, deface, or, in Jefferson's case, enslave. Lincoln, the founder of the Republican party, believed as much as Jefferson that people are endowed with inalienable rights. People "do not have a right to do wrong," however, Lincoln insisted. Although Reagan had convinced himself that only government can do wrong, as governor he was not above making it do right.

—

REAGAN'S SECOND TERM (1970–1974) was devoted to welfare reform, part of a reelection campaign to "squeeze, cut, and trim" the costs of government. The welfare state came into existence as a generational need, prompted by the insecurity of the Depression years, when FDR assured Americans: "The only thing we have to fear is fear itself." Government would ease such anxieties with Social Security, unemployment benefits, disability insurance, and protection of bank deposits. Many such programs came to enjoy a certain legitimacy and went unchallenged. However, one New Deal measure, Aid to Families with Dependent Children (AFDC), became so controversial that it was regarded not so much as a generational blessing but as a curse that would afflict future generations.

Reagan's efforts to reform AFDC created the impression that he had no compassion for the needy and that he had declared war upon the poor. What disturbed Reagan was not the program itself but its seemingly uncontrolled growth. The case load of AFDC had expanded from 375,000 in 1963 to 769,000 when Reagan took office in 1967. Reagan also sought to revise the program to meet the needs of the desperately poor who had nowhere else to turn and to remove from the rolls those who misused the system with false claims. Although their numbers may have been exaggerated, Reagan objected most strenuously to welfare recipients who spent their checks at the liquor store or the racetrack. He succeeded in reducing the number on welfare while increasing the amount of weekly payments. The California Welfare Reform Act of 1971 allowed reduced work time for fathers whose families received support, drew up regulations to prevent fraud, and established a one-year residency requirement. The truly needy benefited from the new policies and within three years the case load dropped by 300,000.

Welfare reform was the major achievement of Reagan's second term, and his success with the program augured what would occur during his presidency. In the 1970 election, he was unsuccessfully opposed by Jesse Unruh, who chased Reagan all over the state trying to debate him and claiming California's governor was in the pocket of the wealthy elite. In his last years in office Reagan supported a complicated property relief bill that failed to pass. He let up in denouncing students activists, particularly after four had been killed by the National Guard at Kent State, Ohio. In his later budgets, it turned out that Reagan proved to be far more generous to the University of California than would be his successor, Jerry Brown, the ascetic who asked professors to teach more classes and likened the university budget to a squid, a creature that grows by issuing black ink.

In 1975, at the age of sixty-four, Reagan left office. He had been written up in the conservative press as the leader America needed to fight the good fight. Reagan won the deep admiration of *National Review* editor William F. Buckley Jr. Reagan was the hero of the Right for putting down the leftist demonstrators on campus during the sixties. What went unnoticed, however, was what would happen on campuses throughout the country after the sixties.

Jefferson believed in "a little rebellion now and then," and the students at Berkeley believed in a lot of it all the time, even every day, pro-

viding it did not rain. The standoff between the radical students of the
sixties and the conservative governor in California represents one of
the great ironies in American political culture. Both saw the state as the
enemy of freedom, a monstrous, oppressive bureaucracy demanding
higher taxes from citizens and higher tuition from students. Yet the students who thought they could overturn the authority of the state succeeded in making the governor a national hero who rode his reputation
all the way to the White House. The irony, however, is twofold. When
President Reagan left office in 1989, many of the campuses across the
country had been taken over by the radicals who were now professors:
Marxists, Trotskyites, feminists, poststructualists, new historicists,
deconstructionists, and other -ites and -ists who left street politics
behind to succeed not in revolution but in infiltration, boring into the
institutions of higher education from within, termites on their way to
tenure, masters of erudition who kept young conservative scholars at
bay. Nonetheless, Reagan ultimately won the political struggle by changing politics in ways that made the Democratic Party almost indistinguishable from the Republican Party, so eager were liberals—both those
under his sway and those opposed to him—to rush to the center. In the
meantime, the few aging radicals who remained on campus seemed
largely unaware of or, finally, indifferent to their political impotence
beyond the classroom.

Many contemporary professors of history, coming from the tumultuous sixties generation, would find it hard to evaluate Reagan as one of
the great or even near-great presidents—indeed, the idea of greatness is
forbidden in the "new social history," where "history from the bottom up"
excludes the exceptional, extols the common, and regards the event-
making hero as a conceit. Yet it must be said that the judgment of history itself belongs to Ronald Reagan. He correctly saw Tom Paine as a
rebel against authority in the name of freedom, not a revolutionary who
would impose authority in the name of the proletariat. Like Lincoln,
Reagan understood that America was about "the right to rise" economically and not only about the right to complain politically. Aware of the
meaning of American exceptionalism, Reagan would never ask students,
as did some professors who wrote textbooks, to compare the American
Revolution of '76 to revolutions that would erupt in France, Russia,
China, Cuba, and Vietnam. In addition to his intuitive Tocquevillian

wisdom, Reagan also had a better grasp of the meaning and direction of history. He was far ahead of radical academics who used to tell their students that socialism was on its way in when, in reality, as ex-Marxist scholars in Europe recognized, it was on its way out to make room for market capitalism.[36]

After leaving the governorship Ronald Reagan had no need to concern himself with campus politics. As a leader with thoughts about running for the presidency, however, he did have two geographical handicaps. The two previous presidents from California had left office under a cloud of shame. Many years earlier, Herbert Hoover was saddled, perhaps unfairly, with the Great Depression. In the mid-seventies, Richard Nixon resigned the presidency under the ignominy of the Watergate scandal. Vice President Gerald Ford succeeded Nixon, and he too suffered the stigma of pardoning the former president in order to prevent prosecution. Reagan had no use for Ford, a president by default, unelected, uninspiring, unacceptable. Ford would be easily defeated by Jimmy Carter in 1976, but the nation was about to hear from California once again.

CHAPTER FIVE

A Reagan Revolution,
or the End of Ideology?

"Why Shouldn't We
Believe in Ourselves?"

R ONALD REAGAN SERVED eight challenging yet satisfying years
as governor of California. Some of his children hoped he would
retire from politics after leaving office, though Nancy Reagan
believed he was destined for greater roles. Reagan could put up with the
daily grind of politics, and he enjoyed its ceremonial side, but he never
composed an address urging young people to enter politics as a vocation,
as did Theodore Roosevelt. Reagan felt, as Abraham Lincoln had, that
economics, not politics, was the way up in America. Lincoln relished
politics, but he also saw it as "the wriggle and struggle for office," simply
"a way to live without work."

The day-to-day details of seeing bills through the assembly, sitting in
on strategy sessions, fund-raising, and so forth had no great appeal to
Reagan. Even when president, he preferred writing and receiving private
letters to official public communications, staff memos, briefs without
brevity. An impression spread that he would often doze off at cabinet
meetings or fail to follow the line of conversation. If he was inattentive,
it may have been that the subject at hand bored him. Speaker of the
House Tip O'Neill remembered several occasions when Reagan, sitting
at a meal with his mind elsewhere, would come alive only when someone asked him about his days in Hollywood or on the football field. In
an August 1984 letter to a friend, Reagan described how he enjoyed the
physical work he did away from the White house and back on his California ranch: driving his jeep in search of flat stones, pruning dead
leaves, trimming tree limbs, mending fences, pouring concrete, gathering firewood. "Of course there were still some things to do that go with
my job, reports, meetings, phone calls and signing laws passed by Con-

gress. I manage to get most of that done in the early morning . . . so I still had time for the fun things."[1]

Even though politics was burdensome, as departing governor Reagan never for a moment thought of withdrawing from the fray. After leaving Sacramento, he would describe himself as a retiring citizen with no public aspirations, but he could hardly take his mind off the fragile state of the world and the despondent mood of the country. In 1975, the United States had just withdrawn from Vietnam, the longest war in its history, lasting fifteen years and costing more than 58,000 American lives. Vietnam was the only war that America fought with so little prospect of success that eventually it became impossible to deny it could not be won. Reagan avoided committing the mistake of Barry Goldwater, who left the impression that the United States could prevent defeat by resorting to nuclear weapons. Yet he did blame the failure of the war on the federal government's incompetence and what he considered its lack of will to victory. To the chagrin of advisors, Reagan once proclaimed the Vietnam War "a noble cause." He was saddened by the sight of returning soldiers, some wounded, others drugged out, and publicly announced that America should never again ask young men to go off to fight in "a war our government is afraid to win." This "No more Vietnams" shibboleth resonated with those who thought America should have won a war fought for "a noble cause" but also with those who thought the war was ignoble in the first place. Reagan had it wrong. Presidents Kennedy, Johnson, and Nixon were not afraid of winning the war but of losing it, and hence the tragedy dragged on. Vietnam was a war that had less to do with international communism than anticolonial nationalism. Reagan and other conservatives were so fixated on communism that they never appreciated the forces of nationalism sweeping through the third world. Nor did the Kennedy liberals, especially Defense Secretary Robert McNamara, who later confessed his blindness to what was going on in Vietnam, a country whose history of colonialism had created a movement determined to drive out the Americans just as they had once driven out the French, Chinese, and Japanese.[2]

In domestic politics, Americans were weary of the Watergate scandal. As a fellow Californian and anticommunist, Reagan was close to Nixon, and he would face a not entirely dissimilar situation in the Iran-Contra affair of 1987, when subordinates took it upon themselves to engage in illegal acts. Both episodes turned on the problem of trust in the exercise of authority. In a letter written in 1973, Reagan unwittingly lays out what will happen to him fourteen years later. "I also share your frustration about Watergate. I have to tell you it is not hard for me to accept that this could have gone on without the president's knowledge. Just judging it by my own much smaller shop. If my staff wanted to keep something of this kind from me, it would be very easy for them to do so."[3]

When Nixon resigned in disgrace in 1974, Gerald Ford filled out the remaining half-term administration, Spiro Agnew having resigned earlier in an unrelated scandal. Ford's leadership was clouded by the national uproar that greeted the pardon he granted his sullen predecessor, and by the outrage of stunned conservatives who saw Ford appoint their nemesis, New York governor Nelson Rockefeller, to the now-vacant vice presidency. Conservative Republican leaders throughout the country urged Reagan to challenge Ford for the party nomination in 1976. Reagan agreed and organized a campaign team headed by his friend Senator Paul Laxalt of Nevada, and the old California veterans, Stu Spencer and Bill Roberts. In the primaries, Reagan emphasized his success in California in reducing taxes, balancing the budget, and reining in the bureaucracy. Reagan lost many early primaries, however, and failed to undo Ford's control over the convention in Kansas City, where he won the nomination by a thin margin on the first ballot. Then the unexpected happened.

After he completed his acceptance speech and the applause had quieted down, Ford looked high up in the convention arena, where Reagan, Nancy, and their team were seated in a sky box. Ford beckoned with his arm for Reagan to come down, and the crowd shouted, "Speech! Speech!" When Reagan appeared at the podium and started to speak, the entire crowd was standing. Reagan had no prepared text, but he spoke like a prophet, reminding his audience that he would also be addressing "people a hundred years from now, who know all about us." President Ford, said Reagan, had spoken of "a world in which the great powers have poised and aimed at each other horrible missiles of destruction." Peace and freedom: "These are our challenges," Reagan exhorted. "We must go forth from here united, determined that what a great general [Douglas MacArthur] said a few years ago is true, 'There is no substitute for victory.'"[4]

The crowd rejoiced, and when the applause died down murmurs could be heard coming from delegates who wondered if they had nominated the wrong person. Yet the "no substitute for victory" peroration could hardly be a premise on which to face the cold war or to address a people living a hundred years in the future. When he had to deal with the Soviet Union a decade later, Reagan would realize that there had to be a substitute for victory. Going to war with missiles of destruction would leave only survivors in an atom-smashed universe.

Ford lost the election to Jimmy Carter, the Democratic governor of Georgia, who campaigned on a promise to protect civil rights at home and human rights abroad. Actually, Carter was as antistatist as Reagan. A southerner and outsider, Carter was the first modern president to tell Americans not to look to government for solutions; a New Democrat whose party ceased displaying pictures of FDR or playing "Happy Days Are Here Again." Carter was a devout Baptist who believed in voluntary good works and walked down the street to his inauguration rather than ride in a limousine; a man so frugal that the White House was allowed to deteriorate while he lived there, its furniture tattered, floors worn out, and lawns parched. Nancy Reagan couldn't wait to refurbish a mansion whose resident thought more about budgets than beauty.

To the Reaganite Republicans, Carter seemed weak and soft, a wimp more interested in human rights than national security and more concerned about arms control than weapons development. Carter committed the cardinal sin: He didn't take the Soviet threat seriously and, in a speech at the University of Notre Dame, told Americans to get over their "inordinate fear of communism." Carter also cut diplomatic relations with Taiwan and completed Nixon's outreach to China by recognizing its communist government. Carter's popularity was more seriously threatened, however, when he seemed helpless in the face of events in the Mideast. The fall of the shah of Iran in 1979 and the taking of sixty-six American hostages, followed by the Russian invasion of Afghanistan on Christmas Day, indicated to conservative Republicans that the cold war had entered a new phase. That interpretation turned out to be erroneous, as Islamic fundamentalism had little to do with Soviet communism. Yet Carter, who desperately increased military spending and attempted a failed rescue operation of the hostages, was just as helpless to do anything about soaring gasoline prices that had cars lining up for blocks waiting to fill up. Carter was vulnerable, a victim of circumstances.

Carter also seemed weak to Reagan for proposing to turn over the Panama Canal to the Panamanians. Most conservatives, with the notable exceptions of Barry Goldwater and John Wayne, opposed the treaty that would relinquish U. S. control over the canal. At first William F. Buckley Jr. opposed it as well, but after a five-day trip to Panama in which he felt the emotions of the Panamanians, he changed his mind and came out in support of the move. Buckley challenged Reagan to debate the issue on *Firing Line*. Reagan, who believed that Panama's communists were exploiting the nation's patriotic sentiment, would not acknowledge Buckley's point that anti-American emotions would be exacerbated if the United States rejected the treaty. In his later account of the debate, Buckley surmised that Reagan opposed the treaty to corral conservative votes in 1980. With Reagan one could never tell, however, if such matters were political or deeply moral or even psychological. The Panama Canal, he declared during the debate, was only one aspect of American foreign policy, and if we gave it up "I think we cloak weakness in the suit of virtue." Reagan questioned Buckley's reasoning. Will the people of the world see the treaty "as the magnanimous gesture of a great and powerful nation? I don't think so in view of our recent history, not in view of our bug-out in Vietnam, not in view of an administration that is hinting that we're going to throw aside an ally named Taiwan. I think that the world would see it as, once again, Uncle Sam putting his tail between his legs and creeping away rather than face trouble."[5]

In 1980, Reagan was clearly the Republican front runner. His main challenger was George Bush, a former Texas congressman and Ford's Central Intelligence Agency (CIA) director. Bush dubbed Reagan's tax and monetary policies "voodoo economics," and Reagan accused Bush of catering to liberals on gun control and women's rights. At the Republican National Convention, Reagan would make Bush his running mate. Reagan was later asked how he could name as vice president someone who dismissed his economic policy as goofy black magic. Reagan turned toward Bush and gave him a big wink, then turned back to the questioner and deployed all his powers of persuasion to make the case for what would come to be called supply-side economics. The American public may have been unsure of what had persuaded them. Few under-

stood what eighteenth-century philosophers called the "mundane science" of wealth making, but all liked the promise that America would get
more bounty for the buck.

The 1980 national election was closely fought. In October, polls
showed the president trailing challenger Reagan by only a few points.
Americans were angry. Iran's Ayatollah Khomeini and his followers held
their countrymen hostage, burned American flags, and shouted "Death
to the United States," and President Carter seemed unable to do anything about it. Reagan's campaign strategists feared that the hostages
might be released just before the election, in what was called the October Surprise. Carter would then be the statesman who negotiated to
save lives rather than resorting to war.

Ever since the election of 1980, there have been ugly rumors about
the timing of the prisoners' release. Did someone in the Reagan camp,
or the CIA, approach the ayatollah's men with a deal? If the hostages
were not released until after the election, it was said, the new administration would reverse Carter's policy and resume weapons sales to Iran.
No credible evidence of such a back-channel deal has been established,
but the hostages were freed within hours of Reagan's inauguration. Iran
had agreed to their release in return for U.S. help in unfreezing Iranian
assets held by Western banks. Carter himself was desperately working
on this arrangement. On inauguration day, January 20, 1981, at seven in
the morning, he had called Blair House, the official White House guest
residence, to let Reagan know that a plane was about to take off from
Tehran with the hostages on board. Reagan's staff refused to awaken the
president-elect, and Carter left office without receiving credit for bringing the hostages home safely. Seven years later, Reagan's efforts to help
American hostages would result in disaster.[6]

Opinion polls showed that Reagan won his television debates with
Carter during the campaign, and both candidates' remarks suggest why
America was moving far away from the "city upon a hill" no matter how
many times Reagan repeated the phrase. It was Carter the workaholic
who was the true Puritan: He spoke of hardship and sacrifice, while
Reagan simply responded: "Are you happier today than when Mr. Carter
became president of the United States?" When Carter criticized his
stand on Medicare, Reagan avoided the intricacies of the issue by joking, "There you go again." The audience roared, as they did when Rea-

gan parodied what the national malaise was all about: "A recession is when your neighbor loses his job. A depression is when you lose yours. And recovery is when Jimmy Carter loses his." The more relaxed and witty Reagan outperformed Carter. He seemed warm and spontaneous in contrast to his opponent's persistent manner, tense forehead, and a smile so steadily fixed it could only, many thought, be forced.[7]

Although Reagan himself stood for individualism and self-reliance, he depended on a diligent political network to raise money, frame issues, and market his message. Ironically, Goldwater's devastating defeat in 1964 had energized conservatives to redouble their efforts. However, it took the disgrace of Watergate to reorient conservative efforts away from pure party politics and the next election campaign. In the mid-1970s, after observing the disgrace of Nixon, the fumbling of Ford, and the cynicism of Kissinger, conservatives determined to build a movement.

The first task was to identify fellow conservatives. Richard Viguerie and Terry Dolan, two entrepreneurs who discovered the political uses of direct-mail marketing, put together large mailing lists of conservative activists who were potential donors to conservative causes. Their list of fifteen million willing contributors would underwrite a diverse assortment of political interest groups (antifeminist, antitax, and anti-UN; progun and proprayer). The marketers of the New Right composed extraordinarily long form letters filled with short paragraphs that featured underlining and multiple exclamation points. The letters generated millions of dollars that were used to put Republican politicians' feet to the fire and saw to it that the Right would be heard.

In the late 1970s, as we have seen, Jerry Falwell's Moral Majority gathered together Christian conservatives to rally for righteousness. It stood firmly for family values, condemned to damnation godless communism, and prayed for the wayward souls of liberal secularists. Falwell, Dolan, and Viguerie cultivated the grassroots. Wealthy conservatives like the Colorado beer baron Joseph Coors and Pittsburgh publisher Richard M. Scaife, heir to the Mellon fortune, directed their philanthropy toward the creation of conservative think tanks, such as the Heritage Foundation and the American Enterprise, Manhattan, and Cato Institutes. They prepared concise briefing papers filled with bullet points that effectively dispensed conservative arguments to busy news reporters and distracted congressional aides. Many of the think tanks had libertarian tendencies at odds with religious fundamentalism. However, Reagan would absorb contradictions rather than face them, and he found a place in the conservative consensus for those who read the Bible and those who read *Playboy*.

Reagan won a resounding majority of the popular vote, 44 million to Carter's 36 million, with third-party candidate John Anderson taking 6 million. More impressive was Reagan's sweeping of the electoral vote, 489 to 49, and coattails that pulled in thirty-three GOP representatives and secured eleven senators, giving the Republicans control of the Senate for the first time since 1945. A significant segment of young white males strongly supported Reagan for his stand on military defense. Women and older people, concerned about social programs, gave Reagan less support. However, there was not so much a gender gap between men and women as a cultural divide between single women who voted for Carter and married women who voted for Reagan, especially Catholics and evangelicals, who saw the women's rights movement as a threat to the family. Geographically, Reagan ran strongly in the Far West, the Deep South, and across the Midwest. If Republicans became a majority party with a popular president, would there be a "Reagan Revolution"?

Reagan's inaugural address promised as much. "It is time for us to realize that we are too great a nation to limit ourselves to small dreams," the president declared, urging people to overcome the humiliation and frustration of recent years. He promised to return power to the people in the tradition of the eighteenth-century antifederalists. "All of us—all of us need to be reminded that the federal government did not create the states; the states created the federal government." He then spoke the familiar bromides of big, bad government, runaway inflation, the national debt, the menace of communism. However, the most moving part of the text is typically Reaganesque (though in part composed by speechwriter Ken Khachigian). Reagan told the story of a soldier, Martin Treptow, who was killed during World War I and left "My Pledge" scribbled in his diary: "America must win this war. Therefore, I will work, I will save, I will sacrifice, I will endure." Reagan brought the message up to date.

> The crisis we are facing today does not require of us the kind
> of sacrifice that Martin Treptow and so many thousands of
> others were called upon to make. It does require, however,

our best effort, and our willingness to believe in ourselves and to believe in our capacity to perform great deeds; to believe that together, with God's help, we can and will resolve the problems which now confront us.

And, after all, why shouldn't we believe that? We are Americans.[8]

Treptow's pledge to "work," "save," and "sacrifice" could have been taken from "A Model of Christian Charity," John Winthrop's seventeenth-century sermon written aboard the vessel *Arbella*, which contains the metaphor of "a city upon a hill." The more Reagan tried to get Americans up on the hill, however, the more we slipped back. To work, save, and sacrifice is truly Puritanism. However, Reagan also asked Americans to believe in themselves while asking "God's help" to resolve the country's problems. Without saying what those problems were, people were not asked to do anything about them, certainly not to save money in a society that regards the spending of it as a sign of status.

The election of 1980 proved a turning point. Not anytime soon would a presidential candidate, whether Democrat or Republican, return to Jimmy Carter's conscience politics of sin and contrition. Liberalism would have to run for its life—and to the Right. The first Democratic president after Ronald Reagan was William Jefferson Clinton, who had gone to college in the sixties and had to downplay his antiwar stance to win the presidency. Once in office, Clinton declared: "The days of big government are over." And so were the ideas of "work," "save," and "sacrifice," which lived on in political rhetoric long after they disappeared from political reality.

Choosing a Cabinet

MEMBERS OF THE Reagan staff love to retell stories of how casually "Ronnie" took his election and inauguration as the fortieth president of the United States. Late in the evening on Election Day, he was taking a shower when the phone rang. It was President Carter, gracefully calling to concede. Reagan came out of the bathroom and into a living room full of advisors and guests and took the call dripping wet with a towel around his waist.

Reagan overslept the morning he was to take the oath of office and deliver his inaugural address. An aide knocked on his door and, hearing nothing, tiptoed in to see an inert lump under the blankets. "Governor, it's time to get up." The covers moved slightly. "Governor, it's the day of your inauguration, you need to get up." A sleepy voice grumbled from beneath the blankets. "Do I have to?"[9]

Yet Reagan hardly took the office casually. Unlike President Carter, who would appear in the Oval Office wearing a cardigan, Reagan insisted that the dignity of the office required he wear a suit and a tie. According to Edmund Morris, Reagan often could not resist stopping to look at himself in the mirror and, fixing his tie and clicking his heels, say with a smile: "I'm President of the United States." It would be the actor's greatest part, "the role of a lifetime," as Lou Cannon aptly put it.[10]

Reagan knew, as Presidents John Adams, Ulysses S. Grant, and Warren G. Harding did not, that good cabinet choices are crucial if an administration is to have any hope of success. The challenge is to be surrounded by people of different minds and to welcome competing points of view. FDR was a master at starting policy discussions with conflict and working toward consensus. He would tell his impassioned cabinet secretaries to go into another room and "weave together" their differences before coming back to him. The last thing a president needs is the loyalty of a lapdog.

Reagan's appointment of James A. Baker III as his chief of staff indicated he was hardly rushing to embrace the Right. A close friend and former campaign manager for George Bush, Baker was dubbed a pragmatist by conservatives intoxicated by their own principles. He was selected to help steer Republican bills through a Democratic Congress. Suave, a sharp dresser, relaxed and witty, poised and well connected, a Princeton graduate with the patience of a scholar and the persistence of a salesman, Baker carried weight at cabinet meetings, in crisis situations, and among congressional leaders. In addressing a group, he came quickly to the point, though he talked at such a pitch that it seemed he spoke with a whistle in his mouth.

Many thought that Edwin Meese III would be named chief of staff, and he was bitterly disappointed to have been passed over. A Yale graduate, Meese had worked with Reagan for many years in California and was a loyal, reliable, and tough law enforcer who backed up the governor in showdowns at Berkeley and on other campuses. His portly gait, jovial manner, and pink skin belied the intensity with which he argued positions and an enthusiasm that caused him to become involved in more issues than he could handle. His office bulged with stacks of unfinished business, and his briefcase was mocked as bottomless because whatever went into it never came out. Although many thought the hardworking Meese would be the manager of Reagan's White House, others on the transition team saw him as too unorganized and overcommitted to be effective and questioned his political experience, which was limited to Oakland and Sacramento. With reluctance, he joined the Reagan team as a counselor and was forever feuding with Baker and Michael Deaver.

It has been remarked that no man got close to Ronald Reagan, but Michael Deaver, deputy chief of staff from January 1981 until May 1985, was close enough to be his shadow. Deaver was the one who tried to get the governor out of bed on inauguration day. He handled the president's schedule, organized press conferences, relayed messages from cabinet members, excelled at public relations, became Nancy's confidant, and was so omnipresent as to be a member of the Reagan family. A small, balding man with horn-rimmed glasses, taciturn and tense, but ready to gossip and relish a joke, Deaver had no credentials in foreign policy and no expertise in the many issues of domestic politics. Yet although he would defer to specialists, he could make his presence felt. Martin Anderson, an economic advisor to Reagan, records a moment when Deaver entered the Oval Office and announced, "Mr. President, I have to leave." Reagan asked why, and Deaver replied that he could no longer take the horrors of the bombing and killing of children in Lebanon by Israel. "My God!" Reagan exclaimed, and got on the phone to Menachem Begin, Israel's prime minister, to tell him that the assault upon Beirut had to stop. It did, and Reagan marveled: "I didn't know I had that kind of power." Deaver left the Reagan administration late in the second term and ran into legal and personal difficulties—too much lobbying and liquor. However, while he was at Reagan's side he served as a discreet advisor whose keen sense of the dramatic turned many humdrum presidential appearances into public relations spectaculars. A moderate, he opposed the hiring of Pat Buchanan as a speechwriter, saying,

"Ronald Reagan does not need anyone to the right of him." Buchanan, envious of Deaver's proximity to the first family, dismissed him as "Lord of the Chamber Pot."[11]

At Nixon's urging, Reagan chose Alexander M. Haig Jr. as secretary of state. A former air force general and member of Nixon's staff, Haig had experience in foreign affairs and a reputation as a diplomatic hardliner. Handsome, with high cheekbones and clear blue eyes, Haig was nonetheless a difficult, haughty, abrasive personality, quick to annoy others with his conceit of superiority. He was always seeking more authority, even letting it be known that he thought he should be president. He served only a year and a half before Reagan asked him to step down, possibly because Haig opposed Reagan's demand that Israel cease bombing Beirut.

Reagan's foreign policy only began to take shape when George P. Shultz became secretary of state in June 1982. Like Reagan, Shultz in his youth had loved the game of football, until a leg injury cut short his playing days. With the build of a lumbering linebacker, he projected strength, determination, confidence. Yet Shultz, unlike Haig, was courteous and patient, the right qualities for a diplomat who prefers negotiation to escalation, as he did with the Soviet Union. Shultz had graduated from Princeton, received a Ph.D. in economics from MIT, had taught at Stanford University, and served in Nixon's cabinet as secretary of labor and then treasury before becoming president of the Bechtel Corporation. He was a team man who believed in deliberate procedure and group consensus, distrusting mavericks in the National Security Council. The Lone Ranger mentality that would produce the Iran-Contra scandal outraged Shultz no end. He was one of the few members of Reagan's staff to emerge from the affair with his integrity intact.[12]

Secretary of Defense Caspar Weinberger believed in international law but showed even more respect for military power. During Reagan's California governorship, Weinberger had worked as state finance director, and during the Nixon administration he had two of the hardest jobs in the federal government: director of the Office of Management and Budget and secretary of Health, Education, and Welfare. He brought to Washington a cosmopolitanism as an Episcopalian with a Jewish surname who had an affinity for the Arab world and a special fondness for Saudi Arabia. Harvard educated, a Renaissance man of many cultural

curiosities, he looked like a professor with his tweed jackets and possessed a penetrating mind at once analytical and tenacious. Reagan
came to office determined to economize and appointed a determined
budget director, David Stockman, to cut out "waste, fraud, and abuse"
in federal spending. At every step of the way, however, Weinberger succeeded in protecting the military budget and even increasing it. Weinberger held to a position that might be called military readiness and martial restraint. America must do everything to prepare for war but not fight
one unless it was clearly popular and absolutely winnable. Colin Powell,
George W. Bush's first secretary of state, drew the same lesson from the
Vietnam War. The difference was that Weinberger would threaten to
resign if he concluded the administration was not heeding his views and
was allowing Russia to move toward military superiority. Shultz, Baker,
and Reagan all believed that they had to negotiate a halt to the arms race
before the United States became involved in a war that was neither
winnable nor popular.

Another option remained. If nuclear war could not be won and a conventional war could not be sustained, there still were secret, covert operations that would halt any Soviet advance in the third world. Reagan
found the ideal candidate to head such operations in William Casey,
whom he appointed CIA director. Casey had eagerly sought the office of
secretary of state, but he ended up in the right position. A devout
Catholic who had studied with the Jesuits, Casey carried on his own private crusade against atheistic communism. He was willing to take risks
and, like the Vatican hierarchy, carry out policies in secrecy untroubled
by democracy. The grandson of an Irish saloon owner, with solid girth
and drooping jowls, Casey was a sixty-eight-year-old self-made multimillionaire when he joined Reagan to become one of the most influential
member of the administration. Few knew what he was saying when he
mumbled his words, the ideal idiom for the head of the CIA. Convinced
that the cold war would not culminate in an apocalyptic nuclear
exchange, he saw as even more dangerous the Soviets penetrating the
underdeveloped world to support wars of national liberation. As head of
the CIA, he funneled covert action funds through the Catholic Church
to anticommunists in Eastern Europe and South America. After the
Soviets invaded Afghanistan, he eagerly allied the United States with the
mujahideen, Saudi intelligence, and Pakistan's military. He helped hatch

the Iran-Contra scandal, but when its revelations broke out in the press, he was in the hospital, dying of cancer.[13]

The covert activities of Casey and the CIA had the support of neo-conservative intellectuals (discussed in the following chapter) convinced that the real battleground of the cold war was the third world. The hawks consisted of Casey, Weinberger, United Nations Ambassador Jeane J. Kirkpatrick, and several other members of the National Security Council. Less militant were Baker, Shultz, Deaver, and, increasingly by the mid-eighties, Ronald and Nancy Reagan.

On domestic issues, Baker, Meese, and Deaver came to be known as the troika, competing voices seen as the stage managers of the first term of the Reagan administration. Each jockeyed to have his position become central to the administration. Baker settled for practical political achievement, Meese aimed for philosophical purity, and Deaver emphasized good public relations.

Less competitive but just as dedicated was Richard Darman, director of the Office of Management and Budget, and the diagnostician of the early Reagan administration. A young liberal Republican from Harvard's Kennedy School of Government, Darman worked hard on briefing papers, and, like Stockman, he doubted it would be possible to cut taxes, increase military expenditures, and balance the budget all at the same time. He worked diligently in the White House and later at the Treasury Department, always trying to stay far away from the attention of right-wingers who had nothing better to do than out a closet liberal. The sensitive Darman grasped what troubled American politics: Those who want to get things done are always at odds with those who want to get reelected. Darman was in the first category, and he suffered from what he called "a kind of Potomac fever."[14]

William P. Clark was an old friend of Reagan's from California who shared a fondness for horses and the outdoor life. Governor Reagan had appointed Clark to the California Supreme Court but talked him into coming to Washington to "clean up the mess," which usually meant feuds and rivalries in the cabinet. After a year as deputy secretary of state, Clark took Henry Kissinger's old job as national security advisor, restoring coherence and purpose to the National Security Council, whose power had been weakened by the imperious Alexander Haig. Though he had a knack for handling people, Clark had no relish for politics itself and was thrilled to return to his California ranch, to Reagan's disappointment.

If Clark was happy to leave the administration, treasury secretary Donald T. Regan left in bitterness. Like a character in old Bogie movie, Regan trusted nobody. His time spent fighting as a marine on Guadacanal and Okinawa did more than his Harvard education to give him the gruff features of a George Raft or Rod Steiger. Son of an Irish cop, Regan worked his way out of South Boston's lace curtain neighborhood on his way to college, law school, and Wall Street, where he became a multimillionaire and the head of Merrill Lynch. The president and secretary had a natural affinity for each other's Irish humor, tales of youth, and faith in free enterprise, and both were skeptical of the creatures of corporate capitalism, the "cartelists" who would rather conspire than compete. Outspoken, with a large ego and little patience, Regan soon tired of his routine functions as Treasury secretary and changed positions with Baker to become chief of staff. In his new role, Regan was rash where Baker had been prudent; he was insensitive to the feelings of other cabinet members and seemingly unaware that his laid-back, poorly informed president needed attention, guidance, and even protection from making poor decisions. Resentful cabinet secretaries called Regan's staff subordinates "mice," four sycophants who competed with each other for Regan's approval and remained more loyal to him than to the president. Regan's end came after a falling-out with Nancy. The everwatchful first lady noticed how Regan would step forward to answer questions addressed to the president and how he had allowed her husband to be misled into going along with a scheme that resulted in the Iran-Contra affair. In Janauary 1987, she made up her mind and told her husband and the administration that Regan had to go.[15]

The Reagan cabinet was too full of diverse personalities and conflicting positions to forge a coherent national policy, not to mention a real revolution. In his farewell address in 1989, Reagan proudly claimed that he had set out to change America and he had helped change the world as well. His second claim has validity, since communism was collapsing as he left office. As far as the nature of American society and the presence of the state are concerned, however, one sees far more continuity than change. The American people elected Reagan to relieve the country from the frustrations of the Carter presidency, particularly the hostage situation in Iran, high gasoline prices, and high inflation and interest rates. They would gladly accept lower taxes, but whether they would accept cutbacks in their benefits and entitlements was another matter entirely. How to make good citizens out of grasping consumers?

Supply-Side Economics and Social Security

A FTER REAGAN TOOK the Oath of Office and delivered his inaugural address, he and Nancy had lunch, watched the inaugural parade down Pennsylvania Avenue, and made their way to the entrance of the White House, with its iron grill fence and spacious green lawns. Reagan had been in the awesome dwelling before; as a labor negotiator, he had met President Truman, and as governor he had meetings with President Johnson. The building "had a mystical, almost religious awe for me since I was a child," recalled Reagan. He and Nancy walked hand in hand through the Central Hall and upstairs to look at the guest quarters, the Oval Office, and the Truman balcony. All the while, Nancy was planning the refurbishing that critics would call extravagant at a time when her husband was calling for budget cuts.[16]

Reagan was especially taken by the Lincoln bedroom, impressed that it remained furnished exactly as it was when Lincoln slept there. "In it," Reagan observed, "was a large oversize wooden bedstead that Lincoln's wife, Mary, was having made for her husband at the time he was assassinated; he'd died without ever returning to the White House." Future presidents regarded the Lincoln bedroom with less awe and opened it up to an organized stream of campaign contributors.[17]

The most conservative members of the Republican Party saw in Reagan's election the promise of a real revolution in government policymaking. James Baker's appointment seemed a betrayal of their expectations. Rather than undertake an exciting reorganization of government, including a promised close-down of the education and energy departments created by Carter, Reagan let well enough alone and chose moderation. With Baker, ideology gave way to pragmatism, principle to politics as usual. In his first year in office, Reagan shied away from several issues dear to conservatives: school prayer, abortion, pornography, tuition tax credits, affirmative action, the Equal Rights Amendment to the Constitution, radicalism in the classroom, and feminism in the workplace. Such controversial cultural issues seemed less pressing than foreign policy and the economy. As the administration got under way, Reagan and his cabinet decided to focus on the economy, especially with a public upset over the country's double-digit inflation, high unemployment, and a prime interest rate of 20.1 percent.

Reagan had studied economics at Eureka College, and a half-century later he became enamored of a school of thought that came to be called supply-side economics. Applying the principles of classical economic theory to government tax policy, it was enthusiastically promoted in the 1970s as a solution to the nation's economic problems by a crew of true believers that included University of Chicago economist Arthur Laffer, *Wall Street Journal* writer Jude Wanniski, the late Robert L. Bartley, then editor of the *Journal's* editorial page, and Buffalo, New York, congressman Jack Kemp. In explaining his theory to Richard Cheney, then President Ford's chief of staff, Laffer drew a curved line on a napkin to show that as tax rates increase they have the perverse effect of producing less tax revenue for the government. Laffer explained that people will work more and produce more when taxes are lower. The chart on the napkin would be called the Laffer curve, and it excited considerable controversy inside and outside the administration. Even the conservative economist Milton Friedman, who supported supply-side policies, wondered how taxes could be lowered and defense spending increased without exacerbating the deficit. One White House aide told the journalist Elizabeth Drew that the economic discussions were more like "a religious debate" than a "scientific debate."[18]

In 1978, Jack Kemp and Delaware Republican senator William Roth introduced the Kemp-Roth proposal to cut tax rates by 30 percent. Wanniski and Bartley carried on a campaign for tax cuts and against what they called root-canal economics, which they associated with the policies of Herbert Hoover. Instead they continually praised President Kennedy, who had used the phrase "a rising tide lifts all boats" when he presented his tax cut proposals in 1962. The Kemp-Roth proposal adopted the same politics of populist optimism in crafting its message, which appealed to Ronald Reagan.

—

ECONOMICS IS ABOUT supply and demand, and liberal economists argued that the key was consumer demand. Without consumer demand, without buyers ready to purchase goods, they said, producers would make no goods, hire no workers, and see no profit. To break this vicious cycle, which liberals said was responsible for the Great Depression, required a theory of government economic policymaking that has come to be called Keynesianism.

The English economist Sir John Maynard Keynes once came out of a room after interviewing President Franklin D. Roosevelt and said, "That man knows not a thing about ecnomics." Perhaps. However, the Roosevelt administration experimented with Keynesian economic policymaking in the thirties and fully embraced it during the World War II years, when heavy government spending was essential. With Keynesianism, government is indispensable to the economy. In contrast, free market advocates argue that the economy is like an organism that creates its own, unplanned, spontaneous order so long as there is no government interference in the operation of open markets. During the Depression years, the economy seemed dead in the water, and the question was how to jumpstart it.

The key to the economy, according to Keynes, is money, not simply its acquisition and possession but its flow and circulation. The more money moves from hand to hand—from the employer who pays the worker, who then gives rent to the landlord, who in turn purchases a car from a dealer, who goes on to acquire a home—the faster the economy revives and prosperity returns. In a depression, the circulation of money slows down and the role of the government is to create consumer demand by spending money, usually in the form of public work projects, support to farmers, loans to business, unemployment payments, Social Security— anything that will put money in motion and increase its velocity.

With Keynes, however, the taxman cometh. Keynes thought taxes should be lowered and government spending increased during a depression. Yet when recovery takes place and prosperity returns, the government has to pay off the debt that generated consumer demand. Government must now do what politicians hate to do—raise taxes.

Reaganomics, based on supply-side principles, took the opposite view. Its proponents argued that the economy worked best when individuals made their own choices to work and save, produce and consume. Prosperity—that is, jobs and goods—is the result of millions of their choices. Supply siders insisted that the most important thing government could do was to reduce the rate of taxation. If Americans paid a higher percentage of their income to taxes as their incomes increased, then they would lose the incentive to work and save and that would harm the economy. Conversely, reducing taxes would spur the economy.

Justice Oliver Wendell Holmes Jr. once advised that taxes are the price one pays to enjoy the blessings of "civilized society." Reagan saw taxes as theft, the price one pays to suffer the bane of existence. More than once he cited the 90 percent rate used to deduct taxes from the salary he earned as a movie star, and he insisted that after making two or three films a year he and other actors would chose not to work rather than be ripped off by the government. In a report submitted to the California State Legislature, the governor explained why a constitutional amendment was necessary to allow people to vote to rein in the tax rates that supposedly had gone off the charts. "Have we abandoned or forgotten the interests and well-being of the taxpayer whose toil makes government possible in the first place? Or, is he to become the pawn in a deadly game of government monopoly whose only purpose is to serve the confiscatory appetites of runaway government spending?"[19]

Although in his first inaugural address Reagan repeated the words "ideals" and "idealism," the president tried to talk Americans out of a sense of civic responsibility to pay their taxes for a government that provides schools, public health, military security, and general well-being. He relieved them of guilt and convinced citizens that government is the enemy. With a touch of Paine and Emerson, the president indicated he would have Americans believe that government was no longer based on the consent of the people but, rather, was alien to their will. Government was bureaucracy, which represents its own interests and the special interests of its favored clients, unlike the market, which is responsive to the demands and desires of individual citizens. Reagan believed that, because business responds to the laws of the market, it is more efficient and accountable than government, whose scope and reach are unrestrained. However, is government, no matter how much a bloated bureaucracy, unrelated to the people who called upon it to meet their needs? Reagan assumed so. He did not need to read the writings of anti-statist "public choice" economists like James M. Buchanan Jr., who won the 1986 Nobel Prize in economics, to make the case that government is the problem, not the solution, because it lets politicians help special interests at the expense of unorganized individuals. Yet when Reagan went after Social Security, he learned differently.

The principle of supply-side economics appealed to the Reagan administration not only because it would minimize the role of government but because it also reduced tax rates. The beauty of supply-side economics, according to its supporters, was that as the economy takes off and wealth spreads throughout society, the new, lower tax rates actually generate increased tax revenues off a much larger base of taxpayers. Supply-side theory offers the best of all worlds: less taxes paid by the people and more money collected by the government.

That was the widespread impression. Martin Anderson, an economist who served under Reagan, insists that supply theory did not claim to increase revenue but only that a tax cut would "not lose as much revenue as one might expect." The psychological assumption was that people would work harder if they could keep most of what they earned, and thus their rising incomes would compensate for the revenue loss due to lower taxes. Reagan himself was certain, based on his own experience with 90 percent taxes, that people lose all motivation for work when they are excessively taxed. One might ask, however, why people work hard *after* they become rich and are tempted to join the leisure class and conspicuously display their status as consumers rather than producers? Supply siders responded that the wealthy will use their money to invest and spend, and thus the private sector can stimulate the economy. However, why can't the government just as effectively use taxes to stimulate the economy? The real question is whether there is any relationship between work and wealth. [20]

The conviction that lower taxes would motivate people to work harder and expand the economy may or may not be the case. After all, productivity expanded and America saw the coming of an affluent society, with two cars in every garage in the 1950s, when tax rates were exceedingly high. In the early 1990s, President Clinton raised taxes, and the country enjoyed significant prosperity while reducing the national debt. In the Reagan eighties, more and more people wanted to take off work and play golf, drive their recreational vans, vacation with the kids, travel on cruise ships, retire at sixty and move to Florida and wait a few years until they could collect their Social Security checks before they went to the bank and then to the beach. For all of Reagan's reference, in his inaugural address, to "work," "save," and "sacrifice," the eighties relaxed without a guilty conscience. The work ethic, historically born of anxiety over the state of one's soul, dies of luxury in a soulless society.

—

LIBERAL DEMOCRATS SCOFFED at the claims of supply siders. The economist Lester Thurow even argued that Reagan's tax proposals were Keynesian because tax cuts enabled people to buy products and thus created the demand that stimulates supply. Treasury secretary Regan strongly denied the argument, claiming that the administration's tax cut enabled people in the upper income brackets to save and invest. The question of what they were investing in, productive enterprise or junk bonds, went unanswered. To supply proponents, the question mattered not at all. The point was to free up the flow of money so that stockholders could sell their holdings untroubled by capital gains and reinvest their earnings again and again. Even junk bonds, they have argued, led to the financing of retail and manufacturing companies.

Reagan was by no means an intellectual, but the policy positions he and his administration took on many issues on the economy, politics, and society had profoundly intellectual dimensions. Economists who served in the Reagan administration paid deep respect to the economic theories of Noble Prize winners like F. A. Hayek, Friedman, and Buchanan. In contrast to Keynes, who thought economies went into depression due to a decline in demand, Hayek thought that money must flow to investment to produce capital goods. In short, supply comes first.[21]

Reaganomics had four objectives: cut taxes, reduce the size of government, control inflation, deregulate the economy. The administration's greatest economic achievement was to bring inflation down. Taxes also were cut (and soon raised), but the size of government grew, and deregulation led to some financial scandals that will be dealt with later in the book. The eighties saw two serious recessions, but interest rates remained low and employment was stable. Yet Reaganomics willingly

yielded to a temptation that had actually started with the Kennedy presidency in the sixties, a temptation that turned into a taboo—once tax
cuts are enacted, they are almost impossible to restore, since no politician then dares to propose raising taxes. Reagan may be faulted for
increasing the deficit by lowering taxes and raising defense spending during his term of office without making any comprehensive cutbacks in
domestic spending. The national debt tripled under Reagan. No matter
what is said about taxes, it is spending that is the issue, and few politicians can resist their constituencies when they turn to government for a
favor. Although Reagan promised to reduce the size of government, its
continual growth stems from his refusal to ask the people to discipline
their desires so as not to grind themselves into debt and continue to
make demands upon the government itself.

—

IN FEBRUARY 1981, Reagan went before a joint session of Congress
and unveiled his economic program, the most comprehensive since
Roosevelt announced the New Deal in 1933. Called America's New
Beginning: A Program for Economic Recovery, it attacked the "waste
and fraud" in the federal government and called the national debt a
"national scandal." Specifically, the program stipulated:

a) a new budget to cut back the rate of growth of federal
   spending
b) initiatives reducing personal income tax 10 percent over
   a three-year period and business taxes 30 percent over
   the same period; reduction in capital gains, lower estate
   and gift taxes; accelerating depreciation in business
   investments in plant equipment to create jobs
c) reform of Social Security; trimming or eliminating many
   welfare programs; a transfer of social problems over to
   the states

After considerable debate, the tax cuts passed Congress in July. Anger
lingered over cuts made in job training programs, limits on eligibility for
food stamps, and the scrutiny given to anything that smacked of welfare.

The Reagan administration promised a safety net for those truly needy, but Democrats ridiculed the administration when officials in the Agriculture Department proposed to cut the budget for school nutrition programs by reclassifying ketchup as a vegetable.

Of all his reform efforts, Reagan's attempt to revamp Social Security stands as the major blunder of his first administration. Tip O'Neill called Social Security the "third rail" of American politics: anyone who tried to touch it would face electrocution. Reagan's hand grazed the rail and recoiled from the voltage just in time. Reagan, treasury secretary Donald Regan, and budget director David Stockman had no idea how their effort even to address the subject would backfire. Without consulting Congress, they took up a subject in a way that seemed to violate a contract made between the government and hardworking Americans contributing to a program that assured their economic security as senior citizens. By the 1980s, Social Security was a half-century old, and its costs had risen due to more people retiring and living longer. Nonetheless, Reagan's approach seemed an assault on promise keeping.

Reagan mistakenly assumed that Social Security was another welfare program subject to the often-denounced vices of fraud, waste, and abuse. That was hardly the case, but Reagan believed that the system created a disincentive for citizens to take care of themselves by savings and investment, that it did not distinguish between women who worked and those who stayed home as dependent spouses, that the system was collapsing under the burden of cost of living increases, and that the rising number of people taking early retirement was breaking the system economically. The administration advocated extending the retirement age, which at the time was set at sixty-five, with full benefits, or sixty-two, with slightly reduced payments. The administration recommended increasing the retirement age to sixty-seven, with a 25 percent reduction in benefits. The bill had almost no support in Congress, even among conservative Republicans. Representative Carrol Campbell of South Carolina, a staunch Reagan supporter, lit into Stockman. "You absolutely blind-sided us with this Social Security Plan," he exploded. "My phones are ringing off the hook. I've got thousands of sixty-year-old textile workers who think it's the end of the world. What in the hell am I supposed to tell them?" The Reagan administration backed off, and no future president would ever again dare to touch the third rail of American politics, not until the second administration of George W. Bush, who also found the issue more sensitive than he had imagined.[22]

In September 1981, eight months after Reagan presented his economic program and a little more than a month after it had won congressional approval, America went into a deep recession. A shadow of doubt seemed to have fallen on the bright promise of Reaganomics. Then the president faced a political shoot-out with air traffic controllers. The 13,000 members of the Professional Air Traffic Controllers Organization (PATCO) defied a no-strike clause in their union contract and seemed indifferent to public safety when they walked off the job, assuming they were so indispensable as to be irreplaceable. The union had backed Reagan in the presidential election, and although its members received a sizable pay increase, they claimed their job was so stressful they deserved much more. Reagan fired any employee who did not return in forty-eight hours, and he brought military personnel to airport towers to keep commercial aviation in operation. "I'm sorry for them," Reagan said of the thousands of defeated workers. "I take no joy in this." At the time, Reagan seemed unaware of the symbolic significance of his stand. Nevertheless, throughout the country, and especially in an England fed up with strikes, he came off as a gutsy leader who displayed confidence and decisiveness, a man who meant what he said.

About the national debt and the need to reduce it, Reagan said nothing, and it went unmentioned in his outline for economic reform. He even avoided discussing it with David Stockman, seemingly leaving the issue to his budget director's discretion. Unlike the president and congressional members, who were reluctant to cut into programs like Medicare, pay down the national debt, or reduce massive outlays for defense spending, Stockton took the initiative and went after everything—farm subsidies, student loans, veterans' hospitals, school lunch programs, payments to mothers on welfare. After his brush with Social Security, Reagan learned that about 80 percent of the federal budget was committed to popular programs and was thus politically off the table. Stockton, on the other hand, wanted to cut the deficit even if it meant taking on existing entitlements and out-Reaganizing Reagan. He became the butt of cartoonists, depicted as the Scrooge who had once been a Marxist and was now a monk. In his college days, Stockton had

been a member of Students for a Democratic Society, which had promised to revolutionize society by ridding America of the beast of capitalism. Rather handsome but intense, with a pointed nose, eyes focused
all-knowingly beneath glasses, hair over the ears, Stockton looked a
cross between an anarchist and an accountant. Members of Reagan's
cabinet often clashed with Stockton, but they valued him as a wunderkind who knew every line of the budget like the back of his hand. Senator Daniel Patrick Moynihan, a former Harvard professor, resisted many
of Stockton's proposed budget cuts while remaining amused by a radical
activist turned conservative economist. "Stockman is peerless. I have
never known a man capable of such sustained self-hypnotic ideological
fervor. One day he arrives at Harvard preaching the infallibility of Ho
Chi Minh. Next thing you know, he turns up in Washington proclaiming the immutability of the Laffer curve."[23]

Stockton had much on his desk. Outgoing president Carter had
handed over to Reagan a deficit of fifty-eight billion dollars, and the
nation's debt was about to go over a trillion. Stockton took seriously the
contradictions in Reagan's economic program, the challenge of lowering
taxes, increasing defense spending, reducing inflation, and balancing
the budget. The free market system aims at the creation of wealth, he
insisted, the welfare system at its redistribution. However, without cor-
responding cuts in government spending, a huge tax cut, such as Reagan advocated, would produce a dangerously unbalanced fiscal policy.[24]

The difference between Stockton and Weinberger, the budget director and the defense secretary, was the difference between a slasher and
an enhancer. Weinberger was convinced, as were the neo-hawks in the
administration, that the Soviets were winning the arms race, and that
anyone who would cut the military budget "wanted to keep us behind
the Russians." Weinberger told Reagan that America's B-52s were older
than aging veteran Russian pilots. The historian Michael Schaller
records a scene of Weinberger presenting Reagan with a blown-up cartoon the size of a poster depicting three soldiers: one a pygmy with no
rifle, symbolizing the Carter budget; the second "a four-eyed wimp who
looked like Woody Allen, carrying a tiny rifle" and signifying Stockman's
budget; the third "GI Joe himself, 190 pounds of fighting man, all
decked out in helmet and flak jacket and pointing an M-60 machine
gun" and standing tall for the Department of Defense budget. Stockman

was dumbfounded. That "a Harvard-educated cabinet officer" could stoop to such a "disreputable and demeaning" demonstration before the president compelled him to wonder whether Weinberger thought the White House was on *Sesame Street*. Weinberger prevailed.[25]

In December 1981, the journalist William Greider wrote an article in the *Atlantic Monthy*, "The Education of David Stockman," based on a series of interviews with the budget director. Stockman all but ridiculed the assumptions of supply-side economics, implying that the administration knew it would not work. He also revealed Reagan's indifference to the national debt and depicted the president's policies as a "Trojan horse" that would bring tax relief for the rich and render the government too broke to support social programs for the poor. The article was widely publicized and was seen as a betrayal of the administration. Moynihan humorously likened Stockman to St. Augustine, another aging radical who sought to confess his earlier sins in order to die a saint. The Reaganites saw him as an apostate, and thought Reagan would fire him on the spot. After a contrite admission of his political thoughtlessness, Stockman survived, with Reagan giving him a warm handshake after a tense meeting in the Oval Office.

Like Stockman, Reaganomics had had a rocky start. The recession of late 1981 lasted two years, until the economy turned around in 1983. Employment picked up with 18 million new jobs, while interest rates fell from a historic high of 20 percent to 11 percent. At the same time, imported oil prices dropped, and, most dramatically, inflation declined, from 14 percent in the Carter years to under 2 percent in 1983. The public agreed that Reagan was right to urge the country to "stay the course." In the 1982 congressional elections, the Republicans had lost two dozen seats in the House because of the recession but held control of the Senate. The recovery would continue throughout the eighties, and much of the public identified Reagan with the good times, which his 1984 reelection campaign touted as "morning in America." Did supply-side economics make a difference? During his second term, Reagan would promote a series of tax increases rather than tax cuts. A final estimate of his economic policy will be addressed in chapter 10.

Reagan's indifference throughout his two terms to the growing national debt is troubling. Critical of Carter's "runaway deficit of nearly $80 billion" in 1980, Reagan was uncritical of the $200 billion deficit of his own administration in 1988. To stay solvent, the government borrowed from the financial world and paid interest on the debt, a good thing for the rich and for foreign investors who loan money to the government but not necessarily for the middle class, whose taxes go to debt servicing. The core of Reagan's political philosophy was the principle of freedom, the individual's capacity for autonomy and self-determination, and an Emersonian faith in America as the land of tomorrow. Jefferson once declared that each generation is sovereign and that the dead cannot govern the living. But Reaganomics defied Emerson and Jefferson by practicing the politics of postponement. Inheriting a massive national deficit, America's children are neither sovereign nor free of the dead and find that they must pay for the past itself.

A Wounded President
Laughs at Death

IT TOOK DEMOCRATS some time to come to realize that they had underestimated Reagan as "an amiable dunce," longtime Democratic presidential advisor Clark Clifford's description. More than any leader since FDR, Reagan touched millions of Americans who believed in what he was saying about the promise of American life. His aides may have perfected the art of media management, and some journalists had little patience for Reagan's simple formulations and redundant jokes. There would be no doubt, however, of his popularity. Ben Bradlee, the *Washington Post* editor, stated that his paper and many others were "kinder to President Reagan than [to] any president I can remember." Michael Deaver agreed and praised the generous treatment Reagan received in the press. He was also a natural at television, with a rare face so real, genuine, and handsomely etched that he required little makeup. At the same time, many claimed that Reagan's presentations were scripted and that he simply knew how to read the TelePrompTer and check his cue cards. Those who begrudged his popularity claimed that the former actor was a master of manipulation. Yet what impressed many others was his spontaneous transparency. Often his best comments were impromptu. A hostile journalist, determined to reveal his ignorance, asked Reagan if he knew who the leader was of some obscure country that was giving the United States trouble. "No, I don't know his name," replied Reagan, "but after the election he'll sure know mine."[26]

One traumatic event, however, occurring at the beginning of his presidency, was hardly scripted. When in the worst condition of his life, Ronald Reagan was at his best.

On March 30, 1981, two months and ten days into his first term, Reagan was leaving the ballroom of Washington's Hilton Hotel after concluding an address to a room full of union officials. As he stooped to get into his limousine, six shots suddenly rang out. Two policemen were wounded, and Reagan's press secretary, James S. Brady, received a bullet to the head that would leave him paralyzed on the left side for life. Visually it seemed that Reagan had escaped unscathed as the limousine raced back to the safety of the White House. En route, the president began bleeding from the mouth. Instantly the driver made a U-turn and rushed to nearby George Washington University hospital, where it took doctors twenty minutes to find a bullet hole. Nancy sped separately to the hospital, and Deaver, assuming there was no wound, told her, "He hasn't been shot," only to learn from the doctors that he had been. At the time, few people were aware of how serious the near-fatal wound was. A vivid description by White House correspondent Laurence I. Barrett suggests how death's approach was deflected:

> FBI ballistic tests later would show an interesting aberration. The .22-caliber "Deavastator" bullet fired by John Hinckley did not ricochet directly off the side of the limousine. Rather the slug skidded for an inch along the Lincoln's armored right rear panel. The hollow-nosed explosive projectile flattened out, taking the shape of a circular saw blade the size of a dime. As if directed by some malevolent homing device, the bullet deflected off the black metal, found the gap between the car's body and the open rear door, sped under the raised left arm of its target, penetrated his torso below the armpit, struck the top of the seventh rib, glanced off the bone, plunged into spongy lung tissue. By the end of its trajectory, its velocity spent, the bullet no longer sliced neatly like a tiny knife. When piercing the skin it had created a slit that was

almost invisible. Now, wobbling through the lower pul-
monary lobe, it gouged a hole large enough to accommodate
the tip of a surgeon's finger.[27]

The assassin, twenty-five-year-old John W. Hinckley Jr., was acting
out a fantasy to impress the film star Jodie Foster, who appeared with
Robert De Niro in *Taxi Driver*, the story of a disturbed cabbie who
believes he can clean the filth from New York City's streets by rescuing
a prostitute. Several years earlier the film's director, Martin Scorsese,
had received a threatening letter warning him what to expect if Jodie
Foster won the Academy Award for best supporting actress. "If little
Jodie wins on March 29 for what you made her do in *Taxi Driver*, you
will pay with your life. I am serious. I am not a sicko." Scorsese and his
film team called the FBI.[28]

Allowed into the hospital room, Nancy was devastated to see her husband as pale as the sheets, grimacing with pain, struggling to breathe.
Even Reagan's soon-to-be-known joke, "Honey, I forgot to duck," did little to relieve her fear and anxiety. Doctors and nurses were rushing in
and out of the room, politely telling her to get out of the way. She
retreated to the hospital's chapel.

When Reagan's staff grasped the seriousness of his wound, which left
a bullet lodged in his lung, they worried about his capacity for a full
recovery and speculated about the chain of command. Vice President
Bush was in Texas, while the press was demanding to know who was
running the government and who, if need be, would declare that the
president was incapable of performing his duties. The Constitution provides for the sequence of presidential succession, but it is vague about
emergency situations. It was clear that Bush would be in charge once his
plane arrived in Washington, but in the meantime Secretary of State
Haig had called the cabinet together to meet in the White House's Situation Room. While Reagan was on the operating table, Haig, an out-of-
shape man who smoked two packs of cigarettes a day, rushed pell-mell
up the stairs and entered the press room to spurt out to reporters:

> Constitutionally, gentlemen, you have the President, the
> Vice-President, and the Secretary of State in that order and
> should the President decide he wants to transfer the helm to

the Vice President, he will do so. He has not done that. As of
now, I am in control here, in the White House, pending the
return of the Vice-President, and in close touch with him. If
something came up, I would check with him, of course.[29]

Haig may have only sought to assure the nation and the world that
things were under control in the capital, but his tense, assertive words
alienated the cabinet and made it appear to the public as if the secretary
of state were power intoxicated; that this former general would rather
give orders than obey the Constitution—which, in any event, puts the
Speaker of the House next in line after the vice president.

Most close observers of Reagan maintained that the assassination
attempt had no lasting effect on him, either politically or psychologically.
Nancy, however, would remain forever affected by "the thing that happened to Ronnie," and she became increasingly protective of her husband, and dependent on a San Francisco astrologist named Joan
Quigley. The stargazer was asked to explain why every president since
William Henry Harrison who was elected in a year ending in zero had
been killed in office (Lincoln, 1860; McKinley, 1900; Kennedy, 1960).
Quigley said she would consult her charts.[30]

What impressed the American people about Reagan was not Jupiter
and Saturn but character and courage, and his never-failing instinct for
self-deprecation and the comedic. Everyone knows that Reagan quipped
to the doctors as he was wheeled into the operating room, "I hope you
are all Republicans." When he came to after the operation, he wanted to
know who the gunman was, whether he had been caught, and what his
motive was, or, as he put it, "What's his beef?" Michael Reagan visited
his father in the hospital room and was given a lecture on making sure,
if he was ever in a position to be shot at, not to wear a good suit. The
president's had been left in shreds. "I understand the parents of the
young man who shot me are in the oil business. Do you think just maybe
they'd buy me a new suit?" When some of his staff visited him and let
him know that he would be happy to hear that the government was running smoothly while he was in the hospital, Reagan smiled and replied:
"What makes you think I'd be happy about that?" To make light of near-
death is life's best revenge.[31]

The public followed the president's recovery as though he were a member of the family. A vigil was held outside the hospital, and when Reagan, wearing a bright red sweater, put his head out the window, it could have been the Second Coming. The surge of public sympathy led Deaver to suggest to Reagan that he address a joint session of Congress to reaffirm his economic program. From Congress he received a thunderous standing ovation. Emerson said, "Every hero becomes a bore at last," but even the poet knew that democracy needs a hero at first. There was something about the old man that seemed indestructible. He was the aged ruler relishing memories of youth, the King Lear of American democracy who was not betrayed by his progeny but instead rose triumphant in the eyes of his children and the public. Surviving an attempt on his life, quizzical about his assassin, still laughing in the face of death, he conquered the king of terror.

—

THE STORY OF the American presidency from the Eisenhower fifties to the end of the twentieth century seemed to be the story of frustration and failure. After a thousand days in office, John F. Kennedy was assassinated. The Vietnam War forced Lyndon Johnson to withdraw from seeking reelection. Richard Nixon resigned under threat of impeachment after Watergate, and Gerald Ford lost reelection to Jimmy Carter. Reagan's successor, George Bush, lost to Bill Clinton, whose two terms were tainted by his impeachment for lying about having engaged in oral sex in the Oval Office. The Reagan eighties stood out as an exception to the record of embarrassment, defeat, and death. Few doubted that Reagan had character and integrity, but some of his foreign policy advisors doubted his intelligence and vision. Chief among them were intellectuals who convinced themselves that the cold war could not end unless it could be won. Haunted by memories of the Vietnam War, they dreaded defeat and tasted victory.

CHAPTER SIX

Neoconservative Intellectuals and the Cold War

The Conservative Realist
and the Political Romantic

IN APRIL 1981, only three months in office, and while stretched out on a hospital bed recovering from the assassination attempt, President Reagan asked for a notepad and started to write in long-hand a letter to Leonid Brezhnev, the grim, bushy-browed general chairman of the Communist Party of the Soviet Union. Reagan, eager to begin a dialogue on the cold war, continued the letter in the White House's solarium after his release from the hospital. His Soviet experts, nervous about a president with no experience in foreign affairs, asked to see the letter, at which point they proceeded to rewrite it. "This isn't what I had written," Reagan said to Michael Deaver after the letter was returned to him, "but they are the experts." As he started to hand back the revised letter to Deaver, his assistant chief of staff blurted out:

> You know, Mr. President, those assholes have been running the Soviet business for the last forty years, and they haven't done a very good job of it. None of them ever got elected to anything; you got elected. Why don't you just tell them to stick it and send the goddamn letter?[1]

Reagan sent his original letter. It was a thoughtful document that tried to get to the bottom of the dangerous distrust the United States and the USSR had toward one another. Brezhnev's response disappointed Reagan, but when Mikhail Gorbachev came to power in 1985, the president's efforts at rapprochement began to bear fruit. Reagan's outreach eventually would lead to dramatic disarmament negotiations between the two powers and to the end of the cold war.

—

THE BEGINNING HAD NOT been promising. In the election of 1980, the Republicans campaigned as though on a warpath. They talked aggressively about the Mideast, about getting tough with Russia and standing tall in the eyes of the third world, brandishing the weapons of a superpower, and riding to victory with the Valkyries. What later came to be called "morning in America" almost started out with signs of a dark night of war.

Actually, the election outcome presented America with an odd cold war juxtaposition: a president who was a romantic surrounded by a staff of advisors who were realists. Reagan's vision of a better world was taken down a notch or two by the foreign affairs agencies of government, staffed mainly by Machiavellians who were convinced that policy was largely a question of using tactics to cope with intractable realities. To dare to change was not in the realist vocabulary. The conservative realist clings to what is, the political romantic imagines what ought to be. When Reagan began to negotiate disarmament with Russia in his second term, conservatives turned against him. After he left office some hard-liners, like Dick Cheney, insisted that the cold war would be resumed and warned America to prepare for the reemergence of an aggressive communist state in Russia. Liberals were at a loss to understand how Reagan achieved what they had been advocating all along. Had the Democratic Party advocated a rapprochement with the USSR, it would have been dubbed "soft" on communism.

Neoconservatism is the term that distinguishes more recent conservative intellectuals from an older generation of American conservative political minds, many of them southerners who believed in states' rights or midwesterners who were isolationists. The neocons were nationalists and interventionists who rejected the liberal diplomatic policy of containment. Convinced that America must go on the offensive and turn back communism in the third world, neocons declared that détente, the relaxation of tensions between the United States and the USSR, was a dangerous delusion. At first Reagan accepted the advice of neocons, particularly in respect to the third world, but he would reject their intransigence toward the Soviet Union as he attempted a rapprochement with Gorbachev. Many neocons were glad to see Reagan retire to California while they awaited their next chance to advise a president on deploying power and bringing America's enemies to their knees. The neocons believed that they had won the cold war and gave little credit to the anti-communist dissidents behind the Iron Curtain. Because they knew, or assumed that they knew, how to effect "regime change," they would lead America into war with Iraq in 2003.

In the early eighties, however, the impression was widespread that while Jimmy Carter had wobbled, Ronald Reagan roared. This was more apparent than real. Actually, Carter had begun a vast program of military weapons expansion after the Soviet invasion of Afghanistan in 1979. When Reagan took office in 1981, he remained as much a sentimental-ist as a strategist about foreign policy. The cold war had not changed Reagan from a populist into a militarist. Rather, Reagan always saw power as a conspiracy against freedom and believed that political insti-tutions stood in the way of human aspirations. In the early eighties, he replied to a letter from a California couple who happened to have met Leonid Brezhnev on board a passenger ship. Referring to one of his own letters to Brezhnev, Reagan wrote: "I almost described your own ship-board meeting in that I suggested that if a Russian family and an Amer-ican family found themselves thrown together they would begin to get acquainted and discover how much they had in common. I even said they would agree to get together again. Then I asked him why govern-ments couldn't do that. His answer was something less than satisfac-tory. But you have proven that people don't start wars. Only govern-ments do that."[2]

At times Reagan sounded like a sixties radical who called for "all power to the people" and believed in resolving conflicts in "rap sessions," where barriers came down once personal relationships opened up. Indeed, Reagan approached the cold war with a soft diplomacy of dialogue that was anathema to those who would confront the enemy. Whether or not Reagan was right that governments start war, the real question was who would prevent it. Reagan truly believed that the role fell to him. In 1975, while he was still governor of California, he insisted that America had a special destiny to rescue the world. "We did not seek world leadership; it was thrust upon us. . . . If we fail to keep our rendezvous with destiny, or, as John Winthrop said in 1630, 'Deal falsely with our God,' we shall be made 'a story and byword throughout the world.' "[3]

Winthrop and the seventeenth-century Calvinists, fleeing what they saw as the moral corruption of Europe, had no interest in leading the world. They were isolationists, not interventionists, and they sought to "purify" New England as an example to the world. Reagan, however, could rarely resist interpreting the cold war in cosmic terms. Unlike his affectionate antagonist, House Speaker Tip O'Neill, who once declared that "all politics is local" to indicate that members of Congress put the interests of their constituencies first, Reagan declared that cold war politics was universal and ideological; but that was before he met Mikhail Gorbachev.

What was the cold war all about? Capitalism versus socialism? Freedom versus totalitarianism? Religion versus atheism? Was it what social scientists call "bipolarity," when two superpowers struggle for supremacy and neither side is capable of relinquishing its hegemony? Scholars of the cold war usually divided into two schools of thought. The "idealists" believed that America behaved aggressively in establishing military alliances to surround the USSR and thereby exacerbated Soviet suspicions. The "realists" believed that America was not aggressive enough in allowing Stalin's Red Army to establish its hegemony over Eastern Europe. However one sees the origins of the cold war, or however one defines it, the way it ended is unprecedented in the annals of the past. Historically, most thinkers believed that conflict was inevitable. Thucydides concluded that men, moved by pride and fear, are tragically fated to go to war. Hobbes taught that the only solution to the state of nature, where everywhere there is war of each against all, was the consolidation of all power into the Leviathan state. Hegel asserted that truth resides in power and war is its ultimate expression. Marx believed revolution is necessary because a ruling class will never give up power peacefully. With Ronald Reagan's achievement, the president disproved the philosophers. He sought peace and helped bring an end to the cold war without resorting to violence against America's major antagonist. To the historian Jacob Burckhardt, such an achievement could only be carried out by a political leader who had "greatness of soul."

Reagan also proved thinkers of his own time too fatalistic. In the Reagan era, many intellectuals, on the Left and Right, treated communism as both a theory destined to inflame the underdeveloped world and a reality certain to oppress the totalitarian world. Where it threatened to take over, as in Nicaragua, it would create social justice; where it already had taken over, as in Russia, it quashed political freedom. Good or bad, communism was apparently immutable, a law of nature, part of both the inexorable tide of history and the irredeemable curse of history.

Reagan's deep, instinctive desire for peace was often lost in his overly combative political language. It's unfortunate that the rhetoric of religiosity and militancy with which Reagan approached the cold war has tended to obscure his deeper concerns. In commenting on the 1960 book *On Thermonuclear War* (an event that the book's author, the futurist Herman Kahn, regarded as more plausible than unthinkable), Reagan replied to his correspondents in this way: "Lately I've been wondering about some older prophecies—those having to do with Armageddon. Things that are new today sound an awful lot like what was predicted would take place just prior to 'A' day. Don't quote me." Armageddon is the scene of the ultimate battle between the forces of good and evil foretold in the Bible. It is difficult to know whether Reagan was serious. It may be that what he feared was not a struggle of good against evil but one of evil against the evil that America would become were it to use nuclear weapons to preemptively destroy an enemy or even retaliate after a first strike. If Reagan saw the cold war in ways scholars have since ridiculed ("the whole eschatology of Armageddon," in Frances Fitzgerald's phrase), why then did he come to believe that the cold war could not be won through military means? God offers no guarantee that the forces of right will prevail, as Lincoln recognized. During the Civil War, Lincoln understood that evil means had to be used with no certainty that good ends would result. Reagan was no religious zealot dragging the world to the brink of war. On the contrary, he realized that the greatest challenge posed by the cold war was to prevent nations from taking up arms. Lincoln also did his best to prevent the outbreak of the Civil War, and his tragic vision of history could only conclude that it was fated to happen. How and why Reagan succeeded and Lincoln failed is addressed in the book's coda.[4]

In 2003, the United States went to war to get rid of "weapons of mass destruction" that turned out not to have existed. Reagan, the first president to use that expression, in a letter to Gorbachev, had asked the Soviet leader to allow on-site inspections, and he urged Gorbachev to join him in getting rid of such weapons. Reagan's conviction about peace and disarmament was there from the beginning of his presidency, even while he concentrated on domestic tax and budget issues. Less than a month after taking the oath of office, Reagan received a letter from F. A. Hayek, whose 1944 treatise against socialism, *The Road to Serfdom*, was much admired by conservatives. Hayek wrote to Reagan in order to "to urge on you the only peaceful solution" to the arms race: "submit the whole issue to the International Court at The Hague."[5]

There was no consensus in the Reagan administration on the question of whether to prepare for war or work toward peace. In the first years, Secretary of State Haig brought his military background to bear. He itched to have the United States do something about Cuba, perhaps even carry out bombing raids. Defense Secretary Weinberger also rattled his saber, insisting that the United States must move beyond the balance of power with the Soviet Union to achieve nuclear superiority. James Baker, Michael Deaver, and Nancy Reagan, whose influence should never be minimized, all insisted on pursuing diplomatic negotiation and avoiding military confrontation.

If the Reagan administration was divided over the cold war, so was conservatism. In domestic policy, conservatives believed that ideas, values, moral principles, and truth should prevail. However, in foreign policy, conservatives were just as likely to assert that there is no substitute for power. Henry Kissinger likened power to an aphrodisiac, but Reagan, who knew there were better ways to make love, was never quite comfortable with power politics except as a last resort. Kissinger's *realpolitik* had few friends among conservative true believers, especially when it was used to rationalize accommodations with communist powers— détente with the Soviet Union, the opening to China, and the withdrawal of America from Vietnam.

Reagan intuited what social philosophers had long taught—that economic progress and political freedom depend on cultural values, on ideals and mores, and not on the "laws" of historical development or on the logic of power, a calculus that sees power either spreading or shriveling: use or lose it. Many liberal thinkers in the Western world viewed the primacy of culture as the catalyst of change and progress: in France, Montesquieu and Tocqueville; in England and Scotland, Adam Smith and David Hume; in Germany, Max Weber and Werner Sombart—all argued that individual moral choice was paramount. But in twentieth-century America, the moral dimension of human nature was marginalized by the scientific interpretation of history. Moral ideas were shunted aside as irrelevant to an agenda of social reform. However, that perspective was changing by the time Reagan became president. Those writing for *The Public Interest* challenged a scholarship based on fact alone, an empirical social science that dismissed culture and values in the study of society. Conservatism would take its stand for morality, not scientific neutrality; for the politically principled subject, not the rationally calculating observer, for individual obligation and not statistical predictability. The neoconservative intellectuals who wrote for *The Public Interest* were profoundly skeptical about the promises of social engineering, and they had in mind the disappointments with such liberal projects as the war on poverty, school busing, and public housing. The use of state power even for altruistic purposes may have unintended consequences.

How odd, then, that when it came to foreign affairs, some conservatives were disposed to see power and brute facts as the key to understanding international relations. Power, the ability to predict and produce intended effects, is the real weapon of diplomacy, and American nuclear power may be an instrument for moral ends. Reagan, never wanting to see nuclear missiles unleashed, preferred persuasion to power.

Reagan felt an empathy for Gorbachev; they were almost fellow libertarians contending with the power of the oppressive state. It is well known that Gorbachev at first assumed that communism could be reformed, but that illusion only made his predicament all the more tenuous. The Czech dissident Václav Havel glimpsed Gorbachev as "rather short and stocky, a cuddly ball-like figure hemmed in by his gigantic bodyguards, giving the impression of someone shy and helpless. . . . All of the sudden I find myself feeling sorry for him."[6] That is how the Soviet leader appeared in 1987. The following year, Reagan toured Moscow with Gorbachev and was impressed by how the general secretary's new path of reform "has really moved the Russian people. We couldn't believe their friendliness and warmth. I'm talking about the people in the street—not the world of officialdom. Wherever we went they were massed on the curb, waving, smiling, cheering. And I'm convinced that he is sincere about wanting to make a change. He'd have to be to take on the bureaucracy the way he has." A few years earlier, Reagan wrote Gorbachev and advised that if any progress toward peace was possible, both governments must ignore their "respective bureaucracies."[7]

Reagan faced the cold war convinced that the deadly inertia of bureaucracy could be overcome by populist faith in the people and the personal force of charismatic leadership. He stood almost alone in holding that conviction. Most of his advisors had little faith in the people and less faith in the possibilities of personal diplomacy.

The Reagan-Brezhnev Communication

IT IS COMMONLY BELIEVED that President Reagan started out as a nuclear escalator and ended up as a diplomatic negotiator, that he went from first-term cold warrior to second-term peacemaker. Reagan always knew, however, that preparing for war increases immensely the power of government. As he listened to his advisors speculate over how to fight the cold war, without explaining how to win it, Reagan could go along with their proposals for military preparation, even though he had his own reservations about Armageddon. But as soon as he finally concluded that a nuclear war could not be won, he shunned his advisors and their weapons strategies and war games. Reagan seemed to have a deep conviction that an all-out war would jeopardize American freedom not only because a nuclear holocaust would leave the world in a rubble of radiation but because war takes away a country's freedom of choice, as events get out of control, and history is at the mercy of necessity. Centuries ago, Thucydides warned that a country may choose whether or not to fight, but that once the battle commences, the power of choice is gone and freedom is lost in the fog of war. Reagan valued freedom above all else, and he would do everything to preserve it.

Reagan's letter to Brezhnev was a response to a communication from the Soviet leader. After a formal congratulation to Reagan for having taken office, Brezhnev insisted that nothing had changed in the cold war. Quite likely Brezhnev had been misinformed about an easygoing, laid-back president who was recovering in the White House solarium, surfing television channels in search of old films to watch. Reagan, a victim of violence, knew the world was more real than any cinematic representation. He was also aware of his reputation of a warmonger, a shoot-first gunslinger, a tool of the imperialists and the "running dogs of capitalism." He had heard all this before, of course, in his Hollywood days, when his antagonists spit in his face the word "fascist." The cold war, however, was real, and Reagan had to deal not with fellow actors and scriptwriters but with Russian political leaders who had proudly used techniques of terror and looked to revolution to liquidate Western freedom. George Bernard Shaw once said of Trotsky that when he "cuts off his opponent's head, he holds it up to show there are no brains in it."[8]

Leon Trotsky had once been a hero to many of the New York intellectuals of the 1930s and 1940s who became neoconservatives in the 1970s and 1980s. They had seen Trotsky as an alternative to Stalin until they heard revelations about his brutal behavior during the civil war in Russia. Still, few could forget that Trotsky, the brilliant Bolshevik who led the Red Army to victory in the October Revolution of 1917, "the pen" of the proletariat who wrote persuasive prose, had been assassinated in Mexico in 1940 when a Stalinist agent smashed his skull with an ice ax. The fate of the "old man" confirmed their view that communism was no alternative to a "bureaucratic collectivism" that produced the totalitarian state. Trotsky, unlike Stalin, believed world communism was still possible, and some American Trotskyists had once believed in a new Fourth International that would emancipate the world. But it is not enough to be right when you are, as Isaac Deutscher described Trotsky in the words of Machiavelli, "The Prophet Unarmed." The lesson American ex-Trotskyists learned is this: never again to be among the defeated, unprepared and unarmed. Years later, when the ex-Trotskyists were Reaganite revolutionaries, they (and their sons) now believed, perhaps in expiation, that the world could be emancipated not by communism but by democracy.

Brezhnev, dour and humorless, was the son of a worker in a Ukrainian steel town. He went to college, studied engineering, directed a vocational school, survived the purges of the 1930s, went on to take command of the Kremlin, and never for a moment doubted the legacy of Leninism and party dictatorship.[9] He died in 1982, shortly after Reagan wrote his letter, and his successors, Yuri Andropov and Konstantin Chernenko, also died almost as soon as they took office. "How am I supposed to get anywhere with the Russians," Reagan asked Nancy, "if they keep dying on me?"[10]

Brezhnev represented the darkest years of the cold war. In 1968, the year of the Prague Spring, when Czechs tried to break away from the Soviet Union and Poles took to the streets in sympathy protests, the so-called Brezhnev doctrine was promulgated. Workers and intellectuals seemed to have lost everything but their chains. The doctrine held that Soviet satellite countries could chose their own road to socialism at home, but that they had no right to defy Moscow and risk the solidarity of international socialism, which history had shown to be permanent and irreversible.

Reagan actually wrote two letters to the Russian leader. One, rather stiff and provocative, was nothing less than a challenge to the Brezhnev doctrine, which Reagan called an infringement upon the sovereign rights of countries to determine their own political future. The second letter was gracious and a little sappy. He sent both to Brezhnev. The president was so fond of the second letter that he quoted the full text in his memoir. He recalled his first meeting with Brezhnev, at Nixon's summer White House in San Clemente, California, and reminded him of how they embraced, how they exchanged hopes for a better world, how both wanted dignity and reward for their own workers, how American and Soviet families should be able to live in peace and security. Then, noting that Brezhnev had sent him a letter of "intemperate tone," Reagan responded in kind. "Will the average Soviet family be better off or even aware that the Soviet Union has imposed a government of its own choice on the people of Afghanistan? Is life better for the people of Cuba because the Cuban military dictate who shall govern the people of Angola?" Anticipating Brezhnev's response to these questions—that such actions were defensive moves necessary to thwart America's territorial expansion—Reagan denied that America had any aggressive designs, even when it had the possibility of carrying them out:

> When World War II ended, the United States had the only undamaged industrial power in the world. Our military might was at its peak—and we alone had the ultimate weapon, the nuclear weapon, with unquestioned ability to deliver it anywhere in the world. If we sought world domination then, who

could have opposed us? But the United States followed a different course—one unique in all the history of mankind. We used our power and wealth to rebuild the war-ravaged economies of the world, including those nations who had been our enemies. May I say there is absolutely no substance to the charges that the United States is guilty of imperialism or attempts to impose its will on other countries by use of force.

Reminding Brezhnev that the United States had lifted a grain embargo on the Soviet Union, Reagan called for starting a "meaningful and constructive dialogue" to lessen the conflicts between the two superpowers. He concluded by emphasizing a point he would repeat again and again to Gorbachev: that conflicts are created when government acts apart from society and its citizens, whether in the USSR or in the United States. "Isn't it possible some of these obstacles are born of government objectives which have little to do with the real needs and desires of our people?"[11]

A week later Reagan received "an icy reply" from Brezhnev, who blamed America for starting and perpetuating the cold war and insisted the United States had no business telling the Soviets what they could or could not do in Eastern Europe or the rest of the world. In some respects, the Reagan-Brezhnev communication represents a profound misunderstanding between the two superpowers. Whoever started the cold war, Afghanistan and Angola had little to do with it. The Soviet takeover of Kabul in 1979, as we shall see, had very little to do with communist expansionism. Rather, it was an attempt to quell certain manifestations of Islamic fundamentalism and prevent the coming to power of what later was called the Taliban. As to Angola, Russia sent troops to Africa, and America supplied covert aid to anti-communist tribal leaders, while Castro sent Cuban fighters for reasons that scholars are still debating. The neocons were convinced that Cuban soliders were Soviet "proxies." Actually, Brezhnev chastised Castro for sending troops to Africa, furious that Cuba's actions would upset any possible new relationship with the United States. With time, Brezhnev grew less intransigent toward Reagan, and as he knew he was dying he wanted desperately to negotiate an arms treaty and go down in history as a peacemaker.

However, Castro stubbornly went ahead with his plans in order to prove that he could act independently of Moscow.

The Reagan-Brezhnev correspondence presages the scholars' debates over the origins of the cold war. The Russian leader scorned the president's claim that America after World War II was able to dominate the world but refrained from doing so. Brezhnev, feigning bewilderment, cited NATO as evidence of U.S. imperialist intentions and of Pax Americana. "One would wonder what the need for it was. After all, fascist Germany had been routed and militarist Japan destroyed." Could not Brezhnev admit at least to himself that NATO was created because the Soviets occupied Czechoslovakia and overthrew its democratic government? In other exchanges, Reagan lost his patience but retained his humor. When Brezhnev insisted both sides freeze their current level of nuclear arms, he wrote: "I would ask you, Mr. President, carefully to consider this proposal." Reagan, convinced the Soviets had far more nuclear capacity, wrote in the margin of the letter: "I have, and it's an apple for an orchard." When Brezhnev claimed to speak in the name of the "people," Reagan quipped: "He's a barrel of laughs."[12]

One of the more remarkable aspects of the correspondence was not Brezhnev's predictable replies but the consternation the letters created among Reagan's advisors. Reagan showed his first letter to Secretary of State Haig and to some Soviet specialists in the administration, among them Richard Pipes, a member of the National Security Council. As noted earlier, they revised it beyond recognition. Alexander Haig composed one draft, which national security advisor Richard V. Allen found lacking in diplomatic finesse. Allen cautioned that Haig's "draft borders on the truculent," reading like a "brushoff," whereas Brezhnev's letter "cleverly maintains a statesmanlike air." The more moderate Jack F. Matlock, ambassador to Moscow, advised Reagan to insist to the Russian leader that the Brezhnev doctrine be discarded. Richard Pipes advised against sending Reagan's first draft, calling it "undiplomatic." The Russian experts who provoked Deaver's profanity saw Reagan as an innocent who foolishly thought he could do something to end the cold war. They believed the superpower rivalry would last indefinitely, as though the world had inherited an incurable disease. The "Soviet business" was steady work.[13]

Ironically, the conservative hard-liners were actually carrying out the work of their antagonist, the allegedly "soft" Jimmy Carter, who had ceased formal diplomatic relations with Russia after the invasion of Afghanistan in 1979. While the neocon intellectuals, along with Nixon and Kissinger, remained convinced that the United States must avoid negotiating with the USSR until it changed its ways, George P. Shultz saw changes taking place even before he replaced Haig as secretary of state. On a trip to the Soviet Union, Shultz spoke to intellectuals and playwrights who reported a relaxation of restrictions, and he saw that government officials kept their promises when he agreed to an interview only if his advice urging Russia to withdraw from Afghanistan was not edited out. Perhaps the best evidence that negotiation was possible involved the fate of the Pentecostals, religious dissidents who had taken sanctuary in the American Embassy in Moscow. Shultz and Anatoly Dobrynin, Soviet ambassador to the United States, worked quietly together to secure their release, and Soviet authorities were encouraged to see Reagan keep his word and not crow about a diplomatic achievement.[14]

The Neocon Intellectual as Master of Suspicion

OCCUPYING CENTER STAGE among the Soviet experts in the administration was Pipes, a distinguished professor of history at Harvard and the author of several books on Lenin and the Bolshevik revolution. Pipes's Polish ancestry and Jewish background perhaps explain his unrelenting distrust not only of communism but of the Russian national character. On the National Security Council, he had much more on his mind than dealing with a president who knew little about military tactics and seemed unaware that U.S. submarines were armed with nuclear missiles. Reagan wanted to prevent war, Pipes to prepare for it.

Foreign policy in the first phase of the administration had been shaped by Defense Secretary Weinberger and Secretary of State Haig. It was a period when Americans were told that they could survive a nuclear attack if they were to dig underground fallout shelters in their own backyards and "if there are enough shovels to go around."[15] In 1983, French

president François Mitterrand went before the United Nations and
pointed out that the United States and the USSR both had "a nuclear
system of 2,000 to 3000 launchers, carrying 8,000 to 9,000 war heads,"
enough to "reach and destroy each other seven or eight times over."
France too was able to obliterate thirty Soviet cities, but continued to
enhance its nuclear capacity. Similar alarming statistics were cited by
Marshal Nikolai V. Ogarkov, chief of the Soviet General Staff, and former Carter secretary of defense Harold Brown. For the Reagan hawks,
however, the nuclear balance of terror was deceptive and dangerous,
since it sanctioned the status quo, rendered legitimate Soviet rule, and
failed to prepare America for what the Kremlin had in mind. Secretary
Weinberger believed that increasing American nuclear forces could tip
the balance so that the United States could call the shots. The American arsenal "must prevail and be able to force the Soviet Union to seek
the earliest termination of hostilities on terms favorable to the United
States." The Pentagon's new strategy, wrote Theodore Draper, "represents a monstrous perversion of the doctrine of deterrence." The new
Weinberger doctrine implied that America must be prepared to use
nuclear weapons to achieve objectives and as a means of self-defense.
Even though the United States might have no intention of launching
a preemptive attack, it must be prepared to take a hit and retaliate
massively with nuclear warheads launched from missile sites and
submarines. The new doctrine assumed that the Soviet Union now
had "a definite margin of superiority" over the United States in the
armaments race.[16]

   This frightening assumption originated in the mid-1970s, when a
fierce debate developed over American foreign policy. Neocon intellectuals had grown frustrated with the CIA. They believed that the agency
was overestimating Soviet economic strength and dealing with Russia's
military growth with insufficient alarm, seemingly untroubled by the
Soviet development of strategic weapons or the intentions behind them.
The Ford administration tried to ward off the hard-liner attacks by
appointing neocons to an oversight panel of experts to evaluate the CIA's
intelligence estimates. The result was the report of "Team B," which
claimed that the Soviet Union had been secretly undertaking an "unpar-
alleled military buildup." According to the report, the Soviet aim was not
to deter nuclear war but to fight and win a war to conquer the world. The

Soviets had no reluctance to fight, since they saw "an enormous persuasive power accruing to a nation which can face the prospect of a nuclear war with confidence of its survival." Much of Team B's estimates and projections of Soviet military capability and the dangers facing America were grossly exaggerated, as Frances Fitzgerald, Gary Dorrien, Robert W. Tucker, and Fareed Zakaria have pointed out.[17] Although the Soviets had outspent the United States in weapons development in the late seventies, throughout the entire Reagan eighties military expenditures in the USSR remained a steady and skimpy 8 percent of Soviet gross national product (compared to America's 6.5 percent). More important than Team B's economic and military miscalculations, however, were the misperceptions of Soviet motives. The claims Team B made about the Russian national character were intended to demonstrate that Russia believed it would prevail and that America would perish.

Team B was headed by Pipes, and his report was published in an article with the telling title "Why the Soviet Union Thinks It Could Fight and Win a Nuclear War." The analysis was reminiscent of George Orwell's essay years earlier on James Burnham in *Partisan Review*. The American cold warrior, Orwell argued, seeks to strike fear in us as he describes the irresistible movement of power and the helplessness of liberals to oppose it. Like Burnham, Pipes portrayed Soviet power as inexorable. However, the irony is that Orwell thought Burnham was defending Stalin. Burnham would later write *Suicide of the West* (1965), which depicts the weakness of liberalism as it capitulates to communism—a theme that ran through the entire cold war.

Pipes's analysis is similar to Orwell's, and it is understandable in light of the political context of the late 1970s. At that time, Carter and the liberals were more concerned about human rights and arms control than about Soviet weapons and machinations. As for what the Soviets were up to with their alleged mania for missiles, Pipes provided an unnerving quote from an "authoritative Soviet publication" warning that "there is a profound erroneousness and harm in discounting claims of bourgeois ideologies that there will be no victor in a thermonuclear war." It is hard to see what such a statement was supposed to prove. Perhaps Pipes was warning U.S. policymakers against such reasoning in order to stiffen their resolve against the Soviets. Herman Kahn said much the same thing in *On Thermonuclear War*, his account of megathon bombs, fallout shel-

ters, and postnuclear survival after millions are incinerated. No U.S.
president took Kahn seriously. The overweight theoretician was called
by a contemporary "a roly-poly second strike Santa Claus."[18] Warnings
that there would be no victors in a nuclear war were not just emanating
from "bourgeois ideologies." Both Pope John Paul II and Nikita Khrushchev had said as much, and so would Reagan, who would soon come
to appreciate the existential madness of the armament race.

Pipes insisted that the Soviet doctrine of warfare differed from the
American doctrine, and that this put the United States at a disadvantage
in any confrontation with the USSR. American military theory was
rational, and its conduct was based on the minimal use of force. In Russia, violence was as ubiquitous as vodka, and a preemptive war was perfectly plausible. If the Russian national character posed an even greater
threat than Soviet communism, as Pipes supposed, then a cold war confrontation was tantamount to a clash in cultural anthropology between
two systems of life with diametrically opposing values. Contrasting
America and the Soviet Union, Pipes assumed that Russia possessed
the superior traits of a combative culture. Speaking of America, Pipes
emphasized: "Now this entire middle-class, essentially Protestant ethos
is absent from Soviet culture, where roots feed on another kind of soil,
and which has for centuries weathered tougher climes." The Russians
had, of course, defeated Napoleon and Hitler. But now, Pipes argued,
the communists had replaced what there was of the Russian bourgeoisie
and "installed in power the *muzhik*, the Russian peasant," who knew
from "historical experience that cunning and coercion alone ensured
survival: one employed cunning when weak, and cunning coupled with
coercion when strong. Not to use force when one had it indicated some
inner weakness."[19]

Pipes thought a Protestant commercial environment was a source of
weakness when Americans were confronting the alien culture of peasant Russia. Reagan believed it was a source of strength. While Pipes
worried that a Protestant culture rendered America soft, other important
thinkers, including Tocqueville and Max Weber, saw such a culture as
conducive to social stability and an honest work ethic. In the 1770s,
Edmund Burke warned Great Britain, in a speech to Parliament, that
the American colonies would not be subdued precisely because they
were Protestant and would fight to the end. Reagan always believed that

the greatest threat to liberty was from governments grown too large for their own good. Pipes was relatively unconcerned about the Communist Party, bureaucracy, or even totalitarianism. It was the Russian people themselves, with their historic capacity for cunning and coercion and, more recently, tactics of torture and terror, whose actions could lead to a preemptive attack.

There are rich ironies in this perspective. While Pipes feared the enduring ethnic character of the Russian people, another neocon intellectual, Daniel Patrick Moynihan, suggested that ethnicity would lead to the breakup of the Soviet Union, a polyglot empire that would be unable to resist its own "fragmentation," as Hélène Carrère d'Encausse had predicted, as early as 1978, in *L'Empire éclaté*. Pipes saw Russia as powerful and America as vulnerable. Such a perspective was shared by communist and anticommunist alike, by Fidel Castro and Whittaker Chambers.

Pipes, as we have seen, taught at Harvard, a liberal campus whose professors were mainly anti-Reagan. Many neocons came from the University of Chicago, a genteel campus with no football team but a ferocious faculty staffed by some wizards of weaponry strategy. Chicago theoreticians believed they could win the cold war without too many people being hurt. Many neocon students worshipped Leo Strauss, a German émigré classicist who taught, with Aristotle, that reason should govern life and, with Maimonides, that some beliefs, while not true, are necessary to survival. Those who went into the foreign service learned more from Albert Wohlstetter, a political scientist who taught that power governs life and that might can be right if the arms race is approached as a branch of mathematics. A legendary figure among nuclear strategists, Wohlstetter served as a model, with Herman Kahn, physicist Edward Teller, and others, as the title character in Stanley Kubrick's movie *Dr. Strangelove* (1964). Wohlstetter also makes a cameo appearance in Saul Bellow's portrait of the University of Chicago philosopher Allan Bloom in the novel *Ravelstein*. A master of how weapons of minimal and maximun destruction work, he tutored Richard Perle, a hawk who believed it wiser to live with the danger of nuclear war than to cooperate with the Soviet Union and let down our guard. In the early Reagan administration Perle was the Iago of foreign policy, a voice whispering its hatred of treaties and its suspicion of the other. Rather than work toward peace,

Perle urged the Reagan administration that we must learn to live with threat and even love it.

While Wohlstetter obsessed over missiles, Pipes worried about the *muzhik* whose ferocity threatened a self-satisfied culture of commerce and consumption. Leo Tolstoy had depicted the Russian peasant as stubborn and surly, yet less concerned with winning than with enduring. However, the novelist did leave the misimpression that the Cossaks would do no harm, despite their bloody pogroms. Pipes's comparable analysis would perplex Reagan, who trusted people far more than institutions. However, Tolstoy also observed that Russia's military leaders believed that "the two most powerful warriors are *patience and time*," and thus, General Kutuzov said to Prince Andrei, "When in doubt, my dear fellow, do nothing."[20] Pipes and Team B had no doubts and sought to do almost anything possible to expand America's nuclear arsenal.

"The Finlandization of America":
Norman Podhoretz and The Present Danger

I N POLITICS, if not in intellectual life, Ronald Reagan became the voice of the neoconservative anticommunists. In his Hollywood days, as we have seen, Reagan's staunchest allies were William Holden, Olivia de Havilland, and Elia Kazan, who remained Democratic liberals. At that moment in American history, in the late 1940s and early 1950s, anticommunist conservatism meant McCarthyism. Then there was fear that it was too late, that the enemy had already entered the gates. It was not paranoid to believe that American communist spies were stealing secrets, as the case of Julius Rosenberg confirmed, and in Britain it was discovered that communist spies had been among Cambridge University's brightest graduates. McCarthyism, on the other hand, saw communism seeping through the State Department, brainwashing children, and spreading its poison through the country's water supply because a fluoridization policy recommended by the American Dental Association to fight cavities was actually a foreign conspiracy to allow communism to enter the mind by way of the mouth. The anticommunism of the neocons who influenced Reagan hardly emanated from the McCarthyites and their conspiratorial fixations. Neocons were less concerned about spooks within the country than specters without. They did, however, continue the old accusation that the successes of communism were caused by failures of liberalism in staying alert; and no one was more persistent on this theme than Norman Podhoretz, editor of *Commentary*, the Reagan administration's intellectual house organ.

The story of Podhoretz is the story of rags to recognition. Born in a working-class Jewish neighborhood in Brooklyn, Podhoretz graduated from Columbia, won a scholarship to Cambridge University, studied literature, and came to worship George Orwell and Lionel Trilling. As editor of *Commentary* in the 1960s, he invited intellectuals to write against the Vietnam War and to contribute pieces on "Liberal Anti-Communism Revisited," and he supported the New Left that Reagan confronted as governor of California. Then Podhoretz underwent a conversion and he himself became an anticommunist, defended the Vietnam War (after America had lost it), championed Aleksandr Solzhenitsyn and the cause of freedom, and claimed that *Commentary* and neocon intellectuals had helped Reagan win the White House. He sent his essay "J'Accuse" to Reagan, politely questioning the president's demand that Israel stop bombing Lebanon. Eventually he would become bitterly disillusioned with Reagan when the president sought rapprochement with Gorbachev in the late eighties. In 1980, however, Reagan was the neocon's political beau ideal. He campaigned as a hawk, deemed Vietnam "a noble cause," dubbed the Democrats the party of appeasement, and promised to stand tall against the Soviet Union. In that election year, Podhoretz also published *The Present Danger*, and the public was told that America was losing the cold war, especially what Podhoretz called the second cold war, which threatened to be the wave of the future in the undeveloped world.

The first cold war, as we know, began in 1946–1949, with the Soviet occupation of Eastern Europe, which caused America to respond with the Truman Doctrine, NATO, and the Marshall Plan, giving military and economic assistance to Western Europe. To America, the fall of democratic Czechoslovakia was shocking, the loss of China distressing, Russia's exploding an atomic bomb frightening, and the outbreak of the Korean War confusing and frustrating. President Eisenhower had the good sense, however, to withdraw America from Korea, and in the fifties he dared not lift a finger to help Hungary when the Soviets sent tanks into Budapest to crush a brave uprising. The Republican Eisenhower and the rest of America watched the Budapest bloodbath in 1956, and the country watched as Democrat Kennedy forced Khrushchev to withdraw missiles from Cuba in 1962. With the communist victory in Vietnam in 1975 and the apparent spread of communism elsewhere in the world, conservative Republicans blamed liberal Democrats for holding to the delusion of "peaceful coexistence" between the two superpowers. In the Carter years especially it seemed that liberalism had no answer to communism. Then in 1979 came a series of shocks, and for Podhoretz the second cold war began.

First came the overthrow of the shah of Iran in early 1979, then the seizure of American hostages in November, and shortly afterward the Russian invasion of Afghanistan in December. At the same time there was the communist struggle for power in Nicaragua and a civil war in Angola that had already been won by a Marxist regime. Reagan's neocon advisors not only saw the long reach of the Kremlin behind such events but concluded that the real communist revolution was taking place globally beginning in the third world. They claimed the Soviets had undertaken a massive arms buildup of missile systems and nuclear submarines and were becoming involved in insurgencies in Africa and South America. Thus for the neoconservative, the case for containment and the hope for détente had proven foolish. In the so-called second cold war there would have to be a new Reagan doctrine to prevent any country from falling to communism. Rather than just contain communist revolution, the West would have to act decisively to overthrow it using counterinsurgency strategies in the third world and nuclear dominance through rapid missile development and deployment in Western Europe.

Reagan's own position was not as rigid as the doctrine implied. Yet at the same time he accepted the thesis that came out of the Committee on the Present Danger, a group formed in the seventies by political and labor leaders, neocon intellectuals and CIA officials, all convinced that the Soviet Union was massively arming for an ultimate showdown. Podhoretz in particular was convinced that communism expands irresistibly and that liberalism retreats inevitably. Indeed, he depicted the Russian menace the way Thomas Carlyle depicted old regime aristocrats standing before the French commune: dumb, inert, squeamish about power, guilty in the face of history. Like Carlyle, Podhoretz did not feel it necessary to explain events; rather, he simply narrated them so that we responded fearfully to the drama itself. Thus: "On November 4, 1979, the day the American embassy in Teheran was seized and the hostages taken, one period in American history ended; and less than two months later, on December 25, when Soviet troops invaded Afghanistan, another period began."

Podhoretz acknowledged that we were unsure where history was heading, but he urged us to clear our minds of "cant" and to renounce "the general idea that before Iran and Afghanistan we have moved from 'cold war' to 'détente' and that the old political struggle between 'East' and 'West' was yielding in importance to a new conflict between 'North' and 'South.'" Podorhetz rejected the notion that the cold war between Eastern Europe and the West had given way to a new confrontation between the wealthy, industrialized North and the poor southern hemisphere, especially Africa. On the contrary, the cold war was entering a new and more dangerous second phase. Iran and Afghanistan represented "the final collaspe of an American resolve to resist the forward surge of Soviet imperialism." Podhoretz would never reconsider his conviction that the events of 1979 were all about communism. As late as 1999, after the cold war was long over, he remained certain that when Reagan took office twenty years earlier, the Soviet Union "began taking advantage of the post-Vietnam demoralization of the United States to resume its expansionist thrust." In an earlier essay in *Commentary*, also published in book form as *The Present Danger*, Podhoretz made the astounding observation that America was about to fall to communism more out of cowardice than weakness. Americans were entering a new era, he insisted, one in which "we would be forbidden to speak its name aloud: the Finlandization of America."[21]

In 1939, Russia went to war against Finland, a Nazi-leaning country that put up a short fight and then settled for a compromised status under the Soviet behemoth. As a metaphor the fate of that country had all the truth, when applied to America, of sheer spectral evidence. Yet such pronouncements buttressed Reagan's undying conviction that communism spreads while liberalism sleeps. Podhoretz's claims that events in Afghanistan and Iran represented "the forward surge of Soviet imperialism" turned out to be historically inaccurate and tragically wrong. Not only did they signify an Islamic reaction to both Western liberalism and communism, but the erroneous impression misled America into arming both the *mujahideen* as "freedom fighters" and Saddam Hussein as America's "ally" in Iraq's own war with Iran. The details of these policies will be treated in the next chapter. Suffice it to say that in the later war on terrorism, Reagan's allies would become America's enemies.

"Dictatorships and Double Standards"; Jeane Kirkpatrick and the Idea of Totalitarianism

O F ALL THE PRESIDENCIES in American history, Ronald Reagan's received perhaps the most input from intellectuals, both academic and think tank specialists. In 1918, Woodrow Wilson had formed the Inquiry, an organization of intellectuals and scholars who submitted studies on the reconstruction of Europe after the First World War. In the 1930s FDR had his Brain Trust, namely economists and law professors who offered some guidance on domestic policies; in the sixties JFK had his Harvard connection, Niebuhrian liberals who sought to bring back into politics what Reagan would later purge—the idea of original sin. The infusion of ideas from intellectuals during the Reagan administration occurred not only in domestic policy but even more so in foreign affairs, where the administration pondered ways to bring down the "evil empire" without contemplating the riddle of evil. Reinhold Niebuhr's question—how much evil must America do to achieve good?—was one that rarely bothered neocon intellectuals. In their mind, the problem of liberal America was its reluctance to use power to do good or evil.

Culturally the situation was quaintly ironic. One of Reagan's favorite writers was Louis L'Amour, the popular novelist of lightweight Western sagas. For public affairs he read William Buckley's *National Review* and the weekly conservative newspaper *Human Events*. Reagan's advisors read Aristotle, Machiavelli, Shakespeare, Hobbes, Burke, Marx, Trotsky, Nietzsche, and others who taught the truths about human nature and the ways of the world. If knowledge is power, then applied knowledge is wisdom; one must know not only how to think but what to do. In 1979 Reagan read an essay in *Commentary*, "Dictatorships and Double Standards," and he felt both the power and wisdom of its author, Jeane J. Kirkpatrick.

Like so many neocon intellectuals, Kirkpatrick started out on the Left. Born Jeane Jordon, daughter of an Oklahoma oil-drilling entrepreneur, she went to school in Missouri and college at Barnard. She joined the youth section of the American Socialist Party and did graduate work at Columbia, receiving her Ph.D. with a dissertation on Perónist Argentina, and later taught international relations at Georgetown University. In 1955 she married Evron Kirkpatrick, head of the American Political Science Association and a liberal close to Hubert Humphrey. She put together a collection of essays, *The Strategy of Deception*, dedicated to S. M. Levitas, the former editor of the *New Leader*, perhaps the most important anticommunist voice in America. The *New Leader* had begun publication in the 1920s and drew upon the writings of Europeans, including the Russian Mensheviks, ousted by the Bolsheviks after the Revolution of 1917. Some of Kirkpatrick's work might be thought of as the revenge of the Mensheviks. In her anthology's introduction, "The Politics of Deception," she emphasized how ideas are manipulated in revolutionary situations. Communists claim to be expressing the inexorable movement of history, as though Marx had set in motion amorphous historical forces, when in reality Lenin, Castro, and others simply sought to capture power. The disparity between theory and practice was one of her deepest concerns.

The *New Leader* published important clandestine documents, such as the writings of Solzhenitsyn and Khrushchev's "Crimes of Stalin" speech, and also Martin Luther King Jr.'s historic "Letter From a Birmingham City Jail." The magazine was in the forefront of the civil rights movement as well as the cause of anticommunism. Its leading editors on the board, however, including Sidney Hook and Reinhold Niebuhr, were never persuaded by the economic philosophy that Reagan would preach, especially F. A. Hayek's conviction that only free enterprise could guarantee freedom and that socialism was the first step down the slippery slope to communism. The magazine brilliantly debated that issue in the 1950s. Many years earlier, in 1935, Hayek declared that the Soviet Union was on the verge of imminent collapse. Fifty years later it was still there, and Kirkpatrick's task was to explain why.

Her essay "Dictatorships and Double Standards" is one of the most important documents in American foreign policy, a turning point text similar to George Kennan's "X" essay articulating the case for containment in 1946. However, Kennan's doctrine, focusing mainly on the European continent, was no longer viable, because the Soviets circumvented containment by moving beyond Europe, even into Latin America, thereby violating the Monroe Doctrine of 1823, which had warned European powers that the western hemisphere was America's sphere of influence. Whether the Soviets were as determinedly expansionist as Reagan and the neocons insisted, whether communism was exported to Latin America or whether it was indigenous, is a question scholars have long debated. The latest archival research, based on the files of the KGB, the secret intelligence apparatus of the Soviet Union, suggests a complex picture. While the KGB believed that the third world was the place to win the cold war, the Soviet foreign office was more hesitant and ambivalent. By the time Reagan became president, Russia was bogged down in Afghanistan and in no mood for adventures elsewhere, and even the KGB thought Castro's aspirations to export revolution in Latin America contained "delusions of grandeur."[22] This subject will be taken up in chapter 9, when we consider Senator Daniel Patrick Moynihan. Nonetheless, Reagan was so deeply persuaded by Kirkpatrick's essay that he appointed her ambassador to the United Nations.

In her theoretical writings, Kirkpatrick's targets were Marxism and liberalism and their common assumption about the progressive stages of history. Kirkpatrick put both ideologies on trial by questioning what might be called the "fetishism of the following," the idea that what comes next in history is always and everywhere preferable to what went before. In a way, Reagan also subscribed to that vision with his reiteration of "a new dawn," but there are certain parts of the world where morning arises only to fall to darkness before noon.

The events that precipitated Kirkpatrick's essay were the overthrow of Anastasio Somoza in Nicaragua and of the shah of Iran. The Carter administration, which had sought to rid America of the psychosis of the cold war, supported both events. Carter and his advisors were convinced that autocracy cannot resist the winds of change and the will of the people. America must identify with the future instead of the past. Carter's national security advisor, Zbigniew Brzezinski, believed American foreign policy should forget Marxism and find the formula for the future in the theory of modernization. Other theorists of international relations believed that the status quo must yield to the forces of opposition, whether socialist or Islamic. While Reagan believed that the "Iron Curtain" could not last forever, Kirkpatrick taught him that what would happen in Nicaragua and Iran had already happened in Vietnam, Cambodia, and Laos. As in Russia and Eastern Europe, the communist regimes that have overturned their autocratic predecessors turn out to be more repressive. Traditional autocracies do not penetrate every aspect of society, whereas communism organizes society from top to bottom, leaving no space for civil society, economic initiative, or political rights. Authoritarian governments can change and reform, but communist systems can do neither. Hence Kirkpatrick's warning:

> It may not always be easy to distinguish between democratic and totalitarian agents of change, but it is also not too difficult. Authentic democratic revolutionaries aim at securing governments based on the consent of the governed and believe that ordinary men are capable of using freedom, knowing their own interest, choosing rulers. They do not, like current leaders in Nicaragua, assume that it will be necessary to postpone elections for three to five years during which time they can "cure" the false consciousness of almost everyone.[23]

At the time, Kirkpatrick's description was accurate. Nicaragua's leaders were the Sandinistas, Marxists who had come to power as liberators and quickly became masters of the masses. CIA director Casey persuaded Reagan that America should secretly support the Contras, the opposition guerrilla forces. The struggle for Nicaragua became an obsession for the Reagan administration and led to further secret operations in the Mideast. After Reagan left office, Nicaragua evolved in ways that neither he nor Kirkpatrick had expected. A democratic election would depose the communists.

When Hannah Arendt's great book *The Origins of Totalitarianism* appeared in 1951, she upset many intellectuals on the Left by equating Hitler's Germany with Stalin's Russia and by failing to leave open the possibility that a Marxist revolution could produce something better than a fascist nightmare. Arendt made a point that is relevant to Kirkpatrick's analysis: she held that totalitarianism is a phenomenon of large, industrial countries like Germany and Russia and far less likely to take hold in small, agricultural countries that lack the concentrated masses or the modern techniques of propaganda and control. Arendt's thesis may have to be qualified. In China Mao's Great Leap Forward herded hundreds of millions of peasants into collectives, and intellectuals who dared ask questions were shot on the spot. Cuba is a small, underdeveloped island where Castro has remained in power for over a half-century. That Nicaragua would become a permanent totalitarian state seemed unlikely. Arendt claimed that the rise of totalitarianism reflected the beginning of the end of the bourgeois world. When Sandinista leader Daniel Ortega and his wife, Rosario Murillo, visited New York, they went on a buying spree on Fifth Avenue and brought back to Managua fashionable clothes and designer sunglasses. Castro the incorruptible wore guerrilla dungarees to prove his proletarian virtue.

The idea of totalitarianism was one of the most controversial concepts of the cold war. The French neoconservative Jean-François Revel, whose work appeared in *Commentary* and who was a staunch Reagan supporter, wrote *The Totalitarian Temptation*, accusing the Left of focusing on the faults of free societies, even implying that they were totalitarian out of a fear to face the realities of communist systems. In America, many political scientists denied the validity of the concept of totalitarianism, and younger "revisionist" historians denied that Stalin's Russia was totalitarian. Communist Russia was no prison house of stagnation and repression; they argued that it was open to "opportunity," "mobility," and "initiative from below"—which indeed it was, when so many of those above were taken from their jobs and executed.[24]

How to interpret totalitarianism became one of the most urgent concerns of neocon intellectuals connected to the Reagan administration. If Kirkpatrick's thesis was correct, then communist regimes cannot change and the cold war cannot end. Reagan believed that communism and fascism were two expressions of the same Big Brother mentality that drove people to submit to the all-powerful centralized state. Yet the most interesting aspect of the idea of totalitarianism is not how Hitler's Germany and Stalin's Russia are similar but how they are different. One outstanding difference between fascism and communism is that the former comes and goes while the latter seems to stay forever. No fascist regime has ever survived the loss of its leader, whereas communist regimes remain in place regardless of who is in charge of the party or state. Reagan watched Brezhnev, Andropov, and Chernenko die within a few years of one another, and yet the Soviet Union continued on as though it had solved the secret of perpetual motion. Or did it?

Herewith a puzzle. Reagan, a political leader who believed that communism could not last, appointed as ambassador to the United Nations a scholar who believed it could. Kirkpatrick's thesis about totalitarianism came to be called the doctrine of irreversibility—once a communist system takes hold, there is no turning back and no way out, no possibility of change or reform. That view held through the mid-1980s, but once Reagan began negotiating with Gorbachev, *Commentary* expressed a quiver of doubt and published Revel's "Is Communism Reversible?" While a few neocons grew hopeful, many others remained doubtful, and the French author was firmly skeptical. "Despite what so many in the West appear to regard as an extremely easy process," he observed, referring to liberals, "we cannot name a single *completed* instance of Communist reversibility."[25]

The *Commentary* article appeared in January 1989. The month many neocons were denying that communism was reversible, Reagan left office, giving his farewell address. Usually modest, Reagan couldn't help but remark that he had hoped to bring change to America when he was elected and that, as it turned out, he brought change to the world as well. The neocon intellectuals failed to feel the changes taking place, or they misinterpreted them as false changes, intended to mislead the United States. Kirkpatrick's thesis must have been the most unsettling of all the positions; "Dictatorships and Double Standards" seemed to argue that the future was already over, that for the communist world history had come to an end in totalitarianism.

The collapse of communism caught not only neoconservatives by surprise but liberals as well. Throughout much of the cold war liberals had hoped there could be "a third way" between Soviet communism and Western capitalism.[26] If the pessimism of the neoconservatives misled them into assuming that communism was irreversible, the optimism of liberals misled them into assuming it was reformable. Gorbachev also thought so, and if his hopes proved wrong we may be thankful that at least he started the changes that led to the dissolution of an "evil empire" that even some Americans had once seen as the hope of humanity. "I've been over into the future," the popular journalist Lincoln Steffens said upon returning from the Soviet Union in 1920, "and it works." Two years later, Steffens visited Mussolini's Italy and told his readers that fascism also worked. The American Left liked the first message; the Right, the second.[27]

In the 1980s, it was a strange *mesalliance* between the president and the professors, the romantic dove and his conservative hawks. He saw history as open to change and freedom. They saw history as dark and foreboding, the liberal world too naïve to understand what needed to be done and the communist world forever stuck with communism, as though condemned by a curse. Fortunately for history, Reagan had ceased listening to his advisors and started listening to himself.

CHAPTER SEVEN

Into the Heart of Darkness: The Reagan Doctrine and the Third World

Words and Deeds

IF HISTORY TURNED on language alone, on words rather than deeds, there would be little grounds on which to criticize Ronald Reagan, the Great Communicator, whose admirers often equated his rhetoric with reality. However, here we encounter an awkward irony. Both radicals and conservatives are comfortable with what has come to be known as "the linguistic turn" in modern thought. Leftist practitioners of deconstruction wish to make us aware of how our understanding of things arises from language constructions, written texts or speeches, where words and expressions are all we can know by virtue of reading and listening. Some conservatives, surprisingly enough, would also have us focus on the text and nothing but the text. In *When Character Was King*, speechwriter Peggy Noonan's homage to Reagan, we are treated to lengthy passages from the president's two most famous addresses, which she hails as expressions of "the power of truth." The first was delivered to the British Parliament at Westminster in London, on June 8, 1982; the second was the "evil empire" speech, given, as we have seen, to a convention of the National Association of Evangelicals, on March 8, 1983.[1]

In the case of both speeches, Reagan later said that he had come to the conviction that it was time to take off the kid gloves, tell "the truth about" the Soviet Union, and lay down the Reagan doctrine, which he defined as supporting "those fighting for freedom against communism wherever we find them." The old era of polite, soft diplomacy aimed not to offend the Kremlin as the United States continued policies of containment and détente. Like an old prophet, Reagan could do no other than to rage against hypocrisy and mendacity.

To the members of Parliament, Reagan spoke of the Berlin Wall, "that dreadful gray gash across the city"; of the Solidarity movement in Poland and the "so-called new philosophers in France" (former Maoists shocked by Solzhenitsyn's *Gulag*); of the long historic struggle for world freedom, from the diaspora in Egypt, the stand at Thermopylae, the revolt of Spartacus, and the storming of the Bastille, to the Warsaw uprising and Churchill's heroics in World War II. Reagan also cited the dark record of contemporary history: the Soviets crushing the spark of freedom in East Germany in 1952, in Hungary in 1956, in Czechoslovakia in 1968, and in Poland in 1981. The Soviets must learn, Reagan exhorted, "that the very repressiveness of the state ultimately drives people to resist, if necessary, by force." Invoking the United Nations Universal Declaration of Human Rights, which guaranteed free elections, Reagan promised to work toward fostering in captive nations democracy's infrastructure, consisting of a free press, unions, political parties, and open universities. "This is not cultural imperialism, it is providing the means for genuine self-determination and protection for diversity. Democracy already flourishes in countries with very different cultures and historical experiences. It would be cultural condescension, or worse, to say that any people prefer dictatorship to democracy."

In his speech to the American evangelicals, Reagan spoke more of morality than of history. He challenged Lenin's claim that ethics is, in Reagan's words, "entirely subordinate to the interests of class war. And everything is moral that is necessary for the annihilation of the old, exploiting social order and for uniting the proletariat." To counter such tactics, Reagan invoked God against the Devil. "Yes, let us pray for the salvation of all of those who live in that totalitarian darkness—pray that they will discover the joy of knowing God. But until they do, let us be aware that while they preach the supremacy of the state, declare its omnipotence over individual man, and predict its eventual domination of all peoples on the Earth, they are the focus of evil in the modern world."

The "evil empire" speech upset many European allies. Even Margaret Thatcher, Reagan's closest supporter, "blanched" upon hearing the expression. What is interesting is that Reagan warned listeners that evil is not exceptional conduct but could very well be normal. As with Hannah Arendt's "banalty of evil," Reagan believed that ordinary people could carry out diabolical deeds almost without lifting a finger:

It was C. S. Lewis who, in his unforgettable *Screwtape Letters*, wrote: "The greatest evil is not done now in those sordid 'dens of crime' that Dickens loved to paint. It is not even done in concentration camps or labor camps. In those we see its final result. But it is conceived and ordered (moved, seconded, carried and minuted) in clean, carpeted, warmed, and well-lighted offices, by quiet men with white collars and cut fingernails and smooth-shaven cheeks who do not need to raise their voice."

Reagan's account attributed evil to the quiet workings of bureaucracy, to government functionaries who pushed papers from one desk to another and apprehended suspects for no other reason than that they were carrying out orders—the world of Franz Kafka. However, Reagan's real targets were those who barely knew the harm they do in doing good, especially the advocates of a nuclear freeze. "I urge you," declared Reagan, who could easily have had in mind his pacifist daughter Patti, "to beware the temptation of pride—the temptation of blithely declaring yourselves above it all and label [*sic*] both sides equally at fault, to ignore the facts of history and the aggressive impulses of an evil empire, to simply call the arms race a giant misunderstanding and thereby remove yourself from the struggle between right and wrong and good and evil."

In his important essay "Morality and the American Experience in the Cold War," Yale University historian John Lewis Gaddis has argued that Reagan rescued American foreign policy from "moral relativism" and "power politics" and returned it to the democratic idealism of human rights and national self-determination. "By 1989, there was a closer correspondence between traditional American ideals and the actual conduct of American diplomacy than at any other point since the Marshall Plan. The country did once again have a foreign policy it could be proud of, but it had achieved it under Ronald Reagan's watch." Gaddis assumed, as did many defenders of Reagan, that the proof of his foreign policy lay in words rather than actions; the reality was more troubling than the rhetoric.[2]

In 1982, the year the president told the British Parliament that he defined the Reagan doctrine as supporting "those fighting for freedom against communism wherever we find them," he chose not to find them

in Poland, to the dismay of Lane Kirkland, the leader of the AFL-CIO
who sought the White House's help in aiding Solidarity. For all of his
dedication to freedom, Reagan supported what he called friendly dictators, the leaders of right-wing regimes in Central America. His administration allowed the American ambassador in Honduras to deflect reports
of atrocities; called Jonas Savimbi the Abraham Lincoln of Angola,
though the rebel murdered and tortured his rivals, even bombing a Red
Cross hospital that was making artificial legs for victims of the mines he
had laid; clung to the autocratic government of Ferdinand Marcos in the
Philippines; sent Stinger shoulder-launched missiles to the Afghan
mujahideen, the very terrorists America would subsequently have to
hunt down; and supplied Iraq with materials to develop such weapons
as poison gas. The country would later blame Saddam Hussein for
killing tens of thousands of people with those weapons, and then find
him so dangerous as to justify America unilaterally launching a preemptive strike.

If such activities could be justified as necessary to support the anticommunist struggle in the third world, Reagan's conduct in the first
world seemed baffling when he was doing everything to reach a rapprochement with Gorbachev. In 1985, Reagan made a pilgrimage to
the Bitburg cemetery in Germany and inadvertently, but stubbornly,
paid homage to the Nazi Waffen SS. Reagan's anticommunism was so
febrile that he could convince himself he was defending the friends of
freedom when he was actually defending its foes. And conservatives
like Pat Buchanan urged him on, quite willing to wink at fascism in
order to win the war against communism. The biographer Lou Cannon
suggests the Bitburg fiasco was due to Reagan's traditional tenacity. As
in the past, he had made a commitment to make a speech, and when
it was pointed out to him that his appearance would be a political
embarrassment, he stuck to his commitment. Yet, as we shall see in
chapter 10, the Bitburg affair occurred just when European scholars
were debating fiercely whether the Germans were the victims of
Nazism or its willing accomplices. Whatever the answer, it is hard to
see the ceremony at the cemetery as evidence that Reagan rescued
American diplomacy from "moral relativism."

Of course, Reagan was no "fascist," as he was labeled by some of the
Hollywood Reds of the 1940s, or a mindless reactionary interested only

in power and clinging solely to the past. The fascist worships the state and hates democracy, the reactionary fears modernity and loves authority. All the same, the notion that the cold war ended because Reagan symbolized democratic freedom overthrowing totalitarian tyranny is a comfortable myth. The democratic impulse had long been challenging communism in Eastern Europe, and the Reagan administration hesitated to support openly the Czech and Polish dissident movements, understandable in light of Reagan's effort to work with Gorbachev. In his memoir, however, Reagan expressed the same reluctance to support the Chinese students in the Tiananmen Square massacre of 1989, fearing they were rash in wanting to bring down communism. "I understood and sympathized with them," he wrote, "but I knew there were people in their government trying slowly to increase democracy and freedom in China, and the students' revolt, as courageous as it was, might in the long run have made it more difficult for them to carry out what they were trying to do."[3]

Not the students' revolt but the subsequent crackdown made it impossible for democratic reformers to have any influence in communist China. Many of them were jailed. Gorbachev had visited China just as students and workers were massing at Tiananmen, and he, unlike Reagan, supported the students and urged his communist hosts to consider the changes the young were demanding. Deng Xiaoping, however, saw Gorbachev losing control in Russia precisely because he tried to carry out *perestroika* and *glasnost* at the same time. Economic restructuring and political opening could not occur together, Deng believed. That China could proceed simultaneously with economic liberalization and political repression complicated Reagan's conservative vision of freedom as the product of a market economy.

In his speeches spelling out America's new cold war doctrine, Reagan surveyed history from classical antiquity to the present, dramatizing the courageous struggles against oppression and the tragic setbacks. Curiously, Adolf Hitler, the Third Reich, and Nazism in general rarely figured in Reagan's account of modern history, though he did mention the Warsaw uprising of 1944. At the Geneva summit in 1985, Reagan speculated that the United States and the USSR would unite with each other in the face of an invasion from outer space. When the perplexed Gorbachev, thinking the president was indulging in Hollywood fantasy, changed the subject, Reagan thought he had made a point, but some of his staff wondered whether his remark about an extraterrestrial military force was sheer delusion. A national security advisor reassured them that he was referring to Hitler, the fascist freak of nature who would arrive to unite the United States and the USSR as they had been united during World War II. Small comfort to Gorbachev, who could only remember how America stood by in the thirties while Germany rearmed to invade Russia.

Even more perplexing is Reagan's claim that "Democracy already flourishes in countries with very different cultures and historical experiences" and that it would be a matter of "cultural condescension" to believe otherwise. On the contrary, in the modern Western world, all democratic cultures took their intellectual inspiration from the eighteenth-century Enlightenment, and in the third world only those colonies that were once part of the British empire have enjoyed democracy. Democracy rarely springs from the mystique of free elections alone but evolves from the historical development of constitutions and the rule of law, institutions that provide procedures to guarantee the exercise of rights and make freedom possible. When America became involved in South Asia, the Middle East, Africa, and East Asia, Reagan was attempting to bring democracy to regions where it never took root. To bring the spirit of Tom Paine to Russia (where Catherine the Great welcomed the Enlightenment) was one thing; to bring it Afghanistan, Iraq, Lebanon, Angola, and Cambodia quite another.[4]

Reagan's speeches read like perorations. Yet the moving language may belie the historic context. Even if words themselves convey "the power of truth," they must be measured against the vicissitudes of reality. If the Soviet Union was the "focus of evil in the modern world," and opposition to it became the "struggle between right and wrong and good and evil," must anticommunism, wherever America found it, always be right and good? Until the cold war, the campaign against communism was waged by fascist Italy and Nazi Germany, regimes whose people preferred a duce to democracy and a führer to freedom. To reverse Orwell's formulation, the conservative wanted to be anticommunist without being antitotalitarian.

When Reagan took office in January 1981, America was well into the second cold war. If the first cold war ended in a stalemate in Europe, with the forces of NATO and those of the Warsaw Pact poised against one another, the second cold war was waged in the turbulent third world, where insurgencies and counterinsurgencies seemed to break out everywhere. Speaking to evangelicals in Florida, Reagan denounced communism for treating morality as an instrument of class war. A Leninist, he insisted, is convinced that what is good promotes the cause of the proletariat and that what is bad thwarts it. On the contrary, Reagan held, morality must become an instrument of the anticommunist struggle. America's allies stood for what was right and good and their antagonists for what was wrong and evil. Yet in Afghanistan the CIA supported Islamic "freedom fighters," whose jihadist followers would later highjack jet airliners and crash them into the World Trade Center and the Pentagon. America also supported Saddam Hussein (as did Russia and France) with materials enabling Iraq to carry out chemical warfare against Iran and the Kurds. If, as Henry Adams observed, politics has no time for truth, diplomacy has less time for morality.

The cold war may have ended on a happy note at the end of the 1980s when Reagan and Gorbachev negotiated disarmament treaties and communism collapsed. Throughout the decade, however, another war was carried out in the third world, where fighting against communism was all that counted, no matter what the cause, whether for freedom or for Allah, power, oil, gold, diamonds, or opium. In deserts, mountains, and jungles American morality descended into the heart of darkness.

Afghanistan: Massoud, the Lion of Panjshir; Osama bin Laden, "Islam Is Coming"

THE CARTER ADMINISTRATION had little hesitation in coming to the aid of Afghanistan after the Soviet Union invaded the country on Christmas Day, 1979. At first the United States covertly supplied only medical kits and small arms to tribal warlords. However, some liberal Democrats and many conservative Republicans viewed the invasion as the first stage of Soviet penetration into the Middle East and its valuable oil fields. Saudi Arabia, already unnerved by the fall of Iran's shah, feared the royal family might be the next victim of communist expansion. Saudi leaders began a campaign to convince the CIA to send money and supplies to Afghanistan through Pakistan. With Saudi and American money, Islamic fundamentalists were supported throughout the Middle East, and they convinced the State Department that Islam's war against Marxist atheism was America's war against Soviet Communism.[5]

Ronald Reagan also saw the war in Afghanistan through this prism, and his simple categories of good and evil blinded him and much of the American public to what was really going on in the Middle East: Islam's war against communism was a war against liberalism in general. What Islam wanted to defeat was Western modernity.

The Soviet Union had no great trouble imposing modernity on the surrounding countries of Uzbekistan, Tajikistan, and Kazakhstan, transforming rural Islamic environments into godless police regimes. In Afghanistan's capital, Kabul, however, local communists and the Soviet KGB engaged in bloody struggles with the native populace over political power and cultural control. When the communists prevailed, they embarked on a terror campaign against religious and political leaders, jailing thousands and executing hundreds. Pressing for secular reforms, they started a literacy program for girls, abolished dowries for brides, allowed freedom of choice in marriage, confiscated large land holdings, and mandated universal education based on the dogmas of Marxism.

The attempt by the secularists to convert the Afghans to communism provoked a violent reaction. Reagan would see Afghanistan as the theater of the cold war, and neocons like Norman Podhoretz insisted that the turmoil in the country represented the "forward surge of Soviet imperialism." The situation was far more complex. Russia, a country that had not allowed capitalism to develop, was trying to impose communism on a country that wanted neither communism nor capitalism. Afghanistan would fight for its own culture and religion. The Brezhnev government was more surprised by the ferocious Afghans than the Reagan administration was alarmed by the Soviet surge. "Afghan resistance to the regime," write Christopher Andrew and Vasili Mitrokhin, was "transformed into a *jihad* in defence of Islam whose significance was grossly underestimated by the KGB."[6]

An Afghan army captain, the charismatic Ismail Khan, organized a jihad against the communists in the city of Herat. His followers tracked down and hacked to death a dozen communist officials, including their wives and children. On the city streets long pikes were waved high, displaying dangling Russian corpses. From Kabul came Soviet-trained pilots flying bomber jets that devastated Herat. Ismail Khan escaped the city to continue the rebellion in the countryside. In Russia, leading party officials recognized that Afghan communists had tried to push things too far and too quickly and as a result had produced a counterrevolution. The Soviets replaced the leader of the Afghan communists, and, fearing that the CIA had been stirring up the Afghan resistance, they dispatched planes and tanks to Kabul. With the invasion, Pakistan, Saudi Arabia, and other regimes sought to convince the CIA that Russia was carrying out an historic ambition to capture the Straits of Hormuz and that the oil-rich Persian Gulf, which the British empire once protected, would fall to communism. Yet nothing in the Soviet archives, released since the fall of communism, indicates that the Afghan invasion was a staging point for a Soviet advance into the Middle East.[7]

Reagan moved prudently in Afghanistan. After Vietnam and Watergate, the CIA worried about being discovered in secret political struggles and violent clandestine operations. In Afghanistan the United States would at first stick to what Steve Coll has called "its legal authority: mules, money, and mortars." The invasion caught the CIA by surprise, and while the agency and the State Department sought to aid the guerrilla resistance, the *mujahideen*, the question was how to do so. The administration told Henry Hart, its CIA officer in Islamabad, a bright multilinguist with considerable experience in the Middle East: "You're a young man; here's your bag of money, go raise hell. Don't fuck it up, just go out there and kill Soviets, and take care of the Pakistanis and make them do whatever you need them to do." The rules of engagement were such that American money went through Pakistan, which meant to the militarist Mohammed Zia-ul-Haq, bitter rival of India, the only democratic country in South Asia. Hart recommended that the Pakistanis put a bounty on every soldier killed by the *mujahideen*.[8]

Whether the Reagan administration believed that the resistance could drive the Soviets out of Afghanistan or simply make the occupation costly was a debated issue. Some believed that the president could have put more emphasis on diplomacy to compel the Soviets to leave; others advocated more covert operations. For CIA director William

Casey, the Afghan war was a dream come true. He delighted in the alliances forged among America, the Saudis, Pakistan, and the Afghan rebels. He reminded his staff of how cost effective it was to pay for others to do America's fighting and the vast amounts of money Russia was pouring into what he saw as a lost cause. Unlike the later Reagan, who wanted to sit down and talk with Gorbachev, Casey refused to believe that the cold war would come to an end over a negotiating table, with the two sides bargaining about disarmament terms. He looked to the third world as the final showdown. "Here's the beauty of the Afghan operation," he told colleagues. "Usually it looks like the big bad Americans are beating up on the little guys. We don't make it our war. The *mujahideen* have all the motivation they need. All we have to do is give them help, only more of it."[9]

Another enthusiast for the Afghan war was Charlie Wilson, an influential Texas congressman who saw himself, in his heady moments, as a Lawrence of Arabia, albeit less ascetic and more alcoholic. Wilson frequently met with Zia at the Khyber Pass to gaze down upon the valley and dream about the glories of desert warfare. He traveled first class, usually drunk and accompanied by former beauty queens, and stayed at swanky hotels, all at government expense. He knew little about Afghan history, but his "whiskey-soaked romanticism," to use Steve Coll's phrase, led him to envision the *mujahideen* as noble warriors carrying out Reagan's war against the secular Satan of communism. Starting in 1984, the representative obtained from Congress increasing funds to transfer to the CIA's classified Afghan budget. At the time Congress was more divided about the civil war in Nicaragua than the struggle in Afghanistan. Wilson's pleas to Congress played upon a bad conscience: Because the *mujahideen* have the courage to fight to the last man, he exhorted, it is up to America to provide them with the means not simply to endure but to win and prevail. CIA director Casey thrilled to the pleas.[10]

But the annals of history offered little encouragement. Prussia's Frederick the Great, France's Napoleon, and Hitler were all unable to emerge victorious over mighty Russia. What chance had poor, backward, feudal Afghanistan? The obvious answer is that the Afghans had no need to defeat Russia but simply had to drive Soviet forces out of their homeland, just as the Vietnamese drove America out of theirs. Proclaiming themselves liberators, the Soviets roamed the streets of Kabul, a brutal force of occupation—the worst position for the promise of liberation.

Reagan's passion for free will had no patience with fate and defeat, and Afghanistan seemed the proper battleground for a struggle against communism. In the mountains and valleys of Afghanistan, however, the lust for vengeance had less to do with the cause of freedom and liberation than with the will to power and domination. The *mujahideen* had several charismatic leaders, none more legendary than Ahmed Shah Massoud, a brilliant young warrior steeped in the writings of Mao Zedong, Che Guevara, and the French theorist of revolution, Régis Debray. Massoud came to be called the Lion of Panjshir for the mountaintop tactics he used to block the Panjshir valley below, the only reliable overland supply route between the USSR and Kabul. Repeatedly Massoud and his men destroyed Russian tanks, captured convoys, and brought back supplies to his forces living in the caves above.

Another legendary figure was Osama bin Laden, son of an enormously rich Saudi family, the "heaven-sent man" who lived to organize jihads and announce that Islam was coming. The CIA was wary of bin Laden and hesitated to supply him with arms. Saudi wealth and American money passing through Pakistan helped him establish camps for Arab volunteers so that the Muslim Brotherhood, Islamic militants united against the West, could carry out the war against the infidel. Soft-spoken and mild-mannered, bin Laden was not a great orator but a superb organizer who arranged for money, food, trucks, tractors, and medicine to be shipped to the Afghan resistance. Years before he became known as the world's most famous terrorist, he was regarded as a humanitarian and one of the "authentic freedom fighters."[11]

But appearances were deceiving. Bin Laden and other *mujahideen* leaders were influenced by the writings of Sayyid Qutb, a young Egyptian radical who spent time in a jail cell while awaiting execution for writing a tract that formulated a Leninist strategy for Islamic revolution. Qutb called for a strict party dictatorship to direct secret conspiratorial cells. He had visited Colorado to study American education, but he came away with a deep repugnance for the United States, complaining about its rampant materialism, obsession with sex and cheap amusements, tawdry films and dance halls, drunken barrooms, and abiding

loyalty to Israel. "Humanity today is living in a large brothel!" he protested of the American way of life. The Hollywood that gave Reagan such
fond memories reminded Qutb of a whorehouse. Qutb and his devoted
followers saw in Christianity and Zionism forces that would annihilate
Islam through their cultural hegemony if not through politics and warfare. But Qutb and bin Laden had one thing in common with Reagan
and America's neoconservatives: They wanted to see religion restored to
public life. Their enemy was liberalism as practiced by Ataturk, the
reformer who secularized Turkey in the early twentieth century, or by the
American founders, deists who separated church from state.[12]

While the Reagan administration knew little about the religious culture of Afghanistan, some hard-line neocons saw the *mujahideen* as fellow religious believers fighting against the same encroachments of secularism. In 1982, the Heritage Foundation's James Phillips declared:
"The Afghans' courage is fortified by traditional Islamic beliefs; if he kills
an enemy in the jihad (holy war) and is revered as a *ghazi* (Islamic warrior) and if he falls in battle he becomes a *shaheed* (martyr) who reaps
great rewards in paradise." The description is accurate, but those once
seen as America's allies have become the suicidal terrorists of today.[13]

When Reagan left office in 1989, he was unaware of the deadly forces
that the Afghan war had unleashed. Neither was his vice president,
George H. W. Bush, who would organize a coalition to drive Iraq out of
Kuwait in the first Gulf War in 1991; nor was Bush's son, who claimed
in 2003 that the Islamic world would welcome America as liberators. It
was Osama bin Laden who desired to lead that first campaign against
Iraq. Bin Laden returned from Afghanistan to Saudi Arabia to plead with
the royal family to allow him to take charge of destroying Saddam Hussein and his secular regime. Instead the Saudis supported the United
States, letting it establish army camps and air bases in Saudi Arabia, a
sacrilege to bin Laden. Throughout the 1990s the CIA was aware that
bin Laden posed a threat to America's foreign bases and its embassies,
and to the homeland. The CIA even sent supplies to Massoud in support of the Northern Alliance against bin Laden and the Taliban. On
September 10, 2001, bin Laden's disguised agents, on the pretext of
interviewing Massoud, exploded a bomb in his headquarters, assassinat-
ing the hero of the Afghan resistance. The next day, in New York City
and Washington, D.C., came the horror.[14]

Most Americans reacted to the horror of September 11 with bitter incomprehension, deeply puzzled that there could possibly be any motive for the attack, completely unaware that the forces their country armed to drive out the Russians from Afghanistan were the forces America refused to support to drive out the Iraqis from Kuwait. Two decades before September 11, in 1999, President Reagan's biggest decision regarding Afghanistan had little to do with ideology and everything to do with weaponry. Following the invasion of Afghanistan and its occupation at the start of the Reagan administration in 1981, the Soviets dominated the air and pulverized the rebels on the ground, who had only rifles and heavy machine guns. The *mujahideen* pleaded for effective antiaircraft weapons. America had developed the Stinger missile, a shoulder-placed launcher with shells that could track and explode bombers and helicopters. The missiles cost only sixty thousand dollars each, and one firing could bring down a twenty-million-dollar Russian MIG, but the CIA worried about the consequences of supplying such weapons covertly to the Afghans. The State Department anticipated an uproar against weapons made in America to kill Soviet soldiers, and Colin Powell reported that the Joint Chiefs of Staff feared the missiles might fall into the hands of terrorists who would use them to shoot down commercial airliners. In the end, however, conservative politicians pressured Secretary of State Shultz to approve sending the Stingers.[15]

U.S. involvement in the Afghan war reflected a series of misperceptions and failures of judgment by the Reagan administration. Although the *mujahideen* were authentic antagonists of the Soviet Union, it was discovered that the Afghan rebels sold some of the Stingers to Iran, suggesting an alliance between the Islamic regimes. On two occasions Iranian boats opened fired on American helicopters with these Stingers, which were rumored to have made their way to the Taliban and al-Qaeda. While the neocons influencing Reagan saw events in Afghanistan and in Iran as evidence of an inevitable march of communism, what was really unfolding were events of an entirely different nature. The fall of the shah of Iran and Russia's march into Kabul were not "the present danger" (as in the neocon thesis) that America would immediately have to face but a future danger; and it was not of a communism that was on the wane but of a fundamentalism that was on the rise. America chose as allies a group of men in cave redoubts who would prove they were freedom fighters by detonating two massive ancient statues of Buddha.[16]

Misjudgments about Russia proved even more telling. The Stinger became the symbol of America's historic success in defeating Soviet aggression in the Middle East, but the decision to send missiles to Afghanistan was made in March 1986, long after Gorbachev made clear his intention to withdraw Russian troops. Even as early as 1984, before he was in power, Gorbachev declared the war a "mistake," and in his memoirs he termed Afghanistan a "hopeless military adventure." Evidence now shows that Gorbachev decided to withdraw from the war the moment he was appointed general secretary in March 1985. All of this remained unknown to the administration, some of whose members confidently placed bets that Russia would never leave Afghanistan before Reagan left office. America's intelligence services proved inadequate in Afghanistan as well as in other episodes of the cold war, including the failure to foresee the coming collapse of Soviet communism. Reagan may have had poor eyesight, but, compared to the CIA on the Soviet Union, he had better vision.[17]

The Middle East:
"A Disordered Mind"

"BILL," REAGAN WROTE to William F. Buckley in January 1984, "the Middle East is a complicated place—well not really a place, it's more a state of mind. A disordered mind." Yet America could not withdraw, the president told Buckley. "There would be instant chaos if a wrong or precipitate move is made. I could use all the cliches— 'walking a thin line,' 'juggling with too many balls in the air,' and so on and so on. The truth is most of the cliches would fit the situation. Let me just say, there is reason why [we] are there."[18]

What was the reason? The Reagan doctrine hardly applied to the Middle East. Iran and Iraq were not fighting communism; they were fighting each other, and America felt it had to get involved, on the side of a regime it would be fighting two decades later.

The rise of Iran's Ayatollah Khomeini in 1979 brought to power a fierce Shia Islam with a long-standing enmity toward Iraq's Saddam Hussein and the country's Sunni Muslims and his own Baath Party. The Baathists were secularists who once saw themselves as the Mideastern expression of Italian fascism. In 1980, a bloody war broke out between Iran and Iraq that lasted eight years, the length of the two Reagan administrations. The administration tried to present a stance of neutrality, but neocon advisors worried that Iran might turn out to be the terrain through which Russia marched into the Persian Gulf, and they urged Reagan to support Iraq to protect Saudi Arabia and other oil sources. Ambassador Jeane Kirkpatrick had advised that America should always side with an authoritarian moderate regime against an impervious totalitarian system. Apparently Hussein was the rational autocrat and Khomeini the totalitarian fanatic.

Reagan's special envoy to Iraq was Donald Rumsfeld, who joined Vice President Bush in embracing Hussein and secretly supplying the dictator with whatever he asked for in his fight against the Kurds, Iranians, and other opponents. Reagan instructed Rumsfeld and other officials to do whatever was "necessary and legal" to support Iraq and prevent Iran and its Shia allies in eastern Saudi Arabia and elsewhere in the Mideast from dominating the distribution of oil. A national security directive of November 23, 1983, aided the counterinsurgency campaign with money and materials (anthrax, botulinum toxin, tabun, a lethal nerve gas, cluster bombs) with which Iraq was able to develop and use chemical weapons, resulting in the systematic slaughter of one hundred thousand people. When stories of the atrocities reached the press and the world reacted in horror, the U.S. Department of State launched an "Iran, too" gambit, claiming that both sides used poison gas. "It was a horrible mistake," observed Kenneth Pollack, author of The Threatening Storm. "My fellow CIA analysts and I were warning at the time that Saddam Hussein was a very nasty character. We were constantly fighting the State Department." The abuse of human rights and the ghastly spectacle of genocide seemed to have left Reagan's neocon advisors coldly unmoved.[19]

The United States became even further involved in the Iran-Iraq war in 1987, when American naval vessels escorted Kuwait's oil ships through waters mined by Iran. On May 17 an Iraqi missile struck the USS Stark, a navy frigate operating in the Persian Gulf. After Iran attacked foreign tankers, several European countries sent mine sweepers to the region. While America was scuffling with Arab powers on the seas, Iran, Iraq, and Syria were sending soldiers to Afghanistan to fight the Holy War against the Soviet Union.

One of the most troublesome Arab states that Reagan had to deal with was Libya, and its leader, Muammar Qaddafi, a flamboyant figure who delighted in taunting America and was rumored to be behind terrorist activities in cities ranging from Chicago to London. The Reagan administration ordered the Libyan embassy in Washington closed, and Defense Secretary Weinberger recommended that the Sixth Fleet resume its annual exercises in the Gulf of Sidra. Qaddafi had claimed that the entire gulf was Libya's territorial waters and that it would repel any intruder crossing a "line of death." In August 1981, Libyan combat planes fired on two U.S. F-14s on aerial maneuvers sixty miles off the Libyan coast. After a quick dogfight with America's top gunners, Qaddafi's aircraft went down in flames.

In 1986, investigators concluded that Libyan terrorists were responsible for planting a bomb in a Berlin disco that killed an American serviceman. In retaliation, Reagan ordered U.S. Air Force and Navy bombers stationed in London to attack the Libyan cities of Tripoli and Benghazi. The bombs struck Qaddafi's residence, killing his adopted two-year-old daughter and wounding two of his sons. The strongman, sleeping in a tent outside, escaped injury. Many civilians were killed in the raid, which was widely criticized. "I don't believe you stop terrorism by killing 150 Libyans who have done nothing," protested French president François Mitterrand. However, the raid on Libya was popular with a certain segment of the American people because it indicated that Reagan would take action rather than settle for denunciation. Even some Europeans were happy at last to see a country respond rather than quail before international terrorism.[20]

Almost every modern president comes to office resolved to try to stay as far as possible from the problems of the Middle East. Yet they all (Truman, Eisenhower, Nixon, Carter, Bush, Clinton, the second Bush) found themselves bogged down in the land of the supposedly "disordered mind." Reagan was no exception. His obsession with the menace of communism everywhere in the world led him to believe that America had a constructive role to play in working with Israel, Egypt, and Saudi

Arabia to thwart any Soviet designs in the region. Like other presidents, yet for different reasons, Reagan allowed himself to be dragged into the festering morass of the Middle East, the most tragic blunder of his administration. In his speech to Parliament, Reagan claimed that the war against communism was a war for democracy. In the Middle East, the many endless wars among the diverse factions were about neither communism nor democracy. The region festered with religious rivalries, struggles over land and oil, territorial boundaries, and other geostrategic objectives. The Reagan doctrine, intended for the cold war, had no capacity to adapt to wars that had no class basis or secular objectives. No wonder Reagan would despair of America's having lost hundreds of its young soldiers in Lebanon, a calamity that haunted him the rest of his life.

"The last temptation is the greatest treason: to do the right deed for the wrong reason," wrote T. S. Eliot in *Murder in the Cathedral*. Reagan's involvement in the Middle East reverses the poet: The right reason was his long, abiding support of Israel and the Jewish people. Reagan never forgot how his father refused to stay in a hotel that did not allow Jews. After World War II, horrified by the Holocaust, he supported the establishment of the State of Israel, denounced anti-Semitism in his radio broadcasts, and once almost came to blows at a party when a guest accused Jews of war profiteering. His reasons were right, his actions the problem.

When Reagan took office in January 1981, Israel and Yasser Arafat's Palestine Liberation Organization (PLO) had been engaged in a ferocious war in Lebanon. In an attempt to wipe out the PLO, Israel crossed the Lebanese frontier with tanks and jet fighters and launched a punishing bombardment of Beirut. Reagan rebuked Israeli prime minister Menachem Begin, canceled future sales of F-16 fighter planes to Israel, and proposed to solve the conflict by allowing Palestinians to have a zone of self-rule in neighboring Jordan. However, the Palestinians sought an independent state in Gaza and the West Bank, and the Israelis would settle for nothing less than having the territories they annexed in war recognized as legitimate settlements.

Although Israel withdrew from Lebanon in the summer of 1982, the country remained a cauldron of violence and instability, and Israel returned later in the year. The Maronite Christians sided with the

Israelis, who again fostered attacks on the PLO. In particular, Reagan learned that the Phalangists, a Christian Maronite party, had been massacring Palestinian women and children as well as soldiers in refugee camps. Then, on April 18, 1983, sixty-three people lost their lives when the U.S. embassy in Beirut was bombed. Druze forces were also beginning to shell the city from mountain heights, and Syrian terrorists had entered Lebanon with plans of their own. In Beirut bombs exploded every hour, blood covered the streets, and ambulances screamed through the city.

The Reagan administration agonized over what to do about the lesion of Lebanon. It was not enough to denounce the atrocities on all sides, as Reagan first did when he telephoned Prime Minister Begin and called Lebanon a "holocaust" that must end. "Mr. President," Begin replied sarcastically, "I think I know what a Holocaust is." Begin did call off Israel's attacks, suggesting to Reagan that his demands carried more weight than he realized. The question was whether to use power and how. The Reagan administration found itself so divided that the president's advisors could barely speak to one another.[21]

Those who worked in the Reagan administration have written about his apparent passivity in the midst of the deepest controversies. Perhaps memories of the tempestuous ways of his alcoholic father led him to shrink from open conflict in the presence of others. "What they saw," wrote Lou Cannon of Reagan's advisors, "was a president who hated discord but lacked the means of achieving consensus." Reagan could think for himself in the privacy of his study, but he avoided thinking aloud in the midst of a room full of contentious protagonists. The two most antagonistic were Shultz and Weinberger, and here one encounters a curious reversal of roles.[22]

Shultz had an analytical, managerial mind, and as secretary of state he most often chose the route of negotiation. Weinberger came from a legal background, and the defense secretary believed in quickly taking a position and defending it. However, in the Lebanon crisis, it was Shultz the diplomatic broker who called for sending in the marines and Weinberger the militarist advocate of massive arms development who recommended restraint. Shultz had served in World War II, and as a former marine he saw U.S. forces as a tool of diplomacy. Weinberger and his assistant, Colin Powell, remembered the Vietnam War and concluded that it would be difficult for America to defend any foreign intervention that lacked the support of the American people. After some vacillation, Reagan sided with Shultz and, in late August 1982, ordered American marines to join a multinational force (MNF) of French paratroopers and Italian contingents to interpose themselves between 30,000 Israeli troops and 15,000 Syrian and Palestinian soldiers. The American marines landed on the beaches of Lebanon to the surprise of sun-tanned, bikini-clad bathers.

At first Reagan's policy seemed a success, as Syrian and Palestinian troops withdrew from Beirut and the Lebanese government appeared to gain control of the situation. The marines even returned to their troop ships in the harbor. However, on September 14, 1983, the Maronite Christian leader Bashir Gemayel fell victim to a bomb explosion just before he was to assume the presidency of Lebanon. Immediately, Israeli troops reentered West Beirut, in defiance of an agreement that had evacuated the PLO. Street fighting broke out, with mass slaughter of civilians, pictures on television of mutilated victims, and mental images of Nazi atrocities. The Reagan policy appeared to be in shambles as demands arose for the MNF to return to Beirut. Some of Reagan's staff, including the joint chiefs, opposed redeploying the marines no matter how horrid the massacres. Reagan felt that, in refusing help, America would avoid its responsibility to take "actions we can and must take to bring that nightmare to an end." He had the support of Congress, whose members believed that the trouble began when the marines left Beirut and that it could be resolved by sending them back. Weinberger remained adamantly opposed, claiming that Reagan was being manipulated with the Hollywood line that "Marines don't cut and run."[23]

The returning marines managed to help Lebanese forces successfully put down insurgents, but Americans were then looked upon by the Druze, Palestinians, and Syrians as the heathen enemy. On the early morning of Sunday, October 23, 1983, a marine barracks was stormed by a truck loaded with bombs, which violently exploded, tearing the building from its foundation and killing 241 marines and navy personnel. A similar attack close by against France's military installation killed fifty-nine people. It was the greatest loss of life in one day that America had suffered since the Vietnam War.

Reagan was sickened when he heard the news, reeling with doubt

about his judgment, his eyes staring painfully down at a carpet. Weinberger, grieving that he had not tried to be more persuasive, suggested
that the attack on the barracks be blamed on marine officers for failing to
guard the compound. Reagan accepted full responsibility for the tragedy.
He and Nancy attended the funeral services at Camp Lejeune in North
Carolina. Years later, in his memoirs, he regretted that "we didn't appreciate fully enough the depth of hatred and complexity of problems that
make the Middle East such a jungle." October 23 was the "saddest day
of my life." "The sending of marines to Beirut was the source of my greatest regret and my greatest sorrow as president." To parents who wrote him
seeking comfort that their son did not die in vain in Beirut, Reagan could
only say that the marines had died in the cause of peace.[24]

The president refused to admit to himself and to the country that the
decision to send in the marines was a colossal miscalculation. He even
tried to describe the mission as a success. "The multinational force was
attacked precisely because it is doing the job it was sent to do in Beirut."
Reagan turned on his Hollywood best and waxed sentimental about
America's presence in the Middle East. "We arrived and were well
received by the people there," he told the press of Beirut. "As a matter
of fact, our marines in the typical American military fashion pretty soon
were organizing helpful things for kids, teaching them to play ball and
all other sorts of things." The truth was that, after the massacre, marines
had to go into hiding. "They lived like moles," a U.S. defense attaché
reported.[25]

Some in the Reagan administration recognized Lebanon for the
tragedy that it was. The saddened Shultz remarked that if ever again he
were to say, "Send in the marines," someone should take him out and
shoot him. Although Reagan told William Buckley that America had
good reason to be in the Middle East and described Lebanon in particular as of "vital interest," a few doubted Lebanon was of any interest
whatsoever. "If Lebanon had disappeared," noted advisor Robert McFarlane, distressed at having recommending that the marines go in, "it
wouldn't affect the United States' security interests very much."[26]

Although some members of Congress complained about "the stupidity of the original decision," Reagan escaped public criticism for one of
the most tragic disasters in American military history since Pearl Harbor.
He did seem to be the "Teflon" president, the phrase coined by Con-

gresswoman Pat Schroeder to suggest that no stigma could stick to the man. Americans were easy on Reagan's failure in Lebanon perhaps because of an apparent smashing success closer to home. Three days after the strike in Beirut, the president announced that America would send troops to the tiny Caribbean island nation of Grenada. The reason the invasion was necessary was perfectly clear: communism, exactly what was never a menacing presence in the Middle East.[27]

The "Sordid Truth" about Angola

LONG BEFORE GEORGE W. BUSH allowed reference to the "axis of evil" to become associated with the war on terrorism, CIA director Casey had referred to the "Soviet, Libyan, Cuban axis in Africa" to describe the war on communism. *Webster's* defines an axis as "a real or imaginary straight line passing through a body that actually or supposedly revolves upon it." In cold war parlance, the body was the Soviet Union, and the straight lines that it revolved upon were those countries that functioned as its satellites and those about to fall to a communist coup.[28]

Armed with the axis metaphor, conservative Republicans saw communism almost everywhere in the world, making little distinction between a Muslim sect and a Marxist splinter. Even when two brands of communism were vying with each other for power, America saw only the axis and missed the antagonist. Such was the case in Cambodia when the Vietcong communists, shortly after the end of the war in Vietnam in the mid-1970s, invaded to put down Pol Pot and the Khmer Rouge. To Reagan and the neoconservatives, such a move could only mean that the dominoes, those mental images that never fell as predicted when America pulled out of Vietnam, were now toppling over as Vietnamese troops marched northward and crossed the border into Cambodia. The United States tentatively and briefly sided with the genocidal Khmer Rouge as the CIA desperately searched for alternative factions to support. In Cambodia the "killing fields" took over a million lives. The origins of the tragedy occurred before Reagan took office, but he used it to argue for the correctness of his cold war policies.

Anarchy in Africa also predated the Reagan presidency. When a civil war broke out in central Africa in the late 1970s, the CIA suspected trouble, especially when Fidel Castro dispatched Cuban troops to Angola. Among Reagan's neocon advisors, it was an axiomatic, unquestionable, absolute article of truth that Cuban soldiers were "proxies" for the Soviet Union, sent there on the orders of Leonid Brezhnev. The conflict in Angola became a symbol of the cold war spilling over into the third world, even into dimly understood tribal cultures.

Angola was a Portuguese colony barely surviving though rich in resources. It was badly administered only because Portugal was so poor. It had fared better than Congo, a Belgian colony brutalized by Western European powers. In the late nineteenth century King Leopold II of Belgium authorized the plundering of lands surrounding the Congo River. Unlike the British, the Belgians had no goal, as patronizing as it was, of educating the African populace in preparation for democracy and self-government. Belgium went in solely to take out Congo's rich resources, to extract, dominate, and oppress. Congo was a squalid example that Angola was imitating. In central Africa, capitalism had no conscience, thereby making communism a preferable alternative to some native African leaders more interested in exploiting their people than educating them. After World War II the disappearance of European empires in Asia and Africa took place within a generation. Except for British territories, European colonialism left behind a hellish residue of fear, poverty, and brutality.

Reagan accepted completely the "proxy" myth about Angola. When, as we have seen, he asked Brezhnev if Cuba was better off because the Cuban military intervened in Angola, Reagan assumed that Brezhnev could compel Castro to remove his troops, since presumably the Soviets had ordered him to put them in Angola in the first place. He also assumed that the communists in Africa were the first to make a move to obtain total power in the civil war. How accurate were these assumptions?[29]

In Angola the CIA advised Reagan to support Jonas Savimbi's UNITA, an opposition movement to the existing Marxist government that was defended by Cuban troops. At first Reagan's efforts to provide assistance were blocked by the Clark Amendment, passed in 1976, barring all aid to insurgent factions in Angola. In 1985, however, the House voted for its repeal, and Reagan was able to send Savimbi fifteen millions dollars of annual covert support.

Jonas Malheiro Savimbi was as colorful as he was controversial. A powerful orator, his speeches rang with the missionary zeal of a prayer meeting. He spoke a half-dozen languages and had studied at European universities. At a time in African history when many tribal leaders drove their silver Mercedeses to their banks, the charismatic Savimbi was in the fields organizing the bush people. Liberals regarded him as an African Uncle Tom and CIA puppet who was willing to accept support from South Africa's apartheid regime. However, in the 1960s Savimbi went to China to meet with Mao Zedong and to learn how to build revolutionary movements among the peasants. He also encountered Che Guevara in Dar es Salaam at an African liberation conference. He debated with the legendary figure and concluded that Che's theory of revolutionary leaders operating from a stationary camp outside the country was elitist, the "superiority complex of the outsider." It was Savimbi's deep roots in the emotions of the local populace that made his UNITA a strong counterforce to the arrival of Cuban and Russian troops in Angola. While Savimbi was receiving 500 tons of arms from China, he was also hailed as an ally of America by the Reagan administration.

Savimbi was just what the neocons were waiting for—a third world leader who would take communism away from the communists by adopting their guerrilla strategy and using it against them. Conservative think tanks talked excitedly about the possibility of organizing an "Anti-Communist International" led by Savimbi's rebels, the Afghan *mujahideen*, and Nicaragua's Contras. It would be the Reagan doctrine's answer to the Brezhnev doctrine, which had maintained that the Soviet Union had the right to intervene in any communist country seen to be backsliding from the party line. In a trip to Washington in 1981, Savimbi was introduced by Ambassador Kirkpatrick as "a linguist, philosopher, poet, politician, warrior . . . one of the few authentic heroes of our time," an anticommunist who needed all the help America could give him.[30]

In Reagan's eyes, Jonas Savimbi could well have been the Tom Paine of Africa. Both black and white leaders saw themselves fighting against colonialism. Although Savimbi was a nationalist and Paine a universalist, each saw his land being exploited by the mother countries. What

Britain had done to Americans in the eighteenth century, the Portuguese colonial administration did to Angolans in the late nineteenth century—force them to pay taxes and accept regulations. "I believe that in Angola the farmer must be exempt from all taxes," declared Savimbi. "The state cannot claim the produce of a farmer's hard work. That would be theft." Music to Reagan's ears.[31]

By the end of Reagan's administration, the warring factions in Angola had exhausted themselves, and the able assistant secretary of state, Chester Crocker, saw come to fruition a project he had thoughtfully worked on for years, a political settlement that specified a two-year time-table for both Cuba and South Africa to withdraw from Angola and independence to be granted to neighboring Namibia.

However, until the settlement was worked out, Angola's Marxist government was winning, with help from Cuban troops. The number of Cuban soldiers in Africa was staggering, beginning at 20,000 in the mid-1970s and increasing to 50,000 by 1988. Castro's motives are a matter of speculation. He had lost his trust in the Soviet Union after the Cuban missile crisis in the early 1960s, when the Soviets agreed to withdraw their missiles from Cuba without consulting him. And Castroism had lost its appeal in South America; in Bolivia, Castro's comrade Che Guevara had been captured and killed. Some argue that Castro was motivated by an Afro-Cuban sense of race solidarity, but the American black leader Stokely Carmichael doubted that Cuba took racial equality seriously and protested that there were no blacks in Cuba's top leadership. The novelist Gabriel García Márquez claimed that Cubans went to Angola to express their national pride and overcome a history of humiliation. Whatever the reason, the longer Cuba stayed in Africa, the more Cubans, both troops abroad and civilians at home, grew disenchanted, even calling Angola "Cuba's Vietnam." By 1987, Cubans had suffered 10,000 casualties, either killed, wounded, or missing. Reagan was right to point out the human waste; there was nothing Brezhnev could do about it. Castro's adventure was the desperate attempt of a communist internationalist who found himself isolated.[32]

The CIA director who replaced Casey, Robert Gates, called Angola "a win for U.S. diplomacy," and the Reagan administration would hail it as a success in the cold war against communism. But one wonders whether Angola figured much in the cold war or communism. Were Cuban troops proxies, and did the United States back the faction closest to the principles of the Reagan doctrine?[33]

The latest archival research contained in *Conflicting Missions*, by Johns Hopkins University professor Piero Gleijeses, suggests that the story is far from the scenario offered by the CIA and Reagan. When, on August 15, 1975, Castro sent a message to Brezhnev asking for his support of Cuban troops in Africa, Moscow balked, fearing the move "would hurt détente and offend most African countries." Likewise, William Colby, CIA director at the time, told the National Secruity Council that then-Soviet ambassador Anatoly Dobrynin earnestly wanted to go before the Congress of the Communist Party with assurances of "significant progress" in Soviet-American relations. In the late 1970s, Brezhnev was ill and thought to be near death, and he sought a significant treaty as his contribution to peace. "A meeting with Ford, the Politburo hoped, would produce a SALT agreement. Clearly, Castro and Brezhnev were on different wavelengths," Gleijeses wrote. The CIA was correct to see Castro as an "impulsive revolutionary" who thought in worldwide terms. "Internationalism is the most beautiful expression of Marxism-Leninism," he exhorted, and his comrade Che Guevara had called for "two, three, or many Vietnams." The Soviet Union, however, would have no part of revolutionary adventurism.[34]

Ironically, in Africa the CIA covertly financed the National Front for the Liberation of Angola (FNLA), which behaved as the Bolsheviks had in 1917 by refusing to allow an election of a constituent assembly. "It was the U.S.-backed FNLA that had violated the Alvor power-sharing agreement of March 1974 in a daring bid to seize total control of the state apparatus," writes diplomatic historian Willian R. Keylor, in *A World of Nations*. "The first foreign combat forces to enter Angola were the Zairean units that invaded in July 1975 in support of the FNLA with the tacit support of Washington. . . . The United States began to complain about foreign interference in the Angolan Civil War only after the tide had turned against the faction it had been covertly backing since the beginning of the conflict." The Marxist regime in Angola continued to do business with American oil firms and did not allow Russia to obtain naval or air bases or any other strategic advantage. However, administration officials worried that the Soviet Union would use Angola and its Cuban surrogates to support liberation movements elsewhere in the third world. America, Keylor wrote, "chose to interpret the political out-come of the Angolan Civil War in the worst possible light."[35]

In his address to Parliament, Reagan cited "the new philosophers" of France as among those who had become staunch anticommunists. One was Bernard-Henri Lévy, who was in Angola at the time the CIA was supporting the FLNA during the civil war. His eyewitness account tells us that Angolans were astonished to look out their doorways and see truckloads of Cubans and Russians in Luanda, as though they had arrived from outer space. Later, when most of the outsiders left, Angolans joked that the few who remained stayed on to become "den-tists." The long civil war was no laughing matter. Nor did it make ideo-logical sense along class lines, with the poor fighting the poor and the better off working out "gentlemen's agreements" on sharing the loot, namely petroleum and diamonds. According to Lévy, the "sordid truth" about the war between Savimbi's UNITA and its antagonists had to do with the ongoing struggle over apartheid in South Africa. Each faction exploited a superpower rivalry for its own purposes, not to establish com-munism but to enjoy the spoils of unearned wealth. The squalid story is but a chapter in the long history of greed and folly conveyed in the writ-ings of Rudyard Kipling, Joseph Conrad, Eugene O'Neill, Barbara King-solver, and others. In Africa, the communist and the capitalist alike are both kleptocrats who, even more than a lust for power, would grab the money and run.[36]

The Reagan doctrine was too dualistic; it always saw only two sides, right and wrong, good and evil, freedom and communism, and it failed to provide a clear view of the complexities of the world. Moving on to South America, Reagan's cold war view grew more intense without nec-essarily becoming more accurate. The vision blurred in Grenada before coming into focus in Nicaragua.

"The Nutmeg Invasion"

GRENADA IN THE LATE 1970s was a battleground for two Marxist factions that struggled to control the socialist New Jew-ell Movement (NJM), which dominated the politics of the tiny tropical island. For Ronald Reagan the struggle spelled the start of a

Grenada-Cuba-Soviet alliance in the Caribbean. It may have had more to do with two leaders who challenged each other about the right road to the goals of Karl Marx.

One, Bernard Coard, the deputy prime minister, sought to model NJM after the Soviet Union of the 1920s, a Leninist dictatorship that collectivized the economy and eliminated all opposition. The other, Prime Minister Maurice Bishop, hoped to set his country upon a social democratic path of justice and freedom. On little Grenada, the cite of tourist hotels and an important medical college, the political drama reprised a theme acted out many times in European history—the deadly conflict between a Stalinist and a socialist.

Interestingly enough, Fidel Castro sided with the socialist. Cuba offered to send help to NJM and Bishop with promises of doctors, teachers, and engineers. American ambassador Frank Cruz warned the prime minister to stay clear of Castro; however, when NJM was told that America would provide an aid package of a mere $5,000, Bishop grew incensed and warned against taking Grenada for granted. The Cubans continued to provide military arms, fishing trawlers, and tractors to build an airport strip. When Reagan took office, Grenadians feared the CIA would try to destabilize the island, as America had elsewhere with leftist regimes in South America. Preparing for the worst, Coard arrested Bishop in October 1983, and when Grenadians rose up in mass protest, the Stalinist leader used his Soviet tanks, the gifts of Cuba, to blast apart a fort and kill Bishop supporters. Trying to save the crowd from further slaughter, Bishop walked out with hands up to surrender, only to be executed along with his mistress and three other civilians.

International opinion denounced the brutal killings, and Reagan was certain that the communist coup had sinister international implications, unlike Margaret Thatcher, who saw it as thug politics as usual. With the Reagan administration and its neoconservative advisors, third world communism was almost always seen as something to be feared in its simplicity before it was faced in its complexity, not as an indigenous phenomenon from within a country but as a foreign effort from without, not an internal civil war along class lines but as an international struggle of geopolitics that had power and domination as its object. If the geopolitical cold war view had reflected the actual realities on Grenada, however, Castro would have welcomed Bishop's execution. Instead he condemned it:

No doctrine, no principle or proclaimed revolutionary position and no internal division can justify atrocious acts such as
the physical elimination of Bishop and the prominent group
of honest and worthy leaders who died yesterday. . . . The
death of Bishop and his comrades must be cleared up. If they
were executed in cold blood, the guilty should receive exem-
plary punishment.[37]

Was Reagan unaware of Castro's condemnation, or did he choose to
ignore it? In a speech delivered right after the murders, the president
went on television and used maps to demonstrate that the tiny island,
with Cuba nearby, was building "a naval base, a superior air base," and
"facilities for the storage of munitions, barracks, and training grounds for
the military." Referring to the island's major crop, Reagan emphasized:
"It isn't nutmeg that's at stake in the Caribbean and Central America; it
is the United States' national security." Convinced that the militarization
of the island could only mean communism and its will to domination,
regimentation, and expansion, Reagan ordered the invasion of Grenada,
Operation Urgent Fury.[38]

Much of the American public was perplexed, wondering how a small
island posed a threat to the United States. The operation, carried out
under a ban on all media coverage, was far more grim than anyone had
anticipated. First to land was an elite squad of navy Seals. They secured
the governor's residence but soon found themselves surrounded. Then
400 marines landed at the airport and 800 army Rangers followed by
parachute. Within hours the attacking force numbered 5,000. The fighting, it was later reported, was ferocious. American troops were unprepared, with command confusion and radio communications so poor the
troops had to rely on telephone booths and were forced to maneuver
with obsolete naval charts and tourist maps. The invaders mistakenly
shelled a hospital, and the United States suffered several casualties from
friendly fire. Grenadian soldiers and Cuban construction workers fought
tenaciously, some armed with AK-47s. After two days of bloody fighting
the island was captured. The United States suffered 19 deaths (half
noncombatant) and 115 wounded. The Cubans had 24 deaths and 59
wounded. The Grenadians had the greatest number of losses, with 67
killed and 358 wounded.[39]

Was the Nutmeg Invasion necessary? "We blew them away," declared Vice Admiral Joseph Metcalf, commander of the American task force. A century earlier Secretary of State John Hay told Theodore Roosevelt that America's quick victory against Spain over Cuba in 1898 was "a splendid little war"; a journalist called Grenada "a lovely little war." That it was little and swift was all that mattered. Coard was captured, order restored, and an enormous cache of arms was found together with military vehicles and patrol boats. However, the telling sight came a week later, with the return of American students who had been enrolled at St. George's University School of Medicine in Grenada. Dramatic television shots showed students descending from planes to kneel down and kiss the tarmac. Reagan had made clear that one of his aims was the safe return of Americans, and once again he basked in the role of rescuer.[40]

Many found the war's rationale unconvincing. Margaret Thatcher condemned the invasion as violating the sovereignty of a former British colony. Senator Moynihan chided Reagan for trying to bring democracy by bayonet. House majority leader Tip O'Neill believed Reagan chose little Grenada to get America's mind off the larger blunder of Lebanon. Because of press censorship, few knew how botched the operation was until months later, when stories leaked to the press.

What about the threat of communism? Brezhnev, who had rebuked Castro's involvement in Angola, was seeking good relations with the United States and had no desire for any adventurism in the Caribbean. Reagan claimed that the Cuban-built airfield at Point Salines was intended to service Soviet aircraft. Why would not Russian planes simply land at nearby Cuba? Reagan also insisted that the airport was a possible refueling station for Libyan aircraft bringing supplies for Nicaragua. In reality, the airfield under construction on Grenada was less than 10,000 feet long, large enough to accommodate island puddle jumper prop planes but too short for jet bombers and large cargo planes.

In politics, truth seldom lies in such details. Images, especially first impressions, are what count. And the administration kept track of the immediate response. After Reagan's evening speech announcing the invasion, the White House received thousands of telephone calls and wires. Those who were positive about America's action numbered 4,272, those negative only 320.[41]

Reagan's popularity once again soared against a historical memory of malaise and passivity. America's reluctance to intervene in the struggles of the rest of the world came to be known as the Vietnam Syndrome. Vietnam was the longest war in American history, lasting more than a dozen years, with enormous American casualties and a humiliating defeat. When Americans could bring themselves to think even for a moment about that gruesome war, all they knew was that it should never be repeated—and, interestingly enough, no American statesman has ever bothered to explain why the war should have been fought in the first place. Reagan, the Great Communicator, had the verbal skills to do so, but the most he would say was that Vietnam was "a noble cause." His staff advised against using the expression, but Reagan went ahead with his three words and no elaboration. Before he was president, Reagan told his radio listeners that Vietnam "has to be our most lied about war." He cited a book by Professor Guenter Lewy, which claimed that American atrocities were highly exaggerated. He did praise Joan Baez for speaking out against the Vietnamese prison camps and asking Americans to assist the boat people after the war. The fate of Vietnamese refugees desperately escaping on makeshift crafts became the cause of leading French radicals, many of them former Maoists now making amends for their misplaced hopes in revolution. In America, Baez was one of the few opponents of the Vietnam War who tried to organize support for rescue and relief, in a letter appealing to the nation. Reagan quite rightly noted that Jane Fonda callously refused to join Baez; and the radical activist William Kunstler showed his true colors in calling the writing of Baez's open letter "a cruel and wanton act."[42]

The Vietnam War, though an episode of the 1960s and early 1970s, haunted the American mind in the Reagan eighties. A trauma in America's collective consciousness, the war was more denied than acknowledged. Reagan did not bother to attend the dedication of the Vietnam Veterans Memorial wall in Washington, D.C., and Interior Secretary James Watt held up the construction permit as long as he could.

As for Grenada, Operation Urgent Fury turned out to be a political godsend. After Lebanon, it was a relief to see that, in Grenada, America could do something competently, even though the 133-square-mile island seemed less an enduring threat than a momentary pest. America had not had a successful foreign intervention since World War II, an entire half-century that saw the Korean War end in stalemate, Vietnam in defeat, and Lebanon in disaster. Reagan could not deny the deaths of the marines in Beirut, but he still tried to retaliate and salvage the disaster in Lebanon by ordering the bombing of an Iranian army barracks in Baalbek, a mission that cost the downing of two American A-6 bombers. Lebanon had little to do with the cold war, but Reagan could not restrain himself from linking it everywhere—to Iran, Syria, Russia, Cuba, Nicaragua, and Grenada. He would also connect it to the Soviet downing of a South Korean airliner and to terrorist attacks throughout the world. The adminstration's fixation explained history better than history could explain itself. "The events in Lebanon and Grenada, though oceans apart, are closely related," said Reagan in a nationally televised speech, delivered on October 27, 1983. "Not only has Moscow assisted and encouraged the violence in both countries, but it provides direct support through a network of surrogates and terrorists. It is no coincidence . . . ," Reagan went on to explain, unwittingly reiterating the Marxist refrain that there are no coincidences or accidents in history, only a succession of struggles that are interconnected. Even the admiring Reagan biographer Lou Cannon is outraged with this desperate subterfuge of linkage. "The president and his White House staff were shameless and successful in using the easy victory over Grenada to wipe away the stain of the unnecessary disaster in Beirut."[43]

Reagan may have used the Lebanon-Moscow-Grenada linkage for election purposes. We now know that the Nutmeg Invasion was small potatoes on an island whose politics could have been handled by the Organization of American States, as suggested by Moynihan, Thatcher, and others. Even years after retirement, however, Reagan could not resist dramatizing the "lovely little war." His memoirs record his final thoughts: "The price we had to pay to ensure the freedom of Grenada had been high," he admitted, citing the casualties. "But the price would have been much higher if the Soviet Union had been allowed to perpetuate this penetration of our hemisphere. It would have only spread out from there."[44]

What was Grenada to Brezhnev or Brezhnev to Grenada? Reagan never knew, and his hawkish advisors would never allow their complacent certitude to be disturbed by trying to know. The larger campaign was in Nicaragua, where the Russians were involved, at least indirectly, and America was reluctant to be involved. In the struggle between the

Contras and Sandinistas, Reagan's arts of persuasion would be tested to the hilt. So would his judgment.

Nicaragua: "Ronald Reagan Is the Che Guevara of Imperialism"

NICARAGUA BECAME the most controversial issue in American politics since the Vietnam War. The tragedy of this Central American country represents an ironic reversal of a passage in one of Byron's poems:

> There is the moral of all human tales;
> 'Tis but the same rehearsal of the past,
> First Freedom, and then Glory—when that fails,
> Wealth, vice, corruption,—barbarism at last.

 The poem reflects the dilemma of Western liberalism, whether in old England, France, or colonial America. As a country modernizes and allows commerce to develop along with democracy, corruption inevitably follows. However, the notion that wealth would spell decadence had no place in Reagan's vision. His advisors looked to market economics as the solution to political problems. The Leninist vision would smother capitalism before it could breathe to prevent the rise of the bourgeoisie and all opposition parties. Yet as the Russian people discovered, the glory of the original October revolution enabled the country's leaders to capture power in the name of freedom, only to cling to it in the name of communism. Not "wealth, vice, corruption" but power, terror, deception led to "barbarism at last." Communism would have us believe that only wealth corrupts. Reagan believed that only the state corrupts, and that wealth liberates. However, Nicaragua would not only be a test of ideologies; it was also a conflict of generations. Reagan was to face the same radical activists he had confronted as governor, on the campuses of the University of California.

The coming to power of Marxists in Nicaragua in 1979 rekindled the same hopes and fears of Castro's revolution in 1959. While Reagan saw

Nicaragua as a possible beachhead for communism in Central America, the New Left, defeated by the governor decades earlier, hailed it as inspiring "a renewal of belief in the possibility of revolution." What failed in Berkeley and San Francisco could succeed in "backward Nicaragua." "To be in Managua," wrote one enthusiastic journalist, "was like being in a time machine. Here was a place seemingly run by the kind of people who were Sixties radicals. Wherever one went, people were young, singing political folk songs and chanting 'Power to the People.' "[45]

Reagan's antagonists in Nicaragua were the Sandinistas, named after a revolutionary leader, Augusto Cesar Sandino, who earlier in the century waged a war of liberalism against a conservative regime in Managua, and not, as legend has it, a radical revolution against the occupation of U.S. Marines. Older Nicaraguan fighters were sometimes called Browderistas, after the American communist Earl Browder, who had been sent by the Soviet Union to make sure workers in Central and South America supported the Allied cause during the Second World War. Nicaraguan politics largely consisted of socialists committed to the working class, agrarian radicals interested in land reform, and liberals and conservatives championing a free press, civil rights, and constitutional government. Religion was also a force in political life: Catholics devoted to the teachings of the Church and the symbol of the Virgin; evangelical Christians devoted to the Gospels and to redemption through faith; and a core of liberation theologians worshipping el Dios de los pobres (the God of the poor). No faction could speak for all Nicaraguans; inevitably one military and political " united front" would claim to do so.

The Sandinistas came to power in 1979 by outmaneuvering their allies after the weakened dictator Anastasio Somoza, facing the collaspe of his military forces, stepped down under international pressure. The Somoza dynasty had run Nicaragua for decades, with the usual corruption and violation of civil liberties, and the United States was no longer willing to send in the marines. FDR's Good Neighbor Policy promised a future of nonintervention as long as order was maintained and investments protected. Of Somoza's father FDR was reported to have said: "He's a son-of-a-bitch, but he's our son-of-a-bitch."[46]

During the Carter administration the CIA and Secretary of State Brzezinksi believed that the Sandinistas had little chance to seize power,

and when the Marxist revolutionaries did so, Washington seemed little
concerned, despite the fact that the insurgents enjoyed support from
Cuba. Jeane Kirkpatrick regarded Washington's blithe acceptance of
Somoza's demise as the typical liberal illusion: authoritarian dictatorships fall and democracy takes their place, bringing a better future for
everyone. On the contrary, Kirpatrick insisted, a moderate authoritarian
regime would likely be replaced by a totalitarian communist system that
was permanent and irrevocable.

Nicaragua's present may cast doubt on her thesis, but Cuba's could
well affirm it. Cuba's Fidel Castro came to power much the same way as
Nicaragua's Daniel Ortega, leading a revolution that promised freedom,
justice, and constitutional rights. After forty-five years, however, Castro
continues to head a regime that has suppressed newspapers, abolished
political parties, and sent middle-class opponents to jail or into exile.
Castro has outlasted numerous European statesmen and ten American
presidents. The American trade embargo has also prevented the growth
of a confident middle class and enables Castro to blame Cuba's economic failures on the Yankee dollar. The embargo, which perhaps helps
more than it hurts Castro, is insisted upon by Cuban exiles in Florida
and acquiesced to by American politicians fearful of any tilt in the
Florida electorate's vote.

In the 1960s, when Reagan was governor of California, elements of
Berkeley's New Left went to Cuba and joined the *campesinos* and
venceremos to help with the sugar harvest, claiming that communism
succeeded economically precisely because it was idealistic. In the third
world, Castro is not the first communist but the last Calvinist. To the
bearded Fidel, economic well-being matters less than the moral idealism that arises not from comfort and pleasure but from austerity and
sacrifice. Reagan could deal with Gorbachev, who at least recognized
that communism was an economic disaster. How could he deal with
Castro, who hailed hardship as a sign of revolutionary virtue?

In the early Reagan administration, only Clark and Haig insisted that
America do something to bring down Castro. In Central and South
America, however, the Reagan doctrine was not to reverse the past but
to prevent any future defections to communism. The test case would be
Nicaragua.

The neocon intellectuals at *Commentary* magazine had no doubt that what was happening in Nicaragua was part of a communist strategy of world conquest directed from Moscow. Reagan himself, as we have seen, was a devoted reader of the right-wing journal *Human Events*, which reprinted a speech by a businessman who had fled Managua and claimed that his country was quickly becoming another Cuba, a "Soviet-controlled base, complete with a Russian combat brigade." Reagan refused to follow the advice of right-wingers to send in American troops to overthrow the Sandinistas, but he agreed with Casey, Haig, and Clark that "all of Central America is a target for a Communist takeover." The possibility of doing something short of intervention presented itself when the Contras, a collection of anti-Sandinista factions drawn from Somoza's disbanded national guard, the middle-class business community, and disillusioned radicals, all grew convinced that Daniel Ortega had betrayed the Nicaraguan revolution. In America, the Left insisted that the Contras were mainly ex-Somocistas who, determined to restore the power and privileges of the old order, were terrorizing the peasants and committing counterrevolutionary atrocities in the countryside. Conservative Republicans sought to Americanize the Contras and to see in them what Reagan hailed as the "moral equivalent of our Founding Fathers." Some claimed they were the political equivalent of the partisans of the French resistance. The old Hollywood radical Reagan once described them as the ideological equivalent of the Abraham Lincoln Brigade of the Spanish civil war.[47]

These historical analogies are curious. The French resistance and the Lincoln Brigade fought on the side of communists, while our founders sought to drive out of America the very country that endowed the colonies with natural rights. Reagan's hero Tom Paine would also be of little use in Nicaragua, for Paine believed a revolution was meant to be fulfilled, not betrayed. What concerned Reagan most, however, was not analogy but proximity. After the CIA proposed secret aid to the Contras, originally twenty million dollars enabling Argentina to train Honduras-based guerrillas, Representative Edward P. Boland had Congress pass by unanimous vote legislation prohibiting the CIA from becoming involved in any activity aimed at overthrowing the Nicaraguan government. Perhaps the unanimity of the vote dissuaded Reagan from attempting a veto, and he signed the Boland Amendment into law on October 12, 1984. This obstacle, Reagan angrily recorded in his diary, allowed Congress to deprive the president of his constitutional authority in foreign affairs. In a prime-time nationally televised speech, he explained in detail what the Sandinistas were doing to destroy any possibility of freedom in Nicaragua, and in a speech to a joint session of Congress he pointed up the perils of proximity. "El Salvador is nearer Texas than Texas is to Massachusetts. Nicaragua is closer to Miami, New Orleans, Houston, San Antonio, Los Angeles and Denver than these cities are to Washington where we are gathering tonight." Although the United States prevented "the tiny island of Grenada" from becoming a Soviet stronghold, Nicaragua had established thirty-seven military bases for a 25,000-man army supported by a militia of 50,000 trained by "eight thousand quote-unquote Cuban advisors." All the usual suspects were in Nicaragua: East Germany, Libya, Syria, Russia, and even the PLO. Against this massive military buildup, the plight of the people remained pathetic: "hopeless, helpless, and hungry." All of Central America was a powder keg, and it was exploding.[48]

According to Christopher Andrew and Vasili Mitrokhin, the Soviet Union was "ambivalent" about the prospects of communism in Central America. Russian officials could not help but notice that Che Guevara, for all the adulation on America's campuses, failed to recruit a single peasant and alienated even Communist Party members. Weary of provoking the new Reagan administration, Moscow sought to distance itself from the bloody civil war in El Salvador. "In an attempt to diminish the risks inherent in the challenge to U.S. influence in Central America, Moscow was happy to leave the most visible role to Fidel Castro," write Andrew and Mitrokhin. Although the Soviets supplied Cuba with abundant arms for use in Nicaragua, making that country the most powerful military force in Central America, Castro was angry that Moscow refused to take a stronger stand against the United States. With the rise of Solidarity in Poland, and speculation that Russia might send in the army to suppress it, Castro feared that a Soviet invasion of Warsaw would provoke the United States to invade Cuba. He even recommended that the Soviets seriously consider rearming the missile sites in Cuba that had been dismantled two decades earlier.[49]

Reagan believed the "focus of evil" in the world was the Soviet Union; Castro believed it was "Yanqui America," and the Cuban leader hysterically compared the inauguration of Ronald Reagan in 1981 to Adolf

Hitler's appointment to chancellor in Germany in 1933. Much of the third world sided with Castro against Reagan, as did many American college students and cultural figures. Only an Orwell could figure out these twisted loyalties. Those who believed in human rights, feminism, and gay liberation, and who were against capital punishment, ended up supporting a dictator who denied political rights, executed prisoners, and jailed homosexuals.

In the early 1980s covert aid had been funneled to the Contras in spite of the Boland Amendment. The emergence among Contra ranks of Eden Pastora, "Comandante Zero," once the dashing hero of the Sandinista revolution, gave the Contras a certain legitimacy. Pastora traveled through Latin America explaining how the Marxists stole the revolution, a stance that won the backing of liberals in Washington. To skirt the Boland restriction, Pastora received U.S. aid in Costa Rica, south of Nicaragua.

For a while the great outrage came over events in El Salvador, where death squads appeared to be sanctioned by a military government willing to have its opponents murdered off as though the country was run by the Mafia. In 1980 a Salvadoran death squad killed Archbishop Oscar Romero, and nine months later the same death squad murdered four American Catholic nuns. An impression grew that the CIA was collaborating with the squads, and the American press was, wrote future director Robert Gates, "flaying us alive." Reagan admitted in a private letter: "It is true that El Salvador was supportive of repressive and violent forces even after the coup which overthrew a military dictatorship." However, he was happy to report that José Napoleón Duarte, once "imprisoned, tortured and exiled," was now El Salvador's president-elect, and there could be a brighter day.[50]

The Boland Amendment was ambiguous, as Daniel Patrick Moynihan pointed out, leaving it unclear whether aid to the Contras was meant to overthrow the government, destabilize the country, or simply harass the Sandinistas. One thing was clear, in the war against communism Reagan was a prudent warrior, preferring negotiation or the support of foreign anticommunist fighters to direct intervention by American troops. In discussing U.S. policy toward Nicaragua, Reagan's advisors were struck by his aversion to military invasion. One official noted that "Ronald Reagan has the reputation of being a gunslinger,

but he [was] the most cautious, conservative guy in those meetings."
In response to congressional criticism, the Reagan administration
announced it would suspend aid to the Contras, but it kept quiet about
another plan to halt communism in Central America—the decision to
place conical-shaped explosives on ships in Nicaraguan ports and mine
the country's river outlets. The plan was devised by the National Security Council and approved by the CIA. Casey loved the idea of America
using fast cigarette boats to glide silently in the night up to the side of
ships and attach time bombs. A few sinkings, Reagan thought, could
well intimidate Russian ships carrying arms to Nicaragua. When the
mining operation was discovered by the press, however, a patient Congress broke into fury and even the cool Secretary of State Shultz lost his
temper. In the Senate, Barry Goldwater, who had been supporting Contra aid, rose from the floor to announce how he had been deceived: "I
am pissed off." Equally outraged, Senator Moynihan reminded America
that mining another country's harbors violated international law. Senator Jake Garn visited Moynihan's office and tried to talk him into seeing
things the CIA's way, and when the listener refused even to raise his
head, Garn lost his temper and threw his briefing book across the room,
yelling at Moynihan, "You're an asshole!" The room fell tense and silent.
Then Moynihan's eyes rose over his glasses, and he broke the ice by saying quietly, "Smile when you call me an asshole."[51]

Nicaragua presented the Reagan administration with one of its worst
nightmares—a regime that it legally could not overthrow and politically
could not tolerate. In 1984, elections were held in the country, and Sandinista leader Ortega won over 60 percent of the vote. However, the
election was boycotted by much of the anti-Sandinista opposition:
middle-class professionals protested the suppression of civil liberties,
peasants were angry about land confiscation, Catholics and evangelical
Christians listened to their church rather than to the state. The election
bestowed little legitimacy on the Sandinistas, who continued to receive
aid from Cuba. Still, in America and around the world, liberals and the
Left praised *Sandinismo*, a movement that stood up to the powerful and
had the support of the poor, defied the Vatican and had the blessing of
the *Cristianos Revolucionarios*—or so it seemed.

To what extent was Nicaragua a theater of the cold war, a staging
ground for a march by the Soviet Union into all of South America? That

the Sandinistas sought the support of the Soviets did not necessarily mean that the Soviets would risk a confrontation with the United States in the Caribbean, as they did in the Cuban missile crisis—with ignoble results. "For the Soviets," wrote Robert Kagan in his definitive book on Nicaragua, *A Twilight Struggle* (1996), "the region was at most a target of opportunity, worth exploring but only if success seemed likely." No doubt the Soviets would exploit communist insurgencies in the third world, if only to claim loyalty to class solidarity and to prevent China from making such claims. Sandinista leaders never understood why the Soviet Union had any fear of the United States, however, since its own socialist economy was strengthening while America's capitalist economy was, as their Marxist teachers had assured them, succumbing. Gorbachev knew otherwise, and he was not about to withdraw from Afghanistan to get bogged down in the Caribbean. American intelligence scarcely appreciated Gorbachev's problems, and the Sandinistas thought they knew which way the wind was blowing. Was not communism the wave of the future? Unless action was taken, Ronald Reagan feared so, Daniel Ortega thought so, American radicals hoped so, conservatives dreaded so—and history proved them all wrong.[52]

—

"YANKEES BEATEN!" When Conor Cruise O'Brien saw the headline YANQUIS VENCIDOS! in a newspaper in Managua in 1986, he wondered how Nicaraguans could think that they had managed to win a battle against mighty America, "the Colossus of the North." Upon reading the story he discovered that the New York Yankees had been beaten by the Cleveland Indians. He also came to sense how affectionate the "gentle" Nicaraguans were toward America and how their country sent to the major leagues so many outstanding baseball players. "There is," O'Brien reflected at the time, "very little personal hatred in Nicaraguan anti-Americanism. Not even personal hatred for Ronald Reagan." The president may have been ill-advised or allowed himself to be "a victim of diabolical possession," but Nicaraguans respected the power of America even if they resented how it was mistakenly wielded. "There has been nothing in Nicaragua, about Reagan, that at all corresponds to, for example, the torrent of frantic and obscene iconography which Buenos Aires directed at Margaret Thatcher, at the time of the Falklands War. Sandinistas, indeed, understand Ronald Reagan better than most foreigners do. They understand, and up to a point respect, his talk about 'standing tall,' because 'standing tall' is what *Sandinismo*, too, is all about. They recognize in Reagan, *to that extent*, a partly kindred spirit. 'Ronald Reagan,' one Sandinista told me, 'is the Che Guevara of imperialism.' "[53]

That epitaph may have to be revised when one considers how the Nicaraguan story turned out. However, before the story came to a remarkable end, the Iran-Contra scandal erupted in 1987. It will be treated in the next chapter. The scandal left the blackest mark on the Reagan presidency, coming close to prompting calls for his impeachment. The story of Nicaragua itself is more positive and more edifying, culminating in the extraordinary election of 1990, when former Vice President Bush resided in the White House. The election outcome was one of the great political surprises of the Reagan-Bush years, and there is a reason why it had to take place after Reagan left office.

In America both the Left and the Right, both the radicals who taught in the universities and the neoconservatives who scribbled in think tanks, proved to be less than accurate about Nicaragua. If the former believed that the Sandinistas were popular because they had a "social base" in the masses, the latter believed that the Sandinistas were strong because they had the support of Cuba and Russia. Election Day was set for February 15, 1990, all sides predicted a Sandinista victory, and even the Bush administration was thinking of ways to reach out to Daniel Ortega. Former President Jimmy Carter was in Managua to supervise the election, and performer Bianca Jagger stirred the crowds, belting out revolutionary songs. The outcome astounded everyone. The liberal publisher Violeta Chamorro overwhelmed Ortega, winning 55 percent of the vote to his 41 percent. What happened?

There had been mass disaffection with the Sandinistas (young people were fed up with the draft, peasants wanted their own land, journalists and intellectuals resented the rigidity of dogma), but no one seemed to notice it in America, with a few exceptions—Shirley Christian of the *New York Times* and Paul Berman of the *New Republic*. What happened was not supposed to happen, according to many of Reagan's neoconservative advisors. Jeane Kirkpatrick had claimed that a Marxist regime in power stays in power, the outcome Ortega himself thought he was directing by agreeing to elections. He, too, was taken in by the myth of the Left and its assumption that whatever the elites may do, the people will stand by the revolution. "The people," Castro warned Ortega, "can be wrong." In communism, to be wrong is to be unworthy of your rights. In liberalism, the right to be wrong is an inalienable right, and resistance to authority is based on disobedience, which is not exactly a conservative value, but certainly an Emersonian principle through and through.[54]

Reagan's persistent policy of support for the Contras worked in an ironic way. Robert Kagan, the leading scholar on the subject, has emphasized that without the pressure of a growing armed insurgency in the countryside, the Sandinistas would have had no need to hold an election. Kagan also provides a telling observation that adds a curious twist to the story. With Reagan in power, Kagan notes, the civil war in Nicaragua could have continued indefinitely, because the Sandinistas were convinced that Reagan would not accept an electoral victory. Ortega could not forget that Reagan had dismissed the 1984 elections (boycotted by some of the population); nor could others forget a whole history of America moving against democratic elections in Central and South American countries (for example, Guatemala and Chile). Since the 1850s Nicaragua itself had been invaded by U.S. forces so many times (ten in all) that the country might well have been an American boot camp.

However, the desperate Ortega assumed that Reagan's successor, George H. W. Bush, would accept his reelection. Indeed, with the approach of Election Day Bush had started to think of ways to establish good relations between the United States and Nicaragua even with a communist regime in power. As it turned out, it was not just Reagan but the Nicaraguan people themselves who would not accept a Sandinista victory. No doubt they still respected Reagan as one who stood tall and stayed with them during a ten-year ordeal that finally brought democracy to their country.

"Reagan and the Return to Idealism." The title is the section heading of an important essay written by the Yale diplomatic historian John Lewis Gaddis. His argument is that Reagan rescued American foreign policy from "realistic" power politics and realigned it with a more honorable tradition. Carter's preoccupation with human rights, Gaddis insists, actually exacerbated the cold war by stiffening Russia's resistance to liberalization. Détente was discarded, he points out, and the cold war moved into Afghanistan and the third world. Reagan, in contrast, stood by democratic ideals while seeking rapprochement with the Soviet Union. "Our mission," Gaddis quotes Reagan addressing Congress in 1985, "is to nourish and defend freedom and democracy and to communicate these ideas everywhere we can." Gaddis observes of Reagan: "And he added, two years later, in words that could have easily come from Carter—or for that matter, from Truman: 'A foreign policy that ignored the face of millions around the world who seek freedom would be a betrayal of our national heritage.' "[55]

If only words alone accurately mirrored the reality of history. The Nicaraguan story may have represented reality as well as rhetoric. But U.S. policy in Angola had more to do with opposing communism than promoting democracy, and in El Salvador America's allies would rather kill nuns than hold an election. As to Afghanistan and the *mujahideen* as "freedom fighters," let that pass. However, where America turned its back on the students slaughtered at Tiananmen Square, and Reagan went along with Nixon and Kissinger in approving Bush's policy of quiet diplomacy rather than loud protest, one can only conclude that America had indeed "ignored the face of millions" seeking freedom. After all, these youths were rebelling against communism, the very meaning of America's mission in the cold war as Reagan defined it. In no uncertain terms, the Reagan doctrine had called for supporting "those fighting for freedom against communism wherever we find them." In Bejing, the students' makeshift Statue of Liberty expressed admiration for America and its political ideals. But the "city upon the hill" looked the other way.

CHAPTER EIGHT

History as Tragedy, History as Farce

"Losing Freedom by Installment"

I N HIS VALUABLE MEMOIR, *In Confidence*, Anatoly Dobrynin, Russia's ambassador to the United States for over a quarter-century, offers a section with the title "The Paradox of Ronald Reagan." The apparent riddle was that Reagan entered the White House to revive "the worst days of the Cold War and then brought about the most significant improvement in Soviet-American relations since the end of World War II." Many Americans and Russians, noted Dobrynin, have been preoccupied with this paradox, unsure whether the positive outcome was the result of an accidental chain of events or in fact was the conscious design of both Reagan and Gorbachev.[1]

Dobrynin's observation needs to be qualified. In the early years of the Reagan administration, the president did increase America's arms buildup and made his much-discussed reference to the Soviet Union as an "evil empire," leading many into misbelieving that the United States was about to embark on some aggressive military adventure against the diabolical enemy. Actually, the cold war was over, a fait accompli for more than a half-century. The historic cold war—which could be said to have begun either in 1917, with the Bolshevik seizure of power, or in 1948, when the Soviets moved into Prague and our old World War II ally established its brute hegemony over all of Eastern Europe—had been on a set course since 1956, when the tanks of the Red Army drove through the streets of Budapest and left a bloodbath for the world to see. No president, whether Republican or Democrat, believed there was much America could do about the tragic fate of Eastern Europe.

Yet ever since World War II, conservatives had complained that President Franklin D. Roosevelt had "sold out" Poland and Eastern Europe at the Yalta conference of 1945. The liberal Roosevelt, it was alleged, allowed the Red Army to remain to occupy the conquered areas. By 1945, it became clear that Stalin was not about to allow Poland to have free elections, and Winston Churchill fumed that Roosevelt failed to exercise any restraining influence over the Soviet dictator. Reagan, Whittaker Chambers, and other conservatives believed that Churchill was the hero and Roosevelt the fool. Earlier, however, when Roosevelt replied to Churchill that the only way to deny the Soviets' conquests was by fighting them, even the British leader had to come to his senses, a point demonstrated in the writings of Conrad Black and Sir Max Hastings. Indeed, Churchill was willing to settle for Soviet hegemony over Poland in exchange for Stalin's recognizing a British sphere of influence in the Aegean, which he did by opposing the Greek communists' bid for power. Churchill rarely expressed dedication to the principle of national self-determination, as did Roosevelt and later Reagan. As Hastings put it regarding the start of the cold war when Churchill was in a funk: "Virtually no one in either the United States or Great Britain had any appetite for a war against the Soviets. In this sense, Roosevelt was entitled to say he was the realist and Churchill was the fantasist in not being prepared to face this reality squarely."[2]

Like Roosevelt, Reagan was the realist when it came to the Soviet Union. Even had nuclear weapons not existed, there was no way that the United States could defeat massive Russia in a conventional land war. Reagan was also a romantic when it came to the arms race, a leader who believed that history was not predetermined by ideology and that a world without nuclear weapons could be possible because it could be imagined. Fate only falls on a country that does nothing, Reagan announced in his first inaugural, and America can remain free only by employing power, not because it seeks to dominate but precisely because it seeks to liberate. Yet in Europe there was no way the United States could use power other than by amassing more and more missiles as symbols of deterrence. The only place America could use its power as an instrument of freedom was outside of the European continent.

The challenge that faced Reagan, what came to be called the "second cold war," raises the question whether there was any direct continuity between the two wars. The second war had its origins in 1979, long after Stalin's death, and it involved uprisings in the Mideast and communist activities in the third world. Although he accepted the stalemate of the first cold war, in fact if not in rhetoric, Reagan went all out to fight the second cold war, by supporting counterinsurgencies in the third world, covertly supplying arms in order to side with what he called "friendly dictators," and, in one minor instance, by direct American intervention. In engaging communists, Reagan operated under the assumption that the same logic and historical experience that explained the first cold war provided the reasoning on which to fight the second. Since communism was not a phenomenon indigenous to the countries of Eastern Europe but instead brutally imposed by the Soviet Union in the aftermath of World War II, the impression grew that communism in third world countries could only be an international phenomenon, as though the world consisted of a chessboard of dominoes about to fall. This chapter deals with Reagan's peculiar views of the history of both America and the communist world. Reagan entertained a questionable attitude toward communism, not with regard to its coercive politics but with regard to the way in which it came to power.

After World War II, the American people were forced to experience the victory of our arms and the defeat of our aims. Few foresaw that the elimination of fascism would mean the perpetuation of communism. Since communism did not come to power in any European country (with the exception of Yugoslavia) independently of the Soviet Union, it stood to historical reason that any country in Latin America moving toward communism must be dependent upon the Soviets, and that revolutionary insurgencies would not have taken place unless Moscow had instigated them. Reagan began to back away from this view as he started to negotiate with Gorbachev in the late 1980s. He continued the struggle against communism in its second phase in the third world, however, while working vigorously to bring about nuclear disarmament between the two superpower rivalries. When communism unexpectedly collapsed as a result of the reduction of military tensions, the first cold war passed into history and the second cold war faded away. What America would face in the post-Reagan era was not Soviet communism but Islamic fundamentalism, a phenomenon that the CIA's William Casey missed comprehending, as he still thought he was fighting the old cold war in the new context of the Mideast. If it could be said that liberalism failed to prepare America for communism, it could also be said that conservatism failed to prepare America for terrorism.

In addition to addressing the Reagan administration's ways of histor-ical reasoning, this chapter also deals with two episodes of the cold war that involved both the pride of American science and the perils of Amer-ican statecraft: Star Wars and the Iran-Contra affair. One policy was her-alded to the world as a possible technological breakthrough that would render nuclear war obsolete; the other was hidden from the public to conceal its illegality.

—

REAGAN'S VIEWS ON the cold war had been shaped long before he became president. His experiences in Hollywood and his reading of Whittaker Chambers had led him to believe that liberals bore some responsibility for the advances of communism, since they denied that it posed a threat to the United States. The defense of Alger Hiss by liberal intellectuals led Chambers to conclude that "every move against Com-munism was felt by liberals to be a move against themselves." What Hiss understood, Chambers claimed, liberals would have to face. "Hiss understood so quietly, or accepted with so little fuss or question the fact that the revolutionist cannot change the course of history without tak-ing upon himself the crimes of history."[3] Reagan's unfortunate hostility toward John F. Kennedy should be understood in the context of Cham-bers's teachings.

During the 1960 presidential election, Reagan wrote the Republican candidate, Vice President Richard Nixon, a private letter to warn him about his Democratic opponent. Listening to Kennedy's speeches, Rea-gan had "heard a frightening call to arms" in the liberal's promising to "free this and free that" around the world. "Shouldn't someone tag Mr. Kennedy's *bold new imaginative* program with its proper age? Under the tousled boyish haircut it is still the old Karl Marx—first launched a cen-tury ago. There is nothing new in the idea of government being Big Brother to us all. Hitler called his 'State Socialism' and way before him it was 'benevolent monarchy.' "[4]

Reagan had already learned from Chambers that New Deal liberals were unwittingly moving America toward a communist state. His refer-ence to "State Socialism" and "benevolent monarchy," however, derived from F. A. Hayek's *The Road to Serfdom*, which became a bible to con-servatives after World War II and throughout the cold war. Hayek became a refugee in America in the 1930s, and he worried that his newly adopted country would follow Europe in losing its freedom to the forces that had overtaken the Old World. His book, addressed to Great Britain and the state of socialism, had perhaps more influence in America. Hayek made two arguments, one regarding the domestic economy, the other regarding the pattern of history that allegedly led to totalitarianism.

In the mid-1970s Hayek won the Noble Prize in economics for his theory of monetarism, the thesis that money supply and interest rates are the key to a society's state of wealth. With the Great Depression in mind, Hayek argued that economic expansion based on high inflation leads to an economic bust unless credit and money are restricted, not by government but by natural market forces or by an independent institution, such as today's Federal Reserve system. The monetarists held that the private sector of the economy is more accountable to democracy than the public sector of government. Market competition assures that the economy will be competitive and productive and responsive to people's interests and demands. When liberals countered with an argument for social justice, conservatives replied that an economy should be more concerned with sustaining freedom than with redistributing wealth.

Hayek made a valuable contribution by showing how the Soviet economies would fail for lack of a resource-allocation system responsive to the market. However, there is a double irony here. While the Soviet system came to be called a "command economy," Gorbachev tried to reform it by commanding it, only to find that the *apparat* refused to change its ways. Many of Reagan's advisors regarded the Soviet Union as a totalitarian system completely resistant to change or collapse. The second irony is that Hayek had been predicting that the Soviet Union was on the verge of collapse as early as 1935, and fifty years later it remained standing, with an economy that could neither be commanded nor transformed. Still, if economics alone cannot explain why communism unexpectedly fell, what might explain how it rose?

The Road to Serfdom's second argument addressed that question. Hayek insisted that communist and fascist regimes come to power as the political state expands its reach into all sectors of society, especially the collectivization of the economy. Marxists also believed that whoever controls the means of production exercises all power in a given society and that the state is an instrument of oppression. Hayek thought that

Marxists profoundly erred, however, in thinking that achieving freedom
and justice is merely a matter of organizing the economy; that the good
society can be the result of planning, of human design and intention. On
the contrary, argued Hayek, market capitalism is a natural phenomenon,
arising spontaneously in response to cultural conventions and people's
desires, rational or irrational. To Reagan, who believed that the desires
God bequeathed to us are "good," Hayek's economic theory was irresistible. So, too, was his theory of history.

Shortly after Kennedy became president, Reagan made a speech in
Fargo, North Dakota, on January 6, 1962. Reagan addressed a topic that
haunted conservatives, "Losing Freedom by Installment." It was essentially a Hayekian argument that purported to show how the citizen's liberty became alienated by degrees as it lodged itself in the labyrinth of big
government. Reagan convinced himself that communism emerged even
in democracies—because of "creeping socialism" that resulted when
government encroached on the lives of the people with programs for
farmers, for health, education, medicine, and so on. In America, Marxist terms like "class conflict" and "the masses" may be not be familiar to
everyone, Reagan acknowledged, but he was still convinced that communism could emerge even in democracies as a consequence of the
overregulated, centralized state. "This was the very thing that the Founding Fathers sought to minimize. They knew that governments don't control things. A government can't control the economy without controlling
the people. And they knew that when a government sets out to do that,
it must use force and coercion to achieve its purposes. They also knew,
those Founding Fathers, that outside of its legitimate functions, government does nothing as well or as economically as the private sector of
the economy."[5]

Thomas Paine may well have agreed with Reagan, and perhaps
Thomas Jefferson, but neither had a hand in the making of the Constitution. The framers of the document, the authors of the *Federalist*, were
the original conservative thinkers in American history, and they were convinced that the young republic had to address the task of state-making
if liberty were to survive. Contrary to Reagan, the *Federalist* authors
believed the people had to be controlled. One of first major acts of the
presidency of George Washington was to put down the Whiskey Rebellion of 1794, led by distillers of Pennsylvania who refused to pay taxes.

To use Reagan's own language against his reasoning, one of the "legiti-mate functions of government" was to exercise authority and even impose its will, something European countries failed to do when faced with fascism and communism.

Hayek's *The Road to Serfdom* led its readers to believe that commu-nist and fascist regimes came to power as a result of a centralized state that had collectivized the economy. Reagan absorbed the argument com-pletely, convinced that Marx and Hitler imposed the "idea of govern-ment being Big Brother." Hayek and Reagan got the story backwards.

In reality, communism and fascism came to power as political move-ments that toppled governments that were neither big nor imposing but weak and antiquated, as in czarist Russia, or that appeared alien and ille-gitimate, as in Weimar Germany. When Reagan bestowed the Presiden-tial Medal of Freedom on Sidney Hook, the philosopher might have told him what he had demonstrated years earlier in his debates with the con-servative economists Reagan admired.[6] Communism and fascism did not collectivize the economy as the first step on the road to power; instead each movement first seized control of the state. The Bolsheviks abol-ished the Constituent Assembly in Moscow, the Nazis burned the Reichs-tag in Berlin. As Marx forewarned, the political will to power refused to wait upon economic development. Contrary to Reagan's conviction, the fate of Russia had less to do with Hayek's prognosis than with Toc-queville's prediction; it was less a matter of suffocating an existing free market that had yet to breathe than of trying to bring to birth a liberal-ism that had yet to be born. It is when societies have been weakened by reforms that they start down the road to collapse. The path to serfdom lies in a failing state.

In one rare instance, Reagan stated that communism "arises from feudalism," but instead of following up on his insight, he waxed Hayekian and continued to fix on the state as the threat to freedom. On the contrary, communism took hold of backward countries emerging from feudalism, countries like Russia and China, neither of which had a strong state or a liberal tradition. Reagan's "installment" theory of com-munism and fascism saw statist ideologies creeping step by step toward power as liberal government expanded. Historically, however, liberal government had done little to pave what conservatives like to call "the road to serfdom"; indeed, it actually overthrew "benevolent monarchy."

Rather than evolving from liberalism, communism and fascism had to destroy it as the last bastion of resistance to totalitarianism.

Citing the specter of Big Brother and the image of European totalitarianism became a temptation for both the Left and the Right in America. In his Hollywood period, Reagan heard radical scriptwriters claiming that McCarthyism would bring fascism to America. Decades later, he accepted the right-wing view that liberalism could well bring communism to America. The idea that "it can happen here" was ludicrous paranoia consuming the Left and Right fringes. Both thought the tragedy of Europe would repeat itself in America as a result of the actions of government. If the Left saw government expressing the "contradictions" of capitalism, Reagan and the Right saw it expressing the conspiracy of power; but the historical record defied the political imagination. In truth, Lenin, Mussolini, and Hitler did not have much to do with the existing political state and its flabby authority, into which they rushed as air into a vacuum. The Bolsheviks seized the Winter Palace in 1917; the Blackshirts marched on Rome in 1922; the Brownshirts stormed the streets of Berlin in 1932. The "universal charm of October," wrote François Furet of the Russian revolution of 1917, appealed to intellectuals who hated liberalism and its bourgeoisie. And Il Duce's formulation of the corporate state appealed to Thomas Lamont of the J. P. Morgan Company, to President Herbert Hoover, to *Fortune* magazine, and to other Americans financiers who loved capitalism. The road to serfdom had many footprints.[7]

However, Reagan saw only the footprint of liberalism moving through the corridors of government to reach the pinnacle of power. As with liberalism in North America, so with Leninism in South America. Referring to El Salvador, Honduras, Guatemala, Costa Rica, and Nicaragua, Reagan wrote in his memoirs. "I have been told that Lenin once said, 'First we will take Eastern Europe, then we will organize the hordes of Asia . . . then we will move on to Latin America; once we have Latin America, we won't have to take the United States, the last bastion of capitalism, because it will fall into our outstretched hands like overripe fruit.'"[8]

Reagan could be terribly cavalier about where he received his information. Apparently he felt that to have been told something made it true, especially if he wanted it to be so. Thus he once stated to the press that the inspiration for FDR's New Deal came from Italian fascism and

Il Duce's corporate state and, when questioned, replied that he had "been told" as much by a scholar at Stanford's Hoover Institute. The impression that liberalism had affinities with fascism had been an old carnard perpetuated by the Left in the Depression. Fifty year later it remained the same rumor coming from the Right.[9]

As to Lenin waiting with "outstretched hands" for the United States to fall like "overripe fruit," the metaphors astounded the serious Marxist. Lenin went to his death, in 1924, in despair that the Bolshevik revolution failed to ignite revolutions elsewhere in the post–World War I industrial world. He even cautioned against those minds full of "infantile disorder" that thought revolution could still be possible. Lenin looked upon peasant societies with distrust and suspicion. The third world would be *geschichtelos* ("historyless"), inert, stagnant, passive, until it modernized by means of industrialization.

During the Reagan presidency of the 1980s, the Sino-Soviet rift, which actually broke open in the 1950s, presented the world with an ideological puzzle when it came to trying to calculate the foreign policies of communist regimes, especially those of Russia and China. Russia doubted the capacity of peasant societies to develop anything resembling communism and called for peaceful coexistence with the West. China held out for permanent revolutionary struggle and claimed that the next war would be between the rural countryside and the metropolitan centers of the world. Yet China rarely involved itself in revolutionary insurgencies in the third world, and while Russia sent troops to Angola and elsewhere in Africa, it claimed that socialist revolutions could move toward "communism only after the socialist countries of Europe." The Reagan administration rejected the doctrine of peaceful coexistence as a ruse designed to disarm America. But the theoretical problem is even more telling. Since the socialist countries of the Eastern bloc had no means of reaching communism without going through a capitalist stage of development, communism would remain an ideology that died before it was born. In the third world, the illusion of communism as an economic proposition became one of the cruelest jokes in history, and Castro's Cuba stands as its tragedy turned farce. However, Reagan and many of his neoconservative advisors believed that El Salvador and Nicaragua were involved in installing communism by means of insurgency, and that the United States would not even have to be attacked, as it would drop to the ground—like "overripe fruit." This specter was a variation of what Norman Podhoretz called the Finlandization of America. Like the citizens of Helsinki, Americans would wake up one morning and see the red flag flying in their front yard.[10]

In the 1970s, the Soviet Union's KGB secretly supported communist movements in Latin America. But shortly after Russia's invasion of Afghanistan in late 1979, Soviet leaders, now realizing they had committed a drastic blunder moving into Kabul, grew weary of any adventurism in Latin America, and they criticized Castro for sending troops to Angola and supporting Marxists in El Salvador and Nicaragua. Publicly, Moscow could hardly renounce its solidarity with the third world; privately, it made it clear that, aside from supplying arms, it would not come to the rescue of the Sandinistas or other communist movements.[11] The Soviets had their hands full with Afghanistan and no longer saw the third world as the battlefield where world revolution would catch fire. The Reagan administration viewed the third world not as the terrain of a power struggle, which it was, but as a launching area that posed a direct threat to the United States. No one knew better how unfounded such fears were than Senator Daniel Patrick Moynihan.

In *The Eighteenth Brumaire of Louis Bonaparte* (1852), Karl Marx offered an epigrammatic formulation: "History repeats itself, the first time as tragedy, the second as farce." Marx was referring to the futility of trying to make a revolution without the necessary stages of social development, the illusion that "treats *pure will* as the motive power of revolution instead of actual conditions," and the sad spectacle of workers and peasants following a leader into the false promised land. Marx's epigram is prophetic and presages Lenin's seizure of power in Russia in 1917, certainly a tragedy for the Russian people. Later in the twentieth century, revolutionary uprisings broke out in the third world in the name of Karl Marx, a farce for the people who had to watch tribal leaders and caudillos fighting turf battles that had more to do with the spoils of war than with socialism. Senator Moynihan had many encounters with leaders of the third world, and he knew what was happening there. Underdeveloped countries were desperately impatient, and their radical leaders refused to allow capitalism to develop as a necessary step toward the beginnings of a socialist society. Third world revolutionaries, rather than letting history take its course, were fighting the inertness of their own circumstances, the past itself. "The tradition of all dead generations," warned Marx, "weighs like a nightmare on the brain of the living."[12]

"The Cold War Is Over!"
—Senator Moynihan, 1984

D URING THE ASCENDANCY of the neocons in the 1970s and 1980s, Democrats appeared reluctant to oppose the alarmist convictions of the hawks. Liberals were still reeling from the charge, first made in the McCarthy era, of being soft on communism and of having lost Eastern Europe and China to the forces of evil. They also had to face the older elements of the nuclear freeze movement, pacifists who, in the parlance of the day, preferred "red" to "dead." Then there were the veterans of the anti–Vietnam War resistance, those who claimed that it was the follies of anticommunism itself that dragged America into one quagmire after another. Only one Democratic politician stood out as an exception, a rare liberal who embarrassed the neocons by the brilliance of his presence.

Before becoming senator from New York, Daniel Patrick Moynihan had served in the Nixon and Ford administrations as ambassador to India and to the United Nations. Between Senator Moynihan and President Reagan there appeared to be a world of difference in party affiliations and political outlooks and values. One had been a Harvard academic, the other a Hollywood actor. Tall, sandy-haired, quick-witted, Moynihan was a classic public intellectual, the brainy professor who brings scholarly expertise to bear upon the social and political issues of the day. Reagan was the celebrity politician, a relaxed, talented performer who could project, persuade, communicate, and empathize with people's hopes and frustrations. They had a common Irish ancestry, with a tipple of the bottle plastering the fathers, and strong mothers who compensated for the fathers' absence. Both exuded confidence and charm and had a wonderful sense of humor, and each commanded a popular following and left office in dignity and respect.

Max Weber once remarked that since it is common practice for politicians to smooth over problems, it is up to the intellectual to uncover them. As governor of California in the sixties, Reagan had famously stated in his inaugural speech a thought that had Weberian overtones in suggesting that politics is responsible to truth. "For many years now, you and I have been shushed like children and told there are no simple answers to the complex problems which are beyond our comprehension." The "truth is," he responded, "there are simple answers—there are just not easy ones." Reagan recognized the existence of problems only to better assure America that it had the capacity to solve them if government would just stand aside. Moynihan the intellectual had the type of mind that likes to turn simple answers into harder questions, but he would have agreed with Reagan that nothing is easy that is worthwhile tackling. Moynihan had many disagreements with Reagan over domestic policies, especially concerning the welfare state, which the president would dismantle and the senator would reform. When Reagan was recovering from the attempt upon his life, in the spring of 1981, Moynihan wrote a letter to the *New York Times*, citing Hemingway's definition of courage as "grace under pressure" by way of expressing his admiration for the president while acknowledging their differences. "I pounded pretty well, and he pounded back even better. If you think of him as a great performer, let me say he is an even greater audience, looking up, beaming and glinting, as you try to say things that are both wicked *and* true. We are surely proud of him."[13]

Moynihan was fond of quoting the French writer Georges Bernanos: "The worst, the most corrupting lies are problems poorly stated."[14] One of the problems poorly stated was the cold war, both the first one that had reached an impasse in Europe and the second, which was being fought in the jungles of the third world. Older conservatives claimed that liberals had lost the first cold war by allowing the Soviets to dominate Eastern Europe, and neoconservatives claimed that the United States was losing the second by allowing communists to move toward power in Latin America. To Moynihan, such fears came close to offering "the most corrupting lies." Stating the problem so poorly, the conservative's warning represented little more than "a response to a nonexistent challenge."[15]

When the first cold war settled into the normal power relations of the 1950s, many assumed containment policy was working, and with Nikita Khrushchev's repudiation of Stalinism in 1956, there was widespread expectation of a thaw inside the Soviet Union and détente between the two superpowers. The easing up of tensions was disrupted by the 1962 Cuban missile crisis and the long war in Vietnam, and détente was overshadowed by the Watergate scandal and Nixon's resignation. In the late 1970s, the Carter administration seemed to promise a resumption of détente, especially when the president, in a memorable 1977 speech at the University of Notre Dame, declared that America must get over its "inordinate fear of communism." A series of shocks, however, beginning in 1979, shattered this complacency, and presumably the second cold war was launched in the Mideast with the fall of the shah of Iran and the Russian invasion of Afghanistan. What Moynihan regarded as the delusion of a "non-existent challenge," the neoconservatives regarded as the doom of "the present danger."

In response to these new threats, Reagan advisors like Richard Perle and Defense Secretary Caspar Weinberger insisted that America not only maintain the balance of power but prevail by achieving nuclear ascendancy. Many scientists thought the goal a dangerous delusion, as did Henry Kissinger, former secretary of state under Nixon. "One of the questions which we have to ask ourselves as a country," queried the secretary, "is what in the name of God is strategic superiority? What is the significance of it, politically, militarily, operationally, at these levels of numbers? What do you do with it?"[16]

Moynihan agreed with Kissinger about the perils of an arms race that promised nuclear dominance; he also, and he alone, questioned the anxiety, indeed the near-hysteria, that took hold of the neoconservative mind during the second cold war. In an address at New York University in 1984, and in other speeches and writings, Moynihan questioned whether the Soviet Union was strengthening itself and whether America was faltering and shriveling back into an isolationist cocoon. He pointed to Russia's poor economy, increasing mortality figures, its social pathology of drunkenness and high crime rates, and the absence of legitimacy in a regime that commanded no loyalty from intellectuals within Russia or respect from the rest of the world. The Soviet idea, he declared, is "spent," and the system is becoming "weaker and weaker." In October 1984, before Mikhail Gorbachev took office, Moynihan proclaimed: "The Cold War is over, the West won . . . the Soviet Union has collapsed. As a society it just doesn't work. Nobody believes in it anymore." The best response to the staggering Soviets "is to wait them out." The collapse of communism was only a matter of time.[17]

The dramatic collapse came suddenly, first with the fall of the Berlin Wall in December 1989, then as communism crumbled throughout Eastern Europe the following year, and finally with the breakup of the Union of Soviet Socialist Republics. The dramatic events discredited Jeane Kirkpatrick's old doctrine of "irreversibility," the conviction that once a regime became totalitarian there is no possibility of changing direction, no presence of a viable opposition, no hope for the evolution of democracy. Still, some neocons conveniently forgot their own doctrine as they toasted their triumph over the "evil empire." Meanwhile, the scholarly Moynihan was more curious about why no one had foreseen what was there to be seen all along, and he asked the Senate to order the CIA to issue a report on its estimates of the state of the Soviet economy.[18]

Yet Moynihan had no need to await the judgment of history. Long before communism's collapse, he questioned the neoconservative conviction that with America's defeat in Vietnam communists would be emboldened to seek victory in every part of the world. After listening to Reagan deliver a speech at Fort McNair reminding America of the presence of communism in "Afghanistan, Angola, Cambodia, and, yes, Central America," Moynihan addressed the Reagan doctrine, the new militant stance that would allow no further defections to communism and would have the United States intervene, unilaterally and often illegally, wherever it chose. The doctrine was based on a misunderstanding that the new anticolonialism in the world represented a continuation of the older communist expansionism, that Marxist-Leninism was still alive and well, that the ghost of Leon Trotsky had returned to undertake "permanent revolutionary struggle." Various insurgencies may receive Soviet aid, "but," Moynihan observed, "the misunderstanding was to read the insurgencies as something *new*, as indeed a third phase in the expansion of Soviet empire. They were in fact something old; not the beginning but the end of a historical period. Thus in the regions cited by Mr. Reagan in his address at Fort McNair, a colonial era had come to an end, and preexisting Marxist insurgencies had come to power."

> These insurgencies had their origins in the period of Marxist triumphalism, when it seemed to many that indeed this

was to be the next stage of history. The doctrine [of world revolutionary struggle] had migrated from the metropolitan centers to the colonial periphery. In some instances the various schisms had migrated also. Ho Chi Minh, who was in Paris writing his dissertation at the time of the Peace Conference of 1919, was later to kill his share of Trotskyites in Hanoi. The trouble in Cambodia to which the president referred involved the effort by Ho Chi Minh's red army to overcome the red army of Pol Pot, who had also studied in Paris [and some of whose followers wrote dissertations at the Sorbonne]. When ideas die at the center, it takes time for the news to reach the periphery. The pagans encountered by Christian Rome were often no more than acolytes of the gods of imperial Rome. By the 1970s the French Communist party had commenced terminal gerontological decline; but how was this to be known in Phnom Penh? It was all over for the party in Lisbon, all over in Madrid; but how was this information to reach Maputo or Managua at the level of changed expectation? How could Sendero Luminoso Maoists fighting in the jungles of Peru know that in Tiananmen Square there is now but one portrait left of Mao Tse-Tung, and that verges on the inconspicuous?[19]

One red army was battling another red army; communists against communists. Moynihan saw communism for what it was, not a monolithic phenomenon emanating from Moscow but a series of sporadic uprisings led by revolutionaries who had lost their way, desperadoes clinging to dead doctrines, a hundred Maoists of Peru's Shining Path unaware that millions of Chinese had turned against Mao, as dramatized when students and workers demonstrated against communism at Tiananmen Square. The Soviet Union might exploit jungle insurgencies, but it could neither create nor control them, and, in some instances, the Kremlin even advised against them—as when Brezhnev rebuked Fidel Castro for sending Cuban troops to Angola.

The second cold war, the Reagan administration was convinced, would be won or lost in Nicaragua. Moynihan was furious upon discovering that the administration decided secretly to mine the west coast

harbors of Nicaragua, an act that violated international law. He was furious about the frantic attempt to support the Contras with money supplied from Iran in exchange for missiles, which violated a law of Congress. When Reagan officials tried to lie about the mining, Moynihan
resigned in protest from the Senate Intelligence Committee (he later
was talked into returning). Barry Goldwater, a conservative friend of
Reagan's, wrote a furious letter to CIA director Casey mincing no words.
He also swore in the halls of Congress, so bitter was he about the subterfuge.[20] Once the Iran-Contra affair became public, the White House
lost its credibility and the president's approval ratings sank. Reagan continued to believe that Marxist Sandinistas intended to export revolution
and hence posed a threat not only to Central America but to the United
States. "On November 3, 1986," Moynihan wrote somewhat facetiously,
"President Reagan would allow that we might have to take our final
stand at Harlington, Texas. A prospect of some portent—the missing evidence for which was soon produced. The Sandinistas were providing
arms to Marxist guerrilla factions in El Salvador. The long march north
had continued."[21]

In contrast to Reagan, Moynihan doubted that the long march would
last very long. He had made visits to Managua and San Salvador in 1983.
In Nicaragua, Moynihan dropped in on Comandante Tomas Borge in his
office to join him for lunch at a restaurant across town. The building's
elevator did not work, the bus on the way to lunch belched and sput-
tered and almost broke down, and the cafe owner, after telling the two
he had only rice and beans, returned from the kitchen to say that he had
neither. While Moynihan drank a Pepsi, he listened to poor Nicaraguans
who came to the lunch table, taking their turn to complain to the com-
mandant about lack of jobs, shelters without electricity, inadequate
schools and hospitals.[22]

In San Salvador, Moynihan asked to speak to the rector and vice rector of Central American University (both Basque Jesuits soon murdered
by the regime).

"Were the Sandinistas shipping arms to the Salvadoran insurgents?"
asked Moynihan.

"No," answered the rector.

"But they had been?"

"True."

"Then why no longer?"

"Because you are doing it now."

After the United States successfully interdicted Sandinista shipments, the CIA took over the show, and arms could be had anywhere on the open market. "And, indeed," Moynihan added, "American equipment costing millions of dollars was being flown down, along with military advisors. We had even built a small gem of a central intelligence agency, complete with fountains in the lobby. In the way of that world, the arms were being shared."[23]

When the end of the cold war finally came, it took place not in the third world but in Eastern Europe, not on the periphery but at the center, as Moynihan had predicted. He was puzzled as to why the Reagan administration paid so little attention to the opposition movements behind the Iron Curtain. "In retrospect," Moynihan wrote in *On the Law of Nations* (1990), "the truly important event of 1980 took place in Gdansk, where a Polish electrician, Lech Walesa, having been fired from the Lenin shipyard for union activity, climbed over the wall back *into* the yard and commenced the strike that before the decade was out would put an end to Communist rule in Poland." While Washington worried about Central America, it did little to help dissidents like Walesa, the Czech playwright Václav Havel, and Polish historian Adam Michnik, who were being locked in prison, isolated, and beaten. Years later, a few neocons admitted that they had failed to grasp the significance of a democratic socialist resistance in Eastern Europe. After quoting Walesa's account of his and his fellow workers' struggle, Moynihan observed: "All this while the United States government was translating 'assassination manuals' for use by forces originally recruited in Central America by the Argentine junta that gave us the mothers of Plaza de Mayo holding up photographs of their disappeared children."[24]

The Rule of Law
and the Ethnic Factor

THE NORMALLY CALM and witty Moynihan could turn to rage upon discovering some of the atrocities committed by America's allies in the cold war. Many neocon intellectuals believed in power politics and got on well with autocratic regimes, and a murder or assassination simply went with the territory. Moynihan believed deeply in ethical conduct and the rule of law, a stance that brought him into conflict with Reagan's heroine, Jeane Kirkpatrick. Even as U.S. ambassador to the United Nations, Kirkpatrick had little patience with the UN Charter principles that stipulated that diplomatic or military action must take place collectively with the vote of the Security Council and the consensus of the General Assembly. As if anticipating George W. Bush's attitude a dozen years later, Kirkpatrick insisted that the United Nation's "legalistic approach to international affairs" proved helpless in dealing with communist aggression and subversion. Although neocons saw themselves as the custodians of American morality, when it came to international relations they felt compelled to invoke an amoral relativism. Both Kirkpatrick and the legal theorist Robert Bork denied the validity of international law on the grounds that it was used against the United States while the Soviets escaped scrutiny in their own conduct. In taking action against the regimes in Panama and Grenada, the United States ignored the United Nations and all customary and treaty law that had come down through history. Moynihan urged his country to abide by the UN Charter and that of the Organization of American States. The neocons replied, in Moynihan's words, "the Soviets don't, so why should we?" Yet why, Moynihan asked, should America allow its standards to be determined by what the Soviets do?[25]

In Reagan's mind, liberty and authority always seemed antagonistic to one another, and to entrust an international organization with sovereign power violated the will of a democratic people whose hearts were in the right place. José Ortega y Gasset observed that law is the "despair" of the human condition; it exists to prevent people from doing to others what they would not have done to themselves. Without international law there is only the Hobbesian world of power, force, and violence that would be "nasty, brutish, and short." In that suspicious, distrusting world human life exists "in the state and postures of Gladiators, having their weapons always pointing, and their eyes fixed on one another." Reagan never turned to the United Nations to bring the cold war to an end, and thus in some respects today's neoconservatives can claim him as a fellow unilateralist. But when the president moved away from the Hobbesian world of fear and dread and sought the trust of Gorbachev, the neocons turned against him.

Moynihan's contribution to ending the cold war dealt less with diplomacy than with sociology. Instead of trying to overwhelm the Soviet Union with military expenditure and arms escalation, he advised the Reagan administration to look more carefully at the people living behind the Iron Curtain. Where Kirkpatrick saw Soviet totalitarianism as irreversible, Moynihan saw it as impossible. What would soon bring down the regime was ethnicity, the cultural and religious differences of diverse peoples who had nothing in common save a communism they did not ask for and refused to live with. Relating to events of the previous decade, Moynihan spelled out this argument in *Pandaemonium: Ethnicity in International Politics* (1993). Although the book appeared after the cold war ended, Moynihan reached his conclusions in anticipation of the breakup of the Soviet Union. Hélène Carrère d'Encausse's *L'Empire Éclaté* predicted the breakup ("fragmentation") as early as 1978, and Moynihan fully acknowledged her book, which described Mongols, Tartars, Ukrainians, Muslims, Jews, and other peoples struggling to get out from under the Bolshevik behemoth. Neither her work (later translated into English) nor Moynihan's received much attention in the United States, where some Reaganites still thought that Hayek was right to see the Soviet State as a one-way road to permanent totalitarianism. However, Adams Roberts, of Balliol College, Oxford, where Moynihan presented lectures that went into *Pandaemonium*, offered the supreme compliment in the book's foreword:

> When in early 1992 [Moynihan] presented a doubting Henry
> Kissinger with evidence that some people at least had seen
> what was coming in the Soviet Union, he received what is
> probably the shortest, and certainly the humblest, letter from
> his former Harvard and government colleague: "Dear Pat: I
> stand corrected. Your crystal ball was better than mine."[26]

The kind of crystal ball some hawks stared into may have been less a prism than a mirror reflecting back their own desires. Many conservatives love to cite Aristotle and Aquinas to reassure themselves that truth, moral authority, civic duty, and patriotic unity are still viable in the modern age. Modernity, however, plays havoc with morality. For ethnicity presupposes differences and diversity, the kind of "identity politics" and

"multiculturalism" that would disrupt America in the 1990s. Whatever
the affirmation of ethnic claims did to American society, Moynihan recognized, in the words of Nathan Glazer, "that it would be the ethnic factor that could tear the Union of Soviet Socialist Republics apart and end
the cold war."[27] The ethnic politics that so troubled anticommunist
America actually helped liberate people from communism.

Moynihan dealt with the ethnic enclaves and national minorities that
represented centrifugal forces throughout Russia. His book, a series of
his own writings and speeches that had appeared in such publications
as *Newsweek* and were heard on college campuses from 1979 to 1986,
describes how ethnic strains defied the Marxist promise to eliminate all
conflict by eliminating private property. In some respects Moynihan
anticipated Samuel P. Huntington's *Clash of Civilizations* in suggesting
that future world conflict would have less to do with economics and politics than with culture and religion. He clearly predicted the aftermath
of the former Soviet Union, with the breakdown of authority and the
release of nationalistic impulses bottled up under communism. When
the Strategic Arms Reduction Treaty, formulated in the 1980s, finally
went into effect in 1992, it had to be signed by four independent nuclear
states: Russia, Ukraine, Belarus, and Kazakhstan. A few Western leaders, especially Charles de Gaulle, had predicted that nationalism would
ultimately prevail over communism. In American neocon circles, however, the potential of nationalism received little attention, even as a
revenge against Soviet occupation, while on many American campuses
Marxist professors continued to teach courses on "class consciousness"
and the "contradictions of capitalism." Moynihan remained in touch
with the neocons but chided them for regarding themselves as "realists"
when their ideas had little to do with reality.

While the ethnic factor may have weakened the Soviet Union, it
would be going too far to claim that it brought about the end of the cold
war. When the cold war came to an end, Reagan and Gorbachev were
thinking more about missiles and tanks than about mosques and tribes.
They were also trying to answer a question that Raymond Aron raised as
early as 1967, in *On War*: "If the armaments race does not promise
either of the two Great Powers a decisive advantage, why do they not
agree to end it?" The answer is that the neocons believed that the race
would indeed give the United States the strategic advantage that could
bring the Soviet Union to its knees. Aron, one of France's most revered

political philosophers, believed that peace between the two superpowers could not be maintained through the threat of a suicidal thermonuclear war. He did support Reagan in deploying the Pershing missile in Europe. Having seen little progress in disarmament, however, he went to his death in 1983 in despair, wondering whether democracy, with all its decadent tendencies, could counter despotism, with all its totalitarian temptations. Many years earlier he offered sound advice to both sides:

> It is by drinking at the well of age-old wisdom that our Faust-
> ian civilization has resisted the fascination with the abyss. To
> limit violence by moderation, to renounce the pride of
> absolute victory, to tailor the use of force to the importance
> of the stakes—these precepts, as old as civilization itself, take
> on new meaning in a time when war puts in jeopardy not only
> the independence of nations, but the destiny of humanity.[28]

It was the "pride of absolute victory" that Reagan's neocons refused to renounce. To this day neocon hawks remain convinced that America "won" the cold war, since the Soviet Union and communist Eastern Europe collapsed and disappeared from history. Yet Gorbachev agreed to disarmament treaties on the assumption that he could save communism by reforming it, and Reagan sought to reduce military tensions and eventually eliminate all nuclear weapons, whatever the future of communism. Neocon hawks assumed that the Soviet Union would eventually submit to the will of an economically and militarily superior America; Reagan sought to avoid confrontation in favor of negotiation. The hawks believed overwhelming strength would instill fear in the adversary; Reagan understood that self-respecting leaders do not negotiate out of fear.

The Perils of Pride and
the Virtues of Guilt: "Star Wars"

DANIEL PATRICK MOYNIHAN was not the only scholar to ask the Reagan administration to consider the ethnic composition of Russia and its tendencies. So did national security advisor Richard Pipes. While Pipes believed that despotism and aggressiveness were inherent in the Russian national character, however, Moynihan seemed closer to Aleksandr Solzhenitsyn in seeing Russia as a shattered country with no coherent society, its fragmentation a sign of its people's yearning for freedom. A salient point about Pipes and some of the neocons was their lack of faith in the American character. They believed that a native Protestant religion fed a flabby culture of consumption in America, and they saw Russia as having taken the road to serfdom for which there was no turning back.

The Reagan administration remained under the influence of Pipes and his pessimistic colleagues until George P. Shultz replaced Haig as secretary of state in July 1982. Soon Reagan began to change his mind about the Russia that the neocons had demonized. In his memoirs, Shultz describes how uneasy Reagan became when Pipes and his team entered the Oval Office.[29] The president grew impatient with the hawks' numbers game as they itemized the alleged ascendancy of Soviet weapons—"threat enhancers," Moynihan called them. In his autobiography, Reagan ridiculed the "macabre jargon" of warheads, ICBMs, "kill ratios," and "throw weights," the payload capacity of long-range missiles. The president dismissed his pestering strategic advisors and their numbers, which sounded to him like "baseball scores."[30]

The neocon hawks, who came to be called vulcans, continued in American politics to serve under subsequent presidents and had no qualms dubbing themselves Reaganites. It is conventional wisdom that the Reagan presidency repudiated the older doctrine of containment and faith in détente. It is true that the administration embarked upon the largest peacetime military program in history, adding $32 billion to Carter's defense budgets; and, with planned yearly additions, the budget would rise to $222 billion in 1982. Much of the expenditure was for strategic weapons: the B-2 Stealth bomber; a half-dozen Trident nuclear subs; a hundred MXs, heavy intercontinental ballistic missiles each armed with ten independently targeted warheads; three thousand cruise missiles, and a hundred B-1 bombers. The intense military buildup was based upon a set of assumptions that the Reagan administration learned from the Committee on the Present Danger and its Team B, led by Professor Pipes (discussed in chapter 6). Among the assumptions were that America had fallen dangerously behind in the arms race; that Russia had been building a vast civil defense system of underground bunkers to withstand a heavy missile attack; that the Soviets regarded a nuclear war as fightable and winnable; and that they think differently than we do.[31]

The people of Western Europe believed America's buildup was an overreaction to what Moynihan had described as a "non-existent threat." If anything, it was the Europeans who felt the deadly prospect of a nuclear war. In the late 1970s, the Soviets had modernized their missile system with the SS-20, a long-range missile carrying three MIRVs, multiple independently targetable reentry vehicles, with their own warheads, capable of hitting any city in Western Europe after being launched three thousand miles away in the Ural mountains. Europeans naturally feared that if a nuclear war broke out they would be the targets. European governments pressured Washington to call for armament reductions with the Soviets, and throughout the summer of 1981 peace demonstrations swept through the streets of Paris, Berlin, and London. In November, Reagan proposed what he called the "zero option," which came down to asking the Russians to abandon their recently installed, expensive SS-20s while America would pledge not to embark upon any new missile programs. Most diplomats realized that the proposal would go nowhere. Discussions took place over shorter range missiles, the Intermediate Nuclear Force (INF), but with no result. Meanwhile, the nuclear freeze movement gathered strength in America as well as in Europe. A poll taken in spring 1982 indicated that 70 percent of Americans favored a negotiated halt to nuclear weapons development.

Conservatives praised Reagan for repudiating the doctrine of containment and the premise of détente. They felt he shared their conviction that both stances proved dangerous, since Soviet influence was expanding into the third world, and that hostilities between the two superpowers were intensifying. Reagan's critics, on the other hand, claimed that to maintain an arms buildup while pursuing disarmament was inconsistent and even contradictory. Reagan, however, liked to remind his critics that the stronger the country became, the more likely the Soviets would come to the table to negotiate. It should also be remembered that Reagan came to repudiate the doctrine of deterrence, a strategy based on the threat of retaliation, a second strike. It came to be called MAD, the guarantee of "mutual assured destruction." The president made his famous "Star Wars" speech on March 23, 1983, and his belief in a missile defense system offered a rational option to the irrationalities of nuclear terror, a system he later offered to share with Russia. The program has been ridiculed as well as praised, and it remains one of the most controversial aspects of the Reagan administration.

In his book *Revolution*, the economist and Reagan advisor Martin Anderson explained how the program came about. The problem was how to present to Reagan and his cabinet an aerial ballistic defense system that had yet to be proven to work. The challenge was weighing its technical reliability and costs, and figuring out how to present it as a scientific hypothesis to government agencies, where it "would be seen as a new idea, and nothing threatens an entrenched bureaucracy like a new idea," especially the idea of shifting orthodox military strategy from offense to defense. According to Anderson's account, Reagan solved the problem for his advisors.[32]

In the summer of 1979, Anderson had gone with Reagan, then a presidential aspirant, and a screenwriter on a visit to Cheyenne Mountain, Colorado, to investigate NORAD, the North American Aerospace Defense Command, an underground network of radar detectors designed to alert the country to any surprise attack. Reagan was impressed by the screen monitors gathered in a maze of rooms that burrowed within a solid granite mountain, secured by a massive steel door opened only by secret code. Just before leaving, the visitors asked the base commander what the response would be if an attack was under way. NORAD could only track the incoming missiles, the commander replied, but it could do nothing to stop them. On the flight back to Los Angeles, according to Anderson, Reagan "couldn't believe the United States had no defense against Soviet missiles. He slowly shook his head and said, 'We have spent all that money and have all that equipment and there is nothing we can do to prevent a nuclear missile from hitting us.'" Just before landing, Reagan was still pondering the depressing dilemma. "We should have some way of defending ourselves against nuclear missiles," he commented, as if anticipating his Star Wars idea, which, after his outline of the program in his 1983 speech, was presented to Congress in 1985.[33]

Reagan believed that in proposing Star Wars he was drawing upon the achievements of science to help reduce world tensions by eliminating the danger of a first strike. Reagan's critics, however, saw the program less as a scientific conquest than as a cultural conceit. In her book *Way*

Out There in the Blue: Reagan, Star Wars, and the End of the Cold War, Frances Fitzgerald looked at the birth of the Strategic Defense Initiative and found Anderson's account preposterous precisely because it was too factual and failed to consider the mythical dimensions of Ronald Reagan and the moral arrogance of America itself. The significance of Star Wars, she held, lay not in its military possibilities but in its symbolic ramifications.

Fitzgerald seized upon Reagan's hope of making "nuclear weapons 'impotent and obsolete,'" as evidence of a deep American desire for innocence and liberation from the sins of the Old World. Since SDI had no immediate practical feasibility, Reagan could only have taken "his missile defense idea from a science-fiction film," and in doing so he had also "laid claim to the soteriology, or the salvation doctrine, of the American civil religion." He partakes, she wrote, in the "role of a prophet" who called upon science to engage in "an act of redemptive reconstruction" and bring to an end the danger of nuclear weapons, thereby appealing to evangelicals and others haunted by doomsday scenarios. The "evil empire" speech "had a much more precise theological significance"; the very phrase would "trip-wire the whole eschatology of Armageddon." Reagan was the "American Everyman" descending into the granite core of a mountain to deliver America from a fate worse than death. Anderson was the "Merlin," the angel guiding Reagan on the road he must take. "The NORAD command center in the core of the mountain recalls the caves of Nibelungen in Wagner's *Ring*," and "Reagan becomes Siegfried setting out to end the reign of the mischief-making dwarves and to restore the gods to their rightful place, bringing order once again to the world." Star Wars resonates with "Biblical narratives," "prophetic epiphanies," "Moses going up on a mountain to receive the tablets and descending to destroy the golden idol." It is also the story of the "temptation of Christ" by the devil who offers the kingdom of the world if Christ would only submit to his authority. Above all, Star Wars represented the ultimate expression of "American exceptionalism" on the part of "God's chosen people."[34]

On and on it goes. Fitzgerald was upset that Reagan had the capacity to make people believe in a remote possibility that had no basis in actual reality, another example of the fabulist fooling himself and the nation. The neocon hawks, however, reached the same conclusion as Fitzgerald,

even if for different reasons: communism was an irreversible fact of life
with no possibility of its ceasing to be a reality. As to that abused notion
of "American exceptionalism," it should be remembered that Winthrop
and the Puritans turned their back on the Old World and felt no responsibility to extend "the sacred fire of human liberty" elsewhere. One wonders what Reagan would have thought of Fitzgerald demonstrating to us
how religiosity runs through his rhetoric like a red thread. Emerson and
Nietzsche reminded us that all modern thought is a "concealed theology," a way of keeping alive the religious spirit in a scientific age. With a
nuclear war there could be no "morning in America," no resurrection of
life, and Reagan had no choice but to repudiate the conceit of American
exceptionalism and instead see the American and Russian people as one
and the same.

A most ardent supporter of Star Wars was Richard Allen, assistant to
the president on national security affairs. Allen sided with Pipes's hawkish stance toward the Soviets against the more moderate views of the
State Department. He wrote a memorandum urging a presidential initiative on SDI, insisting the American people would respond to the idea
just as crowds rising in a football stadium shouting, "Defense! Defense!
Defense!" The scientific community, however, was skeptical of the proposal, with the highly significant exception of Edward Teller, a hulky and
thick-accented nuclear physicist who fled Europe in the 1930s to
escape totalitarianism. A member of the Manhattan Project team that
developed the first atomic bomb and later known as the father of the
hydrogen bomb, Teller directed Berkeley's Lawrence Laboratory at Livermore, California, where he promoted pioneering research on X-ray
laser beams. Teller would imagine satellites in space beaming lasers over
thousands of miles at the speed of light, seeking out and disintegrating
their targets, a scheme likened to George Lucas's popular movie *Star
Wars*, where the forces of good and evil battle one another in outer space
on a movie screen as wide as the wide-eyed children viewing it. However, laser technology failed several tests in the Nevada desert, and
doubts arose as to whether the American public would accept extending
the cold war into space. The Department of Defense also questioned the
feasibility of a missile shield, and a scientific group reported that it had
no technical merit. Reagan agreed with Teller that defense is morally
preferable to offense or, to use the title of one of Teller's books, *Better a*

Shield Than a Sword. Teller told Irving Kristol that he sought to replace the menacing doctrine of mutual assured destruction with "mutual assured security."[35]

The project seemed to have lapsed until spring 1983, when Teller appeared on William F. Buckley's *Firing Line*, warning that the Soviets were developing sophisticated antimissile weapons that rendered America more insecure than ever. Why not take up the urgent matter with the president, asked Buckley, a friend of Reagan's? Teller replied that Reagan had shunned him. Eventually the physicist received his audience with the president.

While the two superpowers thought in terms of megaweapons, in Eastern Europe resistance to communism began to express itself without any weapons, a politics of conviction that represented what Václav Havel called "the power of the powerless." Of the Polish dissidents, the historian Adam Michnik wrote: "They do not place their faith in Reagan, or in the Pershing missiles—they have no hopes hanging on the outcome of negotiations in Geneva."[36] In the early 1980s, the dissident movements in Czechoslovakia and Poland were less concerned about the shadow of nuclear apocalypse than with the presence of Soviet tanks. They valued Reagan's support, but they felt on their own. Dissident students and intellectuals had had enough of Marxist dogma, and they sought to move their countries toward liberalism—the very direction that, according to some neocons, especially the disciples of Chambers and followers of Hayek, led to communism. The Solidarity movement in Poland made the Brezhnev regime as nervous as the Sandinista movement in Nicaragua made the Reagan administration fearful. Fear could be a good thing, however, said the hard-liners. Perle and Pipes, adamantly opposed to any opening up to Russia, were convinced that unrelenting fear of the enemy is the best basis for war readiness. In the Senate, liberal Democrat Edward Kennedy and liberal Republican Mark Hatfield spoke out on the dangers of nuclear war, and the growing nuclear freeze movement caught the administration by surprise. Reagan denounced the movement as harmful to the nation's security. In government circles there was a lengthy debate over how to deploy the clumsy MX missiles, which, requiring launching stations safe from attack, were moved from silos to railroad tracks. Gradually, the nation's mood grew wary of the administration's obsession with weaponry. Congress began to resist increases in defense budgets, and as the recession worsened, James Baker and Nancy Reagan saw Reagan's popularity decline. His approval ratings dropped to 41 percent in December 1982, historically low for a president in only his second year in office. It was against the background of such doldrums that Star Wars was announced several months later.

The dramatic announcement of a new mode of strategy in an old cold war led to considerable speculation. At the time there existed no urgent military crisis. Frances Fitzgerald, scrutinizing the speech and its rewording and revisions, noted a sentence that could well have expressed Reagan's conviction, even though it may have originated with an advisor. "Wouldn't it be better to save lives than avenge them?" She rightly observed that the text was burdened with a sense of responsibility and that its promise to protect lives could not be sincere unless Reagan meant to go all the way to his argument's logical conclusion and propose to make nuclear weapons obsolete. Thus Reagan was not unduly worried, Fitzgerald observes, about the scientific unreliability of Star Wars. Deep down he never saw himself as a nuclear warmonger but as one who, like a religious savior and classical hero, was the bringer of peace. Reagan also sensed something else: the connection between confronting the "evil empire" and being tempted by it, the trial of facing a sinful enemy and still claiming the innocence of sinlessness. Star Wars was Reagan's way of having America preclude facing a situation where a second strike would have to be resorted to after the United States had taken a first hit. It would protect America not only from Russia but from itself. To renounce the doctrine of retaliation also meant that America could avoid the guilt of using nuclear weapons. However, at the summit meetings, as we shall see in chapter 10, Reagan had little success convincing Gorbachev that Star Wars was benign, defensive only, as safe as it was harmless.[37]

Reagan was not always successful in resisting the sins of power, the temptation to operate covertly and circumvent the laws of democracy. This flaw brings us to an episode that represents the ignominy of a president who aspired to integrity.

The Iran-Contra Affair

I N HIS CLASSIC ESSAY "Politics as a Vocation," Max Weber presaged the dilemma Reagan would find himself in during the last
years of the cold war. Like Weber, Reagan saw the state as the
enemy of liberty, yet he had to use the power of the state to help liberty
come into existence. Weber delivered his now-famous lecture in 1918,
in part addressed to libertarians and pacifists who saw the state as diabolical. Commenting soon after the end of World War I, Weber wrote,
"Today, however, we have to say that a state is a human community that
(successfully) claims the *monopoly of the legitimate use of physical force*
within a given territory." However, nothing has ever been accomplished
without using force, Weber contended, and in a world of power, the
nation state has no choice. The only question was whether force is used
wisely and morally, with a clear understanding that tragedy is entailed in
all actions where bad means must be used to achieve good ends.[38]

The Iran-Contra affair confronted Reagan with the predicament
Weber analyzed so well. In critical historical situations when a decision
cannot be avoided or postponed, the politician must choose between an
"ethic of principled convictions" and an "ethic of responsibility." The
first gives a leader the moral satisfaction of acting from good intentions,
while the second compels him to consider the outcome of his actions in
the real world. In the first ethic one may be content with a clear conscience and yet still be guilty of refusing to be answerable for the results
of one's actions, even unforeseen results.

Many analysts of the Reagan presidency treat the Iran-Contra affair
as an example of devious diplomacy, the result of Congress's refusal to
aid the Contras or of the president's poor judgment. The affair went
much further, however, in compromising Reagan's political philosophy.[39]

In his first inaugural speech, as we have seen, Reagan exhorted Americans not to look to government for answers to their problems, because
government itself was the problem. There were echoes of previous
speeches, where he had claimed that the "structure" of government had
become so alienated from the people that it stood independently of the
will of their representatives. By his second term in office, however, Reagan had aggravated the very problem he warned against by concealing

from Congress and the American people the actions of his administration. He did so convinced that no other branch of government took the cause of anticommunism as seriously as he did. Perhaps so, but Reagan authorized and accepted activities that created a national nightmare, the specter of a cliquish government within a government, a closed system of rules based on anonymity, compartmentalization, deniability, and secrecy, a veritable cabal impervious to the reach of democracy. Reagan had good intentions but failed to anticipate the consequences of his actions. In Weberian terms, Reagan was a tragic hero, a political leader with character and conviction caught in a historical world of contingency and irony.

Iran and Nicaragua were continents apart, and at first there was no obvious political relationship between the two countries—except for the conviction that all events adverse to United States interests must be related. In Tehran, Islamic fundamentalists had come to power; in Managua, Marxist rebels fought to stay in power. Ambassador Jeane Kirkpatrick convinced Reagan that the fall of Iran's shah and Nicaragua's Somoza represented a common threat to America's national interests, and many hawks were convinced that communists would succeed in Nicaragua just as the Soviets would spread into Iran. However, when the news got out, in April 1983, that the administration had ordered the mining of Nicaragua's harbors, there was an explosion of outrage. In the Senate, Moynihan charged the CIA of taking the "first acts of deception that gradually mutated into a policy of deceit," and Congress revised the Boland Amendment, passed in December 1982, to prohibit all paramilitary support for the Contras and cancel all CIA funding for covert operations in Nicaragua.

While Reagan's advisors were struggling with problems in the Caribbean, the Mideast continued to fester with Islamic hostility toward the United States. Iran, however, sought American help in pressuring Arab states to overthrow Iraq's Saddam Hussein, and Reagan officials asked Iran to help in the release of American hostages held in Lebanon. Iranian clerical leaders were pleased that both countries viewed the Soviet Union as a threat, that Reagan believed deeply in "our Holy Book," and that Allah was on both sides. In politics, however, money speaks louder than prayer, and the man with the most of it was Adnan Khashoggi.

Born in Saudi Arabia in 1935, the eldest son of a physician, Khashoggi was educated at Victoria College, Alexandria, Egypt, and attended California State University, Chico, but dropped out to use his school funds to start a trucking enterprise. He also attended Stanford University for a year but similarly left to return to business. At the age of twenty, he boasted to a journalist that he had become a multimillionaire. He returned to Saudi Arabia and, with ties to the royal family, amassed a fortune through arms deals. He had companies throughout the United States, and magazines wrote up his glittering lifestyle: a jet airliner with three bedrooms on board, a 282-foot yacht carrying a helicopter and Mercedes limousines, an estate in Marbella on Spain's Costa del Sol. He became the tie to the administration, and through him Reagan's aides were able to raise $32 billion from Saudi Arabia to support the cause in Nicaragua, while Taiwan also promised to come through.

Iran-Contra also involved a weapons-for-hostage exchange independent of Saudi money. American aides had heard that Iran was trying to buy TOW (tube-launched, optically tracked, wire-guided) missiles. Eventually a deal was conducted in utter secrecy whereby a hundred missiles America had exported to Israel would be sold to Iran, and the profits would return to the United States to be used to aid the Contras; in turn, Iran would seek to have American hostages released from Lebanon. With the first sale of missiles, only one hostage had been freed, and the story of the money transactions and botched supply drops in Nicaragua broke into the press in November 1986. Much of the public was furious. Years earlier Reagan had assured America that he would make no deals with terrorists; that he would not bargain with hostages or haggle with blackmailers. "The United States gives terrorists no rewards. We make no concessions. We make no deals." On March 4, 1987, a shakened Reagan went before national television and confessed:

> First, let me say, I take full responsibility for my own actions and for those of my administration. As angry as I may be about activities undertaken without my knowledge, I am still accountable for those activities. As disappointed as I may be in some who served me, I'm still the one who must answer to the American people for this behavior. And as personally

distasteful as I find secret bank accounts and diverted
funds—well, as the Navy would say, this happened on my
watch.

   . . . A few months ago I told the American people I did not
trade arms for hostages. My heart and my best intentions still
tell me that's true, but the facts and evidence tell me it is not.
   . . . [W]hat began as a strategic opening to Iran deteriorated,
in its implementation, into trading arms for hostages.[40]

Theodore Draper, who has written the definitive account of Iran-
Contra, says of Reagan's speech that he "assumed responsibility for irresponsibility." Reagan's lapse of judgment was attributed to his hands-off
style of governance, a casual manner in which the president would make
known his objectives without specifying the means to carry them out.
Because some of the president's advisors knew he desired to see the
Nicaraguan rebels receive support, they took it upon themselves to work
out the ways to do so. Given the porous fragmentation of government
offices under Reagan, they had carte blanche to do so.

   The CIA, despite bungling the Bay of Pigs invasion during the Kennedy administration, had continued to operate with little supervision
over its covert activities. Another loose cannon was NSC, the National
Security Council, organized under Truman in 1947. Since the NSC
reported directly to the president, Reagan could easily exclude the secretaries of state and defense from knowing what the White House
approved of in Nicaragua and Iran, and when the affair erupted Shultz
and Weinberger were enraged. Many of those who worked at the NSC
as advisors regarded themselves as independent, almost as autonomous
agents, in some cases disdainful of the congressional restraints imposed
by the Boland Amendment.

   The key NSC advisor, the decent Robert C. McFarlane, was an exception to several of the rogues in the Reagan administration. His father had
been a Democratic congressman from Texas, and he graduated from the
Naval Academy at Annapolis and went on to serve in the Vietnam War.
McFarlane lacked the self-confidence, however, to stand up against the
fervent anticommunist convictions of the Reagan hawks, whose activities violated Boland's injunctions against covert operations. Instead of
speaking out, the sensitive McFarlane suppressed doubts. He resigned

in 1986, and later, hounded by congressional investigations, succumbed
to heavy drinking and tried to take his own life.

More enthusiastic and less anguished was Oliver North. Tall, angu-
lar, combative, and boyishly handsome, with a cocky smile, North came
off, to some, as a tough guy who wanted to go one-on-one with the enemy
(as he boasted to Congress). To others, he seemed willfully immature
and without conscience. He served with distinction in Vietnam and
sported his many medals on his marine uniform as he labored in the
NSC to transfer funds from Iran to Nicaragua. After the scandal broke,
North spent a good deal of time testifying before Congress in nationally
televised hearings. North had no qualms about disobeying the Boland
Amendment, although he denied doing so, because he thought the
United States government had failed to support his fellow troops in
Vietnam, a war he believed America should have won. As to his own
illegal activities, North implied that the president had given him the go-
ahead. The alienation between North and Reagan grew so intense that,
years later, when North ran for the Senate in Virginia, Nancy came out
against him.

The millions of Americans who followed the Iran-Contra hearings
were absorbed by the intrigue, accusations, and counteraccusations.
There was a moment of glamour as attention focused on Fawn Hall,
North's secretary. The tall, attractive Hall did her best to shred documents before North's office was sealed, and the public wondered about
a married military man hiring a stunning blonde for his secretary. Hall
was found to have been sneaking documents out of North's office by
hiding them in her boots, her blouse, and her coat.

One rationale used to justify the Iran-Contra transaction posed a
hopeful possibility. Did the United States have an opportunity to effect
change in Tehran? America had been embittered with Iran after the
seizure of hostages that took place under the Carter administration. In
the middle of the Reagan administration, however, rumors spread that
the Ayatollah Khomeini was nearing death, and the impression grew that
an opposition of "moderates" was rising among students and the professional class. That the NSC might be able to influence a successor
regime became the conviction of Michael Ledeen, a Ph.D. in history
from the University of Wisconsin who spent time in Italy and the
Mideast. Ledeen saw the possibility of working with Manucher Ghor-

banifar, an Iranian nationalist with ties to dissidents and exiles. Although the CIA distrusted Ghorbanifar, a man always making promises and predictions that seldom came to pass, he became the go-between of two hostile nations, Iran and Israel, which would supply the missiles in return for the United States lifting its embargo on Iran.

The transactions in the Mideast were badly bungled. Israel first sent the wrong missiles to Iran, whose leaders threatened to increase the bargaining terms, demanding a hundred times more weapons for each hostage released. Ledeen became skeptical of the whole enterprise, believing the operation should shut down before American policy became up for grabs, agreeing with Ghorbanifar that "we shall all become hostages to hostages." Ledeen's role was assumed by NSC deputy advisor John Poindexter. Former rear admiral Poindexter preferred to serve as a low-profile operator. He worked hard, ate many of his meals at his desk, saw himself as loyal to the president alone, and believed the commander-in-chief was answerable to no one, not even Congress or the Constitution. Poindexter was the consummate yes man. "His expression of fealty to the president," wrote Draper, "resembled that of a vassal in a feudal age."[41]

Events in the Mideast muddled along behind the scenes, despite rumors in the back pages of the press about shady transactions in Tehran and Tel Aviv. What blew the scandal out of the sky was the shooting down of an A-121 supply plane in northern Nicaragua, on October 5, 1986. The Cuban pilot and Nicaraguan navigator died, but an American, Eugene Hasenfus, survived the crash to tell the story of how he had been hired by the CIA, at $3,000 a week, to load and "kick out" cargoes of weapons parachuted to the Contras. Immediately Reagan and his advisors went into a state of full denial. The president dismissed any connection between the government and the flight, while praising efforts to arm the Contras, comparing them to the courageous comrades of the Abraham Lincoln Brigade of the Spanish civil war—the first time an anticommunist conservative president sided with anarchists, Trotskyists, and Stalinists.[42]

The most impassioned spin doctor of damage control was Elliott Abrams, assistant secretary of state under Shultz. "God bless them," Abrams said of those "brave people" willing to bring supplies to the Contras. "If these people were involved in this effort, then they were heroes."

Was America financing the operation in Nicaragua and raising funds in the Mideast? Abrams denied both. "We're not —you know—we're not in the fundraising business," Abrams insisted, even though it was well known that he had solicited money from oil-rich Brunei. "I have never lied to this committee," he reiterated to the Senate Select Committee on Intelligence. An angry Thomas Eagleton reminded Abrams of his earlier testimony:

EAGLETON: Today I asked were you at any time in the fundraising business.

ABRAMS: We made our solicitation to a foreign government.

EAGLETON: Were you then in the fundraising business?

ABRAMS: I would say we were in the fundraising business. I take your point.

EAGLETON: Take my point? Under oath, my friend, that's perjury. Had you been under oath, that's perjury.

ABRAMS: Well, I don't agree with that, Senator.

EAGLETON: That's slammer time.

ABRAMS: You heard my testimony, Senator.

EAGLETON: I heard it, and I want to puke.[43]

In November 1986, Attorney General Edwin Meese announced that the money diverted to Nicaragua came to anywhere between $10 and $30 million in Iranian payments for arms that had been sent to the Contras, a clear violation of the Boland Amendment. Later research indicated far larger numbers: from other countries, $44 million; from private donors, $10 million; and from arms sale profits, $16–$25 million, bringing the total to around $70–$80 million diverted to the Contras. Reagan recognized the transgression, but he saw the whole enterprise as a package deal that had the best of intentions. "Bringing Iran back into the community of responsible nations," he wrote in his memoir, *An American Life*, "ending its participation in political terror, bringing an end to the terrible war [between Iran and Iraq], and bringing our hostages

home—these are causes that justify taking risks." In private letters Reagan protested that the press's publicity had undermined all such efforts.
"I've felt like I have been swimming in a pool of sharks and there's blood
in the water."[44]

A commission led by Senator John Tower and an independent counsel directed by Lawrence E. Walsh offered varying reports. The majority
found that the NSC had violated the Boland Amendment and the
minority argued that the NSC could work legally with other countries
independently of Congress. Indictments were issued against Abrams,
North, Poindexter, and Weinberger for deceiving Congress and obstruct-
ing congressional inquiry, and McFarlane would plead guilty to misde-
meanor charges. All received suspended sentences and pardons from
President George H. W. Bush.

Reagan's flat assertation that there was no trading of arms for hostages
flies in the face of facts. The investigations reported that he condoned
the sales of missiles for that purpose. As to the multidimensional transactions themselves, as Draper rightly concludes: "President Reagan
behaved as if he could get off scot-free if only he could deny that he had
known anything about [them]. His chief defense was a vacant memory
. . . even if Poindexter did not tell the President everything about the
diversion, there was much more to the Iran and Contra affairs than that.
When Reagan complained that he had not been told 'everything,' it
hardly meant he had been told nothing."[45]

It is clear that Reagan knew about the sales of missiles, the attempt
to open up relations with Iran, and the effort to seek the release of
hostages, several of whom were still captive when he left office. There
is no evidence that he knew that North was diverting funds from the
Iranian arms sales to finance covert operations in Nicaragua. His main
objective, indeed his daily passion, was seeing the return of the hostages
from Lebanon. Why was their return so important? In 1980, running
against Carter, Reagan and his campaign manager, William Casey, had no
compunction about negotiating with terrorists. The hostages taken in Iran
after the shah's fall were released exactly on the day of the president-
elect's inaugural. Was Reagan attempting to show that he could solve a
problem that had stymied his opponent Carter? Or did he represent a
classic case of Weber's morally divided politician, a leader willing to
undertake bad means to achieve good ends? Whatever the case, Reagan

remained as a senior statesman what he had once been as a lifeguard: the rescuer who would bring the helpless to the shores of safety.

Reagan has been criticized for failing to go before the public and make a case for the Contras and for refusing to veto both the original Boland Amendment and the second (1984), which gave voice to even stronger opposition to U.S. support for the Contras. His reluctance has seemed to suggest that after McCarthyism and the Vietnam War, the anticommunist cause had lost popular support. Ironically, anticommunism was popular in Russia, haunted by Stalinism and the Afghan war. Reagan's efforts to reduce cold war tensions were welcomed by the Russian people as they were supported by Americans. How different was the response to Reagan's effort to fight the cold war in the third world, which met with bitter resistance in Congress and among the American public.

Perhaps Congress and the people shared Senator Moynihan's insights. The sporadic insurgencies in the third world, observed Moynihan, represented the dying flames of revolutionaries who had nothing in common except their desperate isolation. In the jungles of South America, guerrillas were fighting for causes that had already died in Moscow and Beijing. They were like Japanese soldiers at the end of World War II, who fled to the caves to continue the fight even after Tokyo had surrendered. In the first cold war, involving Europe, Soviet communism with its arsenal of nuclear weapons was a serious danger. In the second cold war, involving the third world, communism was the land of lost causes and pathetic delusions. When Reagan left office in 1989, Cuba was the only remaining Marxist-Leninist regime in all of South America, Africa was suffering from famine and genocide, and in China the urban masses were discarding their bicycles and buying cars as they rushed to embrace the free market.

Marx was wrong. History does not repeat itself; it reverses itself. Marx knew in his head that history progresses from capitalism to socialism; Reagan knew in his heart that it would be the other way around. Yet neither Reagan nor conservatives, especially those of a strong religious bent, have yet to consider what made capitalism so desirable in former communist countries. Communism made consumer capitalism attractive because Marxism in Russia and China had extirpated religion among the young and left them with a bland materialistic atheism. If material reality remained the only reality, if the salvation of the soul no longer could be believed, then the Russian and Chinese people demanded the material happiness promised by communist materialism. They would find it in market capitalism. They returned to a historical stage that their leaders believed could be skipped over as a false path to the future.

Yet what could an American president do with a political culture that neither progresses nor reverses? Ronald Reagan was the ultimate symbol of a conservative president mired in a liberal condition. The Russian people had only to get rid of the Communist Party to move into a different historical epoch. In America, the only chance Reagan had to make government go away was to make the people go away.

CHAPTER NINE

Politics, Economy, Society

Politics and Spin

COMING OUT OF the East Room on March 10, 1982, President Reagan was passing the press corps when he heard a voice shout: "Do you want to overthrow the Nicaraguan government? Tell the truth now!" Reagan glanced at ABC's Sam Donaldson, shrugged, smiled, and walked on. Donaldson thought politics could come clean with "the truth."[1]

"All politics is local" was House Speaker Tip O'Neill's maxim, a warning that no representative rises above the interests of his constituency and that in politics truth yields to pressure. Another maxim is that all politics is visual, a matter of perception and self-presentation. Politics as performance came naturally to Reagan, a former screen actor; he scarcely had to think about it. Others helped, however. Michael Deaver orchestrated the performance, setting the stage and arranging convention balloon drops and the widely watched Fourth of July celebration at the Statue of Liberty. Peggy Noonan wrote memorable speeches, especially the eulogy to the astronauts after the *Challenger* explosion and the memorial at the fortieth anniversary of the D-day invasion. Assistant to the president for communications was the six-foot-five David Gergen, who brimmed with so much restless energy that he spilled out sentences without a pause. What impressed Gergen about Reagan was that the president knew exactly what he wanted to do and would shun resting on his laurels simply because he had won the highest office in the land. From day one, Gergen recalls, Reagan announced: "We didn't come here just to fiddle with the controls. We came to change the direction of the ship."[2]

The die-hard conservatives contemptuously tagged Baker, Deaver, Gergen, and Richard Darman as "pragmatists" to describe their adaptability to changing events and their eagerness to establish rapport with a liberal media thought to be hostile to the president's policies. The pragmatists knew how to play upon the journalists' "access envy," to use Laurence I. Barrett's phrase.[3] They made sure reporters and photographers were well positioned at presidential news conferences and photo opportunities, that columnists and television news anchors were flattered with special invitations to one-on-one conversations with the president, that the media received advanced texts of speeches, and that hot tips were leaked to favored newspapers and reporters. *Washington Post* writer Sidney Blumenthal accused Reagan's assistants of "marketing the president."

However, while Reagan was performing, on the college campus the philosophy of pragmatism enjoyed a revival, and postmodern professors were teaching students that such marketing and manipulation is what life is all about. The irony is that conservatives who hated postmodernism in the curriculum welcomed "performative acts" in politics. The president's men proved that they were masters at poststructuralism and deconstruction as they stagecrafted reality at Pointe-du-Hoc in Normandy or in front of the Statue of Liberty and constructed stunning visual and verbal images of the president. For the pragmatist, ideas are acted out, and for the poststructuralist, nothing is known until it is constructed. So, too, for the media masters. There is no Ronald Reagan until he makes an appearance, and then we know him from what he says and how he looks. Reagan was careful to wear brown suits, to relate intimately to the middle class, and he avoided blue, which conveys distance and superiority. As to what he actually did as president, that, too, could be easily handled, especially if things went wrong, by "spin" and "damage control." With some Reaganites, all politics was constructed and became sheer simulation. They beat the deconstructionists at their own game.

However, Reagan was genuine, a political leader with convictions, not simply an actor of roles and memorized lines. Whatever controversies surrounded his politics, Reagan's personal leadership was cheerful, credible, and courageous, and it carried the day. There was always in Ronald Reagan a charismatic presence. He was brave enough to face down radical students while professors ran for cover, and so courageous he could crack jokes after taking an assassin's bullet. With Reagan, the medium was as important as the message. As a speaker and a performer, Reagan stood before the American people: six foot two, close to two hundred pounds, broad shoulders, narrow waist, as solid as steel. Thick, wavy, dark brown hair topped the handsome, ruddy face of a man in his seventies. When he spoke, his head bobbed and weaved, his body shifting weight with each emphasis. In lighter moments, his eyes twinkled with laughter, and his lips spread with a winning smile as humorous thoughts spilled from his tongue. In rare angry moments, he could roar like a lion: "Mr. Gorbachev, tear down this wall!" More often, his voice crooned the soothing, reassuring melody of a down-home innocent, the corny "gee-whiz, golly shucks crap," as his friend the singer Frank Sinatra fondly put it.[4]

Reagan chose as his model Calvin Coolidge, a president whose behavior was calculated to frustrate any media master. "Silent Cal" was a man of few words and so confident in his convictions that he was indifferent to the press and public opinion. "Calvin Coolidge," observed Arthur Schlesinger Jr., "is the only President on record who did not seem to care what was written about him." Reagan also seemed not to care. He yawned when the first major book on him, Garry Wills's *Reagan's America: Innocents at Home*, came out in 1987. He told Marion Foster, a family friend, that he had not read the book but came across "some supposed quotes in a review that bothered me a little. These were quotes of [Wills's] statements, not those of anyone he'd interviewed. I've come to believe too many press people fancy themselves as psychologists. They claim to know the innermost thoughts of someone whom they've never been closer to than in the crowd at a press conference. One has proclaimed that I'm only reading lines I spoke in a movie." The president knew himself too well to be troubled by what others thought about him.[5]

When Reagan took down a portrait of Harry Truman in the Cabinet Room and replaced it with one of Calvin Coolidge, Washington was abuzz with wonder and derision. Legend had it that Coolidge, who allegedly did his daily exercises on a rocking horse, knew little, said less, and thought there was nothing that the national government needed to do. Coolidge was the president who proved that the country had no need of a president. We now know that Coolidge was a progressive who opposed racism in society and corruption in politics. Reagan admired the simple utterances of Coolidge's carefully crafted rhetoric, his ability to define himself in moral terms that set him apart from the sleazy conduct of his predecessor, Warren G. Harding. Coolidge

believed America awaited a spiritual revival and was convinced that the
economy turns on individual initiatives, not collective demands. "Economy is idealism in its most practical form," declared Coolidge. A century
earlier Emerson said the same thing in his essay on "Wealth," where he
warned Americans that poverty "demoralizes," earning "dignifies," and
failure "diminishes" all "chances of integrity . . . as if virtue were coming
to be a luxury which few could afford, or as [Edmund] Burke said, 'at a
market almost too high for humanity.' "[6] Burke worried that moral excel-
lence was beyond the reach of democracy. Reagan believed that democracy made morality possible by holding individuals responsible for what
they do with their lives.

An ex-Democrat, Reagan became a Republican but remained his
own man. He was less party-oriented than traditional Republicans, such
as Richard Nixon, less concerned with the factions within the GOP
than with his own personal convictions. In his speeches Reagan often
addressed Democrats as well as Republicans, reminding the audience
that he had once been a longtime Democrat. "Let Reagan be Reagan"
was a common bit of advice conservatives dispensed to those who would
try to make him into something other than himself. Reagan relied more
upon prerogative than incumbency, more upon executive leadership
than party-based constituencies, or, as George Shultz put it, he governed
"more in terms of presidential policy than campaign fodder."[7]

In recent years it has been argued that loyalty to the Democratic Party
has suffered because many Americans no longer have a clear idea about
its position on the issues. Some Democrats envy the historic Reagan as
a leader who articulated a consistent ideological message, from the time
he was governor in the sixties until the time he arrived at the White
House in the eighties. If voters depend upon party identification, and
not the vicissitudes of public opinion, Reagan's steady voice and vision
provided it. Few could say of Reagan what has been said of so many
other presidential candidates: "I don't know what he stands for."

A look at Reagan's position on many domestic issues illuminates the
ways a conservative dealt with the political realities of American representative democracy. How a politician stands is one thing; what he or
she does or can do in office is another matter.

The Reagan Agenda

THOSE WHO WORKED for President Reagan often wondered about the casual ways of the man running the White House. Reagan would meet with cabinet members to lay down a policy or political strategy but then left it to his staff to work out the details. In his memoirs he acknowledged, "I've been criticized for what some people call a 'hands off' management style." Reagan believed that the president should set broad policy matters, be available for consultation, and do whatever might be necessary to "fine-tune the politics." He should not be so intrusive as to peer over his subordinates' shoulders to check up on them and "tell them every few minutes what to do." For the most part, Reagan's easygoing governing style worked well. In at least one instance, it turned out to be disastrous.[8]

The appointment of James Watt as secretary of the interior came like a death sentence to the Environmental Protection Agency (EPA), the Sierra Club, and other organizations committed to preserving the American landscape. A religious fundamentalist with a bald dome and a leering smile, Watt was as happy in his office as a fox in a chicken coop. His attitude toward what Jefferson called, in the Declaration of Independence, "the Laws of Nature and of Nature's God," was to decimate whatever was sacred and stood in the way of economic growth. Watt would be guided by the "Scriptures which call upon us to occupy the land until Jesus returns," and he set out to preside over what came to be called the Sagebush Rebellion to turn over the wilderness to timber interests, rivers to energy producers, open ranges to cattle ranchers, coastal waters to offshore oil developers, and national parks to private enterprise. One environmental official said that with Watt in office he felt "as though I've got one foot on the grave and the other on a banana peel." At first, Reagan believed he and his secretary were standing firmly on two feet. The president told an old California friend that the environmentalists were simply another bureaucracy and that there was nothing wrong with private citizens buying public land. "Would you believe it—there is some national forest acreage in my ranch—totally surrounded by my property on all four sides and I'm trying to find a way to buy it?"[9]

Watt was a glutton for gaffes. When he assembled a panel to supervise a coal-leasing project, he boasted to the U.S. Chamber of Commerce that he had selected a diverse group. "We have every kind of mix you can have. I have a black, I have a woman, two Jews and a cripple." He offended young Americans and outraged Nancy when he banned the Beach Boys from a Fourth of July concert on the grounds of the Washington Monument. Nancy liked the rock group and suggested to her husband that it was time for Watt to go.[10] After Watt's resignation, attention focused on Anne M. Gorsuch, a Colorado attorney Reagan had appointed to head the Environmental Protection Agency. She proved inept in dealing with Congress over toxic waste cleanup, acid rain, and the renewal of the Clear Air Act, and resigned under fire. Reagan replaced her with the moderate William D. Ruckelshaus, the first EPA administrator under Nixon, who returned to the agency he helped set up. He improved relations with Congress and helped win the passage of legislation to expand government purchase of wetlands. The EPA would also require environmental reports from builders applying for construction permits. With Reagan's support, Congress passed the Coastal Barriers Resources Act, which reduced federal funding for developments along storm-threatened seashores, whose residents often expected the federal government to pay the costs of repairing storm damage— "socialism for wealthy people." Reagan wanted to impose more cost controls on established programs that environmentalists considered sacrosanct. All in all, his appointments unnecessarily politicized environmental policy and polarized the electorate.

Reagan's hostility to environmental preservation seems puzzling. While Coolidge may have stayed in the White House resting on his rocking horse, Reagan could not wait to leave the capital to fly back to his ranch in the hills above Santa Barbara. There he would slip on his riding jeans and boots, mount his stallion, and ride off into the proverbial sunset before returning home to sit by the fireplace. And while other political figures loved to pose before the camera next to a deer shot dead or fowl brought down by a rifle, Reagan felt no need to prove his machismo by killing animals. Like Barry Goldwater, Reagan resented federal power and relished open spaces, without ever acknowledging that the former protected the latter. The myth of Western individualism enthralled politicians from Arizona and California, who too frequently forgot the federal government's historical role in developing the West—

from allocating land grants and grazing rights, developing railroads and dams, and granting mining patents, to sending in the U.S. Calvary to protect settlers in need of law and order. Westerners scarcely acknowledged how often the federal government rescued them from folly. The more they depended on government, the more they resented it and denied their dependency. And for Reagan dependency was the original sin of the welfare state.[11]

Convictions about dependency also affected Reagan's thoughts on race and civil rights. No one, white or black, should look to the government to be rescued. Reagan opposed the historic Voting Rights Act of 1965, passed overwhelmingly by Congress to eliminate hindrances to the ballot box in the South. He believed the Constitution was on his side, since voting was a state and not a federal matter. He resented the charge that he was pandering to white southern racists to build a national political coalition. He rejected the support of the Ku Klux Klan, and while he accepted the backing of religious fundamentalists, he expressed little interest in pushing their program for prayer in schools. However, Reagan followed up on Trent Lott's recommendation to have his administration support Bob Jones University, a Christian fundamentalist college in Greenville, South Carolina. The school fought the withdrawal of its tax exemption by the Internal Revenue Service, which objected to its ban on interracial dating and marriage. Deaver suggested that Reagan talk to a few black members on the White House staff, in the hope that they could persuade the president to understand that racial discrimination, and not religious liberty, was the key issue in the Bob Jones case. While the controversy simmered, the Supreme Court upheld the IRS policy of denying a nonprofit tax exemption to institutions practicing racial discrimination.[12]

Reagan also offended black sentiment when he first opposed a bill that would honor the memory of Martin Luther King Jr. by declaring a national holiday in his name. He proposed instead that Congress appropriate money for scholarships for black students, but then supported the bill when it became clear that Congress would pass it. Reagan simply could not see why government workers should have another day off. When North Carolina senator Jesse Helms demanded to know whether King had been a communist sympathizer and insisted that Reagan open sealed FBI records on King, the president refused to support the demand but jokingly replied: "We'll know in about thirty-five years, won't we?" It was another one of Reagan's impromptu remarks that he soon regretted, and he called Coretta Scott King to apologize. Thereafter he spoke admiringly of Dr. King; he also paid tribute to black leaders at a commencement address at Tuskegee University, and visited the home of a suburban black family that had been racially harassed.

The NAACP was unimpressed, and its executive director, Benjamin Hooks, told the press that no administration has "demonstrated as much determination as President Reagan to roll back the hard-won gains of black Americans." The hurt Reagan replied to his old friend "Ben," pointing out that awards in discrimination cases had increased by more than 50 percent under his administration and that the black unemployment rate, while high, was decreasing (as it would from 16.8 percent in 1983 to 10.7 percent in 1986).[13]

If blacks and liberals felt disappointed in Reagan for not fighting to expand civil rights, many hardened conservatives felt downright betrayed by his failure to oppose affirmative action, a policy that Nixon authorized by executive order and that his labor secretary, George Shultz, implemented. The policy was also supported by the Ford and Carter administrations. Reagan's cabinet was deeply divided. Labor Secretary William E. Brock strongly advocated that the policy of hiring with racial goals and timetables be continued, and he had the support of several department leaders: Shultz (State), Baker (Treasury), Margaret Heckler (Health and Human Services), Samuel Pierce (Housing and Urban Development), and Elizabeth Dole (Transportation). The most forceful voice in opposition was that of William J. Bennett, the secretary of education.

On college campuses affirmative action was an explosive issue. It was supported by administrators who liked to see themselves as liberals adapting to change; it was hailed by faculty members who championed diversity and multiculturalism; and it was treated gingerly by some white students, who feared accusations of racism if they opposed it. One outspoken figure was Sidney Hook, who wrote Reagan to convey his bewilderment that the administration was dragging its feet on the issue. The White House replied to the philosopher. While it opposed numerical quotas, it did "actively support positive affirmative action programs in the government where the objective is to ensure equality of opportunity."[14] However, critics believed affirmative action was less a demo-cratic proposition guaranteeing equality of opportunity than a policy that would give legal preference to select groups with the aim of producing equality of results.[15]

The telling detail is that affirmative action had the support not only of radicals but of conservatives, especially the National Association of Manufacturers and other businesses that worried about reverse discrim-ination suits filed by white workers. Responding to the "rights revolu-tion" of the eighties, American firms and schools of business profession-alized the field of employment relations with new offices of "human resources," which made racial hiring as legitimate as health care and pension benefits. The Reagan administration believed that the contro-versy over revising the executive order on affirmative action had no legs, and would lose as many popular votes as it would win. Bennett's cam-paign to overturn it died a quiet death.[16]

In the first years of the Reagan administration, the landmark 1965 Voting Rights Act came up for renewal. Why Reagan allowed affirmative action to stand while opposing the Voting Rights Act is puzzling. The act had transformed the South by allowing blacks to participate in politics and enter the polling booth. Reagan, however, went along with the argu-ments of his Justice Department lawyers (including a young staff assis-tant name John G. Roberts Jr., later chief justice of the U.S. Supreme Court), who said a denial of voting rights had to be established by show-ing that state policies demonstrated an "intent" to keep blacks from the polls. A lower percentage of black voters was no proof of racial discrim-ination by the states, they insisted. Vernon Jordan, president of the National Urban league, challenged Reagan, claiming that "intent to dis-criminate is impossible to prove." How could it be documented? "Local officials don't wallpaper their offices with memos about how to restrict minority-group members' access to the polling booth." Congress sup-ported the more expansive version of Reagan's Voting Rights Act, but his demands for evidence of intent to discriminate tell us much about his view of human nature. Years earlier, his mother went out of her way to attend to the sick and the poor, his father had defied racists, and Reagan himself almost came to blows with an anti-Semite. Reagan believed deeply that our desires are good because God had implanted them in us. Even if an "evil empire" existed, he found it hard to believe that men and women could possibly mean to do evil. Intent had to be proven before he would have the federal government step in to remedy it.[17]

The issue of immigration, however, dealt more with consequences than intentions. By the 1980s, the country was being inundated by waves of immigrants and refugees from Asia and Central America. In his farewell address, Reagan declared that America had "doors open to anyone with the will and heart to get there." Did this include illegal immigrants—the millions of poor peasants transported by "coyotes" across the Mexican border for a high price, or desperate Cuban and Haitians escaping economic and political oppression on small, overloaded boats and sinking rafts? America was divided on the question along class lines. Wealthy farmers and manufacturers needed cheap field and factory laborers, and upper-class homeowners wanted maids, nannies, and gardeners, while American workers and their unions felt threatened by the influx of undocumented aliens. The Republican Party in Reagan's era always had a divided soul; its religious moralists worried about threats to family and community, while its libertarian secularists looked to the market to keep the country free of controls. On balance, Reagan sided with the capitalists, and America shied away from the issues of affirmative action and immigration restriction, believing that the country must participate in a global economy where multicultural hiring, low labor costs, and weak unions were the order of the day.[18]

Reagan's legal and judicial appointments also reveal his preference for freedom over control. Reagan appointed a young lawyer, Yale Law School graduate Clarence Thomas, to be his assistant secretary for civil rights in the Education Department and then promoted him to head the Equal Employment Opportunity Commission. A beneficiary of affirmative action at Yale, Thomas came out against it during his professional career and often clashed with minorities, his own as well as others. In Thomas's view, affirmative action policies implied that blacks cannot make it on their own. He believed his own character and sense of self could not be defined by the ethnic categories of identity politics. Later, as a Supreme Court justice appointed by Reagan's successor George H. W. Bush, Thomas was the most insistent advocate of the conservative doctrine of "originalism," which holds that the laws are constitutional only if they are consistent with the meaning of the Constitution at the time of its ratification in 1787–1788.[19]

Most of Reagan's Supreme Court appointees tied themselves in knots trying to square the conservative doctrine of originalism with the conservative doctrine of judicial restraint (which holds that judges should not second-guess the political decisions of legislatures) as well as with the conservative doctrine of *stare decisis* (which says courts should show deference to past court decisions). These conflicting doctrines led to many 5–4 decisions in which the swing vote most often was Justice Sandra Day O'Connor. Reagan's appointment of a female to the Supreme Court was a first in American history. In his correspondence, the president answered conservatives who worried that a female judge would protect the right to abortion. The right wing in Arizona, her home state, spread rumors that as a state senator O'Connor had voted against a bill that would have prevented a university hospital from performing abortions. Reagan challenged the rumors, as did Barry Goldwater, who enthusiastically supported the Stanford Law School graduate. Jerry Falwell of the Moral Majority and officials at the National Right to Life Committee opposed O'Connor, believing she was unlikely to vote to overturn *Roe v. Wade*, the Supreme Court decision that affirmed a woman's constitutional right to abortion. O'Connor also aroused conservatives' ire for having recommended, as an Arizona state senator, that state agencies disseminate information on medically cleared family planning methods. Religious conservatives balked at seeing teenagers taught birth control and actively enjoying the pleasures of the body. And conservatives who believed in freedom would not allow adult women to be free to be in control of their own bodies and to abort unwanted babies. Goldwater, a true libertarian, would oppose all such intrusions of state power. Reagan, a true Republican with a divided soul, thundered against state intervention in economic decisions, while tacitly approving state surveillance over morality and family life.

However, for Reagan and his supporters, the answer to many social questions was not to assert the authority of the nation state so much as to rein in the power of the Supreme Court. Its rulings over decades protected the rights of the criminally accused. It also upheld a rigid separation of church and state, mandated the continuation of school busing, and allowed abortions and birth control. Some members of Reagan's court took seriously the doctrine of *stare decisis* and refrained from overturning *Roe v. Wade*. Such positions provoked religious conservatives,

who sought to protect their faith and families, as well as legal conservatives, who believed the courts were overstepping their authority by overturning laws properly made by Congress and state legislatures. Conservatives advocated judicial restraint, insisting that the courts simply
interpret the law and resist making it.

One of the most influential legal thinkers was Edwin Meese, who had
worked with Governor Reagan in California and became U.S. attorney
general in 1985. Meese criticized the Supreme Court for refusing to
return to the Constitution as it was understood by its farmers and,
instead, reading into the document the partisan biases of the present. He
called for a jurisprudence of original intent and meaning. However, one
wonders whether conservatives desired to return to the Constitution as
Alexander Hamilton intended it. Hamilton felt a "trembling anxiety" if
ultimate sovereignty were not invested in the national government—the
dread of Ronald Reagan.[20]

In 1987 the struggle over the Constitution came to a head when Reagan's nomination of Judge Robert Bork to the Supreme Court set off a
bitter and clamorous national debate. Bork challenged those who
claimed that abortion was a right to choice guaranteed by the right to privacy in the Constitution. Bork was a federal appeals court judge who had
written extensively on constitutional issues as a Yale Law School professor. He denied that any such right of privacy was contained in the Constitution. Bork took an originalist position, insisting that the Constitution
was clear in its meaning and intention from the moment of its framing.

The Bork nomination aroused an impassioned opposition. Senator
Ted Kennedy famously said, "Robert Bork's America is a land in which
women would be forced into back-alley abortions, blacks would sit at
segregated lunch counters, rogue police could break down citizens'
doors in midnight raids, children could not be taught about evolution."[21]
Liberal law professors went to Washington to testify against Bork. Many
of them took a postmodernist view of the Constitution, holding that it is
what the justices interpret it to mean, and hence could be used to overturn laws enshrining old prejudices or reinterpret them to validate new
social reforms. Law is not an ultimate source of authority, the postmod-
ernists claimed, but an instrument to be used in light of its consequences, and not necessarily its intent. Such a position outraged Reagan, Bork, and the conservatives.

The debate over the Bork nomination was as unfortunate as it was misleading, and it generated an extraordinary amount of anger that has yet to subside. Ironically, it could have been a moment of truth in American legal theory. Properly understood, postmodernism could actually have reinforced the stance of conservatives. For if the Constitution is nothing more than what the judge says it is, then the judge has no authority to overturn the actions of a legislature, because he has no grounds for appealing to an objective or natural law or any principle independent of human bias and will. If judges are actually making law in the guise of declaring it, then surely disputed legal issues should be turned over to where they really belong, the legislative branch of the federal government and the states—precisely where conservatives say that sovereignty lies. Reagan himself believed, as did Thomas Paine, that society precedes the state, and hence the will of government must yield to the ways of society lest the expansion of the judiciary leads to the atrophy of democracy.

Liberals defeated Bork's nomination by a vote of 58–42. There was a lengthy Senate debate not only over Bork's legal stances but his haughty personality and alleged incapacity to understand the problems of ordinary Americans. Earlier, Reagan had easily secured the appointment of the even more acerbic Antonin Scalia to the high court, and eventually he filled the position intended for Bork with a mild-mannered Californian, Anthony Kennedy. More difficult was the elevation of William Rehnquist from justice to chief justice. Ted Kennedy led the attack, accusing the former Nixon appointee of being "too extreme on race, too extreme on women's rights, too extreme on freedom of speech, too extreme on separation of church and state." The confirmation hearings, a conservative senator wryly observed, had become a "Rehnquisition."[22]

The Election of 1984

IT WOULDN'T GO AWAY. Weeks before the election of 1984, the Associated Press reported that the CIA had written training manuals for clandestine military operations in Nicaragua. The CIA advocated that the Contras engage in "selective use of violence [to] neutralize carefully selected and planned targets such as court judges, police, and state security officials." Death squads, assassination instructions, the tactics of terror—all prohibited by Congress and even by an executive order, signed by Reagan. Didn't such tactics amount to "our own state-sponsored terrorism," journalist Georgie Anne Geyer asked the president? Reagan, flustered, responded: "We have a gentleman down there in Nicaragua who is on contract with the CIA, advising supposedly on military tactics with the Contras." Knowing that the CIA had been prohibited from such activity, Geyer asked: "Are you implying, then, that the CIA is directing the Contras?" Reagan, visibly shaken, spluttered: "I'm afraid I misspoke when I said a CIA head in Nicaragua. There is not someone there directing all this activity."[23]

The question came up during the debates in the election of 1984, one of the few times Reagan lost his poise. Reagan was facing off against the Democrat Walter Mondale, an energetic, articulate liberal who was twenty years younger than the president and the protégé of fellow Minnesotan Hubert Humphrey, Lyndon Johnson's vice president and the party's 1968 nominee against Richard Nixon. Humphrey was one of the last liberals who tried to keep alive the New Deal and the Great Society against a rising conservative tide.

At first the election seemed as if it might be close. In 1982 and 1983 the country had gone through a deep recession, and Reagan's approval ratings had dropped to an all-time low of 35 percent, while unemployment rose to 10.6 percent. As the election approached, certain subjects were off the table, since few voters could get excited about them. Defense spending and further efforts to revise the tax code seldom came up, and Social Security was untouched after Reagan touched it and got singed in 1981. The massacre of American marines in Beirut and the controversy over Nicaragua did little to help Reagan. The successful invasion of Grenada, the "lovely little war" touted as a great victory over communism, helped Reagan's ratings some, as did the economy, which had roared back from recession to spread prosperity and create new jobs while keeping inflation low due to the fall of oil prices and the lowering of interest rates by Federal Reserve chairman Paul Volker.

Mondale selected as his running mate New York congresswoman Geraldine Ferraro, counting on the appeal of the first female vice president in American history. Would wives, mothers, and daughters turn out en masse to vote the Democratic ticket? The Democrats' platform echoed the Republicans', with talk about old-fashioned values and the need for efficiency in government. Toward the end of the campaign, Mondale unwisely pledged to raise taxes on the rich in order to reduce the national debt. He had touched another third rail in politics and would suffer for it. As the British learned in the 1770s, Americans do not expect to pay for the security they enjoy.

The major issue that seemed to divide the two candidates was age. Reagan, the oldest president, was approaching seventy-five, his handsome features still intact but his mind at times fuzzy and unfocused. Mondale made a refreshing contrast, a young fiftyish man who smiled with such confidence it seemed an upset was in the making. Mondale easily won the first debate. Reagan claimed that he had been so determined to refute his opponents' facts and figures that he overprepared, stuffing himself with information and ending up with too many details to be coherent. "I had crammed like for a final exam and knew I was flat when the debate started," he wrote to a friend. "In sports they call it leaving your fight in the locker room." Some advisors thought that the president took the debate too lightly and was "lazy."[24]

While the nation was abuzz about the president's poor performance, his memory lapses and unsteady concentration, Reagan showed just how alert he could be. In the second debate, he was asked whether age should be an issue in the campaign. "I am not going to exploit, for political purposes, my opponent's youth and inexperience." The audience chuckled loudly, and even Mondale broke out in a laugh. Later he admitted he knew that with Reagan's one-liner he had lost the election.

Reagan's victory came early and it came big, the largest electoral landslide in history. He swept forty-nine states, losing only Mondale's Minnesota and Washington, D.C. He duplicated what only FDR had done in the 1930s and Eisenhower in the 1950s: win two consecutive landslides. The Republican Party had won the support of the young, with 59 percent of voters age 18 to 25 casting their ballot for the oldest president in American history. Reagan also won over women, despite Ferraro's presence on the Democratic ticket, with their support increasing from 47 percent in 1980 to 54 percent in 1984. Perhaps even more surprising, Reagan's vote penetrated ethnic and class lines. He enjoyed majorities among all ethnic groups except Hispanics, where he received 44 percent, and blacks, who voted overwhelmingly and predictably for Mondale. The majority of the working class, especially blue-collar ethnic voters, continued to break with the Democratic Party and vote Republican. This trend of a new alignment began with George McGovern's candidacy in 1972, when labor leaders and the Moral Majority felt the Democrats had succumbed to the extreme antiwar Left. In the 1980s, those who defected from their historic party came to be called Reagan Democrats.

Nineteen eighty-four, the year George Orwell warned that we would see truth "lifted clean out of the stream of history," was actually a time for truth about modern American history. Between Governor Reagan in the 1960s and President Reagan in the 1980s, American politics underwent a sea change. Many books have been written about the sixties generation, all claiming that the radical decade left its indelible mark on the American mind, its lasting influence on American politics, its enduring legacy on popular culture. On cultural matters, the music of the sixties and its permissive life style did indeed prevail as Americans listened to the driving lyrics of hard rock, watched risqué films where nudity became as common as violence, and were no longer shocked to hear of young couples living together. However, the freedoms won on the cultural front seldom translated into politics.

The nomination of Geraldine Ferraro initially thrilled women. Feminists, members of the National Organization for Women, those supporting the Equal Rights Amendment, and other activists thought that at last they would take their place in the theater of American politics. However, Reagan's appointment of conservatives Sandra Day O'Connor, Jeane Kirkpatrick, Carla Hills, and Lynne Cheney helped to offset these gains. With the overwhelming defeat of Mondale-Ferraro, the women's movement was no longer on the move, and by the era of Bill Clinton's presidency in the 1990s, feminists could only watch the Democratic Party abandon its cause.

The election of 1984 was a referendum on the 1960s. Reagan would often insist that he had not turned against the New Deal of the 1930s but that the Great Society of the 1960s had broken faith with him. LBJ went far beyond FDR to embark upon a campaign of social activism in civil rights, busing, the war on poverty, and other issues designed to assist minorities. Those who once voted Democratic but cast their ballot for

Reagan in 1984 represented a growing white opposition to group-specific activism. As liberalism became associated with identity politics and the claims of multiculturalism, older white and middle-class Democrats no longer saw a place for themselves in their party and began to look with favor on the Republicans. In the late seventies, just before Reagan came to office, 51 percent of Americans called themselves Democrats and only 21 percent described themselves as Republicans. After Reagan left office and ever since, America has been evenly divided between the two parties, while a majority classify themselves as independent.

The area of international relations also worked to Reagan's benefit. The Democrats had long been identified as antiwar activists still suffering from a "Vietnam syndrome," and many in the party thought Reagan's policies in Nicaragua would lead to another war. However, a majority of Americans supported a strong military and success in the nuclear armament race. Mondale criticized arms escalation and attacked Reagan's program for a ballistic missile defense system in outer space. Reagan nonetheless benefited from the image of standing tall against both the Soviets and the Muslims, even though his administration actually blundered in the Mideast and was reluctant to pursue an aggressive policy against the growing threat of terrorism.

On domestic matters, the Republican Party represented broad, solid mid-America, while the Democrats appealed to some of the rich on the top and the dispossessed on the bottom. The novelist Tom Wolfe had depicted the very rich, with their summer homes and charity benefits, as "radical chic." Their liberality expressed the Democrats' *noblesse oblige*, while the poor used political activism to provoke liberal guilt and win government handouts. That imagery resonated with the tax-paying public. Wedged between "limousine liberals" and "welfare queens" were middle-class Americans. They became Republicans, closed out their bank accounts, and escaped to the suburbs, away from the thrills and dangers of the city. Democrats became associated with the shock of the new—feminism, gay rights, sexual freedom, abortion, legalization of drugs, single-parent households. Much of middle America objected to the Democrats' giving pride of place to "deviant" lifestyles. Reagan came to the rescue, saving the hardworking citizen from the barbarians and the bohemians.

AIDS, Education, and the Farce at the NEH

WHAT THE GOVERNMENT can and cannot do is based on
how politicians and judges interpret the Constitution, the
founding document that instructs the government to promote the nation's "general welfare." How should we interpret the meaning of that phrase? In the way his administration dealt with homosexuals and the study of history it is possible to see some of the cultural
limitations of the "Reagan revolution."

Many voters have never forgiven the Reagan administration for
responding so reluctantly to the AIDS epidemic. Prime Minister Margaret Thatcher had her government work with the British Medical
Association to carry out research with the cooperation of AIDS patients.
Having obtained a degree in chemistry at Somerville college, Oxford,
Thatcher saw the disease as a challenge that science could tackle and
overcome. Great Britain had only small numbers of evangelicals and
Roman Catholics, many of whom regarded homosexuality as disobedience to God and the disease as God's revenge. England's AIDS epidemic
was also less widespread.

Reagan's surgeon general, Dr. C. Everett Koop, and Nancy Reagan
urged the president to support efforts to fight the epidemic. Reagan
himself hesitated. He was reluctant to endorse either liberal public
health measures (condom use and the distribution of "safe-sex" bro-
chures) or conservative proposals (the quarantine of AIDS patients and
the forced closure of bathhouses). Congress and the administration
authorized substantial funding for AIDS medical research, but they
sidestepped the controversy by emphasizing that AIDS victims included
innocent recipients of blood transfusions and babies born to AIDS-
infected mothers.

Reagan sympathized with victims wasting away in hospitals, and he
found repugnant Patrick Buchanan's charge that AIDS was nature's way
of dealing with those who violated its laws. Surgeon General Koop complained that Reagan's advisors prevented him from seeing the president
to take up the issue. It was not until he learned of the illness of his friend
Rock Hudson in 1985, however, that Reagan took the AIDS plague seriously and ordered the resources of government to fight it.

Reagan's own attitude toward homosexuality is disputed. His biographer Lou Cannon noted that the Reagans were comfortable around gay men. Nancy Reagan's interior decorator stayed overnight in the White House with his lover. However, Reagan's second major biographer, Edmund Morris, writes: "My research cards have him finding it [AIDS] a fit subject for humor as late as December 1986." Some parts of the American public did see AIDS as a kind of gallows humor until it came closer to home in the community, the professions, or the family itself. "To be fair to him," Morris adds about Reagan, "he made no moral distinction between homosexuality, heterosexuality out of wedlock, or abortion on demand. All three were abhorred by God, in his opinion."[25]

Reagan may have been that judgmental in his dotage, but in his Hollywood days he was relaxed and accepting on issues of sexual morality. On many mornings Reagan woke up in bed with a woman who was not his wife. He responded with relative equanimity when his sons Michael and Ron had sex out of wedlock, and he was tolerant of Patti's liberal lifestyle. As we have seen, he advised his old friend Florence Yerly to overcome her sense of guilt about sex; specifically, he recommended that she do so by reading about the "Polynesians. These people who are truly children of nature and thus of God, accept physical desire as a natural, normal appetite to be satisfied honestly and fearlessly with no surrounding aura of sin and shy whispers in the darkness. By our standards they are heathens but they are heathens without degeneracy, sex crimes, psychoneurosis and divorce." Margaret Mead could not have put it better.[26]

Reagan's public comments were not always indicative of his private convictions. In the letter to Yerly, by insisting that "God couldn't have created evil," he hoped to persuade the widow that physical desire between two human beings is natural. Later, as president of the United States, he maintained that the Soviet Union was "the focus of evil in the modern world." In the first instance, Reagan was listening to his heart, which had been informed by his mother's religion; in the second, to his head, which had been informed by his advisors' politics.

Ultimately Reagan the politician was less interested in explaining the mysterious ways of God than in explaining the malignant ways of government. His antigovernment phobia seldom allowed him to appreciate what the state could do or had done in American history. He rarely expressed any interest in the positive benefits of regulation, whether it concerned establishing fair public utility rates, clean water inspection, air pollution controls, or auto safety design. Who, he asked, will "regulate the regulators"?[27] In Reagan's southern California, laws regulating gas emissions successfully reduced smog. However, Reagan was as reluctant to tell people what they should do as he was to tell them what they should not do.

Reagan's reticence about federal regulation had dire consequences in the area of education, where his indifferrence to what and how schools went about teaching could lead one to believe that the widely touted Reagan revolution never happened. During his first campaign, Reagan had hinted he could well abolish the Department of Education, which Meese had called "a bureaucratic joke." Instead he appointed Utah educator Terrell Bell to the department. The Reagan administration was concerned about methods of bilingual education, efforts to remove religion from public schools, and the alarming decline in educational standards, and it supported school vouchers that would let children escape failing public schools by allowing their parents to use tax dollars to pay tuition in private schools, even religious schools, where prayers were said in the classroom. Liberals opposed vouchers as a violation of the separation of church and state; others accepted aid to private schools as long as it did not take money from public education. Bell proposed to the White House that the department be downgraded to a sub–cabinet-level operation. Under his direction, however, his department issued the valuable report *A Nation at Risk: The Imperative for National Reform*, which revealed how far American students were falling behind those in other countries. Still, a federal education policy was no real priority for Reagan. Bell soon left office to be replaced by the director of the National Endowment for the Humanities (NEH), William J. Bennett.[28]

A muscular former football play whose rugged looks belied his eloquence, a learned classics scholar educated by the Jesuits, Bennett became the moralist of the Reagan administration. He was continually giving addresses and writing books on authority, civility, and virtue, and he vigorously defended the ideals of Western civilization, convinced that American values were under attack by academic Marxists, liberal relativists, and third world multiculturalists. After leaving the Department of Education, Bennett accepted the challenge of combating the heroin and crack epidemics sweeping through America. As "drug czar," not a cabinet post but a position created in response to an emergency, Bennett promised to drive the dealers from the streets and win the war against narcotic addiction. He had the support of Nancy Reagan, who told America's youth how to resist the temptation of pot: "Just Say No." Bennett eventually stepped down and returned to private life, where he made millions on the lecture circuit and by compiling collections of moralistic poems and stories. One was published as *The Book of Virtues*. He began spending more time in Las Vegas, where it turns out he could not say no and lost six million dollars to a gambling addiction, earning the epithet "Bookie of Virtues."[29]

When Bennett left the NEH in 1985, he was replaced by Lynne Cheney, wife of Wyoming congressman Richard Cheney, later vice president under George W. Bush. With Lynne Cheney as NEH director, the proper study of history in the schools suffered an embarrassing setback. What was meant to be a conservative reform raising standards in civic education turned into an intellectual scandal that continued well past the Reagan years. It was as though the Old Left of the thirties rose from the coffins, or the New Left of the sixties enjoyed a Second Coming, proving that Marx was right when he said that the second time around history would end in farce.

Painfully aware of American students' woeful ignorance of history, Cheney authorized NEH funds to write up guidelines for teaching history in grade and high schools. Apparently unaware of how radical liberal arts faculties had become on the nation's campuses, she allocated funds to the history department at UCLA to prepare what would become the *National Standards for History*. When they were published, a firestorm of controversy erupted, and the U.S. Senate voted unanimously to condemn them. Cheney rightly complained that, in the document, white male political leaders disappeared from history, along with explorers, scientists, industrialists, financiers, and even labor leaders who had more faith in capitalism than in communism. The history standards would also have history teachers inform their students that the Muslim world exhibited no trace of slavery, hierarchy, or poverty, and that there were few Muslim women devoid of rights and excluded from education and the professions. The *Standards* extolled every society that was premodern—"organic" cultures supposedly uninfected by the virus of modern capitalism. The third world was virtuous, the first vicious. The *Stan-

dards endorsed a new social history that gave voice to all those who had been left out of past narratives, and it depicted the downtrodden as capable of "agency," acting in ways that made a difference. Indivduals in power apparently made no difference and could be ignored. The social historians regarded Reagan as a laughable film star who took America for a ride. The sentiment was summed up by the *Village Voice*, which had the president, standing atop the stairs about to enter *Air Force One* to fly into retirement in California, smiling and waving to the American people. The caption declared, "See you later, Suckers!"

The *National Standards for History*, one of the most embarrassing documents in the history of higher education, was so politically correct that it told students about the horrors of Hitler and barely mentioned the crimes of Stalin. Reagan's struggle with the Hollywood Reds was for naught and dared not be mentioned. Thucydides and Herodotus believed in studying the past to hold on to the memory of the great things people have done; the *Standards* would have American students remember the worst things: enslaving African Americans, wiping out Native Americans, and oppressing the poor and powerless. Not even the ending of the cold war, which was happening as the *Standards* were being written, deserved mention. Devoting absolutely no attention to the world-important negotiations between Reagan and Gorbachev, the *Standards* depicted the cold war as infantile "sword play."[30]

To "Kill the Beast," or "Nobody Shoots Santa Claus": Reforming the Welfare State

THE REAGAN EIGHTIES had an economic as well as a cultural context. In the sixties, Lyndon Johnson and the architects of his Great Society programs assumed that affluence was plentiful and perpetual. Young people were optimistic and carefree. An annual American Council on Education survey found that only one-half of students felt that financial success was very important in their lives. By the eighties, such a cavalier attitude disappeared. The stagflation of the seventies combined high inflation and growing unemployment with a general slowdown of the economy, and the oil crisis of the late seventies intensified a sense of economic gloom. Surveys showed that college students were choosing courses with career possibilities and reliable earnings: law, medicine, business, and computer technology. No longer was income taken for granted. Students worried that they would never live as well as their parents did, and that the affluent middle-class family life was a thing of the past.

With this new apprehension, the generation of the Reagan eighties took a hard look at the programs of the sixties, and it seemed they were all directed toward minorities: welfare payments, job programs, racial hiring quotas, rent subsidies. Society was strapped. How long could politicians continue to assume that money could be poured into social programs and be made to work? Senator Daniel Patrick Moynihan best summed up the mentality of Reagan's middle-class America in his E. L. Godkin lectures at Harvard in 1984. "We have been a generous people, and remain such, but there is not likely to be any widespread renewed interest in the condition of the poor until the prospects of this uncertain, apprehensive middle class are settled, and for the better, and until it gets beyond the seeming selfishness of the moment."[31]

President Reagan's attitude toward the welfare state reflected his ideological affinities with Tom Paine and Ralph Waldo Emerson. It is hard to see his attitude as generational, since most Americans who went through the Depression appreciated how government could help them, and no president attacked the welfare state with Reagan's animosity. From wherever he derived it, nothing could shake Reagan's belief that poverty saps character and renders humankind weak and dependent. Like older programs for the indigent, the welfare system only perpetuated laziness and irresponsibility. It has been said that Reagan's seeming indifference to the rising fiscal deficit was planned and deliberate. By cutting taxes and increasing defense spending, Reagan was creating a huge budget deficit, but he was also making it impossible for politicians to propose new domestic programs. That was one sure way "to kill the beast" and do away with welfare once and for all.[32]

Liberals thought entirely differently. They believed society wanted big government programs designed to help people in all walks of life. Anyone helped by Social Security, unemployment insurance, and laws giving workers the right to organize and bargain with their bosses for wage increases would be grateful to politicians who made such programs possible. They would continue to vote Democratic to protect their self-interest. As the beneficiaries of government programs, voters would dare not kill the golden goose. The liberals' reassuring slogan became: "Nobody shoots Santa Claus."

Liberal Democrats were late to see the coming attack on the welfare state. The Republican Party under Eisenhower in the fifties was one reason why they grew complacent. The Republicans had been out of office from 1932 to 1952, and with the election of Eisenhower, Democrats expected the worst. Instead he accepted Social Security and left much of the New Deal intact. Liberal Democratic thinkers sighed in relief. "Social welfare legislation is almost entirely noncontroversial," wrote the economist John Kenneth Galbraith in 1955. The historian Arthur Schlesinger Jr. was happy to report that the welfare state did not have "many serious opponents left." In his highly influential *The Vital Center*, Schlesinger had contended that "we are all supporters of the welfare state." However, Schlesinger also espoused a "cyclical" theory of American history, and if the country moved to the left with liberalism, could a move to the right not be far behind?[33]

As we have seen, Reagan had reformed California's welfare system as governor, and throughout the late 1970s he delivered radio broadcasts attacking its abuses. By the time he became president, Phyllis Schlafly, Paul Weyrich, and the Religious Right saw welfare programs as the ruin of the republic. The government, they held, had no business feeding the poor, nursing the ill, housing the homeless, and drying out the drunks. At times Reagan saw welfare not so much as the sin of the weak as the selfishness of the wicked. His speeches were filled with stories about schemers who spent more time living off the system than looking for a job. The matter also troubled Senator Moynihan, who noted that most of those collecting unemployment insurance rarely went job hunting until their checks ran out. Reagan told stories of men who would purchase a few groceries with food stamps and then use the change to buy a cheap pint of gin, or of pornography shops with signs that read: "Food Stamps Accepted." But it was the story of "the welfare queen," a staple of his radio broadcasts of the seventies, that simultaneously stirred the public and led many to believe that Reagan had made it up. It was real, but almost surreal, so fantastic and improbable that a Balzac or a Tom Wolfe would have difficulty imagining it.

Her name was Linda Taylor. She was an attractive forty-seven-year-old black woman whom an official of the Illinois Department of Public Aid called "without doubt, the biggest welfare cheat of all time."[34] The *Chicago Tribune*, the *New York Times*, and other papers ran the story in late 1974. She drove three new cars, a Cadillac, a Lincoln, and a station wagon. Using various names, phone numbers, addresses, and Social Security cards, she collected, it was reported, $154,000 in one year. She owned three houses that she rented out. Possibly out of embarrassment, the authorities hesitated to prosecute her, and she continued living flamboyantly, stepping out of her cars in a mink coat. Three years after the story first appeared in the press, Taylor was convicted, in Chicago on March 17, 1977, for welfare fraud and perjury.

The story provoked angry charges of racism from liberals who believed it was blown out of proportion to discredit the welfare system. The amount Taylor collected proved to be exaggerated. But liberals, even if they acknowledged that Taylor was a rip-off artist, thought the controversial black woman ruined a good thing; conservatives pointed to her life as an example of how welfare corrupts by making it easy for anyone to live off the state.

The development of welfare programs is a case study in what social scientists call the irony of unintended consequences. When the system of welfare was first devised, its guiding principle was to uphold American values by keeping the family intact. The most controversial program, Aid to Families with Dependent Children, came into existence during the Depression years and was designed to shore up families that had suffered a loss, not from divorce or a deserting husband but specifically from industrial accidents—a father physically disabled due to a fall from a construction platform or an Appalachian miner killed by the collapse of a shaft. For decades the public supported such a policy, with the specific aim of helping widows and children. However, in the sixties, AFDC focused on the inner city, where unemployment and disability had been less the concern of welfare agencies than the absence of the father in dysfunctional families. AFDC became associated with poor black people, especially single mothers and even young teenagers receiving welfare checks and continuing to have children without a husband.

The absence of a man in the house was the subject of Daniel Patrick Moynihan's "The Negro Family: The Case for National Action," a small,

forty-eight-page document that became the highly controversial Moynihan Report. It argued that although the country was making progress
in civil rights, the black family in the inner city had been falling apart,
wracked by poverty, drugs, and despair; it was a "tangle of pathology."
Moynihan was reluctant to suggest a remedy, but his diagnosis was
denounced as racist, and the report fell out of sight, as the senator never
again raised the issue in a public forum (though he did publish some
essays on the subject). Decades later, black scholars themselves would
write about the crisis of the African-American family and acknowledge
Moynihan's pioneering study.

Meanwhile, liberals and conservatives continued to disagree about the
welfare system and why it was failing. The view of the Left, best
explained in *The Other America* (1962), by the social democrat Michael
Harrington, claimed poverty and unemployment were deeply rooted in
U.S. social and economic institutions and that the nation would have to
make a political commitment to put more money into social programs.
The view of the Right, articulated by the neoconservative Charles Murray, claimed that the problem was moral in nature. The poor lost their
sense of self-reliance and personal responsibility as they became dependent on welfare programs and the expectation of welfare checks from
Uncle Sam. Murray's *Losing Ground: American Social Policy, 1950–
1980* (1984) became the seminal statement on the subject. A social scientist with New York's Manhattan Institute, a neoconservative think
tank, Murray noted that total government budget outlays for social programs had been increasing over three decades and were continuing to
do so under Reagan. The welfare state had destroyed the role once
served by church, family, and community. The dilemma was how to aid
the poor without encouraging their financial dependency. "We tried to
provide for the poor and produced more poor instead," wrote Murray.
"We tried to remove the barrier to escape from poverty, and inadvertently built a trap." Moynihan's Harvard colleague Nathan Glazer
stated the dilemma in the Weberian terms of the irony of unintended
consequences: "Our efforts to deal with distress themselves increase
distress." Perhaps President Reagan said it best of all: "We had a war on
poverty, and poverty won."[35]

There was a telling difference between the earlier Moynihan Report
and Murray's *Losing Ground*. President Reagan fully accepted Murray's

thesis that the plight of poor blacks in the inner city was directly caused by the welfare state, whereas Moynihan demonstrated that Murray was unable to establish such a causal connection. Moynihan suggested that the economically distressed black family was and would continue to be in utter disarray with or without welfare payments. He quoted specialists claiming that the widespread belief that poverty programs contribute to poverty problems was more impression than fact. The notion that black mothers were motivated to have more children to collect more money also had no basis in empirical evidence. While the number of families receiving AFDC increased 68 percent in the seventies, the number of children receiving AFDC benefits increased only 19 percent. Moynihan agreed with Murray that the black family remained in critical condition, but he asked for more precision in explaining how the condition had come about:

> Murray's work is concerned primarily with the growth of an urban minority underclass. But that is precisely what I did predict in 1965, using data series that ended in 1964, before any of the events that he asserts have brought these "turns for the worse." It could well be that the predictions made in 1965 were not warranted, that I saw trends which did not as yet exist and only subsequently came about. Very well, but prove *that*. . . . It comes down to this: *Losing Ground* attributes to government actions that mostly began *after* these development had commenced as clearly recognizable statistical trends. It may be argued that these government actions intensified these developments, but the data are not all conclusive.[36]

Moynihan and the neoconservative historian Gertrude Himmelfarb recognized that government programs to overcome poverty had been a conundrum at least since the Elizabethan Poor Law of 1601. Reagan seemed no more successful in handling the issue than other presidents. In his first administration, he shifted some responsibility for the poor to local government (the New Federalism), reducing the distribution of food stamps, and tightening eligibility for AFDC. By the mid-eighties, however, hunger and homelessness had become major public issues.

Americans did not have to turn on the evening news when they could
see the homeless on their own sidewalks. In Washington, D.C., the
street activist Mitch Snyder led protests and fasts against hunger and
homelessness. The United States Department of Agriculture became the
object of derision for classifying tomato ketchup as a vegetable for
school lunches. On CBS, Bill Moyer, former assistant to Lyndon Johnson, produced a documentary, *People Like Us*, that dramatized the
effects of budget cuts on a working mother who quit her job so her sick
child could qualify for Medicaid, on a teenage girl suffering from
strokes, and on a priest who administered a food program for the poor.
In the middle of Reagan's second administration, even Republicans in
Congress voted against further cuts in the food program and welfare
benefits. In 1987, when Congress and the country began to turn against
Reagan's domestic programs, he was recovering from a prostrate operation and reeling from revelations of the Iran-Contra scandal, and polls
showed public approval of his performance had dropped from 70 percent to 45 percent. Relations with the Soviet Union were much
improved, but at home Reagan's last year in office was one of the lowest
moments in his political career—also the loneliest, as Reagan felt he had
lost the trust of the people.

The debate over welfare reform culminated in the Family Support Act
of 1988. Conservatives had hoped for stringent reductions and controls.
However, the bill, mainly the work of Moynihan, had the federal government take over poorly handled state responsibilities, establish federal
health and job training standards, and increase the allocation by 3 billion over a period of five years. It hailed the idea of "workfare," requiring
able-bodied welfare recipients to seek jobs and providing child care and
continuing Medicaid coverage to women who went to work. The bill
sent a mixed message, since the benefits came more from being on welfare than from being employed. It was not the bill Reagan had wanted,
but he signed it.

The Reagan revolution fell short of ridding the country of the welfare
system—that would have to wait for the 1996 welfare reform bill signed
by Bill Clinton—but it did much much to render it vulnerable by exposing its inefficiencies, scams, and failures. By the time of the Clinton
presidency, the welfare state had become so indefensible that Clinton
supported legislation reducing it to the barest minimal health care pro-

visions. While Reagan "did not make the 'ending of welfare' *inevitable*," writes the Oxford historian Gareth Davis, "he did make it *possible*."[37]

The struggle over welfare troubled the conscience of the country. "Does this administration—does my party—care about the poor?" asked Senator David Durenberger, Republican from Minnesota. "Is the 'new federalism' a smoke screen for a repeal of the New Deal? Is the private sector initiative a fig leaf to cover for a lack of compassion?" Many were eager to portray Reagan as callous. One congressman joked that someone should take the president to a meat market and buy him a heart. Some journalists understood that Reagan's quarrel was not with the poor and helpless but with the institutions failing them. Reagan may "sound terribly cold," Murray Kempton observed. "Yet his problem is that his imagination is incapable of compassion in the general. Show Ronald Reagan a crippled or beaten and broken child and he would be the first to weep and then loot the treasury to make it right."[38]

Economics: Prosperity without Morality

THE PRESIDENCY OF Ronald Reagan marked the reemergence of the fabulously rich in American social life. Not since the gay nineties and the roaring twenties had the public seen such bold, conspicuous elegance at concert halls, museums, Academy Award ceremonies, and inaugural balls. Gone were the tie-dye T-shirts and torn Levis of the youthful counterculture, Jimmy Carter's cardigans and Rosalyn Carter's recycled inaugural gown. The 1980s inaugural balls were resplendent in plunging necklines, dazzling jewelry, and fur coats. The president wore white tie and tails, the first lady a one-shoulder beaded cream satin gown. Long black limousines clogged the streets, and as journalists watched the parade of the prominent enter the ballroom, they gasped at the "staggering splendor." Nancy Reagan became a heroine to the fashion world, wearing designer gowns by Adolfo, Galanos, Oscar de la Renta, and Yves Saint Laurent. In the eighties, *Dynasty* was a popular TV series that dramatized the intrigues of the rich and famous, and Diana Vreeland mounted costume exhibitions at the Metropolitcan Museum of Art that were the social events of the year. The 1984 exhibition "Man

and the Horse" featured a nineteenth-century painting of an English
lord on horseback confidently gazing at the viewer. It could have been
Reagan himself at his California ranch, the Marlboro Man whose belief
in the American dream made it happen. Everywhere America celebrated
wealth and beauty, as though the dream of democracy was opulence
itself, and those who could hardly afford such a lifestyle envied it.[39]

Against this milieu of aristocratic affluence, Reagan's domestic policies appeared almost mean. Indeed, a double standard held sway. What
made Reagan seem so stingy and uncaring when it came to welfare for
the poor was his seeming smiling indifference when it came to windfalls
for the rich. During his administration, some elements of the wealthy
class were doing what some elements of the welfare class did—making
false claims, juggling the books, ripping off the system, and commiting
other misdeeds dedicated to the proposition that dishonesty is the best
policy. It has been said that Emerson had no answer to evil. Did Reagan?
Like the poet, the president believed that human drive is divine and government artificial—the "badge of lost innocence," as Paine put it. In
America, Reagan declared, a "permanent government" had produced a
"federal bureaucracy . . . so powerful it was able to set policy and thwart
the desires of not only ordinary citizens" but their representatives as
well. "Government growing beyond our consent had become a lumbering giant, slamming shut the gates of opportunity, threatening to crush
the very roots of our freedom." How to liberate desire from the strangle-
hold of government?[40]

The answer was to deregulate and contract out to private interests all
the activities that liberals and leftists said were responsibilities of government. Deregulation, however, is a profoundly ambiguous proposition. In the 1980s, while conservatives sought to see it take place in the
economy, professors sought the same in the academy as they assaulted
the idea of the canon and anything that smacked of orthodox authority.
In American political history, deregulation actually goes back to the hero
of modern liberalism, President Andrew Jackson, who refused to renew
the charter of the Bank of the United States in 1832, thereby leaving the
economy to unregulated market forces, just as Reagan wished to do a
century and a half later. In contemporary history, deregulation started
before Reagan, in the Carter administration, and had the support of
many liberals as well as conservatives. Under Reagan, the policy was
inspired by Milton Friedman and the University of Chicago school of

economics. Reagan appointees pored over the catalogue of federal programs looking for opportunities to remove rules that sustained high prices, reduced competition, and limited consumer choice. The policy was applied to the airline, railroad, trucking, and telephone industries, and the public was happy to see prices come down and services improve. However, giving outside parties taxpayer money and authority to provide public services could also be an invitation to corruption.

In the mid-1980s persistent newspaper readers could follow the twists and turns of stories that revealed how private interests abused government programs to line their own pockets. In the Wedtech scandal, John Mariotta, son of struggling Puerto Rican immigrants, started a machine shop in one of the poorest neighborhoods of the South Bronx. His success caught the attention of Reagan, who was delighted to be told that Mariotta would generate $100 million in new business in the inner city while saving the government $25 million by hiring a thousand former welfare recipients. With Reagan's encouragement, the army and navy placed orders with Wedtech to develop parts for helicopters and jet engines. The company benefited from programs the government set aside for minority businesses while secretly bringing in nonminority partners and bribing a federal official to recertify its status as a minority firm. As suspicion of fraud arose, Wedtech hired lobbyists and gained the support of New York congressmen who used their influence with members of Congress and the administration to keep government loans and business orders flowing to the company. Even when the army judged Wedtech's costs excessive and its ability to fulfill orders doubtful, Reagan intimates Lyn Nofziger and Ed Meese did all they could for the company, which continued to pose as a minority firm helping the underprivileged. On the verge of insolvency, Wedtech executives, advised by corrupt accountants, continued to sell millions of dollars in public stock while giving millions in hidden payments to themselves. In 1986, with the U.S. attorney in New York and the Pentagon's auditor knocking at the door, Wedtech filed for bankruptcy.[41]

Scandal also besmirched the Department of Housing and Urban Development. Reagan had no use for HUD, a legacy of the Great Society programs of the sixties that aimed to promote housing for low-income people by using tax dollars to motivate developers. Conservatives saw it as another example of government intrusion on the private sector, and Reagan appointed Samuel Pierce to head the department. A black Republican and Wall Street lawyer, Pierce had no experience with public housing, and he offered little protest when Budget Director Stockman drastically shrunk funding for the department's staff and programs, eliminating the oversight of its cadre of professional civil servants. HUD now "stood out as a cash cow ripe for plunder," writes the historian Michael Schaller, who describes how former interior secretary James Watt earned a half-million dollars merely by placing a telephone call to support a company seeking backing for housing projects, how HUD money was spent to construct luxury apartments, swimming pools, and golf courses, and how friends and relatives of New York senator Alfonse D'Amato made a killing in getting HUD to subsidize local projects. Reagan appointees were convicted of crimes, and Pierce himself remained under a criminal indictment for almost a decade before he was acquitted.[42]

More notorious were the savings and loan scandals of the era. For a half-century, S&Ls served a highly useful purpose in the nation's credit system. They extended low-profit loans to home buyers and accepted deposits by small savers whose accounts were guaranteed by the Federal Deposit Insurance Corporation (FDIC). With the approval of both Congress and the public, deposit insurance was increased to $100,000 per account to permit S&Ls to attract more savers and pay them higher interest rates, and the Reagan administration deregulated the savings and loan industry to allow higher profit margins on its investments. To generate more income, the industry embarked upon highly speculative purchases in everything from commercial real estate to junk bonds. Arizona businessman Charles Keating used his California-based Lincoln Savings and Loan to convince elderly investors to dip into their Individual Retirement Accounts (IRAs) to buy junk bonds on the false promise that they were guaranteed, like regular deposits.

S&L officials made considerable money by extending risky loans to business ventures and paying themselves exorbitant salaries. When some S&Ls began to fail and a government bailout was sought, Ed Gray, appointed by Reagan to supervise the industry, advocated tightening lending rules and employing more bank examiners. His efforts were blocked by White House chief of staff and former treasury secretary Donald Regan, whose former employer, Merrill Lynch, thrived on S&L accounts, and speaker of the House, Texas congressman Jim Wright, who had a partnership with a close friend who owned a savings and loan.

The abuses continued as Keating gave campaign contributions to five leading senators: Alan Cranston of California, John McCain and Dennis DeConcini of Arizona, Don Riegle of Michigan, and John Glenn of Ohio. When Gray's term came to an end, Reagan replaced him with M. Danny Wall, who immediately interceded on behalf of Lincoln Savings by overruling the recommendations of bank examiners to close it down. That the S&L scam had the support of both Democrats and Republicans concealed the enormity of the crisis. By the end of the Reagan administration, hundreds of S&Ls had failed. Most citizens lost none of their savings, since they were insured, but it has been estimated that the bailout of the financial industry cost taxpayers $500 billion, to be paid over several decades. Keating was convicted of fraud and sentenced to a jail term.

The S&L debacle suggests the unintended consequences of Reaganonmics. The idea of deregulation intended to remove government from the private sector of the free market. Yet the program was based on government-guaranteed banking deposits. Capitalism, hailed for its aversion to public policy and willingness to compete and take risks, actually wanted government to minimize all contingency while S&L directors gambled with other people's money.

Behind every virtuous citizen, Mark Twain warned us, may reside a huckster and scam artist. During the Reagan eighties, which came to be called the Me Decade, not only bold bankers but solid citizens seemed to have the urge to "go for it." In his 1981 book *Wealth and Poverty*, George Gilder not only described the striving after wealth as an expression of hard work, but he hailed the profit motive as the foundation of civilization and Christianity. "Greed is good" became a popular saying, taken from the 1987 film *Wall Street*, where actor Michael Douglas showed how far a broker could go by insider trading—from a penthouse to prison. A short time after the Reagan era, the culture of avarice remained to reemerge in the film *Pretty Woman*. Actress Julia Roberts asks Richard Gere what business he is in. "I buy and sell businesses," he replies. "But what do you make?" she insists. "I make money," he answers. "Oh, just like me," reflects the gorgeous prostitute.

The financial scandals of the Reagan era cast a shadow on the economy and made the country a little cynical about the cult of wealth even as Americans wildly pursued it. A popular liberal assumption held that, during the eighties, the wealthy few ruled over the struggling many.

When George H. W. Bush became president in 1989, and stated in his
inaugural address that he would stand for "a kinder, gentler nation," he
and his advisors were trying to distance themselves from the Reagan era,
which had come to be seen as a decade of selfishness that produced
increasing inequality and impoverishment. A stock market crash in 1987
seemed to affirm that government cared only about the rich. "At the
time of the crash," wrote James Reston of the *New York Times*, "the Secretaries of State and Treasury were out of the country, and the President,
as usual, was out to lunch." Washington is "leaderless in following a policy of spend and spend, borrow and borrow," all the while allowing tax
breaks for the rich. A Herblock cartoon depicted the opening of a safe
brought up from the depths of a shipwreck. The safe had the stamp
"Reaganomics" and the sunken ship bore the name *The Great Boom*.[43]

Cynical critics of the Reagan administration scorned the notion that
an economic upswing lifts all the boats in the harbor, whether a dory or
a yacht. The working class have no boats, charged the Left. Such dreams
are only the "false consciousness" of the bourgeoisie. American workers,
however, educated by Reagan's "trickle-down" theory, showed their class
consciousness by emulating the classes above them. They began to buy
Boston Whalers and SUVs. The rising tide did indeed lift all boats. From
1986 to 1988 the top 5 percent of taxpayers paid 45.5 percent of all
taxes, up from 41.8 percent in 1986. The next 45 percent of taxpayers
paid 48.7 percent of all taxes, down from 51.6 percent, and taxes paid
by the bottom 50 percent of all taxpayers declined to 6.6 to 5.7 percent.
The impression that the Reagan era was a time when the rich exploited
the poor must be revised if history is to be faithful to statistics.

Data supplied by the Urban Institute also show income levels
increasing for those at the bottom of the income distribution:

Quintile	1977	1986	Percent Change	Percent of Total Income Gain
Bottom	$15,853	$27,998	77%	28%
Second	31,340	40,041	37	27
Third	42,297	51,796	20	20
Fourth	57,486	63,314	10	14
Top	92,531	97,140	5	11

In view of the overall class benefits of the eighties, how is one to judge "Reaganomics"? There is a consensus among economists that the Reagan administration brought down the high inflation of the Carter years and that, aside from the recession of 1982–1983 and the market crash of 1987, the economy performed well and employment and productivity remained steady. On the other hand, the national debt, the budget deficit, and the international trade imbalance went up substantially. Economic theorists were not entirely happy with the economy. Monetarists such as Milton Friedman complained that Reagan could have done more to facilitate the circulation of money, supply-side economists demanded more tax cuts; fiscal conservatives worried about huge budget deficits; and libertarians wanted to eliminate almost all regulations. In terms of productivity and national income, the Reagan eighties performed reasonably well economically, but no more so than the Kennedy-Johnson sixties had or the Clinton nineties would.

Reagan would have had a hard time cutting federal spending in the best of circumstances. In America's political culture people think far more about their individual rights than about their duties to one another, and their rights include subsidies they think they are owed. The massive amount of domestic spending that kept the country in debt was due in large part to entitlements demanded by middle-class America, especially Social Security and Medicare for the elderly, who, living longer than expected, took from government coffers far more than they ever paid in during their working years. Agricultural subsidies and highway and water projects testified to the power of rural states in the Senate. Yet unlike subsequent Republican presidents, Reagan did not make lowering taxes the stubborn fetish of fiscal policy, and he was willing to raise them several times during his two administrations. Reagan, of course, had no interest in cutting back defense spending, especially his pet project, the Strategic Defense Initiative, "Star Wars." When Reagan left office the government had accumulated close to $1 trillion in national debt. To this day politicians and economists still debate the question: "Do deficits matter?"[44]

The answer Governor Reagan gave in 1975 was that deficits are a disgrace. He was responding to his old labor comrade George Meany, president of the American Federation of Labor and the Congress of Industrial Organizations. Meany believed that unemployment and poverty could be addressed with some deficit in the budget. "He went on to say," in Reagan's words, "a big rich country like ours can afford to go into debt." Reagan retorted that such an attitude is like a family going further into "hock" by doubling the mortgage on its home and borrowing far beyond its capacity to repay. Reagan cited Keynes, FDR, and others to acknowledge that a government should spend during bad times but must use the surplus accrued during good times to pay off its debts. Reagan dared not mention the "T" word—taxes. But he insisted that a national debt meant higher inflation, deeper recession, and more unemployment. What troubled him as governor in the 1970s, however, scarcely seemed to bother him as president in the eighties, although he regretfully acknowledged the debt in his farewell address. He attributed the deficit to expenditures due to the cold war, but even when it was winding down there was no letup in military spending and no effort to reduce the national debt.[45]

The national debt was no problem to Alexander Hamilton because he had a solution to it. The greatest theoretician of public finance in American history, America's first secretary of the treasury knew how to reconcile means and ends. In the 1780s, he had devised a national banking system that gave the states (former colonies) a way to pay off the debts they had accrued during the Revolutionary War. The new federal government would take over the states' old debts in order to allow their people to focus on new plans and projects. Once economic development was under way, the federal government would levy taxes to clear the books. Hamilton even anticipated Reagan in warning that a continuous national debt would lead to high inflation and low productivity. Thus he insisted that the conventional dictum that "public debts are public benefits" can only lead to "a position inviting prodigality and liable to abuse," and the treasury secretary "ardently wishes to see incorporated, as a fundamental maxim, in the system of public credit for the United States, that the creation of debt should always be accompanied with the means of its extinguishment."[46] With his aversion to taxes, Reagan left America without any means of extinguishing its debts.

Although Reagan's favorite president was Calvin Coolidge, our fortieth president seemed to want Americans to live fabulously rather than frugally—or at least some Americans. One wonders, for example, why Reagan went after Linda Taylor and not Charles Keating. The "welfare queen" showed herself to be highly resourceful and imaginative in ripping off government programs. So did Keating, the S&L king whose devious manipulation cost Americans hundreds of billions of dollars. Yet in Reagan's correspondence and public addresses there is no mention of Keating, while Taylor is held up as an example of what happens when government tries to take care of the poor. To judge one social class by one set of values and another by no values at all is called relativism. Those scheming from below are reprehensible, those doing the same thing from above are forgivable. Reagan's Emersonian vision of America had little patience for those who grovel in the shame of charity. Those who are shameless in deceiving investors were apparently another matter.

—

THE REAGAN PRESIDENCY reopened the American mind to the bounties of the free market. His spiritualization of capitalism has had an enduring effect on America's political culture, having lasted longer than Roosevelt's New Deal, Kennedy's New Frontier, or Johnson's Great Society. Reagan allowed Americans to indulge the acquisitive instinct fully, to pursue avarice without angst, and to see welfare programs as ways to make the weak into objects of pity: "the worst of all pamperings," according to Nietzsche. If man simply wanted comfort and pleasure he could settle for the welfare state, the last refuge not of the legitimately disabled and truly needy, for whom Reagan genuinely cared, but of the parasites who make a virtue out of victimhood. However, Reagan demolished the philosophical dualism of matter and spirit. He also saw no conflict between capital and labor, virtue and interest, or a market economy and popular democracy. The conservative leader Ronald Reagan was simply carrying out what used to be called the "liberal consensus," as articulated in the 1950s by Richard Hofstadter and others. Buried deep in the heart of America is the cupidity of a consensus that gives the American the right to covet wealth and the rage to curse taxes.

The Reagan era may have restored the old-fashioned virtues of ambition and hard work, and the dream of upward mobility. While Reagan opened the American mind to the material blessings of freedom, however, he allowed it to stay closed to the requirements of moral authority. Reagan would make no distinction between Bill Gates, the technical genius who became rich by producing according to our need, and Charles Keating, the financial speculator who became rich by manipulating according to his greed. The costly and corrosive savings and loan scandals ballooned as a result of Reagan's determination to get government off the back of business so that the "magic of the market" could show its stuff. It did, in ways less magical than mischievous.

Reagan believed in the virtues of the free market, yet the scandals of his era violated the principles of capitalism. In *The Wealth of Nations*, Adam Smith made it clear that a free society required open competition, profit as a function of the production of some socially useful activity, and transparency, full access to information about the market price of investments. The Reagan administration offered neither political criticism nor ethical judgment about the financial scandals it helped to create. Adam Smith, the seventeenth-century philosopher, worried about how a market economy could be made compatible with Christian morality. Three centuries later America had no such worries.

At least not in reconciling capitalism to conscience. Reagan himself was profoundly worried, however, about reconciling diplomacy with morality. His political philosophy departed from his economic philosophy. In international affairs, he believed that "history is not predetermined" but instead " is in our hands." In economics, the "invisible hand" of the market was self-determining and self-regulating, as fixed as the law of gravity. It was a view that rendered all the more noteworthy Reagan's intolerance for fate when it came to communism. He refused to listen to the advice of the foreign policy specialists who told him that Soviet communism would be around indefinitely, its existence as inevitable as it was irreversible. If the peccadilloes of market economics gave him no cause for worry, he was profoundly worried about reconciling the arms race with the future peace of the world. Disarmament became his highest moral duty, and his negotiations with Gorbachev one of American history's finest hours.

CHAPTER TEN

From Deterrence to Dialogue:
How the Cold War Ended

The Doctrine of Deterrence
and Classical Tragedy

"HE NEVER HAD his integrity questioned before," sighed Nancy Reagan. "And that really bothered him."[1]

The Iran-Contra fiasco brought Ronald Reagan as close to despair as he would ever come. Amid congressional hearings and speculations about the forthcoming Tower Commission Report, which would implicate several members of his administration, there were rumors of impeachment. The immediate reaction to the capture of cargo handler Eugene Hasenfus, after his C-123 crashed in Nicaragua loaded with U.S.-supplied illegal weapons for the Contras, was a blatant strategy of denial and disinformation carried out by the National Security Council, a spin control that might have worked had not Hasenfus spilled the story of secret supplies on national television broadcasts. A poll taken in 1987 indicated that only 14 percent of the public believed Reagan when he claimed that he had not, "repeat not," traded arms for hostages. The appearances of Oliver North, John Poindexter, and other Reagan advisors before Congress amounted to a coverup far more serious than Nixon's Watergate scandal. Iran-Contra involved international relations and trading with terrorists.

All the deficiencies of Reagan's character as a leader seemed to be magnified by Iran-Contra: casualness about details, aloofness from staff rivalries, dependence on advisors who acted on their own and went around the White House. So out of it did Reagan seem that one specialist cited the Constitution's Twenty-fifth Amendment advising what to do if the president "is unable to discharge the powers and duties of his office." The Great Communicator, now seventy-six and the oldest serving president in American history, no longer seemed in command, his credibility and competency questioned along with his integrity.[2]

Reagan's plummeting approval rating registered all the more acutely since it represented a drastic fall from the astonishingly high rating of 83 percent in late 1985, after the first summit with the Soviet Union. Reagan's diplomacy with Gorbachev was formal and open, and the public approved of the rapprochement; but relations with Nicaragua were covert and illegal, and the public disapproved. Why, then, was Reagan unwilling to negotiate with the Sandinista Daniel Ortega and so willing to do so with the Marxist-Leninist Mikhail Gorbachev? Obviously Russia posed a greater threat because of its numerically superior ground forces in Europe and its dangerous arsenal of nuclear weapons. In addition, the two countries were moving in opposite directions. Gorbachev recognized that communism had failed in Russia, and he was determined to make drastic changes; Ortega saw communism as the solution to Nicaragua's problems, and he was determined to go forward with it. Both leaders harbored the same illusion, however, when it came to democracy; both believed that the forces of freedom could work either to transform communism or to advance it.

In the Soviet Union and in Nicaragua, the end of the cold war was carried out politically rather than militarily. Gorbachev's policies of *perestroika* and *glasnost* presumed that Russia's economy could be restructured and its political culture opened to diversity and democratic participation, and Ortega believed that Nicaragua could have free elections to prove that democracy and communism marched together. Recall that Castro warned Ortega that "the people can be wrong." Like many revolutionaries, however, Ortega believed that by definition communism must have a "social basis" in the people themselves. It turned out that democratic elections drove Ortega from power in Managua, and that the process of liberalization that Gorbachev introduced in Moscow eventually brought down the entire edifice of the communist state. One leader thought he could perpetuate communism, the other that he could reform it.

The cold war would end without a shot being fired, and Gorbachev would become a hero in the United States. He was less admired in Russia, where he futilely undertook measures to reform the system of rule and was reluctant, to the very end, to admit not only that the system had failed but that fellow members of the Politburo and other organizations had plotted against him in an attempted coup d'etat. Gorbachev was succeeded by the more progressive and charismatic Boris Yeltsin. By the time of Yeltsin's ascendancy, in 1991, Reagan was gone from office, but what Yeltsin had to say to Gorbachev and the Russian people was pure Reaganism: "Do not look to the Communist Party for answers to our problems. The Party itself is the problem." So is the economy, Reagan could have added, recalling the old Reds of his Hollywood days and their claim that, in the long view of history, socialism would prove to be superior to capitalism as a mode of production. Reagan was not a political leader interested in debating the merits of various -isms, although he was aware that such views of history had been taught on the American campus when he was governor and president. While conservatives started their think tanks off campus, radicals flooded the campus with a plethora of publications, many dedicated to Marxist studies. Whatever the future of the American campus, Reagan became more concerned about the fate of a world possibly imperiled by nuclear holocaust.[3]

Reagan often likened the nuclear standoff of the two superpowers to old western movies, with two gunslingers poised to shoot it out at the OK Corral; but he knew the difference between the two scenarios. In the film world, the good guy is always the quickest on the draw, and the villain goes down before firing a shot. In the real world of the U.S.-USSR standoff, each side has the capacity for a second strike. Reagan drew the obvious conclusion: In nuclear warfare no side will be left standing in the rubble of death.

What Reagan questioned, it will be recalled, was the policy of deterrence as an instrument of international diplomacy. Deterrence may seem like a showdown when any act of vengeance calls for a retaliatory one, but when the aim is "mutually assured destruction," can there be a winner? The idea of massive retaliation horrified Reagan, particularly after he saw the TV film *The Day After*, in which Lawrence, Kansas, is wiped out in a nuclear attack, leaving actor Jason Robards staggering around among the walking wounded, whose bodies begin to decay from radiation. "It's very effective and left me greatly depressed," Reagan said of the film. On the evening the TV dramatization was shown to the nation, on November 20, 1983, the White House received a volume of calls, and when the telephone bank volunteers asked whether the callers thought Reagan was "on the right track" in trying to reduce nuclear weapons, 299 respondents answered yes, only 14 no. Even those who did not support Reagan as a president were overwhelmingly in support of his disarmament policies. Reagan grew even more depressed when he heard American generals claim that a nuclear war was "winnable." "I thought they were crazy," concluded the president. If not crazy, certainly shortsighted. Thomas Watson, head of IBM, was once asked to speak to Pentagon generals about the implications of nuclear war. In a room full of large maps and lighted charts lining the walls, the generals showed him more than a thousand targets on Russian territory. Soviet casualties would be more than one hundred million, he was told.

> "And what about our casualties?" asked Watson.
> They replied that about eighty million Americans and many more industries would be destroyed, just as in the Soviet Union.
> "And what would you do after almost everything was destroyed?" Watson probed. The generals looked at each other and did not have much to say.[4]

The doctrine of deterrence hardly troubled the president's neocon advisors, who were unwilling to accept a political solution to the cold war. The neocons remained suspicious of détente, could never think of accepting parity, and advocated all-out nuclear superiority, supposedly on the assumption that the Soviets would give up the arms race and call off the cold war. The neocons believed that anything less than full nuclear might poised to strike would be appeasement; Reagan believed anything more would be Armageddon.

Reagan had good reason for such fears. In the last months of 1983, superpower tensions reached terrifying, almost paranoiac, heights when the Soviet leaders were certain America was planning a preemptive strike. Oleg Gordievsky, KGB chief in London, recounted receiving orders to be on the alert for the "immediate threat of a nuclear attack on the Soviet Union." The planned deployment of American missiles in Europe convinced the Soviets that an attack was imminent and that the "countdown to nuclear war" had begun. Gordievsky referred to the secret NATO "war games" as "Able Archer 83," and Moscow placed its interceptor aircraft on high alert as well as units of the Soviet army and those of the Warsaw Pact. "The world did not quite reach the edge of the nuclear abyss," Gordievsky wrote, "[b]ut during Able Archer 83 it had, without realizing it, come frighteningly close." When Reagan heard about the alarming situation, he couldn't believe that the Soviets would ever think that he would launch a surprise attack. "Well, if that was the case," he wrote in his memoirs, "I was even more anxious to get a top Soviet leader in a room alone and try to convince him we had no designs on the Soviet Union and Russians had nothing to fear from us."[5]

Reagan's desire to approach the cold war through talk and persuasion would have pleased ancient Greek thinkers, who believed in the saving power of dialogue. The nuclear standoff had all the makings of classical Greek tragedy, as Thucydides described the rivalry between Sparta and Athens. Two powerful states are poised against one another, each fearing the other's growing strength, and each feeling further threatened by the other's cultural and political differences. The mind seems helpless to trace back the causes that have brought on the situation, and once war is launched reason is lost to the fury of combat and the unforeseen contingency of events. Alexander Hamilton, it should be noted, dealt with a similar situation with the framing of the Constitution in 1787. To bring stability to the world is not unlike establishing good government, which Hamilton posed as a decision between "reflection and choice" or between "accident and force." Reagan opted for reflection and choice. In realizing that he had to prove to the Soviets that they "had nothing to fear from us," Reagan recognized with classical thinkers that the presence of fear can be the basis of political deliberation. He chose conversation over escalation.

In so doing, Reagan began to think for himself in his second term. He no longer listened to the neocons, who thought communist totalitarianism irreversible; or to the CIA, whose director had manipulated the Iran-Contra scheme; or to Richard Pipes and the disciples of Alfred Wohlstetter, who insisted that the Russians think in such alien ways that we should cease seeing them as a reflection of ourselves. When Reagan first met Gorbachev and, later, the Russian people themselves, he delighted in how much he had in common with them. Anatoly Dobrynin described well Reagan's behavior at the end of 1984, when it appeared Washington and Moscow could not agree to a summit. Receiving a communication stating that all plans were off, Dobrynin wrote in his memoirs:

> Did this amount to a complete deadlock? Not exactly. Brent Scowcroft told me [that] at his last meeting with Reagan, the president expressed an intuition that something was wrong with his policy toward the Soviet Union[,] but he did not know where the fault lay. In any case, he was prevented from discovering it not only by his own internal arsenal of anticommunist cliches but by the narrowness of his own close advisors, who would be the last to come up with concrete recommendations for improvement. He had to look somewhere else, and as it turned out, he turned to the one person whose self-confidence and determination had guided his political career from the start—himself.[6]

There was, however, a highly significant other whom Reagan listened to almost as much as he listened to his own mind thinking. The evangelist Billy Graham was a dinner guest at the Soviet Embassy in Washington, and Dobrynin asked him "who, in your opinion, had the most influence on the president. Without a moment's hesitation, he said it was Reagan's wife, Nancy." Indeed so, for it was Nancy who pushed her husband toward accepting a summit, discreetly raising the subject with his reluctant advisors. Not since Abigail Adams and Eleanor Roosevelt has a president's wife made such a contribution to peace.[7]

From Deterrence to Dialogue

WINTER WAS APPROACHING on the shores of Lake Geneva, where the first summit of the long cold war was held in a stately chateau in November 1985. As if history might turn on a gesture, President Ronald Reagan looked across the table at General Secretary Mikhail Gorbachev and said: "Why don't you and I just step out and get some fresh air, and let them, for a while, go on with the subject." The "them" Reagan was referring to were advisors assisting each leader, some hard-liners on each side. Gorbachev quickly accepted the invitation to leave the room, and the two men, accompanied by interpreters and followed by security guards, walked down a path to a pool house, where a fireplace had been kept going. Later, when address- ing Congress, Reagan cited President Roosevelt saying that he had learned more from five minutes spent talking to a man than from "any number of briefing books and letters." At the dinner preceding the open- ing meeting of the summit, Reagan reminded the table of a cartoon show- ing the two superpower leaders standing on two sides of a deep abyss. Reagan called across the table, "Gorby, I am prepared to go my part of the way." The Russian leader replied, "Come ahead." Reagan would refer to Geneva as "the fireside summit."[8]

Getting to Geneva was half the task. Few people expected Reagan to be there. Anatoly Dobrynin, who had presided in Washington's Soviet Embassy during the administrations of Kennedy, Johnson, Nixon, Ford, and Carter, recalled in his memoirs: "Those early Reagan years in Wash- ington were the most difficult and unpleasant I experienced in my long tenure as ambassador." These tense years were not made any better when, on September 1, 1983, a Soviet fighter plane shot down Korean Air Flight 007, killing 269 civilians, mainly Americans and South Kore- ans. Reagan was outraged, and he spent Labor Day sitting by a pool in a damp swimming suit writing a speech "so I could give my unvarnished opinion of the barbarous act," calling the tragedy a "massacre." He directed Shultz to persuade members of the United Nations to condemn the act and suspend airport services for a time to Soviet airlines. The KAL incident demonstrated to Reagan how a nuclear war could be trig- gered by an accident or miscalculation. Gradually Dobrynin won the trust of Reagan, and the ambassador helped the president secure the travel of a half-dozen Pentecostals who had sought sanctuary in the American Embassy in Moscow. Gorbachev also helped in obtaining the release of the jailed Jewish dissident Natan Sharansky, and he brought the exiled Andrei Sakharov back to Moscow and set him up with an apart- ment, where the physicist sat at his desk writing articles criticizing Gor- bachev himself.[9]

Reagan may have been depressed to discover that Soviet leaders feared that they were about to be attacked by the United States. The

early Reagan administration, however, had looked upon the Soviet
Union as a deadly, relentless antagonist. Reagan warned America how
threatened it was by a regime that had a "record of deceit in its long
betrayal of international treaties" and by political leaders who believed it
was "moral to lie or cheat for the purpose of advancing Communism."
Members of the administration joined in the chorus of condemnation:
"Soviet promotion of violence as the instrument of politics constitutes
the greatest danger to world peace" (Haig); Moscow's "unrelenting
efforts to impose an alien Soviet model" on other countries (Shultz); the
Politboro sponsors "spying and terrorism" (Casey); Russia's conduct has
nothing to do with national security; it is "neither reasonable nor prudent to view the Soviet military buildup as defensive in nature" (Weinberger); nor is it realistic to believe that communism can change its ways
(Kirkpatrick), or reconsider its errors (Bush), or listen to reason (Perle),
or think objectively (Pipes), or fight fairly (North).[10]

America's enemy stood as a mortal foe that had to be confronted and
challenged, and called to account for its behavior; and the administration's confrontational stance involved three demands: restraint, responsibility, and reciprocity. "What do we mean by restraint?" Reagan had
asked, in his draft letter to Brezhnev. "We are not asking the Soviet
Union to abandon its allies or to renounce its principles," only that critical situations in world politics be resolved by negotiation rather than by
military force. Since Russia had few allies and even fewer principles that
would withstand the test of time, Reagan was actually asking the Soviet
Union to refrain from interfering in the internal affairs of Eastern European countries and intervening in regional conflicts around the world.
The Soviet Union must also be responsible and abide by the terms it had
declared its allegiance to, such as the Helsinki Accords, which called
upon communist countries to honor the commitments they made in
respect to the human rights of their citizens. The third demand, reciprocity, involved "linkage," making American policy conditional upon
Soviet behavior. Thus Russia's withdrawal from third world countries, or
its help with the release of the Pentecostals or Jewish dissidents
("refuseniks"), holds out the possibility of trade, arms reductions, even a
summit. The aim was, as Haig put it, to establish the superpower relations "on a sounder footing by linking improved bilateral relation with
increased Soviet restraint."[11]

The demands of restraint, responsibility, and reciprocity represented the stance of the first three years of the Reagan presidency (1981–1983). During this period no significant emphasis was placed on arms control. The floating of the "zero option" proposal, whereby Russia would scrap its SS-20 missiles and America would forgo developing further nuclear missiles, was so ridiculously advantageous to America that no one was surprised when Moscow rejected it. The Strategic Arms Reduction Talks (START) were also one-sided. The president proposed that land- and sea-based missiles be reduced to the same number on each side, with 2,500 ground missiles the limit. The offer would require the Soviets to reduce their 5,500 land-based warheads, thereby destroying half their arsenal, while the United States continued its nuclear buildup. As everyone expected, the Soviets rejected START as a "propaganda ploy."[12]

Many critics believed the Reagan administration was not serious about arms control. Some people in the nuclear freeze movement feared that the United States was actually preparing for war. Jonathan Schell's *The Fate of the Earth* became a best-seller with its impassioned description of the horrors of nuclear war, and Strobe Talbott, editor at *Time*, argued in *Deadly Gambits* that Reagan was crafting arms proposals designed so the Soviets would reject them, thereby heightening the tensions of the cold war. The neocons, meanwhile, were pleased that the president was refusing to compromise or negotiate with the Soviet Union, so convinced were they that a hardline stance, instead of stiffening the spine of the enemy, would eventually crush it. An impression grew that Reagan and members of his administration were more interested in denouncing the Kremlin than in dealing with it. While liberals wished that Reagan would be more cooperative, neocons were delighted to see him more coercive, and to this day they still believe, as we have seen, that America "won" the cold war because of its militant, unbending posture. "War is an act of force to compel our enemy to do our will," observed Carl von Clausewitz. How could a cold war based on the theory of deterrence and the premise of "mutual assured destruction," however, achieve such a rational objective? Reagan was one the first members of his administration to see that a cold war based on the necessity of nuclear retaliation was politically irrational and morally unacceptable.[13]

Actually, neither liberal critics nor conservative supporters appreciated the extent to which Reagan's attitudes underwent a profound change, one that made defeating communism or winning the cold war a less urgent choice than saving the world from destroying itself. The change is all the more remarkable as it took place long before Gorbachev came to power.

On January 16, 1984, Reagan delivered a foreign policy address that was broadcast around the world. His message, rather than conveying the once-confident voice of Reagan, suggested fear and angst. The perilous danger facing life on earth was not the threat of communism but the threat of war itself. "Reducing the risk of war—and especially nuclear war—is priority number one," Reagan exhorted. "A nuclear conflict could well be mankind's last." Whereas Reagan's cold war speeches had once been confrontational and accusatory, they were now conciliatory and mollifying. The previous themes of restraint, responsibility, and reciprocity had been replaced with three new themes: danger, dialogue, deescalation. The danger that political disagreements could develop into armed conflict could no longer be disregarded, and deterrence was no more rational than the generals who thought war winnable. Clear communication was absolutely essential. "We must and will engage the Soviets in a dialogue as constructive as possible." And we must begin the process of deescalating through discussion and agreement. Our "dream is to see the day when nuclear weapons will be banished from the face of the Earth."[14]

The remarkable thing about Reagan's broadcast is that the old anti-communist, the Ronald Reagan who once fought the cause all the way back in his Hollywood days, had been superseded by a statesman who had a higher priority. In his speech there was no hint of a diabolical enemy, and even the familiar terms that once described the Soviet Union—interventionist, expansionist, adventurist—went unmentioned. Throughout much of 1984 Reagan and Shultz emphasized America's desire for cooperation between the superpowers.

In September Reagan invited Soviet foreign minister Andrei Gromyko to the White House. It would be the first time he had had a full discussion with a leading member of the Soviet hierarchy. The meeting went on for three hours before a blazing fire in the Oval Office and over lunch in the State Department dining room. No one expected any breakthrough on weapons negotiation, but reporters were surprised to learn that Reagan told Gromyko that the United States "respects the Soviet Union's status as a superpower and has no wish to change its social system." A few days later Reagan flew to New York to address the United Nations, and at the Waldorf Astoria's Starlight Roof reporters timed a handshake between Reagan and Gromyko—it lasted twenty-three seconds. The foreign minister teased the president, insisting that in his speech to the United Nations he would be shot full of arrows. Reagan let Kirkpatrick reply for him: "Not even a dart will be thrown." Listening to Reagan deliver the speech, his advisors became aware that he had edited out all direct criticisms of Moscow.[15]

When Gorbachev took office in 1985, both the superpowers proceeded cautiously toward détente, emphasizing cooperation and understanding. Still, Reagan as well as Gorbachev clung to prior convictions even while trying to move forward to better relations. While Reagan made hopeful gestures about possible discussions and meetings, he still reminded America that communism was up to no good and that even if the Soviets wanted to avoid war, they still sought to control the world. Meanwhile Gorbachev acknowledged that Reagan was correct to emphasize the dangers of war and the need for dialogue, and he even went so far as to admit that Lenin had erred in rejecting the bourgeois values of the West; nevertheless, he would still affirm the need to support regimes in Angola, Ethiopia, and elsewhere "that have taken the anti-imperialist path."[16]

The cold war caught both Reagan and Gorbachev in a quandary. For reasons of domestic politics, each leader had to verbally lash out against the other's regime; for reasons of international stability, they had to seek grounds for accommodation. While Gorbachev was having second thoughts about the dysfunctional nature of the Soviet Union, however, Reagan never had any doubts about the superiority of America's democratic institutions and economic system. He did have doubts about the state of the world.

Recognition that nuclear weapons constituted a deadly peril made Reagan fear for the future. "We must never negotiate out of fear," declared John F. Kennedy, in his inaugural address of 1961."But let us never fear to negotiate." Reagan well understood the dilemma of feeling too weak to win and too strong to yield. His encounter with the emotion of fear takes us to the beginning of modern political philosophy in the seventeenth century. Thomas Hobbes believed that anxiety about the preservation of life and the fear of war and death necessitated a strong state, the Leviathan of political authority to which people submitted to guarantee their rights to security and safety. That only a strong state might protect its citizens from fear, however, could be anathema to a libertarian president who would prefer to see the state abolished along with nuclear weapons. Had Reagan fallen for the temptation of the demagogue, he could have followed in Joseph McCarthy's footsteps and magnified the threat of communism, joining the horror of fear with hatred of the enemy. Not only did Reagan refrain from McCarthyism, he went through a process of "new thinking" (to use the term that described Gorbachev's own shifting views) to see his way out of the impasse between the two superpowers. Eventually the cold war would no longer be exclusively about communism but instead about the arms race, a campaign in which Reagan sought to convince the Russians that they could not win but could lose and still survive.

In the early years of his administration, Reagan doubted that the Soviet Union could change its ways any more than "a leopard will change its spots." He believed America must undertake a massive arms buildup since "it is five minutes to midnight for the United States." At the same time, he knew that most offers put forth on arms control would be far from acceptable. Still, there was no harm in making such offers. By doing so, America "would be showing the country which really wanted peace because I'm quite sure the Soviet Union would never sit down with us at a table to negotiate such a legitimate agreement." At what point would the Soviets negotiate? To this day, the hawks in the administration have insisted that Reagan continued the arms race because he realized that America must deal from "a strategy of strength." He did so at first, to be sure, but his subsequent doubts about deterrence and the gory prospect of retaliation, which began to trouble his mind throughout the middle of 1983, eventually gave him pause. Continuous escalation had little bearing on the delivery capacities of the two superpowers. His advisors may have thought nuclear weaponary perfectly rational, but Reagan would come to see that, in his own words, "it makes no sense whatsoever." Power has been defined as "the production of intended effects." Such effects can be realized in many ways, and not only by resorting to the use of weapons of violence. As Reagan combined a sense of danger about war with the necessity of dialogue, he would no longer be thinking about power and force but persuasion and reason. More and more Reagan convinced himself that it was imperative to move from the premises of threat to the promises of trust.[17]

Many in the administration, committed to power politics, believed that trust was the naïveté of the idealist. Reagan was starting to play the angel, forgetting that in a Machiavellian world of force and deception there is only room for the lion and the fox, strength and stealth. The neo-con hard-liners sought victory, not peace, or a peace by fear rather than trust until the enemy collapses in exhaustion. They believed that Russia could be cowed into surrendering. Frederick the Great, Napoleon, and Hitler had also believed so.

Ambassador Dobrynin knew that Gorbachev sought a summit with Reagan, and he had to tell the Soviet leader that much of Congress and most of the cabinet would delay a meeting in order to further the arms buildup. In all likelihood Dobrynin conveyed to Gorbachev a conversation he had had with Robert McFarlane, telling him that an early summit could only handicap prospects for MX funding. Republican senator Robert Dole let the ambassador know that a summit "would mean the collapse of the policy advocated by extreme right-wingers around Reagan." However, for some time Reagan had begun to distance himself from the right wing, dismissing their mathematical calculations about nuclear power politics as a dangerous fantasy. One of the differences between Reagan and his neocon critics involved means and ends. Reagan believed in power as the means to reach the ends of peace and disarmament. His critics regarded power as an end in itself, to be maximized so that America would emerge from the cold war as the only superpower.[18]

One voice of prudence who helped the Reagan administration think freshly about the cold war was Max M. Kampelman. Trained in law, Kampelman wrote books on communists in American trade unions. The liberal Democrat had worked with Senator Hubert Humphrey, the presidential candidate in 1968, an agonizing election year for which the country came apart as a result of the raging war in Vietnam. "Hubert was my good friend," Reagan told Kampelman, adding that the senator spent a night at the executive mansion when he was governor of California. "He told me that Humphrey had been very helpful to him when he was president of the Screen Actors Guild," recalled Kampelman. " 'Hubert,'

said Reagan, 'helped me a great deal as we fought the Communists.'" He
reminded Kampelman that the senator "had been among the organizers
of the liberal anti-Communist Americans for Democratic Action (ADA)."
Then came the ultimate compliment. " 'Hubert would have made a great
president,' Reagan said."

Unlike many of the neocons, whose political beliefs were never liable
to error, Kampelman was modest, patient, thoughtful, and gracious. He
would be appointed ambassador to and U.S. negotiator with the Soviet
Union on nuclear and space arms policies, and he has recalled how he
was assigned the daunting task. He reported to Shultz that his talks with
KGB agents in Moscow indicated to him that changes were being
undertaken in the Soviet government. An appointment was made to meet
with the president in the presence of his staff:

> The president explained that Shultz had suggested he listen
> to an idea from me. I presented it in summary form. White
> House chief of staff Jim Baker, saying that Shultz had made
> a contrary suggestion earlier in the week, said he agreed with
> Shultz and did not support my proposal. Ed Meese spoke up,
> as did two or three others in the room, all agreeing with
> Baker. I did not take this as a personal affront in any way, and
> had not expected to get even this far with my idea. But the
> president, sensing disappointment I did not feel, spoke up.
> "Don't pay any attention to these fellows, Max," he said. "Not
> a single one of them was ever a Democrat!"[19]

A week later Kampelman received a call from the president telling
him he had been appointed chief arms negotiator for the upcoming
Geneva conference.

The Geneva Summit
and the Neoconservatives

MILLIONS HAD WITNESSED the scene on television around
the world. A long back limousine pulled up outside the Fleur
d'Eau, a nineteenth-century lakeside chateau, and out

stepped Mikhail Gorbachev, wrapped in bulging topcoat and covered by a black fedora and, beneath the turned-up collar, a thick scarf. Ronald Reagan, having removed his overcoat to receive Gorbachev in the cold air, bounded down the chateau's steps in a smart suit, with a suntanned face and a broad grin. The hatless president brimmed with confidence and good cheer; the general secretary looked a little tense and reserved until Reagan reached out to shake his hand, and then, beneath his heavy clothing, there were the stirrings of a smile.

It was a historical moment, the heads of the superpowers about to take the lead in forcing history to stop in its tracks. The world's future lay in the hands of two statesmen. Hegel taught that all history is the struggle for self-recognition, and that historical conflicts will end either in a war to the finish or when leaders recognize each other.

No one knew then that they would take an instant liking to each other. Gorbachev delighted in finding Reagan not the brusque warmonger depicted in the European press but a friendly, ebullient player in the world of international politics. Reagan later said of Gorbachev: "There was warmth in his face and his style, not the coldness bordering on hatred I'd seen in most Soviet officials I'd met until then." To Gorbachev, Reagan seemed the embodiment of *glasnost* itself: open to ideas, willing to face reality, relaxed with himself. "I remember the episode when we were sitting down together," Gorbachev recalled years later. "The President said I think the time has come for us to be on a first-name basis. Call me Ron."[20]

The personal meeting may have broken the ice, but opposition to the summit remained strong in Moscow and in Washington. It took French president François Mitterrand to convince Gorbachev that Reagan was not simply a pawn of U.S. militarists but a leader committed to ending the nuclear impasse. British prime minister Margaret Thatcher played a similar role, taking pains to explain to Reagan that Gorbachev was not a typical hardened apparatachik but a forward-looking statesman open to the possibility of cooperation.

That Gorbachev and Reagan hit it off so well is all the more surprising in light of their contrasting life histories. Some of the few points of reference were that each was born and raised in a rural environment; that young Mikhail had toyed with the idea of becoming an actor; and that he, too, had a sense of humor. Gorbachev's Russia, however, was no laughing matter. In the thirties Stalin's glorious five-year plans aimed to

transform the economy and eliminate class distinctions to achieve
Marx's goal of a society of freedom and equality. What it did achieve, as
the poet Joseph Brodsky put it, was "equality in poverty."

Gorbachev was born into a poor peasant family in the Stavropol region
of southern Russia in 1931. He came into the world during the era of
forced agricultural collectivization that left the region in chaos and
famine. While the older Reagan was starting out in his career as a radio
announcer on his way to Hollywood and fame, Gorbachev endured the
purges in a house marked as containing "an enemy of the people." One
of his grandfathers was arrested and sent to Siberia, another imprisoned
and interrogated for fourteen months until he confessed to crimes he
could not possibly have committed. All around, young Gorbachev saw
relatives and neighbors starving. One third of the inhabitants of his village perished. During the early years of the Second World War, the German army occupied the Stavropol territory, and after the war the Kremlin regarded the area as a hive of Trotskyists. According to the Oxford
historian Archie Brown, Gorbachev wisely kept secret these early experiences lest he be regarded as suspect in his later political career, and he
only revealed them to a group of intellectuals in 1990. "Gorbachev's
childhood coincided with the harshest years of Soviet history and some
of the most tragic times in the whole of Russian history," writes Brown.
At that time in history, across the world in another continent, the Hollywood Ten was defending a Soviet regime that caused Gorbachev and his
family such suffering.[21]

Young Gorbachev was a hard field worker and successful student,
receiving recommendations from the Komsomol (Young Communist
League) enabling him to enter Moscow University in 1950. He studied
law and met Raisa Maksimovna Titorenko, an attractive young scholar
in philosophy and sociology. Years later, when she arrived in Britain with
her husband, she surprised the English by saying how pleased she was
to be "in the land of Hobbes and Locke." Gorbachev, however, was
steeped in Marxism, but with the proviso that there be, as Marx himself
insisted, a direct connection between practice and theory, a principle he
used to dismiss teachers who "talked hot air about general principles"
having no bearing on reality. Gorbachev graduated from the Law Faculty
and returned to the Stavropol region and worked as a district prosecutor.
He found the Communist Party bosses tedious functionaries, but he

remained in the party for career reasons. With the fear of another purge always in mind, Gorbachev dared not speak out against the repressive political system and its slave labor camps. In his memoirs, however, he tells us that having heard about what had happened under Stalin, he rejected violence and terror as a means of politics, and recalled that the multiethnic character of his home town nurtured tolerance and respect for others.[22]

While many members of the party were thrown into confusion by Khrushchev's "Crimes of Stalin" address of 1956, Gorbachev took hope from it. Years later he would follow the liberating thoughts of European social democrats like Felipe Gonzalez, Willy Brandt, and François Mitterrand. When Gorbachev was appointed general secretary of the Communist Party in 1985, however, he still regarded himself not only as a Marxist but as an orthodox Leninist. He was convinced that the only way to reform Russia was in and through the party. Yet there remained a touch of pragmatism in Gorbachev's temperament. A month after he became the Soviet leader, a former student remarked of him: "We are talking about a man who attributes more importance to his own experience, lived and felt, than to that which is decreed on paper." For the pragmatist, all of philosophy comes down to one question: Does it work?[23]

When Gorbachev arrived in Geneva that fall of 1985, he had already concluded that the Soviet Union was not working. One of the policies that proved erroneous was rushing into Afghanistan. "You ass, what are you babbling about, giving us advice? You got us into this dirty business, and now you are pretending that we are responsible." Such were the emotions felt (as paraphrased by an onlooker) by Gorbachev as he listened to Andrei Gromyko, furious that his foreign minister had recommended that the Soviet Union invade Afghanistan in 1979. Even before Gorbachev came to power, in March 1985, he had regarded the Afghan war as a "mistake," and as general secretary of the Communist Party he called it "a hopeless military adventure" and "a bleeding wound." The Russian people began to call Afghanistan "our Vietnam." Today it might well be called "our Iraq." The Soviet Union was never able to seal the borders of the country or to stop suicidal ambushes. "The number of *mujahideen* is increasing," the Politburo was told. The Russian people, however, were never told of the dimensions of the disaster. Throughout the eighties, the bodies of 15,000 young Russians were flown back to

Moscow under cover of night, with no official ceremony. Within the ruling elite, Gorbachev was the first Soviet leader to admit that the war in Afghanistan was a failure and that Russia must withdraw.[24]

At Geneva, the subject of Afghanistan came up across the conference table. Earlier, Reagan had seen photos of maimed Afghan children, and he had to hold back tears gazing at them. The president, wondering how a world leader could allow such atrocities, felt like sending the photos to Gorbachev. While Reagan denounced the war passionately at the conference table, Shultz noted that Gorbachev offered no heated response and defended the war only halfheartedly. When Gorbachev stated that he had heard of the invasion over the radio—it took place in 1979, six years before he became general secretary—Reagan took the statement to mean "he had no responsibility and little enthusiasm" for the war. True, but Gorbachev had his own domestic politics to consider. He had resolved to get out of Afghanistan, a severe drain on Russia's economy and a hopeless war with no clear end in sight. However, if he had agreed to a pull-out at Geneva, he would have come off as a weak negotiator who sealed a Soviet defeat. At the same time, continuing the bloody occupation jeopardized his image as an enlightened reformer. Remarkably, his dilemma echoed that of former president Lyndon Johnson, who simultaneously faced Vietnam and worried about the Great Society programs. The Afghan war was unwinnable, withdrawal unthinkable—at least publicly, for privately Gorbachev knew pulling out was inevitable.[25]

During the two-day conference, several issues were on the table. The Soviets' involvement in regional conflicts in Angola and elsewhere was brought up only to be deflected. Cuba's involvement in the civil war in Nicaragua was mentioned more as an irritant than as an issue to be resolved. Gorbachev made it clear that the Soviet Union would not be intimidated by claims that the United States could drive his country into bankruptcy with military expenditures. Yet the question of terrorism could hardly be dismissed, especially after Libya's connection to kidnappings and bombings became an international concern. The Soviet Union, instead of protesting the Libyan involvement in a Berlin discotheque bombing, protested the presence of American naval war ships in the Gulf of Sidra. Reagan was incensed, and in an early letter had demanded to know how Gorbachev could support "a local dictator," Muammar Qaddafi, who "has declared a war of terrorism" on the United

States and much of the world. At the conference Gorbachev avoided responding directly to Reagan's challenge, but Soviet propaganda in support of Libya tapered off and reports of aid to terrorist groups declined.[26]

In a private meeting Reagan had presented Gorbachev with a list of Russian citizens, including Jews, who had been denied permission to leave the country. However, during the conference he refrained from pressing the human rights question, to the dismay of some advisors. Surprisingly, Gorbachev did so, albeit in somewhat different terms, asking Reagan about the human right to a job in a country that puts up with unemployment. Reagan patiently explained how unemployment insurance helps the out-of-work, thereby inadvertently defending the welfare state. And what about women, demanded Gorbachev? He had been told that "American women were downtrodden . . . and treated like black slaves." That's old news, replied Reagan. "Things have changed."[27]

The most troubling issue at Geneva was disarmament. The White House had already convinced the public that the summit could be successful without a major arms control agreement, and a poll indicated that 83 percent of the public favored proceeding with the summit regardless of the issue. As an exploratory conference, the subject was confronted even though both sides intended to avoid any signed treaty. Gorbachev charged America with pouring endless money into the military-industrial complex and developing SDI as its crowning weapon. With Star Wars on the table, the discussion heated up. SDI, he alleged, could only make sense if it allowed America to wage a first strike and then operate the shield to defend its people from retaliation. Reagan insisted fervently that SDI had no offensive implications and offered to share it with Russia once it became operable. Reagan's advisors believed that Gorbachev was furious because he knew that the Soviet economy had no means of developing such a system. According to American ambassador Jack F. Matlock Jr., however, Soviet scientists warned against wasting money on matching the U.S. system since they doubted it would work. When Reagan asked Gorbachev to trust America's intentions as well as its technology, the general secretary exploded:

> GORBACHEV: It's not convincing. It's emotional. It's a dream. Who can control it? Who can monitor it? It opens up an arms race in space.

REAGAN: As I said to you, I have a right to think you want to
use your missiles against us. With mere words we cannot
abolish the threat.[28]

One Reagan advisor, Columbia University's Stephen Sestanovich,
took notes during a private meeting between Gorbachev and Reagan.
The Russian leader asked why Reagan could not change his mind about
building SDI and still save face at home. Or was it the power of military
contractors pushing the proposal? Gorbachev also speculated that the
Pentagon could be behind SDI in order to have an offensive weapon. He
asked Reagan how we could expect to reduce nuclear arms on earth if
we allowed them to spread into space. Reagan tried to reassure Gorbachev that in outer space all would be visible to on-site inspection:

REAGAN: Open labs—you'll know what we're doing.

GORBACHEV: Do you have money to burn?

REAGAN: No—nor do you, I bet.[29]

It was at this point in the discussion, as both leaders grew angry,
accusing each other of harboring aggressive aims, that Reagan looked
across the table and suggested they take a break and get a breath of fresh
air with a stroll outside that eventually led down to the pool house. Later,
they walked uphill back to the chateau and made the important decision
to hold future summits in Russia and America. Technically what was settled at Geneva was an understanding that nuclear warfare was inadmissible. There could be no winners and only losers on both sides.

The personal contact between the two leaders proved most worthwhile. Reagan felt he experienced a "kind of chemistry" with Gorbachev,
who in turn came to believe more and more that America had no hostile
designs. Both leaders, it turned out, loved to spin yarns. Gorbachev
reminded Reagan of Tip O'Neill and his locker-room humor. "Gorbachev could tell jokes about himself and even about his country, and I
grew to like him more."[30]

The Geneva summit also registered Reagan's growing distance from
his hard-line advisors. In preparing briefs for the conference, Ambassador
Matlock struggled with Peggy Noonan, Pat Buchanan, and others who

objected to using any soft language, such as "cooperation" and "compromise," which Reagan liked but which they regarded as "détentist" and therefore "leftist." Noonan and Buchanan refused to take their harsh language out of the speech drafts, and Matlock underlined their passages so that the president would notice them. At a breakfast at the conclusion of the conference, Reagan walked into the room with three drafts in hand. Turning to Buchanan, he said, "Pat, this has been a good meeting. I think I can work with this guy. I can't just keep poking him in the eye." Then Reagan "glanced over at me with a quizzical expression," recalls Matlock, "as if to say, 'How in the hell did you allow that stuff to slip through?' "[31]

Desiring to work with Gorbachev, Reagan had to distance himself from the hard-liners who thought he was wasting his time. Kirkpatrick left the administration in 1985, and Reagan paid less attention to the other hawks, but conservatives were persistent. The Heritage Foundation had forwarded a "Briefing Book" for Reagan to ponder before heading to Geneva. While the Heritage think tankers wisely advised Reagan not to "sign proclamations of good intentions lacking enforcement mechanisms," they also emphasized that he must avoid the worst trap of all. "Do not succumb to Soviet manipulation by guilt. Stalin successfully used the guilt of his Western Allies over the huge losses of the Red Army in World War II to make them agree to the installation of a communist government in Poland." Actually, at the Yalta conference President Roosevelt insisted upon free elections in Poland, and subsequently at Potsdam and at the United Nations Truman protested the Soviets' failure to hold elections—elections that were once acceded to because, according to the historian Hugh Thomas, Stalin thought the communists were popular in Poland! Reagan sought to rethink the cold war all over again, and while he continued to disdain American liberalism, he could hardly invoke what passed for conservative foreign policy in the thirties: a collection of profascists, imperial expansionists, or die-hard isolationists. Not the best background for a rapprochement.[32]

At the Geneva summit, and especially afterward when addressing Congress and speaking to the press, Reagan disregarded the advice of the neoconservatives. He had no worries that Americans and Russians would be unable to communicate and comprehend one another, and hence he called for a People's Initiative of "openness, contacts, and honest communication" consisting of student exchange programs, sport events, and scholarly conferences as the "first successful step" in reducing tension and conflict. "Our young people would get first-hand knowledge of life in the USSR, learn about their culture and suffering in World War II." The afflictions experienced by the Russian people affected Reagan as much as the absence of human rights. "We recognize that you have suffered a great deal, and struggled a great deal, throughout your history." Neocons looked to Reagan to repudiate détente and to go on the "ideological offensive," as Haig once put it, by resuming the Old Right's drive to "roll back" communism. However, Reagan sought to secure the status quo before trying to change it. "If we can radically reduce offensive nuclear weapons and make it possible to shift toward stable deterrence based on non-nuclear defense, we will have set the world on a new, more peaceful course." In communicating with Gorbachev, Reagan had no hesitation citing Roosevelt's penchant for fireside chats and Kennedy's for summit meetings. Some of his advisors were less comfortable with the liberal legacy. When Reagan told Congress it was good to talk to Gorbachev and to emerge with the same sentiments that Kennedy took away from an earlier Vienna summit with Khrushchev— no great accomplishments but no setbacks and at least the beginning of a dialogue—speechwriter Peggy Noonan inserted a note in the text's margin advising dropping reference to Kennedy, reminding the president that Vienna is "remembered as a bad summit."[33]

Past and Future:
Bitburg and the Philippines

WHILE REAGAN DEVOTED his energies to trying to bring an end to the cold war, he found himself facing two other challenging issues, each shedding light on what turned out to be his less than sterling commitment to political freedom. One issue involved Germany and its fascist past, the other the Philippines and its democratic future.

The first such embarrassment occurred when Reagan's plan to visit Kolmeshohe Cemetery, in Bitburg, Germany, created a firestorm of controversy in the spring of 1985. The visit was planned, in good faith, to observe the fortieth anniversary of V-E Day, and it coincided with an economic summit in Bonn. Unknown to the administration, forty-nine of the two thousand German soldiers buried in Kolmeshohe had been members of the Waffen SS, which had been commanded by Heinrich Himmler. Both the SS storm troopers and their Waffen branch had served as Hitler's select corps. Known to have lined up American prisoners and machine gunned them down into their graves, the SS fought in World War II as a firing squad. The American public was furious that the president would pay homage to such assassins. "Reagan's visit to Bitburg," wrote biographer Cannon, "was the seminal symbolic disaster of an administration that placed great store in symbolism." In many ways, Bitburg was a greater embarrassment than Iran-Contra, which, though devious and illegal, at least had a political rationale of attempting to free hostages and assist the Contras. Bitburg was an open, ceremonial affair, arguably immoral and indefensible, though certainly with no political rationale save the president's personal stubbornness, perhaps even his admirable tenacity to honor his commitment to make an appearance.[34]

However, the timing was such that the event was as much political as ceremonial. "It's no coincidence," Marxists love to say, when making the point that historical events are interconncted and that nothing happens without a reason. It may be of the purest coincidence, but the Bitburg affair, which conjured up the ghost of fascism, coincided with a "revisionist" look at modern European history that was nothing less than an attempt to rehabilitate Nazism. At that very time, some German scholars began to insist that the SS as well as the Wehrmacht were fighting not only for fascism but against communism, and hence their country had been shouldering the burden of the cold war long before it came to be named as such. The storm had been brewing at the same time as the Bitburg affair and broke in fury the following year with the publication of a book by Ernest Nolte comparing the Soviet Gulag to the Holocaust. Few Americans like to think that during World War II America sided with one tyrannical murderer to defeat another tyrannical murderer. One member of Reagan's staff, Pat Buchanan, has written a book arguing that Hitler posed no direct threat to the United States and that the world would have been better off had the two totalitarian regimes bled each other to death on the eastern front. In German and French schol-

arship, the revisionist reasoning has led to a *Historikerstreit*, a fierce battle among historians over whether the Third Reich was fighting the
cause of Western Christendom or whether it represented the abyss of
nihilism and racism. In the Reagan eighties, certain conservative German scholars sought to defend Nazism as a response to the threat of Bolshevism, and Professor Nolte even went so far as to state that Stalin's
purges came before the extermination of the Jews and the Gulag was
"more original" than Auschwitz. By implication, America was fighting on
the wrong side when it allied with the Soviet Union in World War II, a
position that had been voiced by conservative isolationists before the
United States entered the war after Pearl Harbor.[35]

Prior to the Bitburg affair, the Reagan administration had sought to
cement good relations with Germany, especially after Chancellor Hel-
mut Kohl's visit to Washington in November 1984. Germany had allowed
Pershing missiles to be installed in the Federal Republic, and the Bonn
government had helped refugees from East Germany emigrate to the
west. Reagan and Nancy attended the ceremonies of the fortieth anniversary of the D-day invasion of Normandy. Reagan gave a moving speech
(prepared by Peggy Noonan) at Pointe-du-Hoc, the sharp cliffs that
American Rangers had to scale, with great casualties, to overcome German fortifications. The president and the first lady walked up and down
the desolate stretches of Omaha Beach, examining the remains of the
German pillboxes and nearby, gazing upon the infinite rows of white
crosses and the Stars of David on the graves of the fallen. The only sound
was the quiet rustling of small American flags. The sight "was a heart-
breaker," Reagan wrote in his memoirs.

All this stood in stark contrast to the series of confusions and miscalculations leading directly up to the Bitburg trip. Originally, Chancellor
Kohl had invited Reagan to honor the V-E Day anniversary by visiting a
concentration camp and a cathedral. In his memoirs, Reagan wrote that
he first learned of an invitation to visit the notorious prison at Dachau
from a Kohl rival, and he rejected it as having "a political motive." According to Cannon, however, as soon as Nancy heard of the invitation to walk
through a concentration camp, she immediately made it known that it
must be turned down flat. The president would have no stomach for it,
she believed. Nancy could never forget that earlier her husband had

been overcome at the sight of aged, disabled patients in a veterans' hospital in Indiana. He had become so distraught and had faltered so badly that she had had to finish his speech for him.[36]

While the people of west Germany themselves were uneasy about a tour of a concentration camp, American Jews objected to Reagan's having either turned the invitation down or canceled it, claiming any such gesture desecrated the memory of the Holocaust. Reagan addressed these objections in several personal letters. In them, he conjured the gatherings in the East Room that he had held for survivors of the Holocaust, which, he reiterated, should never be forgotten and never be repeated.[37]

Reagan eventually accepted a suggestion by Kohl to include on his itinerary a stop at a military cemetery in Bitburg. Weeks before the trip, Michael Deaver and his staff had checked out the grounds, so covered by snow they had no way of knowing who was in the graves. An American diplomat in Germany had told them to stop worrying. "What do you think—Joseph Mengele is buried there?" When it turned out that among the dead were Nazi criminals, Reagan found himself trying to defend his decision to visit. The American Legion and the Veterans of Foreign Wars could only express sad disappointment. Elie Wiesel, the well-known author who had survived Auschwitz, couldn't believe so decent a man would lose all sense of perspective. "I know the president," he said. "I know this is not his sentiment." However, as Reagan stubbornly resisted canceling Bitburg, the public could only ask: What is his sentiment?[38]

Reagan refused to listen to Nancy, who tried to persuade him to bypass the cemetery and end the bitter controversy. Shultz called Reagan's unshakable decision a "disaster." But Pat Buchanan and Donald Regan urged the president to resist both the Jewish community and the liberal media and go forward with the ceremony. Reagan did so, and he claimed never to have regretted it. We can mourn the German war dead, he insisted, because "the evil war of Nazism turned all values upside down," leaving "human beings crushed by a vicious ideology." Kohl told him that his controversial observation—that the dead German soldiers were just as much "victims" of Nazism as were Jews in the Holocaust—had been well received in Germany. "I'm more pleased than I can say that the visit to a concentration camp will be part of the official program," Reagan wrote. In the end, Reagan also paid a visit to Bergen-Belsen, declaring that "the anguish, the pain and the suffering" of the camps compelled us to pledge: "Never again."[39]

To Reagan, the visit to Germany, Bitburg included, was meant "to commemorate not simply the military victory of forty years ago but the liberation of Europe, the rebirth of German freedom and the reconciliation of our two countries." The United States Information Agency worked overtime to get out the message and control the damage.[40]

Was Reagan a relativist? He clearly avoided applying the same standard of moral judgment to Nazi Germany as he did to Soviet Russia. The latter was the "evil empire" and "the focus of evil in the modern world," the former simply the helpless subjects of an "evil war," its people "crushed by a vicious ideology." Were the Brownshirts subjects to whom history happens, or did they actually will what they wrought? The idea that German soldiers were victims of Nazism outraged many Europeans. As even some German journalists pointed out at the time, those in the SS had not been drafted but had eagerly volunteered. A Dutch newspaper insisted that the German soldier may have been "a relatively powerless cog in the Nazi wheel," but it was he and his fellow soldiers who provided Hitler "the means for the armed subjugation of Europe and for carrying out their murderous plans." More recently, a scholar has pointed out that in the Third Reich, "evil lost the attribute by which it knows itself: that of temptation." Nazism was beyond good and evil, beyond morality and all the values of Christianity and the Judaic code. Nazis made sure that "pity was dangerous in the eyes of the Reichsführer SS." Fighting communism was the object of Heinrich Himmler's SS. So was fighting GIs.[41]

History demands to be heard. The liberation of Europe, whether fought for on the beaches of Normandy, or in the undergrounds of the French, Italian, Norwegian, Polish, and Czech resistance, or on the eastern front at Stalingrad, was a victory over fascism, over the very forces that had set out not only to turn back communism but to destroy liberalism. At Kolmeshohe Cemetery, Reagan paid respect to the killers of American soldiers, those who fought bravely at the Battle of the Bulge and were captured and mowed down.

Symbolically, Reagan's appearance at the cemetery came close to supporting the revisionists who claimed that in the Second World War the

German army had been fighting for freedom against the demonic forces to the east. Reagan never met an anticommunist he didn't like. In the early eighties, the administration defended as "freedom fighters" whoever took support from the United States in guerrilla wars against communism regardless of human rights violations. Reagan's behavior in this regard is puzzling. Where freedom was completely crushed, as in the Soviet Union, he spoke of it as though thundering a biblical proverb, as though nothing could stand in freedom's way. However, where freedom was hanging on amid the vicissitudes of politics, or struggling to be born against a decrepit authoritarian regime, Reagan would support almost any means necessary to keep communism out. He felt anguished about the "death squads" in El Salvador, but he refrained from repudiating them. From one point of view, the Reagan policy made sense. Ambassador Kirkpatrick had argued that the overthrow of authoritarianism could very well result in totalitarianism, a thesis demonstrated in the case of Cuba. The United States had helped free Cuba in the Spanish-American War of 1898. It also helped free the Philippines. Cuba had long been lost to Castro, and thus in the eighties the Reagan-Kirkpatrick thesis would be tested in America's handling of the authoritarian Philippine leader Ferdinand Marcos.

On August 21, 1983, the Philippine opposition leader Benigno S. Aquino Jr. was shot in the head as he stepped down on the tarmac at Manila's airport, returning to his country after three years of exile in the United States. The scene had been captured live on television and was replayed around the world. The assassin was immediately killed in a shootout with the police. Reagan, Nancy, and several members of the administration had been friends of Ferdinand Marcos and his wife, Imelda, whose vast collection of style-studded shoes served as fodder for gossip columns. Marcos ruled with the support of the army, and after the assassination of the popular rival leader Aquino, the State Department urged changes to improve the economy and allow for more democracy. A survivor rather than a reformer, Marcos remained content with the way things were, even when challenged to an election by Corazon Aquino, the slain leader's widow. Reagan sent the able diplomatic troubleshooter Philip Habib to Manila, and Habib reported that Marcos had stolen the close election and that an uprising on Corazon Aquino's behalf was under way. When Marcos became ill, Imelda was rumored to be ready to take his place, and Corazon Aquino threatened to put Marcos on trial for the death of her husband. The Catholic Church supported Aquino, the people rose to the call of her party, and the U.S. Senate voted 85 to 9 that an election "marked by such widespread fraud . . . cannot be considered a fair reflection of the will of the people of the Philippines."[42]

Reagan, however, stood by Marcos, both as a loyal friend and as a seeming stalwart against communism. "We love your adherence to democratic principle and to the democratic processes," declared Vice President Bush of Marcos. Kissinger accused liberals of a double standard, charging that they were harder on Marcos than on other, more ruthless dictators. Not until February 25, 1985, did the administration, fearing that violence would erupt into civil war, withdraw support from the Marcos family, which departed for asylum to the United States, later to retire in Hawaii.[43]

Again and again Secretary of State Shultz tried to impress upon Reagan the promises of "people power in the Philippines," of having faith in the forces of democracy. Ironically, Reagan showed little faith in the people, as would Castro when he warned Ortega against holding democratic elections in Nicaragua. During his presidential debates with Walter Mondale, Reagan was asked: "What should you do and what can you do to prevent the Philippines from becoming another Nicaragua?" "I know," Reagan replied, "there are things there in the Philippines that do not look good to us from the standpoint right now of democratic rights. But what is the alternative? It is a large Communist movement to take over the Philippines. I think that we're better off trying to retain our own friendship and help them right the wrongs we see than throwing them to the wolves and then facing Communist power in the Pacific."[44]

Reagan was reasoning in a way consistent with Ambassdor Kirkpatrick's famous essay "Dictatorships and Double Standards." It was the Carter fallacy of "helping to undermine," in Reagan's words, "two friendly dictators who got in trouble with their own people, the Shah of Iran and President Somoza of Nicaragua." Kirkpatrick was convinced that support for soft authoritarian regimes must be sustained; the alternative was a harsh, unchangeable totalitarian system. Reagan also favored "friendly dictators" to whatever unknown might follow, and he convinced himself that after Marcos the army would crumble and there would be "a large Communist movement to take over the Philippines." As it turned out, the Philippines went on under Corazon Aquino to enjoy democracy, however unstable the country's politics, and democracy emerged in Nicaragua through popular elections.

Reagan had to face a dilemma confronting every American president in the twentieth century. Can America, a country founded in revolution centuries earlier, be a model for those countries struggling toward freedom in the modern world? President Franklin Roosevelt liked to boast that he had had a hand in writing a constitution for Haiti in the thirties. In the Reagan eighties, the decidedly unfriendly dictators François "Papa Doc" Duvalier and his son Jean-Claude "Baby Doc" Duvalier ignored the constitution while enriching themselves and driving the people into abject poverty. The French government and the Reagan administration worked together to see the Duvaliers deposed, to live amid their gaudy, ill-gotten wealth in Grenoble, France. The people of Haiti to this day have yet to make democracy work as it does in other Caribbean islands, especially those that once were British colonies.

One might ask whether the episodes at Bitburg and in the Philippines proved Reagan's faith in freedom to be more rhetorical than real. Not exactly, for the episodes highlight perennial problems in political philosophy that characterize conservatism. In the eighteenth century, conservatives defended the *ancien régime* and saw any attempt at reform as subversive to order and authority. While Edmund Burke did believe in the imperative of reform, he equated a specific order of aristocratic heredity and hierarchy with the eternal nature of politics. Burke's antagonist, Tom Paine, defended the French Revolution of 1789 and the rights of man in the name of "Reason," only to find himself imprisoned by Robespierre in the name of "Virtue." The enduring question is how an undemocratic society can undergo change and achieve reform without experiencing either revolutionary tyranny or reactionary oppression. In the case of the Soviet Union, in contrast to Central America, the president would find not simply a "friendly dictator" but a leader who was seeking to do what Marcos refused to do: to transform the country both economically and politically; to take a country in "total darkness," as Gorbachev put it, and bring the morning dawn. Anthony Dolan, the speechwriter who gave Reagan the "evil empire" text, claimed that he was striving not only for semantic effect but for historical truth. "Now and forever, the Soviet Empire is an evil empire. . . . The Soviet Union itself can't let go of it," insisted Dolan. However, Gorbachev and most of the Russian people wanted to let go, or at least not hold on to it as it existed. The cold war was no time for fatalism.[45]

The Road to Reykjavik

T HE GENEVA SUMMIT of November 1985 accomplished one thing. After charging each other with aggressive aims, Gorbachev and Reagan came away from the meeting convinced that nuclear war was unacceptable. Yet both superpowers continued the arms race, for even if their leaders were not planning a first strike, they desperately sought to possess invulnerable retaliatory missiles. Prior to Geneva, the Soviet Union was insecure and militant at the same time. Its older leaders could hardly forget Germany's surprise invasion of 1941, just as America recalled Japan's surprise attack on Pearl Harbor the same year. Referring to the pre-Reagan years, the military historian Lawrence Freedman observed: "Soviet political doctrine is undeniably defensive, speaking of war only in the context of an 'imperialist' attack, but its military strategy is undeniably offensive," sustaining "the need for surprise and initiative." With the Geneva discussions, however, the reasoning of Russia came closer to mirroring that of the United States. It was a case of two diametrically opposed political cultures coming to the same conclusion: We do not want war, but if it breaks out, we are ready, willing, and able to fight. The determining word is "if," which again raises the theory of deterrence and why Gorbachev and Reagan came to reject it.[46]

The impression that the eighties was a decade of superficial politics, and that Reagan himself was an "amiable dunce," ignores the profound intellectual dimensions of the cold war. More than at any other time in American history, human existence depended on the adequacy of conceptual thinking. The presence of power challenged the mind to get it right, for nuclear weapons, if unleashed, promised mutually assured extinction. To some who would advise Reagan, the American mind seemed inadequate to the task of protecting America.

The historian Richard Pipes claimed that the Russian national character was so alien that America could not count upon familiar rational behavior, while the mathematician Albert Wohlstetter advised that we avoid "reasoning in the mirror" so as not to make the mistake of believing that the Soviets think as we do. Deterrence rested on the assumption that America's antagonists would be deterred by the threat of nuclear annihilation because if they were not so deterred they would be, by definition, irrational. Thus Pipes worried that the doctrine of mutually assured destruction had little meaning to a country that had suffered so much destruction fighting Napoleon and Hitler. Wohlstetter's views, which influenced, among others, Paul Wolfowitz, President George W. Bush's deputy secretary of defense, reduced the nuclear arms race to mathematical equations that presumed the world was rational and predictable. Meanwhile, if American advisors had sought to find out the views of their adversaries, they would have learned that Russian Marxist theoreticians believed the superpower rivalry could be understood by studying the "correlation of forces" representing the laws of history, and since the cold war was ultimately about class conflict, there could be no doubt which side would prevail. Communism was going to win one way or the other, either because the Russian character was humanly irrational or because Marxist doctrine was scientifically predictable. Or, to consider the opposite scenario, if America was going to win by resorting to a secondary strike, and hence nuclear retaliation, America had already lost, since deterrence had failed to deter.[47]

Deterrence rested on credibility. America had to persuade the Soviets that we would go to war to defend parts of Europe invaded by Russia and at the same time persuade them how reluctant we were to do so. Reagan, the former actor, had to convince the antagonist that he would do what he knew very well he did not want to do—resort to nuclear weapons.

Deterrence held that fear must be feared. Common sense also advised that the adversary must be fathomed. Military strategists from Sun Tzu to Clausewitz counseled the wisdom of imagination and empathy, the necessity of reaching out to the other in order to know thy enemy. Reagan reached out and, in the end, found a friend.

Throughout the Reagan eighties the doctrine of deterrence was widely discussed in scholarly journals, popular magazines, and televised debates. The entire premise of the doctrine assumed that political deci-

sions are made intelligently and that the arms race could be carried out
rationally, since human behavior was predictable and therefore controllable. What undermined deterrence was not so much human design but
the terrifying possibility of mechanical catastrophe, which both America
and the Soviet Union actually came to witness.

This kind of tragic accident was underscored on the morning of January 28, 1986. Before the eyes of America, the space shuttle *Challenger*
blew up thirty seconds into the blue sky. One of the astronauts was a
high school science teacher, Christa McAuliffe, and throughout the
country students had watched the countdown and liftoff. Spectators initially thought that the fiery explosion was only the booster rocket going
off, then suddenly they knew that the whole crew of seven had perished.
Nancy and Ronald Reagan grieved the loss of the young astronauts who
had boarded the spacecraft with smiles and arm-waving cheers. In a
moving speech, scripted by Peggy Noonan, Reagan voiced the mourning
of the nation. "The future doesn't belong to the faint-hearted. It belongs
to the brave," exhorted the president. "We shall never forget them . . .
as they prepared for the journey and 'slipped the surly bonds of earth'
to 'touch the face of God.' " Tip O'Neill, who had earlier in the day
denounced Reagan's comments about the welfare state as "crap,"
exclaimed with tears in his eyes and a lump in his throat, "He's the best
public speaker I've ever seen."[48]

Reagan had long worried about a nuclear war breaking out due to
human miscalculation or a faulty radar system. The *Challenger* explosion indicated mechanical failure could also set off a war, since electronic warning systems could fail as rocket devices had. Deterrence had
been predicated on predictability beyond pure chance. In Russia on
September 26, 1983, in a secret military facility south of Moscow,
Stanislav Petrov, seated in his commander's chair inside the bunker at
Serpukhov-15, which housed equipment for monitoring the facility's
early-warning satellites over the United States, heard alarms go off and
a light flash "Start." It was the signal to start the electronic system to
launch missiles at the United States. The system indicated that American Minuteman intercontinental missiles were approaching. When
Petrov asked how many and was told only five, he knew that any real
attack would be massive and overwhelming, and he realized that the
launch report had to be wrong. The false alarm, it turned out, occurred

because one of the Soviet satellites had picked up the sun's reflection off the tops of clouds and had mistaken it for a missile attack.[49]

A real and even more terrifying event occurred in Ukraine. In late April 1986, reports spread as far away as Japan and Scandinavia of the fall of radioactive dust. The Kremlin vaguely announced that a nuclear power plant at Chernobyl had had "an accident," and that the plant's reactor 4 had been "damaged." At first the Kremlin tried to cover up the deadly seriousness of the meltdown. More worried than wise, Reagan claimed that "*Chernobyl* means Armageddon in the Ukrainian Bible"; somehow, he was convinced that the name of the Ukrainian city was the expression "Wormwood" in the Book of Revelation, and that the term had something to do with a star falling to earth to poison its rivers. Gorbachev had no time for prophecy, as he had to face the greatest nuclear disaster in history. Scores of Russian scientists rushed into the reactor to shut down the core's valves, knowing they risked death from contamination. For thousands of miles around, radioactivity affected crops, livestock, and air, and seeped into the ground water. Figures vary as to how many died in and around Chernobyl; the number is perhaps in the thousands. Secretary Shultz later wrote of Gorbachev's "seemingly genuine horror" regarding "the devastation that would occur if nuclear power plants became targets in a conventional war much less a full nuclear exchange." Reagan also noted "how deeply affected" Gorbachev had been by Chernobyl. The incident, wrote Reagan, produced "a strong anti-nuclear streak" in the leader's mind. He wrote Gorbachev urging that nuclear danger be the priority at the next summit, and Gorbachev replied, noting that within a decade there had been 152 accidents at atomic power stations involving the release of radio activity. Dmitri Yazov, who became Soviet minister of defense just after the disaster, was reported to have said in private that until the accident at Chernobyl he had assumed that the Soviet Union could fight a nuclear war and prevail. Regarded as inadmissible at the Geneva conference, nuclear warfare now seemed to verge on the suicidal.[50]

Another issue, involving espionage, kept tensions high between the two superpowers. In September 1986, the FBI arrested Gennady Zakharov, a Soviet physicist working at the United Nations. He was apprehended on a New York City subway platform while slipping cash to an undercover agent to purchase classified documents. The following week, the KGB arrested Nicholas Daniloff, the Moscow correspondent for *U.S. News and World Report*, and charged him with being a spy. The drama was pure cold war theater, almost out of a John le Carré novel, with both sides playing the same game while professing how shocked they were. Reagan insisted on Daniloff's innocence, and while he mused about a trade in which the two prisoners would be exchanged, some of his advisors sought to put Zahkarov on trial. It turned out that Daniloff's hands were not all that clean; the CIA had unknowingly set him up to deliver pieces of mail from a Soviet citizen to the American embassy in Moscow. Each prisoner could have been tried and received a substantial jail term. Eventually, after many harsh accusations on both sides, Daniloff and Zakharov were traded, and several Jewish refuseniks were freed. Instrumental in the exchange and prisoner releases was the Soviet foreign minister Eduard Shevardnadze, who came to Washington bringing a message from Gorbachev inviting Reagan to a second summit in either England or Iceland. The president opted for the latter.

—

THE LEADERS AND ADVISORS of the two superpowers landed in Reykjavik, once a fishing village. The "city that never sleeps" lies desolate and storm-scarred; the fishing industry is depleted, and the major sign of life are youths carousing all night in disco bars. In October, when the summit was under way, the sun shone for a few hours before blackness set in and the skies dazzled with constellations and the light show of the aurora borealis. In contrast to the elegant Chateau Fleur d'Eau that hosted the Geneva summit, Reykjavik's small, modest Hofdi House, which had been made from building kits with timber shipped from Norway, was ill suited to serve as a conference center, and some of the secretarial work involving word processors and copiers had to be done in a bathroom. The grounds surrounding the Hofdi House had no trees, lawn, or any vegetation whatsoever, a bleak setting for a conference resting on hope.

As Reagan approached Hofdi House for his first meeting with Gorbachev, the CBS journalist Bill Plante had a question. The reporter had already been misled when he had once asked about the rumor of an invasion of Grenada and a White House spokesperson had told him that the story was "preposterous." Now, standing among a crowd of reporters,

Plante shouted at the president: "Are you going to give away the store?" Reagan answered in four simple words: "Don't own the store." The answer was hardly reassuring to William Buckley Jr., Pat Buchanan, and other Catholic conservatives convinced that Reagan might not want to take on atheists with the vehemence they felt was needed.[51]

Reagan had spent considerable time preparing for the earlier Geneva summit. Inexplicably, he arrived in Reykjavik without having had any strategy sessions with advisors and without having prepared a list of specific issues to be discussed and negotiated. The Soviet team, on the other hand, believed that the United States had walked away with a propaganda edge at Geneva, nothing more than a "cosmetic" summit but nonetheless so skillfully stage-managed that Reagan came off as the world's peacemaker. Thus in the next round Gorbachev brought with him material that represented more than a year's preparation on arms control matters, arriving in Iceland "with a blockbuster in his briefcase." He put on the table a "breathtaking proposal" for a series of drastic disarmament policies, limiting strategic weapons capable of attacking each country, all intermediate-range missiles, and any consideration of military technology in outer space. With only the two leaders and their translators and note takers present, Gorbachev asked Reagan to come forth with a counterproposal. Reagan had none. Reagan listened respectfully, and after forty minutes of a dialogue dominated by Gorbachev, the two leaders were joined by Shultz and Shevardnadze. When the meeting broke up, a worried John Poindexter advised Reagan that he should go before the public and claim he had put forward the comprehensive disarmament proposal. Reagan reprimanded Poindexter for such a suggestion.[52]

In some respects, Reagan needed no counterproposal. The one Gorbachev laid on the table seemed reasonable and familiar, almost reiterating the "zero option" policies that the president himself had put forth as early as 1981. Gorbachev advocated a "complete elimination of U.S. and Soviet missiles in Europe," while allowing England and France to retain their cruise missiles (those which, unlike ballistic missiles, could be called back after launching), and leaving the existence of Soviet missiles in Asia off the table. The old SALT II treaty, from which America withdrew after the invasion of Afghanistan, came up during the conference, but any new proposals would render it obsolete, and any attempt to use it to link arms control to regional issues ought to be put "in mothballs," scoffed Gorbachev. One treaty that could hardly be dismissed was ABM, the anti-ballistic missile agreement signed in the early seventies that prohibited the deployment of any missile system, whether based on land, sea, or space, that intended to target enemy projectiles in flight. ABM applied to Reagan's pet project, SDI. According to Frances Fitzgerald, Reagan and his advisors subscribed to a "broad" interpretation of ABM that would allow the development and testing of matters of physics relating to missiles, such as laser and particle beams. The "narrow" interpretation confined missile development only to research based on land-grounded systems.[53]

Gorbachev was adamant that missile systems should be kept out of space, and he surprised even his own scientific advisors, who believed Star Wars would prove a dud, with the tenacity of his opposition to SDI. At the same time, Reagan saw nothing wrong with accepting the reduction of nuclear arms and continuing to develop SDI, not only in the laboratory but as a space station. He had already justified the system that "might one day enable us to put in space a shield that missiles could not penetrate, a shield that could protect us from nuclear missiles just as a room protects a family from rain." He tried to insist to Gorbachev that a successful SDI would make the elimination of nuclear weapons possible, and he offered, as he had done at Geneva, to share it with Russia. The Soviet leader remained skeptical, and tempers flared:

> GORBACHEV: You will take the arms race into space, and could be tempted to launch a first strike from space.
>
> REAGAN: That's why I propose to eliminate ballistic missiles and share SDI with you.
>
> GORBACHEV: If you will not share oil-drilling equipment or even milk processing factories, I do not believe you will share SDI.
>
> REAGAN: We are willing to eliminate all ballistic missiles before SDI is deployed, so a first strike would be impossible.[54]

The romantic Reagan must have been an enigma to the realist Gorbachev. Here was the leader of the capitalist world, dedicated to competition and the pleasures of possession, talking about cooperation and the principle of sharing. Gorbachev made many concessions at Reykjavik. "He was laying gifts at our feet—or, more accurately, on the table, concession after concession," noted Shultz. He dropped the time period to uphold ABM from twenty years to five, agreed to include human rights and regional issues in disarmament treaties, and concurred with Reagan that the world must do away with all nuclear weapons. On SDI neither leader would budge, however. Exasperated, Shevardnadze turned to Kampelman and said, "You are a creative person—can't you think of something?"

On a piece of scratch paper Reagan scribbled a query and pushed it over to Shultz: "Am I wrong?"

The secretary whispered back, "No, you are right."

Night was falling, and Gorbachev pleaded with Reagan, "Give me this one thing."

Reagan gathered his papers, pushed back from the table, stood up, and said. "This meeting is over. Let's go, George, we're leaving."

TV cameras caught the look of the two leaders as they left Hofdi House, their faces stricken, eyes staring down in dejection, figures as pale, grim, and cold as the frigid Iceland night.[55]

Reykjavik was not the bust the press reported it to be. As Ambassador Matlock has pointed out, almost all the disarmament issues had been resolved except for SDI. Reagan's liberal critics claimed that his stubbornness at Reykjavik over SDI blocked "the most sweeping and important arms control agreement in the history of the world." Had Reagan forsaken SDI, however, any agreement made would have had no chance of winning congressional approval. The truth was that months after Reykjavik Gorbachev, perhaps persuaded by Thatcher, dropped his obsession with SDI and told Shultz that upon settling the INF treaty Russia would destroy its shorter-range missiles in Eastern Europe and leave it up to the United States to persuade Germany to forsake their Pershing missiles, which one Soviet official likened to "a pistol to our head." The Soviets also agreed to on-site inspection, and Gorbachev remembered Reagan's fondness for the Russian saying, "*doveryai, no proveryai*," trust but verify. Gorbachev's change of mind resulted from his realizing that no serious reforms in Russia could begin until the arms race was settled with the United States. Furthermore, there was the persuasive voice of Lady Margaret Thatcher.[56]

Thatcher was one of the first Western leaders to recognize that Gorbachev represented a new political species, a communist who knew communism had to face the truth about its own decrepit system. She did everything to bring the two superpower leaders together. She also remained skeptical of the workability of SDI and urged Gorbachev to put the issue aside. Yet she always worried that the Soviet Union had still not repudiated the Brezhnev doctrine of securing the expansion of world communism and regarding existing communist regimes as permanent. On a visit to Moscow in March 1987, Thatcher patiently but firmly told Gorbachev why the West still felt the Soviet Union had ideological aims and no genuine interest in peace. The scolding lecture made an impression on Gorbachev, who summarized it for the Politburo:

> She focused on trust. She said, "The USSR has squandered the West's faith and we don't trust you. You take grave actions lightly: Hungary, Czechoslovakia, Afghanistan. We couldn't imagine that you'd invade Czechoslovakia, but you did. The same with Afghanistan. We're afraid of you. If you remove your INF, and the Americans do too, then we'll be completely defenseless before [your huge armies]." That's how she sees it. She thinks we haven't rejected the "Brezhnev doctrine." Comrades, we have to think this over. We can't ignore these arguments.[57]

"Gorby" in Washington:
Public Delight, Conservative Despair

MIKHAIL GOBRACHEV arrived in Washington, D.C., in early December 1987 to sign the disarmament treaty that had come to fruition in the months following Reykjavik. The capital city, and much of the country, was overcome with "Gorby fever." The subject of adulation and speculation, Gorbachev improbably became an iconic figure in the United States, the purple birth mark on his head a distinctive aspect of his elegance. Smiling, animated, arm in arm with his tall, attractive wife, Raisa, who warmed to Nancy Reagan, Gorbachev addressed an odd group of celebrities at the Soviet Embassy, including Billy Graham, Henry Kissinger, and Yoko Ono. In the East Wing of the White House Reagan accompanied Gorbachev down the broad red carpet to announce the treaty. Ridding the world of "the sense-less waste of resources on weapons of destruction" meant that "May 8, 1987, becomes a date that will be inscribed in the history books." Every-where the atmosphere thrilled with a sense of historical importance, as though history itself had turned a corner. Outside the White House, on congested Connecticut Avenue, Gorbachev ordered his limousine to stop. He brought traffic to a halt as he stepped out to shake hands with pedestrians who cheered him on. The scene was on the evening news across the nation.[58]

One incident marred the otherwise the joyous spirit of celebration. In the crowded Cabinet Room, Reagan suggested to Gorbachev that he explain *perestroika*'s effort to reform the Soviet Union. The Soviet leader was used to making jokes about his country's creaky bureaucracy, but Reagan made a gaffe when he relayed the story of a Russian-speaking American scholar in Moscow who was asked by a taxi driver what he planned to do when he graduated from college. "I haven't decided yet," the student replied. The American then asked the driver—also a student on the way to getting a degree—the same question, to which the Rus-sian replied, "They haven't told me yet." Gorbachev, who was trying to free his country from a command economy, was deeply hurt. Shultz and other cabinet members were upset at a joke that Colin Powell called downright "offensive." The meeting became a public relations disaster. Thereafter, staff members wrote down bits of advice urging the presi-dent to stick to the script and not meander off with jokes and anecdotes. Reagan was no longer adept at ad-libbing, and in the future he remained alert and formal.[59]

In winter 1988, Gorbachev would travel through America, going out west to deliver an address at Stanford's Hoover Institution, the great library and archive of modern Russian history, rich in materials dealing with the Mensheviks, the majority party that lost out to the Bolsheviks after the October Revolution of 1917. Gorbachev was popular on the West Coast as well as the East. He told the people of San Francisco that his country had no plans to reclaim Russian Hill (with its views of the Golden Gate and Bay Bridge). One group of American thinkers, how-ever, remained completely unmoved by Gorbomania.

Conservatives like Paul Weyrich believed that the Iran-Contra scandal had weakened the presidency and that Reagan was hardly dealing with Gorbachev from a position of strength. Republican senator Dan Quayle, soon to be vice president, expressed worry that Europe would be denuclearized and helpless before Russia's superior ground forces. Another future vice president, Richard Cheney, believed that *glasnost* was a ruse and that Reagan was wrongheaded not to see that the Soviet Union still remained the mortal enemy. Then there was Henry Kissinger, the inveterate contrarian. In the late seventies he lambasted Reagan for questioning his and Nixon's détente policy and insisting that communism should be confronted and the cold war faced and resolved. "Reagan doesn't know what he's talking about and he's irresponsible," fumed Kissinger in the early eighties. Because Kissinger was not negotiating it himself, he expressed "grave reservations" about the disarmament treaty and Reagan's effort to reduce cold war tensions. More distressful to Reagan was the position taken by his own friend William F. Buckley Jr. and his *National Review*. Neoconservative contributors to both *National Review* and Norman Podhoretz's *Commentary* advised against ratifying the treaty, convinced that it would leave the world less safe and not at all convinced that America had seen the last of communism. William Safire, conservative columnist of the *New York Times*, scornfully described Reagan as looking into Gorbachev's eyes and thinking he had seen "an end to the Soviet goal of world dominance." *Newsweek*'s George Will, another friend of the president, bemoaned Reagan's weakness for "elevating wishful thinking to the status of political philosophy" in assuming that disarmament would really follow summits and their treaties. Many of those who later credited Reagan with defeating communism had first claimed that he had lost the cold war. Even after the Berlin Wall came down, in the fall of 1989, many neocons believed that communism would reassert itself and that the United States must be prepared.[60]

In private correspondence Reagan set out to answer his critics on the Right who implied that he had been under the spell of summit euphoria. He assured them that the treaty's verification procedures had been carefully worked out and that Gorbachev sought to end the arms race because he knew he could not win it. "General Secretary Gorbachev is the first leader in the history of the Soviet Union who had agreed to destroy weapons they already have," he pointed out. "He is also the first leader who has not reaffirmed the Marxism concept of a one-world Communist state." He understood Buckley's "anxiety," Reagan wrote to his friend, but the "evil empire" had no choice but to join in arms reduction, a policy America's allies as well as NATO also supported.[61]

Ultimately Reagan's reasoning had less to do with ideology than with weaponry. He informed Dr. Gerald B. Broussard, a letter writer who supported the treaty but worried about trusting the Soviets, that after Chernobyl, Gorbachev and the Russians knew what a war with weapons of annihilation would mean. Reagan reiterated a theme that would appear in his speeches: "A nuclear war cannot be won and must never be fought. In such a war between the two great powers one has to ask if ever we launched those weapons at each other where would the survivors live?" Some neocon critics had claimed, as we have seen, that the Russian historical experience was so different from America's that the two respective leaders could not possibly reach any understanding based on common motives. On the issue of disarmament, however, Gorbachev's reasoning reflected Reagan's exactly. When told that "the main source of Gorbachev's new thinking was Reagan's old thinking," the general secretary replied: "The roots of the new thinking lay in the understanding that there would be no winners in a nuclear war and that in any such event both 'camps' would be blown to kingdom come."[62]

Reagan always prided himself on performing as a negotiator. Between the Geneva and Reykjavik summits he wrote to Laurence W. Beilenson, an old Hollywood friend who had been a counsel to the Screen Actors Guild and knew what it was like dealing with studio executives. Reflecting on what the experience meant to him now that he was dealing with world leaders, Reagan wrote: "You know, those people who thought being an actor was no proper training for this job were way off base. Every day I find myself thankful for those long days at the negotiating table with Harry Cohen, Freeman, the brothers Warner et al." In a speech delivered after Reykjavik, Reagan told the audience: "Before I took up my current line of work, I got to know a thing or two about negotiating when I represented the Screen Actors Guild in contract talks with the studios. After the studios, Gorbachev was a snap."[63]

Reagan believed that in a bargaining session there must be a rough equality of interest claims met on all sides or else there could be no agreement. Negotiating required patience and beginning with high demands and being willing to compromise. Reagan, of course, was unwilling to compromise on SDI, but Gorbachev's position in opposing it also had the opposite effect of increasing the hard-liner's stance in supporting it. In negotiating, Reagan exuded confidence, certain that he could return to a country politically intact and economically sound. Gorbachev had no such confidence, but instead of concealing the problems of the Soviet Union he made the negotiator's error of almost confessing them. At Hofdi House Ambassador Matlock observed Gorbachev across the table, "a man reputed to be a formidable debater" but now "leading with the chin." His position that America was exaggerating Russia's economic problems amounted to a concession that there were such problems while at the same time casting doubt on his own claim that Russia did not seek military supremacy. Gorbachev emphasized the importance of trade, only to lead Reagan to withhold trade agreements unless human rights were addressed. Gorbachev gave away his hand by letting it be known what was of utmost importance. "He obviously had not been briefed on American, and particularly Reagan's psychology as carefully as Reagan had on Soviet thinking, Gorbachev's in particular," observed Matlock. "This is not to say that Reagan had perfect understanding of Gorbachev, but he would not have made the elementary negotiating mistake of highlighting well-known weaknesses by denying their existence."[64]

In some respects, the ending of the cold war, a victory for Reagan's hopeful vision, was also a refutation of his political philosophy. It was not simply that Whittaker Chambers convinced many neoconservatives that communism was on the winning side of history and the anticommunists would be the losers. Reagan also believed that the "road to serfdom" begins with a strong, centralizing state from which there was no turning back. The power won by the state augments itself and cannot be dislodged. Yet the Soviet state that Gorbachev had to deal with faced problems as enormous as those faced by Lincoln during the Civil War. Gorbachev had to bring the armament race to an end along with the cold war, modernize a hopelessly dysfunctional communist system, and deal with the incipient disintegration of the Soviet empire. "It was not Western policy that caused the breakup of the Soviet Union but the failure of the political process within the Soviet Union," Ambassador Matlock correctly observed. However, the failures of that political system had been exacerbated by the tensions of the cold war, where the alleged threat of an external enemy allowed the Politburo to crack down on dissidents and refuse to recognize the gaping inadequacies of Russia's economy. The relaxation of those tensions was the beginning of the end of Soviet communism, a prospect that Thatcher foresaw when she emphasized the importance of mutual "understanding and trust." Senator Moynihan, it will be recalled, judged the cold war over as early as 1984. Still, not until the Soviet Union became convinced that it could count on Reagan did Gorbachev feel confident enough to try out the policy of the "new thinking," a process of liberalization and democratization. After the first summits, he was free to embark on his domestic reforms, to convince his military to go along with budget cuts, and to reassure his people that they no longer needed to worry about the old bogey of "capitalist encirclement." Most importantly, he was ready to renounce the Brezhnev doctrine and informed the Soviet Union's satellite countries that henceforth they were on their own, that no longer would Red Army tanks be sent to put down uprisings. The cold war ended in an act of faith and trust, not fear and trembling.[65]

In his own memoirs, *An American Life*, Reagan expressed bewilderment at those Americans, especially conservatives, who sought to obstruct the ratifying of the disarmament treaty. Convinced that he lacked the qualities of a negotiator and true statesman, some feared that at Reykjavik he in fact did give away the store. Reagan could only wonder what these malcontents wanted. A nuclear war? By 1989, as Reagan left office, the Soviet Union had withdrawn all its forces from Afghanistan, ended support for insurrections in Africa and Central America, and terminated its subsidies to Castro's Cuba. In an address given a few years after his retirement, Reagan expressed what many Americans felt: "The nightmare of annihilation has been lifted from our sleep."[66]

A Hero in Europe

"SHE FOCUSED ON TRUST," Gorbachev said of Margaret Thatcher to the Soviet Politburo. To the much-quoted aphorism "Nobody is a hero to his valet," Hegel added: "Not because the former is no hero, but because the latter is a valet." Or, as Goethe responded: "Of course not, for one must be a hero to understand a hero." Whether or not a heroine, Thatcher deserves credit for persuading Gorbachev and Reagan to have confidence in each other as the beginning of understanding. "Know the men that are to be trusted," is a proverb Thomas Carlyle quotes in his study of heroes and the heroic in history. Carlyle adds: "The sincere alone can recognize sincerity." Most theoreticians of diplomacy and the power politics of international relations take their lessons from Niccolo Machiavelli. The Renaissance philosopher taught that the trusting, good leader comes to his ruin among those who are bad, and that suspicion is the virtuous wisdom of the wicked who must be more feared than loved. The neo-Machiavellians of the eighties regarded Reagan as an innocent abroad unable to protect America from an evil world—in short, Woodrow Wilson all over again. It may be more accurate to see Reagan as a historical character with such integrity of purpose that he was capable of recognizing sincerity. That is how he was seen in Europe, where he was given a hero's welcome.[67]

In June 1987, with the INF treaty progressing toward agreement, Reagan made a ten-day trip to Europe, glad to escape the Iran-Contra scandal festering in Washington. In West Berlin crowds turned out to greet the cold warrior turned peacemaker. Facing the Brandenburg Gate, the symbol dividing the West from the East, Reagan challenged Gorbachev to bring the spirit of *glasnost* to the rest of Europe. Before cameras he spoke loudly, his voice growing in anger with thoughts that seemed to be spontaneous but had been drafted by White House speechwriter Peter Robinson:

> There is one sign the Soviets can make that would be unmistakable, that would advance dramatically the cause of freedom and peace.
>
> General Secretary Gorbachev, if you seek peace, if you seek prosperity for the Soviet Union and Eastern Europe, if you seek liberalization: Come here to this gate! Mr. Gorbachev, open this gate! Mr. Gorbachev, tear down this wall!

Reagan later told Lou Cannon that the bitterness he heard rising in his voice was directed not at Gorbachev but at the sight of police pushing people away from the loudspeakers to prevent them from hearing what he was saying. That evening his words were broadcast all over Europe and heard as far away as Moscow. Months later, in a speech televised to Europe, Reagan suggested that the two leaders get down to real work. "Wouldn't it be a wonderful sight for the world to see, if someday General Secretary Gorbachev and I could meet in Berlin and together take down the first bricks of that wall, and could continue taking down walls until the distrust between our people and the scars of the past are forgotten?"[68] What the poet Robert Frost said of fences of neighbors echoed in Berlin: There's "something . . . that doesn't love a wall."

A year after the speech on the Berlin Wall, in May 1988, Reagan and Nancy made their first trip to Moscow, to follow up with the summit meetings. There he spoke openly about the right of Soviet citizens to emigrate, especially Jews prohibited from practicing their religious beliefs. The president and the first lady planned to visit Yuri and Tatyana Zieman, Jewish refuseniks who had applied to emigrate to Israel a decade earlier. Soviet authorities had spruced up the Ziemans' apartment in preparation for the visit, but Reagan's assistant Rozanne Ridgway was told that, if the visit took place, Gorbachev would be put under such pressure that the Ziemans would never be allowed to leave the country. Instead the Reagans met them, along with ninety-eight other refuseniks, at an inspiring reception at the American Embassy.

Reagan and Gorbachev discussed some aspects of the forthcoming disarmament treaty but never allowed themselves to go into the difficult details; these would be ironed out at the next meeting in Washington. The one item that created controversy was the use of the expression "peaceful coexistence." Gorbachev insisted it be in the formal treaty, and Reagan and his advisors balked. Peaceful coexistence, at least as practiced during the height of the cold war, bore unfortunate associations with the Brezhnev doctrine. It was invoked whenever Russia invaded a neighboring country—Hungary in 1956, Czechoslovakia in 1968, and Poland in 1980: brutal episodes for which Thatcher rapped Gorbachev on the knuckles.[69]

Attending a Moscow summit in June 1988, Reagan had the rich satisfaction of speaking across generational lines to reach the minds of the young—something he never succeeding in doing when he addressed students of the University of California. The scene at Moscow State University has been etched in memory and in photos. Reagan is standing at a podium, behind which is a towering white bust of Lenin. The auditorium is packed and the students and professors are at first quiet and skeptical as Reagan is about to speak. He opens as though a scholar giving a lecture on the future, as though the day of politics has passed and is to be superseded by science, economics, and technology.

> I want to talk about a very different revolution that is taking place right now, quietly sweeping the globe without bloodshed or conflict. . . . It's been called the technological or information revolution, and as its emblem, one might take a tiny silicon chip no bigger than a fingerprint [holds one up between his thumb and index finger]. . . .
>
> Linked by a network of satellites and fiber-optic cables, one individual with a desktop computer and a telephone commands resources unavailable to the largest governments just a few years ago.[70]

The message is rich in irony. Reagan did not hold up a copy of the Declaration of Independence, the U.S. Constitution, the Bible, or Adam Smith's *Wealth of Nations* but instead an almost invisible computer chip. He was right to see that computer technology would be profoundly transformative, but whether it would contribute to reducing the power of the state appeared to be doubtful. Not only did Reagan hope that new technological resources might help in diminishing the "largest governments," he was also echoing the promises of Lenin and those of Tom Paine, who had spent his last years as an amateur engineer designing bridges. It was the hope of the Enlightenment that science would subordinate politics, and when Lenin came to power he was hailed as "the engineer of the revolution." The presence of Lenin's bust was ironic in more ways than one. Shortly after the Bolshevik revolution, Lenin had defined communism as " rural collectivization plus electricity," and the Soviet experiment depended upon science and technology to bring Russia into the modern world. Yet it would be computer technology that would render the Soviet Union vulnerable, since the free flow of information was hardly compatible with totalitarianism.

Ronald Reagan was genuinely excited about the prospects for a noncommunist Russia. Other American thinkers had worried not about communism but about Russia itself. At the turn of the twentieth century, long before the October Revolution, what troubled Americans was the stagnation of Russia and the inertia of its people. "The Russian people could never have changed,—could they ever be changed?" wrote Henry Adams in 1904. Adams had talked to Count Sergei Witte and other liberal reformers who were trying to bring Western capitalism to czarist Russia. With Reagan, Russia got a second chance.[71]

The president drew on his old General Electric days and his speechwriter Josh Gilder to explain "the riot of experiment that is the free market." The audience received a lecture on Economics 101. "It is the continuing revolution in the marketplace" that allows America to proceed in trial and error, "to recognize shortcomings and seek solutions. It is the right to put forth an idea, scoffed at by the experts, and watch it catch fire among the people. It is the right to dream—to follow your dream or stick to your conscience, even if you're the only one in a sea of doubters." Reagan could as well have quoted Emerson: "Whoso would be a man must be a nonconformist." The crowd was in thrall to the president. He explained to them how America had always reconciled and made friends with the people it had once fought—southerners after the Civil War, Germans and Japanese after the Second World War, and now the people of Russia:

> Your generation is living in one of the most exciting, hopeful times in Soviet history. It is a time when the first breath of freedom stirs in the air and the heart beats to the accelerated rhythm of hope, when the accumulated spiritual energies of a long silence yearn to break free. . . .
>
> We do not know what the conclusion will be of this journey, but we're hopeful that the promise of reform will be fulfilled. In this Moscow spring, this May 1988, we may be allowed that hope: that freedom, like the fresh green sapling planted over Tolstoy's grave, will blossom forth at last in the rich fertile soil of your people and culture. We may be allowed to hope that the marvelous sound of a new openness will keep rising through, ringing through, leading to a new world of reconciliation, friendship, and peace.[72]

The audience leaped to its feet with a thunderous ovation. Many people in Russia and throughout Eastern Europe came to trust Reagan and deeply respect him. Everywhere streets were lined with well-wishers. What moved Reagan himself was to experience the Russian people and feel their yearning for change. "Systems may be brutish," he stated, "bureaucrats may fail. But men can sometimes transcend all that, transcend even the forces that seemed destined to keep them apart." Gorbachev agreed, emphasizing to the Politburo how important "the human factor is in international politics," quite a message to give to Marxists who had been brought up to believe that history moves by "vast, impersonal forces." Several times Reagan was kidded about his old semi-biblical curse of the "evil empire." At a dinner speech, Gorbachev reported Reagan's response when he was asked if he still believed in it: "He said no, and he said that within the walls of the Kremlin, right next to the czar's gun, right in the heart of the evil empire. We take note of that," Gorbachev emphasized. "As the ancient Greeks said, 'Everything flows, everything changes. Everything is in a state of flux.' " Journalists reported Reagan shrugging off the question about the "evil empire" with different replies, suggesting "that was way back then," or that "everything changes," or "that was another time, another era."[73]

In a letter to fellow actor and former senator George Murphy, Reagan opened up about his enthusiasm for the Russians. He doubted that *glasnost* could be dismissed as mere "showboating," for things were happening that had never happened before, such as the Estonians demanding their freedom without being arrested and a crowd of two thousand marching in St. Petersburg on the KGB headquarters and the officers of that dreaded organization not daring to step outside. "I have to tell you," wrote Reagan, "we were surprised by the ordinary citizens, not the 'nomenklatura' [party functionaries]. You can't believe how warm and friendly the ordinary people on the streets were. There was an enthusiastic laying on of hands, women were embracing Nancy and crying when she had to move on and there could be no doubt that was for real."[74]

In one of his speeches, Reagan had joked than when he was governor all he had to do was make a visit to one of the campuses of the University of California and there would be an angry demonstration. That was in 1968, the year of rage in America. Twenty years later, at Moscow State University and in Berlin, Reagan received a different reception entirely.

In the eyes of many Europeans, he had indeed joined FDR, the hero who had rescued the continent from fascism. A half-century later Reagan helped free Eastern Europe from communism. In American history, these two episodes were the finest hours of liberalism and conservatism.

Burke versus Paine

REAGAN HELPED RUSSIA liberate itself not only from communism but, in a way, from Russia itself. "The Germans, Scandinavians, Poles, and Hungarians, energetic as they were, had never held their own against the heterogeneous mass of inertia called Russia, and trembled with terror whenever Russia moved." So wrote Henry Adams in 1904. Adams saw precommunist czarist Russia as being as much a threat to others as to its own people. It will be recalled, from chapter 1, that Adams believed that reforming a system of government without changing the nature of society could only make matters worse, while Reagan believed that only government, and government alone, had to be addressed. Yet with Soviet communism, the distinction between the state and society became almost indistinguishable. The Russian people themselves trembled with terror whenever the Communist Party moved, and now the party *apparat* was gone.[75]

A Russia without communism may have been the fulfillment of Reagan's political dream, but postcommunist Russia suggests the limitations of his political philosophy. Peace and harmony by no means flowered with the disappearance of the power of state in a country seething with ethnic conflict in Chechnya and elsewhere. As Adams warned, no matter what the state of government, an unreformed society still may need the political institutions of legitimate authority.

Reagan broke free of the rigidities of cold war thinking to begin negotiating with Gorbachev, who in turn was trying to break away from doctrinaire communism. Many writers have ridiculed Gorbachev for thinking that the communist regime could be reformed, when instead the whole rotten system had to come down, as it did when Yeltsin assumed leadership. It may be, however, as Archie Brown has noted, that for Gorbachev to call for the end of the communist state would have been too radical not only for the party but for many Russians themselves. After seventy years of communism, the people knew no other way of political life and were reluctant to forsake the familiar for the unknown.[76]

Gorbachev has been ridiculed for thinking Russian communism could be reformed, yet no one has regarded Reagan as naïve for thinking American liberalism could be reformed. When Gorbachev left office, the Soviet state had lost its sovereign power and the Russian empire began to fall apart. When Reagan left office, government was larger than ever and sovereignty had yet to be returned to the states and the fetish of states' rights, as conservative Reaganites had demanded. Certain liberal ideals (voting rights, rule of law, and so forth) could be brought to bear on Russia to help it change its ways, but those same ideals seemed helpless to change the political character of America.

It is not enough to suggest that America has always been a popular democracy and Russia an oppressive autocracy. The contrast between what happened in Gorbachev's Russia, the dissolution of the state, and what happened in Reagan's America, the burgeoning of the state, should cause us to reflect whether democracy, always seen as a check on power, is actually its agency of growth and expansion. Tocqueville warned that it is the people's demands and desires that lead to the growth of the powerful state. Reagan's intellectual heroes, however, Thomas Paine and Ralph Waldo Emerson, were innocent of the ways of power, and Reagan believed that power would go away to the extent that the authority of the state disappeared. At times he spoke as though he even assumed that the cold war ended because the governments of the United States and the USSR stepped aside and allowed the will of the people to prevail. It was wishful thinking, for such an impression of Reaganism was more romantic than real and had little to do with the fall of communism.

The ending of communism in Russia, as Ambassador Matlock and historian Brown made clear, offers no example of "history from below," which would imply that the masses stormed the citadels of power and Reagan's virtuous people fulfilled their role in history. Even in Czechoslovakia, once a democratic republic, Václav Havel's Charter 77 dissident organization attracted fewer than two thousand signatures from a population of fifteen million. After the fall of communism, the masses were indeed heard from as the former Soviet empire broke up, political chaos and ethnic violence broke out, and governmental systems broke down. Even though President Reagan's statecraft required the resources of the state to steer the country through to disarmament and peace, he rarely acknowledged that government could do the right thing. With Reagan government amounted to little more than the subject of diatribes and puns. "Government does not solve problems; it subsidizes them."[77] But Paine's antagonist, the progovernment Edmund Burke, put the case for conservatism in ways more relevant to modern times.

In *Reflections on the Revolution in France* (1790), Burke challenged the liberal interpretation of politics and history that he believed led to the disaster of 1789. "Government is not made in virtue of natural rights, which may and do exist in total independence of it," he insisted. Historical rights that have evolved in time, such as the rights of Englishmen enjoyed in colonial America, are moderate and self-limiting. People in the thrall of natural rights, however, "by having a right to every thing, . . . they want everything." The only institution that can stand in the way of the people's urge to want everything is government itself. "Government is a contrivance of human wisdom to provide for human *wants*. Men have a right that these wants should be provided for by this wisdom." Burke argued that a government is based upon consent of the people, its power derived from a *power out of themelves*," and that people should recognize that "the inclinations of men should frequently be thwarted, their will controlled, and their passions brought into subjection." In language with which Reagan strenuously disagreed, Burke insisted that the people need to understand that their liberties depend upon political controls. "In this sense the restraints on men, as well as their liberties, are to be reckoned among their rights."[78]

No statement in the history of political philosophy could be more alien to Ronald Reagan's outlook. That restraint should be regarded as much a liberty as the rights of citizens seemed a contradiction. Yet Burke believed that for a political regime to move from a condition of total submission to one of total freedom invites tyranny. Czarist Russia ended up with communism and Lenin for much the same reason that royalist France ended with terrorism and Robespierre. Both regimes had been weak, failing states, incapable of reforming and granting changes and liberties that would have allowed people to preserve themselves. Reagan

convinced himself of the opposite proposition, that a strong, centralizing state leads to totalitarianism, and hence the only attitude toward the
state is good riddance.

What John Adams said of Thomas Paine applies to Ronald Reagan:
He is more interested in bringing down government than in knowing
how it is to be properly constructed. Some of the Reaganites who steered
American foreign policy in postcommunist Russia advocated a free market economy as the solution to the dissolution of political authority. Yet
in Russia the unfettered market immediately abolished price controls
and wiped out the savings of workers, and the policy of privatizing industry resulted in favoritism and massive corruption. An economy without
a state, Burke warned, would allow the "cash nexus" to give rein to the
"disorderly appetites." It would also engender disrespect for political and
moral authority and bring about a crisis of legitimacy that only enhances
the threat of total power. "Nothing turns out to be so oppressive and
unjust as a feeble government."[79]

The relevance and irrelevance of Reagan's political philosophy applies
to America as well as Russia. He would have no sympathy with Burke's
position that people's liberties need to be restrained, and in fact rights
depend on restraint, or else people with a right to do everything will want
everything. If there was a fundamental core conviction of Ronald Reagan, it was that people's desires are good and they have a right to all they
want. He called it the American dream. Perhaps a Reaganite can look to
religion to restrain the unruly appetites. But America is the most Christian nation in its professed beliefs and the least religious in its practical
behavior. As Tocqueville warned more than a century ago, religion dare
not stand in the way of commerce and the pursuit of self-interest. Americans have trouble remembering the Ten Commandments, the Cross,
and the agony of Calvary as they pursue pleasure in the name of piety.
Thus it could be said of Ronald Reagan that he opened the American
mind to its dreams, wishes, and contentment and left it closed to duty,
wisdom, and conscience.

It is hard to deny that Reagan gave the American people what they
wanted. His conviction that the soul is divine and every American a hero
had no patience with the duties and obligations voiced by authority,
especially the authority of the state. The religion Reagan learned from
his mother, Nelle, was free of guilt and repression, and President Rea-

gan believed the American people should not be burdened with a troubled conscience.

To consider Reagan's outstanding successes abroad and the relative
inertia that met his policies at home is more a matter of meditation than
celebration. He brought the spirit of Tom Paine to Moscow while Washington remained indifferent to his own Emersonian conviction about
freedom as self-reliance and the will to change the institutionalized
structures of power. America may have won the war against the brutal
legacy of Bolshevism, but we lost it to the "iron cage" of bureaucracy.
Reflecting on Reagan's legacy, we are left to ponder a disturbing irony:
American ideals did for others what they could not do for us.

CHAPTER ELEVEN

The Homeric Conclusion

"ISENHOWER HAD THE military-industrial complex to contend with; Reagan had the academic-media complex."[1] The observation was offered by University of Virginia professor Whittle Johnson, at a conference on the presidency of Ronald Reagan held at Hofstra University in 1995. Johnson's shrewd comment suggests that while other presidents had to deal with those who liked the cold war for economic reasons, Reagan had to deal with those who disliked it for political reasons.

In his farewell address, in 1961, Dwight D. Eisenhower had warned America of a complex of forces in the country allegedly perpetuating the cold war with Soviet Russia. He saw this as a collusion between the Pentagon and the weapons industry, the unholy marriage of power and profit. Thirty years later, with the end of the cold war and the collapse of communism, the academic-media complex remained cynical about Reagan regardless of his achievements. During the conference, Ambassador Jack Matlock conveyed the bewilderment of the Russians. Why the reluctance of American intellectuals, scholars, and journalists to give their president any credit for his role in history? To this day, much of the positive writing about Reagan comes from conservative think tanks and staunch Republicans.

Many neocons are certain that America drove the Soviet Union into bankruptcy by escalating the arms race. The assumption is that the United States can always prevail if it remains prosperous and deals from a strategy of superior strength. To the neocons, it remains an axiom of geopolitics that unwillingness to employ power implies self-doubt and denies the possibility of spreading freedom throughout the world. During the cold war this assumption cut both ways, for it had also been projected onto the Soviet Union itself. We were told that the Russian national character always veered toward violence and warfare and was bent on spreading, if not freedom, certainly communism. In the Slavic "peasant" mentality, a Reagan national security advisor insisted, any refusal to resort to power would be seen as a sign of weakness. More recently, the same reasoning was used by Robert Kagan, in *Of Paradise and Power*, to justify going to war with Iraq. America must recognize itself as the country of "Mars" and take up the martial spirit that a weary old world, the continent of "Venus," has forsaken. Not to go to war is to be a wimp.

How the cold war came to an end may well be one of the most misunderstood episodes in all of American history. If conservatives remain convinced that it was possible solely because of America's superior economic might, radicals, especially those of the sixties generation, and particularly the few who have advocated the recent war in Iraq, have convinced themselves that it happened because of America's superior political culture. One of the rationales used to argue the moral necessity of overthrowing Iraq's Saddam Hussein was that he symbolized the historic totalitarianism that America fought against in both World War II and the cold war. Presumably both wars vindicated the cause of democracy. Such assumptions are emotionally satisfying and yet historically dubious. In neither war was democracy the immediate issue. In the cases of Germany and Japan, military defeat and abject surrender led to the acceptance of democracy by countries that already had experience with parliamentary government and enjoyed cultures that were religiously and ethnically cohesive. The collapse of communism at the end of the cold war was no doubt due to the enlightened statesmanship of Reagan, who had the help of Thatcher, who encouraged it, and Gorbachev, who thought he couldn't avoid it. Yet communism's demise, though stimulated by the actions of a courageous few, especially East European intellectuals and the rebellious youth, had little basis in the inert popular masses. The fall of Soviet communism had more to do with a crisis of legitimacy within the bureaucracy than with a mass upsurge of democracy.

Except for Max Kampelman and Ambassador Matlock, the Reagan administration had no liberal spokesperson to provide a different perspective on the cold war. Many liberals had taken their point of departure from George Kennan's theory of containment, a policy that advocated standing strong against the Soviet Union but also sitting back and waiting, a policy of prudent patience. In his now-famous "long telegram," sent from Moscow to Washington in 1946, Kennan insisted that the different historical experiences of America and Russia rendered mutual understanding highly doubtful, at least for the immediate future. Kennan had been ambassador to the Soviet Union and was a brilliant historian and the esteemed author of *American Diplomacy*, which characterized his country as either retreating into isolationism in order to escape the responsibilities of power or intervening moralistically with no sense of the limits of power. Kennan's pessimism increased the more he wrote and reflected. He published two masterly volumes on America's intervention in Russia during the Bolshevik Revolution of 1917–1919. He was attempting to prove that the administration of Woodrow Wilson had not been siding with reactionary forces in order to forge a counterrevolution. What Kennen tried to prove for the period of the aftermath of World War I, Reagan tried to prove for the aftermath of World War II. In the letter to Brezhnev that Reagan started in his hospital bed in 1981, the president tried to demonstrate that the United States had no aggressive intentions, even when it enjoyed atomic superiority after Hiroshima. Kennan failed to convince Russians of America's nonaggressive stance in an earlier period, and he felt that he had to teach Americans that, as powerful as their country was, the United States did not have the might or means to make the Soviet Union go away. As would Ronald Reagan years later, in 1960 Kennan urged that "our foremost aim today should be to keep it [the world] physically intact in an age when men have acquired, for the first time, the technical means of destroying it."[2]

Kennan's prudent reflections proved more reliable than the alarmist convictions of many neocon intellectuals who sought Reagan's ear. Kennan believed that the Soviets were still rational enough to share America's fears about nuclear warfare and that they had no blueprint for military expansion or timetable for world revolution. To the extent that Marxism misled the Soviets into concluding that history was on their side, time was really on America's side, as Reagan well knew, even if some of his advisors saw doomsday around the corner. Reagan, however, was too impatient to wait for the containment policy to demonstrate its efficacy, which rested more on the continuity of stability than the uncertainties of change. Even Kennan himself never imagined it would take Soviet communism almost a half-century to somehow come to an end,

to begin to "mellow," as he put it. A calm endurance in the face of false-
hood was the last thing Reagan's romantic temperament could endure.

Thus while Reagan's hawkish advisors wanted to keep the missiles
ever ready for use, he wanted to start the conversation going. It is erroneous to argue, however, as do some conservative writers, that Reagan
concluded that the time had come "not merely to contain Communism
but to defeat it."[3] Reagan defined his "highest priority" as the elimination of nuclear weapons, not the defeat of the Soviet Union. Communism, in truth, defeated itself. Its raison d'etre was based on the promise that its collectivized mode of production would outproduce the
capitalist West, a desperate delusion that Gorbachev finally recognized.
As Gorbachev dealt with *perestroika*, the Reagan administration spent its
energies on proposals for disarmament. Again and again Reagan made it
clear that he sought to rid the world of nuclear weapons, even if it meant
the continuation of the Soviet regime. As we have seen, it was Gorbachev who unintentionally brought about the end of communism by trying to reform it; and here the ironies are telling. In the eighteenth century, Edmund Burke declared that a political system can only preserve
itself by undertaking reforms. Faced with the inexorability of change, to
reform is to conserve. Gorbachev's predicament was closer to the liberal
truths of Tocqueville's prophecy: When a regime begins to reform its
foundations, it surrenders control of its fate.

Reagan the optimist would never give up on the preference for communication over escalation. He could not bring himself to conclude that
the cold war must remain at the impasse of power politics and historical
misunderstanding. On the contrary, he attempted to show how America
refrained from using power. In the period 1945–1949, he explained to
Russian leaders, America had been the sole possessor of the atomic bomb
and did not threaten its use to win concessions from the Soviets. While
Reagan went along with an arms buildup, he also believed it imperative
to convince Brezhnev and Gorbachev of America's peaceful intentions.

Here the stance of Prime Minister Margaret Thatcher proved crucial.
Boldly she stepped forward to assure many American conservatives that
Reagan was taking the right path to rapprochement with Russia. William
Buckley Jr. and Norman Podhoretz worried that Reagan would be out-
foxed at the summits and leave America weak and vulnerable. What,
however, could they say to Thatcher, who would fight war with the same

determination as she would make peace? It was Thatcher, the leader who did not hesitate for a moment to take on the Argentine generals in the Falkland Islands War, who insisted that the cold war must come to an end on the basis of understanding and trust. When the Iron Lady spoke, even conservatives listened.

While Reagan and Thatcher left office with modesty and dignity, other American political figures couldn't resist the temptations of triumphalism, the conceit that America alone, and not Thatcher, Gorbachev, the Vatican, or East European dissidents, deserves full credit for the outcome of the cold war. In his State of the Union Address of 1992, President George H. W. Bush declared: "By the grace of God, America won the cold war." Bush went further to assure that the American people would know what he meant. The "cold war didn't 'end'—it was won." He then honored those "who won it, in places like Korea and Vietnam" and expressed gratitude to the "American taxpayer [who] bore the brunt of the burden, and deserves a hunk of the glory."[4]

No doubt President Bush was trying to reassure the friends and relatives of those fallen American soldiers that they did not die in vain, but a student of history is obligated to attend to the facts. Where the cold war was actually fought, as in Southeast Asia, it ended in stalemate and even defeat for America. After more than a decade of bloody warfare, communism prevailed, and today North Korea looms as a dangerous nuclear power led by a manic ruler in a country of political prisons and starving children, while communist Vietnam gropes it way toward market capitalism. Where the cold war was not fought at all, as in continental and Eastern Europe, it came to an end peacefully which is how Reagan, Gorbachev, and Thatcher wanted to see it settled. The assumption that America's soaring military expenditures brought the Soviets to their knees is dubious, since the knees had been buckling long before the arms race began. There exists not "a shred of substantiation," the scholar Thomas Risse-Kappen writes, "for the claim that there is any connection between the US buildup and the Soviet turnabout."[5]

Specialists in international affairs may debate how and why the cold war turned out the way it did historically. There are those who will continue to insist that the Soviet Union had its back to the wall and was forced to conclude that it could not afford the war economically. Could America afford it politically and morally? The enduring cold war

posed a challenge to the country's identity as Reagan saw it. A war that
would require endless escalation, with no alternative to defense other
than a second strike of massive retaliation, could only mean the end of
Reagan's optimistic vision of history and his hopes for limited government. It could also mean that America must compromise its moral
principles. It may be no coincidence that the announcement of Star
Wars as a defense initiative came only two weeks after Reagan made
his "evil empire" speech. Reagan had read Winthrop's seventeenth-
century sermon "A Model of Christian Charity." The Puritan is warned
that in the struggle between good and evil the good that is aimed at
may become indistinguishable from the evil one sets out to destroy. All
the moralizing about the "focus of evil in the modern world" does little
to relieve the political leader from the Christian sins of pride. "The
pretensions to virtue are as offensive to God as the pretensions to
power," advised Reinhold Niebuhr. Reagan abhorred the idea of massive retaliation, convinced that it renders the retaliator complicit in
evil. "The power necessary to control the wicked is the danger, not the
wicked," wrote Niebuhr.[6]

What the cold war required of America, the paramount power of the
nation state, was precisely what threatened the conservative idea of freedom in America. Reagan told the audience at Moscow State University
that freedom is the ability to change, and the eminent economist Milton
Friedman defined it as the ability to choose. Both the president and the
professor looked to market capitalism, where things happen freely, auto-
matically, spontaneously, without the conscious control of technical
experts and state bureaucrats. The cold war posed an entirely different
proposition. It called for nothing less than total control, a diplomacy of
calculated nuclear escalation in which nothing would be left to chance.
The Reagan diplomatic doctrine depended upon the diplomacy of deliberate planning, while Reaganomics required the economy of natural
abandon, wherein the market would be left up to "an invisible hand."

—

RONALD REAGAN WAS the exponent of freedom and also the voice of
morality. Can the two be reconciled? If there was one thing most Reaganites were absolutely convinced of, it was the certainty that one could
be a capitalist and a Christian too. George Gilder announced this thesis

in a book, *Wealth and Poverty*, which came out just when Reagan was taking office. The book has many wise things to say about how the poor need to practice the values of hard work, but that advice only suggests that workers should look out for their own interests; that they will be rewarded for being selfish, not for being good and virtuous. What of the rich? Gilder goes even further than Adam Smith in denying that the "invisible hand" of the market place is guided by "avarice." On the contrary, it is not what the capitalist takes out and acquires but what he puts back in and gives in the form of entrepreneurial investment, innovation, and risk taking. Does becoming involved in the circulation of capital render one morally responsible? In Nazareth centuries ago, a rich youth asked what he should do aside from keeping the commandments, and Jesus replied: "Sell your property, give your money to the poor, and . . . follow me."[7]

In "Self-Reliance," Emerson balked at the Christian commandment to look to the down and out. "Do not tell me, as a good man did today, of my obligation to put all poor men in good situations. Are they *my* poor?" Reagan insisted that we are responsible for ourselves, and with Emerson he regarded desires not as something to be ashamed of but as impulses to be pursued. According to Emerson,

> Men such as they are, very naturally seek money or power. . . . And why not? for they aspire to the highest, and this, in their sleepwalking, they dream is highest. Wake them, and they shall quit the false good, and leap to the true, and leave governments to clerks and desks. . . . Each philosopher, each bard, each actor, has only done for me, as by a delegate, what one day I can do for myself.[8]

To those of us who doubt that Reaganite capitalism can rise above a hedonistic egotism, there is a ready answer in Emerson: Why should it? "Take egotism out," advised Emerson, "and you would castrate the benefactor." However, even so thoughtful an admirer of Emerson as Harold Bloom believes that if you start indiscriminately with Emerson you risk ending up with "Ronald Reagan and the Reverend Jerry Falwell." The context is all, advises Bloom, the eminent Yale professor who found himself in an ongoing debate with Harvard professor Stanley Cavell about the implications of Emersonianism and Reaganism for America's political culture. Following the debate, it would seem that the meaning of America depended on how it was argued in the atmosphere of nineteenth-century Transcendentalism, an influence on Reagan's ancestry on his mother's side. " 'Self-Reliance' translated out of the inner life and into the marketplace," Bloom wrote, "is difficult to distinguish from our current religion of selfishness set forth so sublimely in the recent grand epiphany at Dallas." He was referring to the Republican National Convention of 1988.[9]

Catholic admirers of Reagan are even more sensitive to the problem of reconciling a market mentality with religious morality. Michael Novak attempted it in *The Spirit of Democratic Capitalism*, and years earlier William F. Buckley Jr. wrote *God and Man at Yale* to protest the teaching of secularism and socialism to the exclusion of religion and capitalism. Buckley, of course, knew Reagan was a relaxed Protestant and not a zealous believer, but he was sure that the Reagan presidency represented nothing less than a reformation of morals. "No one, with the possible exception of Arthur Schlesinger, can doubt that Ronald Reagan will leave Washington having effected a historical transformation in thought not only economic in nature, but also ethical." Buckley spoke those words in 1988, a year after the appearance of Allan Bloom's *The Closing of the American Mind*. Bloom failed to see the ethical transformation that Buckley hailed, and what he did see reads like a descent into decadence.[10]

When speaking of America's historical transformation, Buckley was praising Jack Kemp for sponsoring a bill that cut taxes. No doubt Buckley was being his usual whimsical self, but there is an assumption that putting more money in the hands of people makes them not only productive citizens but ethical characters. The picture one has of Reagan's America in Bloom's *Closing of the American Mind* is far less reassuring. A text that sold over a million copies at airports and supermarkets as well as in bookstores, *Closing* obviously responded to a public wanting to know what had gone wrong with the country. The prosperity of the era, it seems, made people, especially the young, self-indulgent, glued to visual stimuli, seeking nothing better than to be entertained—or high on cocaine, as described in Jay McInerney's best-seller *Bright Lights, Big City* (1984), or strung out on infidelity, as parodied in Tom Wolfe's

Bonfire of the Vanities (1987). An advertisement for Bloom's book announced: "At last you will know why today's young Americans are 'isolated, self-centered, tolerant of everything and committed to nothing.' " Was the Reagan generation of youth the ultimate expression of supply-side Dionysian romanticism? As Bloom saw it, culture hungered for instant gratification, pleasure on demand, diversion, and narcotic escapism.[11]

Whatever the political accomplishments of the Reagan years, the period from a moral perspective was downright confusing. Consider Allan Bloom. Here was a bon vivant who pursued the good life, the amoral sensualist who took upon himself the task of educating America about sexual morality, personal responsibility, classical wisdom, and the virtues of discipline. The truth is that Reagan's "city upon a hill" was always menaced by modernity and the market; conservatives shied away from blaming the corruption of youth on capitalism and its uninhibited desires. Another culprit proved to be the liberal college, where professors taught cultural relativism and drew on French philosophy to deny that the self had a true identity. "Our sense of selfhood dissolves," wrote the philosopher Richard Rorty, rightly protesting the academic chic of poststructuralism and deconstruction that infected the campus like a mental disease. "We can no longer feel pride in being bourgeois liberals, in being part of a great tradition, a citizen of no mean culture. We have become so open-minded that our brains have fallen out."[12]

If liberals tolerated everything, however, conservatives excused almost anything. What is surprising for a president praised as a moral leader is how untroubled Reagan was by the immorality of the era. During the eighties the evangelist Oral Roberts pleaded to his flock that if he did not raise eight million dollars in two weeks, the Lord would call him home. Jim Bakker raised over six hundred million dollars on television before confessing that, like Jimmy Swaggart, he had consorted with prostitutes. In the Reagan era many ministers who promised to save America's soul ended up in jail, as did even more financiers who promised that they would save the country's conscience from being troubled about selfishness. Ivan Boesky, the central figure of the insider trading scandal that exploded in 1986, preached four words of wisdom to students at the business school of the University of California: "Greed is all right." It was a commencement speech that would send graduates out

into the world of finance capitalism. "I want you to know that. I think
greed is healthy. You can be greedy and still feel good about yourself."[13]

What would Emerson say? To be greedy about one's own need for
autonomy and self-determination is perfectly legitimate. As for manipulating others for one's own purposes, the Transcendentalists believed that
one is only free when self-sufficient and independent of others. "Simplicity, Silence, Solitude!" How can you take that to the stock exchange?

—

IN THE EARLY DAYS of the Reagan administration a marvelous coming
together of Marxism and capitalism occurred. On the eightieth birthday
of Sidney Hook, October 28, 1982, President Reagan wrote to the
philosopher to express his admiration. Hook had been correct about the
"façade of Stalinism," the menace of Nazism, and the danger of Soviet
totalitarianism after World II. Reagan told him how the "logic and clarity" of his arguments had helped him in his own struggles against Hollywood communists. Reagan would also bestow upon Hook the Presidential Medal of Freedom, and one wonders whether the president knew
that the philosopher was not only a socialist but an atheist and an advocate of euthanasia.[14]

Shortly before he died, in early 1989, right before the fall of communism, Hook was asked to reply to Bloom's *Closing of the American Mind*.
He wrote a respectful but telling critique in which he defended relativism on the grounds that human knowledge is shaped by the context
in which thinking takes place. What, after all, was Reagan's reconsider-
ation of the "evil empire" but a relativistic shift of perspective? William F.
Buckley Jr. found Hook's essay "sharp and illuminating," but he was not
altogether convinced by the defense of philosophical relativism mounted
by "my valiant and in some respects misguided friend." Another of
Hook's associates, the Harvard sociologist Daniel Bell, suggested that
"there is material for farce" in America's contemporary cultural situation.
"Mr. Reagan praises you as a great philosopher, but denounced radical
humanism as a scurrilous doctrine, not realizing you are the embodiment of radical humanism (or secular humanism)." Today it is difficult
to imagine a political leader in the thrall of Christian fundamentalists
expressing such deep respect to a nonbeliever.[15]

At the same time, a philosopher could well have good reason to

respect Ronald Reagan, especially in the field of international relations.
There was something Homeric in Reagan's fervent desire to alter the
course of the cold war by addressing the arms race. Thousands of years
earlier, after devastating wars left the once glorious Greek city states bar-
ren deserts, Homer and Thucydides meditated upon the horrible consequences that follow when thinking stops and fighting starts. They
believed that the tragic Trojan and Peloponnesian Wars might have been
prevented by the intervention of politics, by discussion and conversation
that would avert destruction and annihilation. "No people have elevated
talk and debate into a way of life as did the ancient Greeks," writes the
historian M. I. Finley. Reagan, the Great Communicator, also believed
that "constant dialogue" offered the possibility of ridding the world of
"the nightmare of annihilation," the Armageddon of the atomic age. "You
are being given a choice between war and survival: do not make the
wrong decision out of a passion for victory." The line from Thucydides
could have been uttered by Reagan to some of his national security advisors. Reagan rejected the doctrine of deterrence and retaliation for a
diplomacy of negotiation. Some of Reagan's victory-minded advisors, it
will be recalled, doubted there could be any opening to the Soviets. The
Homeric component of Reagan's thought lies in what Hannah Arendt
described, in her study of the ancient world, as "an awareness that even
the most hostile encounter between two people gives rise to something
they have in common," the desire to live and avoid suffering and to build
more reliable relationships. Such hopes, observed Arendt in the early
years of the cold war, found expression in classical literature and were
"limited only to poetry and memory and achieved no direct political
effect." At Geneva and Reykjavik, Reagan's Homeric instincts did
achieve direct political effect.[16]

The Reagan presidency was about not only his economic and political policies but his undying will to peace and his uncanny ability to trace
political problems to their roots in emotions. Thucydides warned how
the threat of thinking about going to war robs us of our reason, render-
ing us incapable of knowing how we came to be in the situation in which
we find ourselves. Reagan was capable of so knowing as he took pains to
distinguish the effect from the cause. At the Geneva summit in 1985, he
said to Gorbachev: "We distrust each other not because we are armed;
we are armed because we distrust each other."

Henry Kissinger, the dean of modern American foreign policy, had trouble taking Ronald Reagan seriously. As far as Kissinger was concerned, Reagan was a politician who had no experience in international relations and no advanced degrees in theories of statecraft, an actor who had been more interested in making movies than in pondering Machiavelli. At first Kissinger believed that Reagan's approach to the cold war lacked finesse, as it seemed to vacillate between "confrontation and conciliation." Kissinger would come to admire Reagan, but he was perplexed by a president who assumed that world historical issues could be reduced to the level of personal contact and good faith:

> If Soviet conduct had been caused by suspicion of the United States for two generations, Reagan might well have assumed that the feeling was ingrained in the Soviet system and history. The fervent hope—especially in so vocal an anticommunist— that the Soviets' wariness could be removed in a single conversation with their Foreign Minister (who moreover represented the quintessence of communist rule) can only be explained by the irrepressible American conviction that understanding between peoples is normal, that tension is an aberration, and that trust can be generated by the strenuous demonstration of good will.[17]

Kissinger was a "realist" who saw international relations as the terrain of incessant conflict and tension; other foreign policy theorists were fatalists who saw no alternative to resignation or escalation, either accepting the communist concept of coexistence or taking action to bring about the final destruction of the Soviet Union. Rejecting both perspectives, Reagan was an idealist who put more trust in words than in weapons. He had to convince Gorbachev that Star Wars had no ambition beyond self-defense; and Margaret Thatcher, who as a scientist recognized that SDI was technically dubious, persuaded the Russian leader not to worry about it. All three leaders proved that "trust can be generated by the strenuous demonstration of good will." The ending of the cold war was history's Homeric moment.

The cold war, having begun in fear, ended in trust. In a way, intellectual history went backwards, beginning with a Hobbesian view of war

and eternal conflict and returning to a classical hope in words and conversation. Classical thinkers did believe that fear provided the basis of
settling disputes short of war, and at times the conversations at Geneva
and Reykjavik read like a Platonic dialogue, if not in profundity, certainly
in sincerity. Whether or not Reagan was an intellectual, he belongs in
American intellectual history.

Critics of Ronald Reagan will continue to blame him for the low moral
tone of the eighties. I prefer to end on a higher note. Reagan was fond
of quoting Fitzgerald's *The Great Gatsby*, particularly the "transitory
enchanted moment" felt by the Dutch sailors as they looked upon the
"fresh, green breast of the new world." Gatsby failed to grasp that his
dream lay behind him, lost to the past, whereas Reagan believed, with
Emerson, that America looks ahead to "a bright new dawn."

Reagan might well be exempted from the corruptions of the age, just
as Fitzgerald's narrator Nick Carraway exempted Jay Gatsby. "If personality is an unbroken series of successful gestures, then there was something gorgeous about him, some heightened sensitivity to the promises
of life," reflected Carraway of Gatsby; ". . . it was an extraordinary gift for
hope, a romantic readiness such as I have never found in any other person and which it is not likely I shall ever find again. No—Gatsby turned
out all right at the end; it is what preyed on Gatsby, what foul dust
floated in the wake of his dreams. . . ."

A CODA

Slavery and Communism:
Abraham Lincoln and Ronald Reagan

PERIODICALLY ACADEMIC scholars and other historians are asked to rank the American presidents. Abraham Lincoln invariably comes out on top, generally followed by Franklin D. Roosevelt and George Washington. The three leaders led their country through a civil war, a world war, and a revolution. Their names are identified with the triumph of right over wrong.

Ronald Reagan falls short of top-ranked presidents. To a certain extent, his lesser rating reflects the reality of political correctness. Recent American historiography has been dominated either by older liberals who came of political age in thrall to Roosevelt and the New Deal or by young radicals from the sixties who blame liberalism for the Vietnam War and conservatism for the wickedness of Wall Street. Reagan presents a special case. While Lincoln, Roosevelt, and Washington fought wars the country was unable to prevent, Reagan saw America's political ideals win recognition abroad without going to war. The three other great leaders were all crisis presidents, and historians tend to treat the wars they faced as inevitable. After the battles have been fought to an end, historians investigate the role of leaders and the circumstances that may have precipitated the war. In situations leading up to war, action frequently precedes thought. The mind does not so much determine events as respond to them. As history unfolds, philosophy arrives too late to be of any use to historical understanding. "The Owl of Minerva takes flight after dusk," Hegel warned, leaving us in the dark when confronting the rush of events. Thucydides said it even better thousands of years ago.

> "Think," said the Athenians to the Spartans, "of the great importance that is played by the unpredictable in war; think of it now, before you are actually committed to war. The

longer a war lasts, the more things tend to depend on accidents. Neither you nor we can see into them: we have to
abide their outcomes in the dark. And when people are entering upon a war they do things the wrong way around. Action
comes first, and it is only when they have already suffered
that they begin to think."[1]

Our own world history does not bear Thucydides out. In the late nineteenth century, for example, the American public, regarding the Civil
War as a "mistake," ceased thinking about it. The same was true of the
aftermath of World War I, when the lost generation found itself bitterly
disillusioned with Wilsonian idealism. While Americans rightly took
pride in World War II, the Vietnam War hardly confirms Thucydides'
observation that it is only when people "have already suffered that they
begin to think." The Vietnam War remains more of a subject of recrimi-
nation than reflection, and Ronald Reagan did not hesitate to exploit the
tragedy for political purposes. In the 1960s, Reagan accused liberal
presidents of not wanting to win the war in Asia, just as in the 1980s
Reagan himself came to be accused, by hard-line conservatives, of not
wanting to win the cold war in Russia.

Lincoln also had his share of accusers, especially those who thought
he failed to pursue the war vigorously enough and those who thought he
planned to treat the South too leniently. Lincoln, however, never claimed
that his opponents did not want to see the war won, nor was he sure why
it had to be fought. He saw the war defying all understanding based
upon historical causality and human intentionality. Contrary to Thucydides, Lincoln had no need to wait until after the sufferings of the war to
try to grasp what had caused it. Even during the war, however, his med-
itations yielded no answer, as though the cause of the war was as
inscrutable as the will of God. Neither the North nor the South wanted
the war, Lincoln observed, only to conclude in four simple words, "And
the war came." Could the opposite be said of the cold war? At the end
of his presidency, Reagan partook of a touch of Lincolnesque humility.
As the U.S.-USSR rivalry receded from history, Reagan refrained from
boasting that he alone had ended it. Neither Americans nor Russians
wanted the arms race, and when trust was established between the two
regimes, the cold war went away. A long, dangerous episode in history

ended, yet a gnawing question remains. Why was one leader able to help bring down communism and the other helpless to bring down slavery?

To begin a reassessment of Ronald Reagan in American history, it may be worthwhile to compare him with Abraham Lincoln, even though the two leaders existed in entirely different centuries: one in a country defending itself with missiles and submarines, the other doing so with canons and cavalries. Still, the similarities are curious, and the contrasts even more striking. Whereas America's leading president failed to attain his goal without going to war, the lesser-ranked president succeeded in doing so.

—

REAGAN WAS BORN and raised in Illinois, the state from which Lincoln had launched his political career. Lincoln was a founder of the Republican Party in the nineteenth century and Reagan became the most popular leader of a transformed party in the late twentieth century. Both were attacked by assassins. They admired Tom Paine and prized ambition and other values associated with an aspiring middle class. Yet they had different political philosophies. Lincoln, as a Whig, believed that the national government should oversee America's economic development. Reagan, a libertarian, saw no role for the state in an economy that was supposedly self-regulating.

While the melancholic Lincoln dwelled in an unfriendly universe with a vindictive God; the mirthful Reagan saw the universe as meaningful and God as benign. Lincoln's critics believed he was mentally too despondent to make a good president, while Reagan's critics saw him as too blithely cheerful. Endowed with contrasting temperaments, they had to cope with similar historical crises. Reagan is worthy of comparison to Lincoln because both presidents, the optimist and the pessimist, confronted the moral dimensions of their century's greatest and most momentous political struggles. Why one president succeeded in the struggle against communism and the other faced greater obstacles in ending slavery may tell us much about America's political culture, its limitations as well as its possibilities.

In his last public address, a speech to the Republican convention in 1992, Reagan noted: "I have seen the birth of communism and the death of communism."[2] It was a death without war or defeat in battle. There was, however, no peaceful death of slavery. On the bloody battlefield of Gettysburg, the stench of corpses still filled the air as Lincoln gave his immortal speech. It took America roughly the same time to get rid of slavery, from its legal incorporation at the framing of the Constitution to the Emancipation Proclamation (1788–1863), as it took Russia to get rid of communism, from the Bolshevik Revolution to the fall of the Berlin Wall (1917–1989). Both presidents initially tried a containment policy: slavery must be kept out of the western territories, communism out of the third world. Both also had to fight off the fatalism of their advisors; those of Lincoln who advised the president to let the South secede as a fait accompli; those of Reagan who were unconvinced that Soviet totalitarianism could undergo its own transformation or would even self-destruct. Reagan saw Soviet communism as Lincoln saw Southern slavery: a grotesque violation of human freedom and the right of workers to the fruits of their labor. At Gettysburg Lincoln announced the purpose of the struggle against slavery—"that government of the people, by the people, for the people shall not perish from the earth." At Moscow State University, Reagan announced the new birth of freedom—"freedom of thought, freedom of information, freedom of communication"—and the promise of reform "in this Moscow spring, this May 1988." America's political ideals were there to be heard, but while Reagan could bring them to Russia, Lincoln could not do so in the South. Ultimately history worked against one president and it worked for another. Reagan and Gorbachev could join together to change history; Lincoln had to contend with a South that wanted to preserve the status quo.

—

RUSSIAN LEADER MIKHAIL Gorbachev received the Nobel Peace Prize for his efforts to bring an end to the cold war. Yet Gorbachev, however courageous in advocating change, believed that communism could be saved by reforming it. Ironically, he brought about the opposite of what he had intended by introducing *perestroika* and *glasnost*. Reagan believed that communism was destined to perish, yet our fortieth president has received little recognition for his vision and his actions. What Gorbachev believed could be corrected Reagan was certain had to be rejected. It took a long time for the cold war to come to an end, for it has emerged from two entirely different histories separating the United States from the USSR.

The October Revolution of 1917 and the American Revolution of 1776 reveal profound differences between Russia and America. In the first instance, the Bolshevik revolutionaries were fighting against the old order, the czarist monarchy and aristocracy, and to win the struggle required (or so Lenin insisted) the concentration of power in a dictatorial party. The American colonial rebels had no native *ancien régime* to struggle against, and thus the American Revolution had little to do with class conflict. America's was the only revolution in modern history where all classes fought on the same side. Tocqueville saw this remarkable consensus in American history, and his fellow French historian Ernest Renan was reported to have said: "Happy is the people who have inherited a revolution, woe to those who make it."[3] America inherited a revolution; the war for independence in the colonies carried out the struggle of Parliament against the monarchy that took place in England centuries earlier. Henceforth in American history, liberty was identified with a weak state and the idea of class struggle would be a foreign notion, whereas in Russia freedom would be identified with a strong party that brooked no dissent, and the idea of world revolutionary class struggle would become a permanent fixation. Yet somehow Reagan was able to persuade Gorbachev to reconsider communism's fixations. A century and a half earlier, Lincoln had no success in trying to persuade the South to reconsider its convictions. Reagan had to deal only with Gorbachev and his ruling party, whereas Lincoln had to deal with a South that believed in states' rights. The actions of the South confounded the political philosophy of Reagan, who was certain that freedom is only possible when the the power of the nation state diminishes. The cold war, however, may have demonstrated the opposite conclusion.

Conservative followers of Hayek believed that the road to serfdom derived from liberalism's tendency toward state centralization, a thesis Reagan completely accepted. However inaccurate that claim was historically, it was only because political authority had been so centralized in the Soviet Union that the system could collapse once the party began to question its own rule. In the American South, on the other hand, the road to slavery derived from conservatism's tendency toward state

decentralization, and slavery flourished because there was no strong
national government to pose a moral opposition to it. Each of the Southern states defended slavery with the same zeal as they defended state
sovereignty, and when citizens of each of the states voted to go to war,
they used their inalienable, natural right to participate in democracy to
assure that other human beings remained in bondage. In contrast, the
Soviet Union was composed of a satellite system, and the Brezhnev doctrine denied sovereignty to Eastern bloc countries and denied democracy to its peoples—all in the name not of a master class, which would
have made communism as reasonable as fascism, but in the name of
Marxism, which made it intolerable. In light of what happened in 1860
and in 1989, the premise that informed cold war thinking in America
may have to be revised. While Jeffersonian democracy in America made
slavery defensible, the centralization of power in a totalitarian state,
the nightmare of conservatism, made totalitarianism not irreversible
but vulnerable.

In 1987, President Reagan delivered a Fourth of July address in which
he announced: "We're still Jefferson's children."[4] Not exactly. Had the
American people remained the children of Jefferson, there would have
been no way not only to do anything about slavery but to end the cold
war. The third American president was not always convinced of the
necessity for an army or navy, and saw few reasons why the nation state
should be strong and vigorous. To the Jeffersonians of the eighteenth
century, and to the libertarian Reaganites of contemporary America, it
would be inconceivable to think that freedom could derive from the
exercise of the state's authority. Yet Reagan could do no less than to carry
out such authority in dealing with the Soviet Union. He would increase
America's military power in order to bring power under control and possibly eliminate nuclear weapons altogether. A Jeffersonian would see
such a stance as a contradiction. Given the country Reagan had to work
with, however, and in light of his willingness to increase the national
debt for political ends, it would have been more appropriate for him to
have said: "We're still Hamilton's children."

Even though Gorbachev first saw himself as one of Lenin's children,
he knew that the Communist Party system was vulnerable unless it
could be reformed. He also knew that Reagan was right to insist that,
once the question of security was addressed with disarmament treaties,

matters of ideology could be reexamined, and indeed toward the end of the eighties Moscow intellectuals started the exciting project of "new thinking."

In American history, however, there would be no "new thinking," no opening of the political mind, no reexamination of the South's ideological fate. More than a century before Reagan and Gorbachev, Lincoln was unable to convince the South to reconsider its political philosophy, which was based on an oppressive labor system that violated the egalitarian principles of the Declaration of Independence. Nor could Lincoln convince the slave states that if they would begin a process of gradual emancipation they would have nothing to fear about their security. For all of America's vaunted pragmatism and alleged capacity to solve problems, it seems remarkable that the impasse over slavery was greater in democratic America than was the inherited curse of communism in totalitarian Russia. One reason for the two different situations is that communism came to be seen as alien to Russia's historical past, while slavery was seen, at least in the South, as consistent with America's past and continuous with history from ancient times. Slavery was even seen as compatible with the American Revolution, and hence while southerners felt no need to renounce Jefferson, the Russian people felt every need to renounce Lenin.

The meaning of the October Revolution had to be repudiated, since it led to the dictatorship of the party. The American South, however, had no need to repudiate the American Revolution, for the right of revolution that led the colonies to separate from England could be readily reaffirmed as the right of secession that gave the South the right to leave the Union. In other words, the liberalism of self-determination (one of Reagan's favorite expressions) could challenge communism in Russia, but it could also serve to protect slavery in America. No wonder Lincoln's tragic despair was as deep as Reagan's romantic hope of possibility. Both leaders identified freedom with eliminating the forces that stood in its way. But history in some respects may be kinder to Reagan, who won the war of words. The more Reagan criticized communism, the more the Russian people listened; the more Lincoln criticized slavery, the more the South defended it. Southerners could hardly acknowledge that they were the oppressors; Russians knew what it was like to be oppressed.

The South defended slavery as an institution that had its origins in the ancient world, but communism was focused on what was to come. "We must draw our poetry from the future," Marx urged. The Soviet system derived from the Marxist conviction that socialism was history's next step beyond liberalism and capitalism. By the Gorbachev eighties, few Russians could any longer believe this. The October Revolution had been an abject failure, and Russians knew that the story of their country under communism added up to "seventy years on the road to nowhere."[5] The South, which had once seen slavery as a "necessary evil," came to praise it as a "positive good," and Lincoln failed to convince southerners that slavery had no future. The South also had no enlightened leader. Even Robert E. Lee, the great Confederate general who hated slavery, fought for his state's right to secede. For Reagan, however, Gorbachev made a difference. Fearing America's growing military superiority, he made concessions on arms reduction, knowing full well that the arms race was bankrupting the economy and reducing Russia to a "third world county." The paradox was that the more powerful Russia became militarily the weaker it became economically. "We cannot live a normal life in our supermilitarized economy," declared Gorbachev.[6] Less well known, however, is that Gorbachev had second thoughts about the ideology on which he had been reared. He came to acknowledge that socialism had no historical destiny and no basis in human nature, a point upon which Reagan always insisted. "Communism works only in Heaven, where they don't need it, and in Hell, where they already got it," quipped Reagan. "The Achilles' heel of socialism," Gorbachev admitted, "was the inability to link the socialist goal with the provisions of incentives for efficient labor and the encouragement of initiative on the part of individuals. It became clear that in practice the market provides such incentives best of all." Even though Gorbachev thought he could save communism by reforming it, he came to realize the efficiency and morality of free market capitalism. Lincoln had no success in persuading the South to accept free soil and free labor.[7]

To Russian thinkers, the example of Lincoln represented the very meaning and tragedy of American history. The pacifist Leo Tolstoy saw Lincoln as "Christ in miniature," a martyr to the violence he had unleashed. In his debates with John Dewey in the thirties, Leon Trotsky invoked Lincoln to argue that taking up arms to defend a revolutionary heritage was absolutely necessary. The Czech intellectual Zdeněk

Mlynář asked Gorbachev why he refused to resort to force to hold the Soviet Union together in 1990 in defiance of Reagan. "Marx's proposition that violence is the midwife of history" was demonstrated, Mlynář suggested to his friend Gorbachev, in Lincoln's waging a civil war to prevent the breakup of the American Union. "Granted that Lincoln remains a hero of his country and of his time," replied Gorbachev. "While granting him his due, I don't forget what the Civil War meant for the people, what torments they had to undergo. Let us recall Margaret Mitchell's novel *Gone with the Wind*. What losses and sacrifices accompanied that war." It should be remembered that in the late 1980s, when communism was on the verge of collapsing, many writers and political leaders feared the outbreak of civil war in the former Soviet Union. It didn't happen then, nor more than a hundred years earlier, when Russia abolished serfdom. What Russia accomplished peacefully, America could only accomplish violently.[8]

Both Lincoln and Reagan believed that it was culture, not politics, that determined the character of a society, and both valued the ideas of property, opportunity, and natural rights. With such values in mind, Reagan hoped to speak directly to the Russian people. He even delved into political philosophy, with observations that would have pleased John Locke and Karl Marx, both of whom believed passionately in the labor theory of value. "The peoples of the world, despite differences in racial and ethnic origin, have very much in common. They want the dignity of having some control over their individual destiny. They want to work at the craft or trade of their own choosing and be fairly rewarded. . . . Government exists for their convenience, not the other way around."[9]

Reagan knew from his Hollywood struggles that many communists regarded liberalism as the real enemy. When Reagan came of political age in the 1930s, writers, intellectuals, and actors were "waiting for Lefty," all convinced that liberalism was finished and the future belonged to socialism. Lenin disdained the "bourgeois liberalism" that America had produced, while Trotsky concocted his theory of "the law of combined development" to claim that Russia could skip the liberal stage of history altogether. When Reagan spoke at Moscow State University in 1988, he was carrying out the wishes of Tom Paine, who believed that the cause of the American Revolution was the cause of the world.

Much of Reagan's cold war took place not in Europe or America but.

in the third world. Such struggles in that part of the world were significant but by no means decisive. Soviet archives indicate that after Russia found itself bogged down in Afghanistan, beginning in 1980, it lost
interest in the third world and, as we have seen, even dismissed Castro
as an adventurer with "delusions of grandeur." In a strict theoretical
sense, a true Marxist had no need to be concerned with the underdeveloped world and entertain a blueprint for global victory. History deemed
that capitalism would eventually fall and the working class arise. In
America, however, capitalism continued to thrive, and much of the working class voted for Reagan. To wait for capitalism to collapse of its own
"inner contradictions" proved to be a lost cause, and no one knew this
better than Gorbachev himself when he embarked on a series of revisions
and reorientations that required what he called "a major conceptual
breakthrough" of party doctrine. At the end of the cold war, Gorbachev
could even joke about the wishful thinking that blinded his generation.
"I remember an anecdote from that time," he recalled of the sixties:

> A certain lecturer, speaking about the future communist
> society, concluded with the following remarks: "The breaking
> day of communism is already visible, gleaming over the hori-
> zon." At this point an old peasant who had been sitting in the
> front row stood up and asked, "Comrade Lecturer, what is a
> horizon?" The lecturer explained that it is a line where the
> earth and the sky seem to meet, having the unique character-
> istics that the more you move toward it, the more it moves
> away. The old peasant responded: "Thank you, Comrade
> Lecturer. Now everything is quite clear."[10]

"I've been over into the future," the journalist Lincoln Steffens wrote
after visiting the Soviet Union in 1921, "and it works." Slavery, however,
had no horizon; it was historical fact. It worked because it is, was, and
always had been. Slavery required no justification, no acknowledging
that the South was passing through necessary phases of existence as a
historical proposition about the future. Thus to Lincoln, slavery was the
curse of the past, and history was his nemesis. Reagan's orientation,
however, was always toward the foreground; and history as it was forthcoming, the "bright dawn ahead," was his hope.

—

IN THE EARLY DAYS of superpower tensions, Bishop Fulton J. Sheen broadcast to millions of Americans his conviction that the curse of communism is the curse of atheism. In grammar schools, nuns told their classes that there would not be peace in the world until the Soviet Union was converted to Christianity, preferably Catholicism. Many of Reagan's admirers were Catholics, and Reagan fully accepted the support of Protestant fundamentalists in the war against the "evil empire."

Viewing the cold war in religious terms may be emotionally satisfying. Yet Soviet leaders believed in historical materialism and conceived knowledge as grounded in science, a way of thinking subjected to verification and revision. It is difficult to see how communism could have been repudiated if it were not a scientific proposition. Many Russian people, to be sure, believed in God and resented the suppression of religious freedom. When they finally bid good riddance to communism and welcomed Reagan's speeches, however, it seemed they were less interested in returning to older pieties than in looking forward to a new prosperity. At Moscow State University, Reagan held up not the Bible but a computer chip, delighted in his hope that with the advent of modern technology, power would gravitate toward science and away from the state. Had Russia defended communism on religious grounds, the cold war may have continued far longer than it did, as the Soviet Union refused to face its own demise, just as the South had once refused to face the sin of slavery.

While Southern apologists for slavery cited ancient history and dabbled in scientific theories that supposedly proved the inequality of the human species, the basic defense of slavery was drawn from the Bible and religious doctrine. The South relied upon scriptural sources to justify labor as the curse of original sin and condemned the worker to be forever in a state of servitude. Southern thinkers quoted the apostle Peter instructing servants and slaves: "Submit yourself to every ordinance of man for the Lord's sake. For so is the will of God."[11] The argument for slavery thus remained beyond the realm of reason and science; the apology was more like a militant religious system that rarely reexamines its foundations.

If conservatives saw Soviet communism as dangerous because of its atheism, liberals committed the opposite error and saw it as dangerous because of its theism. Communism must be seen, we were told in the misleading title to a book, as "the God that failed." While Reagan was fighting communism in Hollywood in the late 1940s and 1950s, intellectuals were writing essays and books depicting it as a religious "messianism," a "disguised theology" promising nothing less than redemption and salvation, a scheme of history where the dialectic of thesis, antithesis, and synthesis was tantamount to the Father, the Son, and the Holy Ghost. Communism, stripped of its scientific verbiage, was actually supernatural "chiliasm," the return of Christ to earth and the end to what Marx called "pre-history," the state of limbo, that abode of lost souls outside the gates of heaven.[12]

No doubt many Russian people believed that a pseudo religion had been imposed upon them, and Reagan the Emersonian knew that a soul without God would surrender itself to the perils of secular authority. When Gorbachev ridiculed the idea of a "horizon," however, it was not salvation he had in mind but deprivation. Because it was conceived as a science and not a religion, Soviet communism could subject itself to "new thinking" to discover what is still living and what is dead in Marxism in order to root out its false theories. Religion induces resignation; science is about expectation; one can endure a society of stagnation, the other must change or die.

For those who may think that the Reagan administration had little to do with intellectual history, one should keep in mind that the fall of communism stimulated intriguing debates about "paradigms," "rhetorical frameworks," "systems theory," and other ideas that tried to explain why a long-established way of looking at things could engender "cognitive dissonance," the intrusion of contradictions and anomalies that threatened to expose the faulty foundations of a rigid orthodoxy. In Soviet communism, in contrast to many religious systems, the explanation of failure was obvious, and Reagan could readily point to it. In Russia the experience of daily life contradicted the premises of its ideology. The egalitarian promise of socialism, rather than being confirmed, was falsified every time a cab driver looked at limousines and saw party functionaries being chauffeured on the streets of Moscow. Had the party apparatachiks read the American writer Thorstein Veblen, they would have feared what Reagan knew, that the instinct of "emulation" compels even the working-class Marxist to desire a Mercedes-Benz. Soviet Russia was supposedly a workers' state under the sway of the forces of production. In reality, it was the temptations of consumption that undermined the regime's mental hegemony, which had been built by decades of propaganda imposed in the classroom.

In most religions, the teachings and indoctrination remain almost invulnerable, since the disparity of wealth hardly matters when the true meaning of existence is the afterlife. In fervent religious cultures, beliefs hold fast because the experiences of life pose no contradiction to spiritual doctrine. Communism, however, presumed to be a philosophical system based on the Hegelian idea of progress and the Darwinian idea of change. Both philosophies combined to claim that whatever is later in life must be, by the progressive nature of history, better than what went before, and better now, not in the hereafter.

A common assumption today is that America "won" the cold war once Reagan deployed Pershing missiles in Western Europe in the late 1980s and the Soviets yielded to fear. Yet Reagan never felt he had to resort to nuclear terror to challenge a philosophical error. His faith in conversation and dialogue expressed a belief in a world beyond power politics and a conviction that truth would out. Reagan was less a warrior than an educator. In the end, the cold war did not have to be fought not only because of the presence of nuclear weapons but also because of the fallacy of an ideology that failed to come through with what it had promised. In the words of Karl Marx, the promise was "reintegration or return of man to himself, the transcendence of human self-estrangement."[13] Those brought up on the teachings of Marxism were well prepared to respond to another message delivered a century later by President Ronald Reagan. At Moscow State University in 1988, those in the audience had been taught to believe that the pursuit of wealth was alienating and led to self-estrangement. Reagan taught them that it was fulfilling and led to self-reliance.

—

ALL THE FORCES of history that worked in Reagan's favor worked against Lincoln, who had to deal with a South that not only claimed state sovereignty but justified slavery on religious grounds. In the midst of the Civil War, Lincoln reflected: "I claim not to have controlled events, but confess plainly that events have controlled me."[14] Lincoln was a tragic hero. The emotions turned to anguish as he saw events stalking freedom at every turn on the field of battle.

In the midst of the cold war, Reagan's heroism consisted in defying destiny and taking control of events. "History is not predetermined," he exhorted the press on his way to the Geneva summit. "It is in our hands." "If I can leave the young people of Europe with one message it is this," he told an Italian audience in 1987: "History is on the side of the free."[15]

Lincoln also saw history as the story of freedom. Yet the Civil War seemed so darkly ambiguous and indeterminate that he refrained from taking credit for the Emancipation Proclamation. The specter of fate haunted Lincoln. Reagan had to struggle against the pessimism of many of his advisors in order to push ahead with his disarmament proposals. The sudden end of communism and of the cold war represented the great political surprise of the twentieth century—perhaps for all of history, for it was the first time an empire collapsed without war or revolution. Reagan responded with characteristic modesty to this unprecedented event. When asked who should take credit for the end of the cold war and the demise of communism, he named Mikhail Gorbachev. At the very moment of victory, Reagan displayed humility, as did Lincoln when the North emerged victorious in the Civil War. Both exceptional presidents were politically wise, humane, and magnanimous. Each had greatness of soul.

Abbreviations for References

HIA, Hoover Institute Archives, Stanford University.

PSRR, *Actor, Ideologue, Politician: The Public Speeches of Ronald Reagan*, ed. Davis W. Houck and Amos Kiewe (Westport, CT: Greenwood, 1993)

RIOH, *Reagan in His Own Hand*, ed. Kiron K. Skinner, Annelise Anderson, and Martin Anderson (New York: Free Press, 2001)

RLIL, *Reagan: A Life in Letters*, ed. Kiron K. Skinner, Annelise Anderson, and Martin Anderson (New York: Free Press, 2003)

RMHP, *Reagan: The Man and His Presidency: The Oral History of an Era*, ed. Deborah Hart Strober and Gerald S. Strober (Boston: Houghton Mifflin, 1998)

RR, Ronald Reagan

RRPL, Ronald Reagan Presidential Library, Simi Valley, California

RRSW, *Reagan's Path to Victory: Selected Writings*, ed. Kiron K. Skinner, Annelise Anderson, and Martin Anderson (New York: Free Press, 2004)

TRP, *The Reagan Presidency: Pragmatism, Conservatism, and Its Legacies*, ed. W. Elliot Brownlee and Hugh Davis Graham (Lawrence: University Press of Kansas, 2003)

TQRR, *The Quotable Ronald Reagan*, ed. Peter Hannaford (Washington, D.C.: Regnery, 1998)

VDSE, John Earl Haynes and Harvey Klehr, *Venona: Decoding Soviet Espionage in America* (New Haven: Yale University Press, 1999)

Notes

INTRODUCTION

1. Allan Bloom, *The Closing of the American Mind* (New York: Simon & Schuster, 1987), 142.

2. Much of the discussion of this introduction regarding foreign affairs is treated in detail in chapter 10.

3. Quoted in Johanna Neuman, "Ronald Wilson Reagan, 1911–2004," a *Los Angeles Times* obituary (June 6, 2004), reprinted in *Ronald Reagan Remembered: CBS News*, ed. Ian Jackson (New York: Simon & Schuster, 2004), 20.

4. The exception is the two-term administration of President William Jefferson Clinton. Clinton not only brought down the national debt but left America with a huge surplus. Ironically, Clinton, who had a hard time controlling his sexual appetites in the White House, exercised amazing discipline in holding back on spending and catering to constituencies. In contrast, Reagan, who in the White House led the life of a faithful husband without a temptation in the world, could not resist the temptation of allocating subsidies to farmers and other interest groups who believed in small government, provided it was large enough to meet their demands.

5. John Patrick Diggins, *Up from Communism: Conservative Odysseys in American Intellectual History* (New York: Harper & Row, 1975).

6. Reagan loved to say that Soviet communism was on its deathbed, and leaders of Solidarity also believed that the system in Poland could be brought down with mass demonstrations forged by the Gdansk shipyard workers. The American labor leader Lane Kirkland, head of the AFL-CIO, immediately sent funds to Solidarity, convinced that the Polish trade union's struggle for independence from the party could put into motion a movement that might topple communism elsewhere in Eastern Europe. On December 15, 1981, Kirkland was invited to the White House to discuss the subject with Reagan, and he proposed that the United States order a halt to the loans banks were making to Poland. The meeting ended without Reagan making a commitment. In the political context of the period, Reagan had to exercise caution about Poland. In the first years of the administration, he was attempting to help Jewish dissidents leave

the Soviet Union, and any overt assistance to Solidarity would raise the charge that the United States was interfering in Poland's internal affairs (RR to Leonid Brezhnev, Dec. 23, 1981, and Feb. 4, 1982; Leonid Brezhnev to RR, Dec. 15, 1981, Box 38; all in RRPL). Yet in his much quoted speech declaring the Reagan doctrine, made to the British Parliament on June 8, 1982, the president announced that America would go "anywhere" in the world to support those fighting against communism. Apparently the doctrine had little bearing on those living under communism and struggling against it, such as labor leader Lech Walesa and the historian Adam Michnik, who were imprisoned for their anticommunist activities. When General Wojciech Jaruzelski imposed martial law and outlawed Solidarity, Reagan and his advisors became more certain that the movement would fail and invite repression from the Soviet Union. "For the duration of the Polish crisis," wrote Arch Puddington, "Kirkland remained critical of the Reagan administration for what he regarded as a consistently inadequate policy toward the Jaruzelski regime. Kirkland believed that the administration's Poland policy was dictated in large means by the Republican party's ties to the world of finance, which vigorously opposed calling in the debt and forcing the Polish government into default." Kirkland knew that Reagan believed deeply in the cause of anticommunism, but he doubted whether the State Department "cared whether Solidarity reemerged as a legal trade union." The administration did impose minor sanctions, such as canceling landing rights to the Polish national airline. Such sanctions were lifted as Jaruzelski called off martial law. "The Reagan administration, despite the continued Solidarity ban, the imprisonments, and the trials, formally eased some of its sanctions." Abandoned, "Solidarity was left to struggle forward on its own underground." Arch Puddington, "Surviving the Underground: How American Unions Helped Solidarity Win," *American Educator* 29 (Summer 2005): 6–17.

The relation of the Reagan administration to Poland during the cold war would require a book in itself. Here two points should be made. Reagan was the only trade union leader ever to become a president, and his reluctance to support Solidarity may have been due to his desire to work with Gorbachev to bring about disarmament. During the tense moments at the summits, both leaders accused each other of interfering in the internal affairs of their respective spheres of influence—Russia in the Caribbean, America behind the Iron Curtain. Moreover, the dilemma Reagan faced was strikingly similar to the one that confronted Abraham Lincoln during the Civil War. Pressure was put on Lincoln to issue an emancipation proclamation shortly after the war broke out in 1861, and Lincoln refused to do so for fear of losing the border states to the South. Similarly, Reagan was reluctant to declare solidarity with the Polish workers for fear of jeopardizing a rapprochement with the Soviet Union. For further discussion of Reagan and Lincoln, see the Coda.

7. RR to Mrs. Van Voorhis, circa 1976, *RLIL*, 277–78.

8. Reagan, of course, had been describing the Soviet Union as a "basket case" on the verge of collapse since his anticommunist years in Hollywood. But such American attitudes began as early as 1917, not long after the Bolsheviks took power and the *New York Times* predicted again and again the regime would not last. The impression was reinforced after V. I. Lenin introduced "NEP," the New Economic Policy of the early twenties that allowed for some measure of market economics to take place in the country so that farmers would deliver their crops, and supposedly Russia was forsaking communism. The impression that the system was in shambles continued through the two "scissors crises" of the twenties, when peasants had overproduced and facto-

ries had held back. The forceful collectivization at the end of the decade traumatized the countryside, though the heralded "Five Year Plan" of the thirties created the false impression that Russia withstood the world depression. After World War II the world became aware of the earlier Ukraine famine, the Gulag camp, and the devastation of the economy due to the war effort. Ultimately it was not what Americans thought about the future of the Soviet Union but what Russian leaders did, and Gorbachev undertook reforms in a desperate attempt to save communism only after he felt reassured that Reagan was not a "war monger" and a tool of the "military-industrial complex." When Reagan was deep into disarmament negotiations, the elimination of nuclear weapons took precedence over the ending of communism. For further discussion, see chapter 10. See also Jack F. Matlock Jr., *Autopsy on an Empire: The American Ambassador's Account of the Collapse of the Soviet Union* (New York: Random House, 1995).

9. Whittaker Chambers, *Witness* (New York: Random House, 1952), 16–17.

10. Stephen Spender, in Richard H. Crossman, ed., *The God That Failed* (New York: Bantam, 1950), 240.

11. Chambers, *Witness*, 476.

12. Harvey Klehr, John Earl Haynes, and Fridrikh Igorevich Firsov, *The Secret World of American Communism* (New Haven: Yale University Press, 1995).

13. From the marvelous memoir of Dorothy Gallagher, *How I Came Into My Inheritance and Other True Stories* (New York: Random House, 2001), 47–48.

14. George Orwell, "Arthur Koestler," in *Collected Essays, Journalism, and Letters of George Orwell*, ed. Sonia Orwell and Ian Angus, 4 vols. (New York: Harcourt, Brace, and World, 1968), vol. 3, 236.

15. Chambers, *Witness*, 471–75.

16. The exception of a Western country turning communist without the direct presence of the Soviet Union is Cuba. In 1959 Fidel Castro came to power promising progressive reforms and constitutional freedoms, and within a year the country became a Leninist dictatorship. In *Listen, Yankee*, the sociologist C. Wright Mills proclaimed that Castro's dictatorship was "part of a phase" and that "Americans should help the Cubans pass through it." The help would need to be endlessly steady work, perhaps carried on indefinitely; the book was written almost a half-century ago. C. Wright Mills, *Listen, Yankee: The Revolution in Cuba* (New York: McGraw Hill, 1960), 183.

17. Among the leading anticommunist cold war liberals was Reinhold Niebuhr, the learned theologian who passed away in 1971. Niebuhr sought to reintroduce the idea of original sin into political discourse, and most likely he would have had no trouble approving of Reagan's reference to the "evil empire," providing America faced the deceptive delusions of its own innocence. More specifically, Niebuhr's recommending that America should reconsider escalating the "game of deterrence" and risk proceeding toward disarmament presages by two decades Reagan doing just that, as he ceased listening to his hawkish advisors and their mathematical calculations about "kill ratios."

18. George P. Shultz, Foreword to *RIOH*, x.

19. Sidney Hook, *The Hero in History: A Study in Limitations and Possibility* (Boston: Beacon Press, 1943), 154.

20. Peter Schweizer, *Reagan's War: The Epic Story of His Forty Year Struggle and Final Triumph Over Communism* (New York: Doubleday, 2002).

21. RR to Dr. Gerald B. Broussard, Feb. 15, 1988, *RLIL*, 421–22.

22. The ending of the cold war and the fall of communism should be regarded separately. The first episode by itself might have strengthened the Soviet Union by reliev-

ing it of heavy military expenditures. Initiatives taken by Gorbachev, especially his repudiation of the Brezhnev doctrine, inadvertently led to the collapse of communism. See chapter 11.

23. Irving Kristol warned that it was not the "grandiloquent declamations" of the Revolution that accounted for America but the procedures of constitution making. Jeane Kirkpatrick advised: "The freedoms of the American people" derive not from "the marvelous and inspiring slogans of Tom Paine"; rather, they are based "on the careful web of restraints, or permission, of interests, of tradition woven by the Founding Fathers into the Constitution and explained in *The Federalist Papers*." Quoted in Harry V. Jaffa, "What Were the Original Intentions of the Framers of the Constitution?" *University of Puget Sound Law Review* 10 (Spring 1987), 373–75.

24. Reagan also wrote an essay called "Return to the Primitive," where he drew upon Joseph Warton's youthful poem "The Enthusiast" (1744) to show the romantic's urge to glorify the self and its relation to nature (*RIOH*, 428–30). As Arthur O. Lovejoy observed, Warton and the Romantics were in utter revolt against classicism and its rules and regulations, a temper of laissez-faire in literature that could carry over to economics. Arthur O. Lovejoy, "On the Discrimination of Romanticism," in *Essays in the History of Ideas* (New York: Braziller, 1955), 237–42.

25. Karl Marx, "The Grundrisse," in *The Marx-Engels Reader*, ed. Robert C. Tucker (New York: Norton, 1972), 223.

26. Alexis de Tocqueville, *Democracy in America*, ed. Isaac Kramnick, trans. Gerald B. Bevan (New York: Penguin, 2003), 858–59.

27. In Reagan's library at his ranch in Santa Barbara was *The Works of Epictetus*, the ancient Greek Stoic, who urged human beings to moderate their desires and be satisfied only with that which is in one's power to achieve and control. Whether or not Reagan read Epictetus, the Greek philosopher's outlook ran parallel to Reagan's belief that those aspects of life that are out of our control may be fated by God (or, for the ancients, "the furies") and those that are presently undetermined challenge us to take control of events. Yet on the subject of desire, Reagan rarely seemed troubled by what concerned ancient philosophers and modern moralists. The Epictetus in Reagan's library was edited by Thomas Wentworth Higginson, the New England Transcendentalist who believed, along with Ralph Waldo Emerson, that desires are meant to be fulfilled, not frustrated. When a nineteenth-century poet of English romanticism was asked what it was he wanted from life, he replied, "Everything!" Reagan was more the romantic than the stoic.

CHAPTER ONE

1. Falwell quoted in James A. Morone, *Hellfire Nation: The Politics of Sin in American History* (New Haven: Yale University Press, 2003), 453.

2. H. L. Mencken, *Treatise on the Gods* (Baltimore: Johns Hopkins University, 1997), 74–75.

3. RR to Michael Reagan, June 1971; RR to Patti Reagan, Apr. 2, 1968, *RLIL*, 60–61, 54–55; son Ron's telling his father about his loss of faith is in the History Channel documentary "Ronald Reagan: A Legacy Remembered" (2002).

4. Lou Cannon, *President Reagan: The Role of a Lifetime* (New York: Public Affairs, 1902), 196–99.

5. Raymond Boudon, *Tocqueville aujourd'hui* (Paris: Odile Jacob, 2005), 229–44.

6. RR to Brad Rumble, circa 1980, RLIL, 680; Alexis de Tocqueville to Louis de Ker-

gorlay, Feb. 2, 1838, in *Tocqueville: Lettres choisies, Souvenirs, 1814–1859* (Paris: Gallimard, 2003), 401–3; to Arthur R. de Gobineau, Oct. 2, 1843, ibid., 525–29; Alexis de Tocqueville, *Democracy in America and Two Essays on America*, trans. Gerald E. Bevan (New York: Penguin, 2003), 510–18, 587–600; for different translations, I have used another edition of Tocqueville's *Democracy in America*, ed. J. P. Mayer, trans. George Lawrence (New York: Harper, 1969), 442–49; Tocqueville on "interests" is quoted in James T. Schleifer, *The Making of Tocqueville's Democracy in America* (Chapel Hill: University of North Carolina Press, 1980), 63–64, 235–37; see also John Patrick Diggins, *The Lost Soul of American Politics: Virtue, Self-Interest, and the Foundations of Liberalism* (New York: Basic, 1984); Joshua Mitchell, *The Fragility of Freedom: Tocqueville on Religion, Democracy, and the American Future* (Chicago: University of Chicago Press, 1995). Tocqueville, influenced by Pascal and carrying the burden of a Catholic conscience, believed that Americans' ability to obey God gave them the strength to resist worldly authority. But the religion that Reagan inherited from his mother had no need to wrestle with the "democratic soul," deriving, as it did, from nineteenth-century Unitarianism, with a strong dose of Emersonianism. The message of the Transcendentalists was that in obeying one's self, one obeys God. Tocqueville asked the Unitarian leader William Ellery Channing whether religion would disappear entirely in a culture devoted to the pursuit of self-pleasure.

7. Bloom, *Closing of the American Mind*, 141–56.

8. Roberts quoted in Todd S. Purdum and John M. Broder, "Nominee's Early Files," *New York Times*, Aug. 19, 2005.

9. *Basic Writings of Nietzsche*, ed. Peter Gay, trans. Walter Kaufmann (New York: Modern Library, 2000), 483.

10. RR to Kenneth Wells, circa 1967–68; RR to Mrs. Van Voorhis, circa 1976, *RLIL*, 259, 277–78.

11. Dolan's formulation is discussed in chapter 10.

12. RR to Florence Yerly, Dec. 17, 1951, *RLIL*, 139–40.

13. Walter Lippmann, *A Preface to Morals* (1929: New Brunswick, NJ: Transaction, 1982), 152.

14. Gay, *Basic Writings of Nietzsche*, 174; William James, *The Varieties of Religious Experience* (1902; New York: Touchstone, 2004), 246.

15. RR to Mr. Norman Lear, June 25, 1984, *RLIL*, 643–45.

16. Office of Press Secretary, "Remarks of the President at Conference on Religious Liberty," Apr. 16, 1985, RRPL.

17. Reagan is quoted in Paul Kengor, *God and Ronald Reagan: A Spiritual Life* (New York: HarperCollins, 2004), 227–28.

18. Morton White, *The Philosophy of the American Revolution* (New York: Oxford University Press, 1978), 114–15.

19. Ronald Reagan, *An American Life* (New York: Pocket Books, 1990), 363; RR, "Killed in Action," *RIOH*, 430–33.

20. Paul Lettow, *Ronald Reagan and His Quest to Abolish Nuclear Weapons* (New York: Random House, 2005).

21. Office of Press Secretary, "National Prayer Breakfast," Feb. 2, 1984, RRPL; Reagan on St. Ignatius (and also Mahatma Gandhi) is quoted in George J. Church, "Holding Their Ground," *Time*, Oct. 8, 1984, 12–19.

22. Quoted in Lettow, *Reagan and His Quest*, 133.

23. Reinhold Niebuhr, *The Irony of American History* (New York: Scribner, 1952), 173.

24. Ralph Waldo Emerson, "Politics," in *Selected Writings of Ralph Waldo Emerson*, ed. Brooks Atkinson (New York: Modern Library, 1992), 378–89.

25. Baxter is quoted in John Patrick Diggins, *Max Weber: Politics and the Spirit of Tragedy* (New York: Basic, 1996), 99. Emphasizing how capitalism arose from Calvinism, Max Weber noted the way it transformed the meaning of religion, how Ben Franklin made not justice and mercy but utility and success the core American values. Weber was profoundly ambivalent about this development, but Emerson saw no dualism between the spiritual and the material, and he hailed the advent of commerce as a liberation of the soul (the expression "capitalism" was not used in his era). See John Patrick Diggins, "Transcendentalism and the Spirit of Capitalism," in *Transient and Permanent: The Transcendentalist Movement and Its Context*, ed. Charles Capper and Conrad Edick Wright (Boston: Massachusetts Historical Society, 1999), 229–50.

26. Ronald Reagan, "Endangered Species," in *RIOH*, 329–31.

27. Quoted in Kengor, *God and Ronald Reagan*, 206.

28. Ralph Waldo Emerson, "Wealth," in *The Complete Works of Ralph Waldo Emerson, Centenary Edition,* ed. Edward Waldo Emerson, 12 vols. (New York: AMS Press, 1979), vol. 6, 85–127.

29. Ronald Reagan, "Government Costs," *RRSW*, 189–90.

30. Ronald Reagan, speech to Republican National Convention, Aug. 17, 1992, *PSRR*, 330–35.

31. A valuable analysis of Reagan's "sacramental vision" is to be found in Hugo Heclo, "Ronald Reagan and the American Public Philosophy," *TRP*, 17–39; a sensitive, endearing portrait of Reagan is Peggy Noonan, *When Character Was King: The Story of Ronald Reagan* (New York: Penguin, 2001); see also her reflections on the Reagan presidency, *What I Saw at the Revolution: A Political Life in the Reagan Era* (New York: Random House, 2003).

32. George Santayana, "The Genteel Tradition in American Philosophy," in *Santayana on America*, ed. Richard Colton Lyon (New York: Harcourt, Brace, & World, 1968), 36–56.

33. On Adam Smith, see Arthur O. Lovejoy, *Reflections on Human Nature* (Baltimore: Johns Hopkins University Press, 1961).

34. Ronald Reagan, speech at Moscow State University, May 31, 1988, in *TQRR*, 338.

35. Karl Marx, "Capital," in *The Marx-Engels Reader*, 303.

36. Santayana could well have warned Solzhenitsyn what not to expect from religion in America. In 1920, the American philosopher described the Protestant beliefs characteristic of the church of Reagan's mother. The old Yankee Calvinist, with his "sour integrity," had given way to a religion that celebrated material plenty. "Was not 'increase,' in the Bible, a synonym for benefit? Was not 'abundance' the same, or almost the same, as happiness?" Piety and prosperity go hand in hand. 'Be Christians,' I once heard a president of Yale College cry to his assembled pupils, 'be Christians and you will be successful.' Religion was indispensable and sacred, when not carried too far; but theology might well be unnecessary. Why distract from this world with talk of another? Enough for the day was the good thereof. Religion should be disentangled as much as possible from history and authority and metaphysics and made to rest honestly on one's fine feelings, on one's indomitable optimism and trust in life." George Santayana, "The Moral Background," in *Santayana on America*, ed. Richard Colton Lyon (New York: Harcourt, Brace & World, 1968), 57–72; Aleksandr Solzhenitsyn, *Comment réaménager notre Russie?* (Paris: Fayard, 1990), 70–85.

37. *Tocqueville: Lettres*, 247–49; Alexis de Tocqueville, *Voyage en Amérique*, in *Oeuvres* (Paris: Pleiade, 1998), vol. 1, 77–99; Diggins, *Max Weber*; William Elery Channing, "Likeness to God," in *Channing: Unitarian Christianity and Other Essays*, ed. Irving H. Bartlett (Indianapolis: Bobbs-Merrill, 1957), 86–108; Alexis de Tocqueville, *Journey to America*, ed. J. P. Mayer, trans. George Lawrence (New Haven: Yale University Press, 1960), 63–65.

38. Joseph Kraft, "Reaganism and the Politics of Piety," *Los Angeles Times*, Sept. 6, 1984; Murray N. Rothbard, "The Reagan Fraud," *Reason* 13 (June 1981): 84.

39. Ralph Waldo Emerson, "Politics," in *The Selected Writings of Ralph Waldo Emerson*, ed. Brooks Atkinson (New York: Modern Library, 1992), 386.

40. Ronald Reagan, Inaugural Address, Jan. 20, 1981, *PSRR*, 178.

41. Ralph Waldo Emerson, "The World-Soul," in *Emerson: Collected Poems & Translations*, ed. Harold Bloom and Paul Kane (New York: Library of America, 1994), 17–20.

42. Channing, "Likeness to God," 92; Patti Davis, *The Long Goodbye* (New York: Knopf, 2004), 196.

43. Thomas Paine, *Common Sense*, ed. Issac Kramnick (New York: Penguin, 1982), 65.

44. Ronald Reagan, "Address at the Captive Nations Week," July 15, 1991, in *TQRR*, 283; Emerson, "Politics," in Atkinson, *Selected Writings of Ralph Waldo Emerson*, 378–89.

45. Ronald Reagan, "French Registry I," "Regulations Go to College," *RIOH*, 293–94, 360–61.

46. Ronald Reagan, "Speech on Agriculture," Dec. 8–9, 1979, *RIOH*, 466–70.

47. Henry Adams, *Democracy*, in *Henry Adams* (New York: Library of America, 1983), 20, 37.

48. Gay, *Basic Writings of Nietzsche*, 563.

49. Alexander Hamilton, *The Federalist Papers*, ed. Clinton Rossiter (New York: Signet, 2003), 500; no. 85; Edmund Burke, *Reflections on the Revolution in France*, ed. Conor Cruise O'Brien (New York: Penguin, 1982), 90.

50. Santayana, "Emerson the Poet," in *Santayana on America*, 258–83.

51. In the Reagan eighties, the school of French poststructuralism had an enormous impact on American academic life; but no American scholar, as far as I am aware, saw the parallels between the poststructuralist's deconstruction of the canon, the body of authoritative texts that were once taught, and the conservative critique of administrative authority in general. The suggestion that the New Left was hungering for "a new spirit of capitalism" is in the special issue "Foucault, Derrida, Deleuze," *Sciences Humaines*, 3 (May-June 2005): 88–91.

52. James Madison, *The Federalist Papers*, no. 51.

53. Henry Adams, *Democracy: An American Novel* (1880; New York: Signet, 1961), 30.

CHAPTER TWO

1. Ralph Waldo Emerson, "History," in *The Portable Emerson*, ed. Mark Van Doren (New York: Viking, 1946), 139–64.

2. RR to Leonard Kirk, Mar. 23, 1983, *RLIL*, 13.

3. RR to Freddie Washington, Nov. 23, 1983, *RLIL*, 12; Anne Edwards, *Early Reagan: The Rise to Power* (New York: William Morrow, 1987), 51.

4. RR to John Morley, May 22, 1984, *RLIL*, 5–6.

5. Reagan, *An American Life*, 28.

6. RR to Monte Osborn, Mar. 29, 1982, *RLIL*, 33–35.

7. Ronald Reagan with Richard G. Hubler, *Where's the Rest of Me?* (New York: Duell, Sloan, and Pearce, 1965), 7–8.

8. Robert Dallek, *Ronald Reagan: The Politics of Symbolism* (Cambridge: Harvard University Press, 1984), 3–21.

9. Reagan and Hubler, *Where's the Rest of Me?* 20–21.

10. Kenneth T. Walsh, *Biography: Ronald Reagan* (New York: Park Lane Press, 1997), 12.

11. George Orwell, *Down and Out in Paris and London* (New York: Harcourt, 1961), 184.

12. On Eureka College Reagan is quoted in *RLIL*, 1; Reagan and Hubler, *Where's the Rest of Me?*, 17–39.

13. Reagan and Hubler, *Where's the Rest of Me?*, 42–44.

14. Ibid., 28–30.

15. Ibid., 15–27; RR to William E. Burghardt, Jan. 9, 1980, *RLIL*, 16, 799–800.

16. William F. Buckley Jr., *Let Us Talk of Many Things: The Collected Speeches* (Roseville, CA: Forum, 2000), 337.

17. It is interesting to speculate what Reagan came away with after his experiences on the football field. Many years later he recalled the "wild exhilaration" of plunging into the scrimmages. He felt the same wildness of freedom reading romantic poetry. "It was a good life," he reflected on his youth. "I have never asked for anything more, then or now. Probably the best part of it all was playing football. Sure, I played basketball, went out for track and swimming, but those were games. Football was a matter of life and death" (Reagan and Hubler, *Where's the Rest of Me?*, 18). No wonder his assistants observed Reagan's difficulties concentrating on the mundane details of politics.

18. Robert Heilbroner, *The Worldly Philosophers: The Lives, Times and Ideas of the Great Economic Thinkers* (New York: Simon & Schuster, 1961), 179–83; Karl Marx, "The Grundrisse," in *The Marx-Engels Reader*, 223.

19. Ronald Reagan, "Return to the Primitive" (1930), *RIOH*, 428–30.

20. RR to Monte Osborn, Mar. 29, 1982, *RLIL*, 33–35.

21. RR to Ron Cochran, May 12, 1980, *RLIL*, 27–31.

22. Edwards, *Early Reagan*, 143.

23. Reagan and Hubler, *Where's the Rest of Me?*, 66–67.

24. Garry Wills, *Reagan's America: Innocents at Home* (Garden City, NY: Doubleday, 1987), 109–23; Reagan's career as a sportscaster and the Knute Rockne legend are dealt with by Wills with wit, perception, and not a little disdain (97–131).

25. Reagan is quoted in Wills, *Reagan's America*, 123.

26. On John Reed, see Bertram D. Wolfe, *Strange Communists I Have Known* (New York: Stein & Day, 1965); Suzanne Finstad, *Warren Beatty: A Private Man* (New York: Harmony Books, 2005), 449.

27. Ronald Reagan, "The Making of a Movie Star," *RIOH*, 433–36.

28. Stephen Vaughn, *Ronald Reagan in Hollywood: Movies and Politics* (New York: Cambridge University Press, 1994), 27; Joan Didion, "In Hollywood," in *The White Album* (New York: Farrar, Straus and Giroux, 1979), 153–67.

29. Wills, *Reagan's America*, 178. Laurence Olivier, *Confessions of an Actor: An Autobiography* (New York: Simon & Schuster, 1982), 20.

30. Vaughn, *Reagan in Hollywood*, 37–38.

31. Ibid., 27–39

32. Ibid., 38–39.

33. RR to "Jim," "Circa 1970," *RLIL*, 128.

34. Quotes from the broadcasts among the generals, admirals, and Reagan are in *RLIL*, 132.

35. Quoted in Edwards, *Early Reagan*, 461.

36. Interview with Sandy Wolfe, a scriptwriter on the show.

37. Quoted in Edwards, *Early Reagan*, 403.

38. For details about Reagan's personal life, his relations with Jane Wyman, Nancy Davis, and the four children, I am indebted to Anne Edwards, *Early Reagan* (previously cited), Edmund Morris, *Dutch: A Memoir of Ronald Reagan* (New York: Random House, 1999), and Bob Colacello, *Ronnie & Nancy: Their Path to the White House, 1911 to 1980* (New York: Warner Books, 2004); and for information about Reagan's high school and college years in Illinois, I am indebted to Garry Wills's research in *Reagan's America* (previously cited).

39. Anne Edwards quotes the actor Eddie Bracken on Reagan: "He was never for the sexpots. He was never a guy looking for the bed. He was a guy looking for companionship more than anything else" (Edwards, *Early Reagan*, 357, 403).

49. Edwards, *Early Reagan*, 480.

50. Quoted in Diggins, *Max Weber*, 251.

CHAPTER THREE

1. Crossman, *The God That Failed*, 101.

2. Kenneth Lloyd Billingsley, *Hollywood Party: How Communism Seduced the American Film Industry in the 1930s and 1940s* (Rocklin, CA: Prima Publishers, 1998).

3. Eric Bentley, ed., *Thirty Years of Treason: Excerpts from Hearings before the House Committee on Un-American Activities. 1938–1968* (1971; New York: Nation Books, 2002), 146–47; unless otherwise indicated, Reagan's subsequent remarks come from this document.

4. In her testimony, the writer Ayn Rand, who had been born in Russia, offered an entirely different testimony from Reagan's, describing in detail to the committee how the movie *Song of Russia* distorted the brutal facts about the Soviet Union (*Thirty Years of Treason*, 111–18; Reagan quoted, 146–47).

5. RR to Hugh Hefner, July 4, 1960, *RLIL*, 146–49; Vaughn, *Ronald Reagan in Hollywood*, 206.

6. Edwards, *Early Reagan*, 418.

7. Compare, for example, the willing verbosity of the Chicago Seven, called to testify before HUAC in 1968 for anti–Vietnam War activities, to the uncooperative silence of the Hollywood Ten. Bentley, *Thirty Years of Treason*, 879–932.

8. Bentley, *Thirty Years of Treason*, 147.

9. On four generations of the twentieth-century Left, see John Patrick Diggins, *The Rise and Fall of the American Left* (New York: Norton, 1992).

10. Mona Charen, *Useful Idiots: How Liberals Got It Wrong in the Cold War and Still Blame America First* (Washington, DC: Regnery, 2003). Whether or not Lenin actually used the phrase "useful idiots," Charen is certain it applies only to liberals. Reagan and conservatives, however, could also be useful to the Soviet Union, if not idiotically, certainly expediently, even under the dark days of Brezhnev. Reagan became president at

the time the Solidarity movement in Poland was asserting its independence from the communist party. As explained earlier, the Reagan administration remained coldly aloof. The decision of American labor to "contribute to the Polish Workers Aid Fund threw Washington, not the Kremlin, into a panic and led the State Department to supererogative assurances to the Kremlin that the American government was not involved in the charitable efforts." So wrote the anticommunist Sidney Hook, who could only wonder if under Reagan America had "developed a vested interest in the stability of the Eastern bloc" (in the words Hook quoted from the democratic socialist Tom Kahn). Sidney Hook, "In Defense of the Cold War," in *Marxism and Beyond* (Totowa, NJ: Rowman & Allenhead, 1983), 195.

11. Klehr, Haynes, and Firsov, *Secret World of American Communism*; the figure assigned by the KGB to influence Hollywood writers was V. J. Jerome, author of the pamphlet *Changing World: A Marxist Approach* (1947); Jerome laid down the postwar line that socialist "reality in art involves partisanship," that the actor or screenwriter could not remain neutral. *VDSE*, 109–11.

12. Bentley, *Thirty Years of Treason*, 294.

13. *VDSE*, 236–49.

14. See the valuable study by Stephen J. Whitfield, *The Culture of the Cold War* (Baltimore: Johns Hopkins University Press, 1991), where Mary McCarthy's acerbic comments are cited, 127–51.

15. Robert Lerner, "Conservations with George Kennan," *Historically Speaking*, 6 (July–Aug. 2005): 11–13.

16. I am indebted to the recent study by Ronald Radosh and Allis Radosh, *Red Star Over Hollywood: The Film Colony's Long Romance with the Left* (New York: Encounter Books, 2005).

17. Mary McCarthy, *The Company She Keeps* (New York: Dell, 1939), 157.

18. Diggins, *Up from Communism*, 435–36.

19. Martin J. Duberman, *Paul Robeson: A Biography* (New York: New Press, 1995).

20. Quoted in Alain Besancon, "Sur l'histoire de la Russie," *Commentaire* 110 (2005): 331–38.

21. Quoted in Radosh and Radosh, *Red Star Over Hollywood*, 52.

22. Reagan and Hubler, *Where's the Rest of Me?*, 127.

23. Garry Wills, *Reagan's America: Innocents at Home* (Garden City, NY: Doubleday, 1987), 244.

24. Ibid., 215–58.

25. Reagan and Hubler, *Where's Rest of Me?*, 31–62; Radosh and Radosh, *Red Star Over Hollywood*, 109–22.

26. Reagan, *An American Life*, 114–15.

27. Wills, *Reagan's America*, 245–46.

28. Reagan and Hubler, *Where's the Rest of Me?*, 166–67.

29. Quoted in Vaughn, *Ronald Reagan in Hollywood*, 130.

30. Reagan and Hubler, *Where's the Rest of Me?*, 142.

31. Bentley, *Thirty Years of Treason*, 446.

32. Reagan and Hubler, *Where's the Rest of Me?*, 139.

33. Ibid., 167.

34. Radosh and Radosh, *Red Star Over Hollywood*, 109–22.

35. Quoted in Edwards, *Early Reagan*, 313.

36. Reagan and Hubler, *Where's the Rest of Me?*, 169–73.

37. Bentley, *Thirty Years of Treason*, 374–75

38. "Dialectical materialism is the world view of the proletariat," declared Mao Zedong. "The proletariat, which has been given the task by history of eliminating classes, utilizes dialectical materialism as a spiritual weapon in its struggle and as the philosophical basis for its various viewpoints." *Mao Ze-dung on Dialectical Materialism: Writings on Philosophy,* ed. N. Knight (Armonk, NY: M. E. Sharpe, 1990), 93. There is a story of a Sandinista teacher who was planning to distribute a pile of books on her desk to her students. Mikhail Gorbachev and his entourage arrived in Managua in 1987, and the Russian leader asked the teacher what the books dealt with. When he was told it was "dialectical materialism," Gorbachev snapped: "Get rid of that junk!" In American intellectual life in the 1930s, the dialectic became something of a mantra among Marxists, as though the future of the world depended upon its philosophical validity. A newer generation of German refugee intellectuals, whose philosophers came to be called the Frankfurt School, attempted to rehabilitate the philosophy of Hegelian dialectics after World War II. But it had already been scrutinized to death in the writings of Max Eastman, Sidney Hook, Lionel Trilling, and Edmund Wilson. See Diggins, *Up from Communism,* 39–73.

39. Reagan and Hubler, *Where's the Rest of Me?,* 174.; Radosh and Radosh, *Red Star Over Hollywood,* 122.

40. Gide's essay is in Crossman, ed., *The God That Failed,* 157–76, based on his earlier *Le Retour de l'U.R.S.S.* (Paris, 1936).

41. Murray Kempton, *Part of Our Time: Some Monuments and Ruins of the Thirties* (New York: Delta, 1967), 209; Whitfield, *Culture of the Cold War,* 120.

42. Lillian Hellman, *Scoundrel Time* (Boston: Little Brown, 1976), 89–90.

43. Reagan and Hubler, *Where's the Rest of Me?,* 269.

44. Sam Tanenhaus, *Whittaker Chambers: A Biography* (New York: Random House, 1997).

45. Chambers, *Witness,* 3–22.

46. Arthur Schlesinger Jr., *The Vital Center: The Politics of Freedom* (1949; New Brunswick, NJ: Transaction, 1998), 129–30.

47. *VDSE,* 246; *As I See It: The Autobiography of J. Paul Getty* (Los Angeles: J. Paul Getty Museum, 2002), 345; "Armand Hammer and the Soviet Union," Case #F00–16, RRPL.

48. David Shub, *Lenin: A Biography* (New York: Mentor, 1948), 120.

49. Lionel Trilling, *The Middle of the Journey* (New York: Viking, 1947), 304–5.

50. Emerson, "Character," in Atkinson, *The Selected Writings of Ralph Waldo Emerson* (New York: Modern Library, 1992), 329.

51. Arthur Miller, *On Politics and the Art of Acting* (New York: Viking, 2002), 38–43.

52. Cannon, *President Reagan,* 37.

CHAPTER FOUR

1. Cannon, *President Reagan,* 22

2. Quoted in "In Need of a Makeover: A Survey of California," *The Economist,* May 1, 2004, 4.

3. The Brown-Reagan gubernatorial race is well analyzed in Matthew Dallek, *The Right Moment: Ronald Reagan's First Victory and the Decisive Turning Point in American Politics* (New York: Free Press, 2000).

4. Dallek, *Right Moment,* 23; Hess told of Nixon's remark at a conference in honor of Daniel Patrick Moynihan, on March 29, 2004, at the City Museum of New York.

5. On Goldwater, the 1964 election, and the Republican Right, see the valuable study

by Rick Perlstein, *Before the Storm: Barry Goldwater and the Unmaking of the American Consensus* (New York: Hill and Wang, 2001)

6. Quoted in Dallek, *Right Moment*, 67–68.

7. Ibid., 68.

8. Perlstein, *Before the Storm*, 513.

9. W. J. Rorabaugh, *Berkeley at War: The 1960s* (New York: Oxford University Press, 1989).

10. RR to Mildred Bell, Sept. 15, 1965, in *RLIL*, 171.

11. Dallek righty emphasizes the significance of FHA in *The Right Moment*, 48–61.

12. For the discussion of Reagan's governorship, I am indebted to the recent work of Lou Cannon, *Governor Reagan: His Rise to Power* (New York: Public Affairs, 2003).

13. Ibid., 199.

14. Wills, *Reagan's America*, 310

15. Cannon, *Governor Reagan*, 208–14.

16. RR to Mrs. Hawkings, Jan. 2, 1967; RR to Mrs. McKay; RR to Mrs. Perez, written in Jan. 1967, *RLIL*, 202–05.

17. Cannon, *Governor Reagan*, 240–42.

18. Quoted in Morris, *Dutch*, 318.

19. RR to Michael Reagan, June 1971, *RLIL*, 60–61.

20. Morris, *Dutch*, 417.

21. Nancy Collins, "Patti Dearest," *Vanity Fair*, July 1991, 90–93, 129–33.

22. The interview with Patti Davis is quoted in Colacello, *Ronnie & Nancy*, 502.

23. Quoted in Rorabaugh, *Berkeley at War*, 122.

24. Reagan, *An American Life*, 180.

25. On San Francisco State and the New Left, see Diggins, *Rise and Fall of the American Left*, 242–56; and Vartan Gregorian, *The Road to Home: My Life and Times* (New York: Simon & Schuster, 2003), 161–76; John Bunzel, ed., *Political Passages: Journeys of Change Through Two Decades, 1968–1988* (New York: Free Press, 1988), 132–61; and Joan Didion, *The White Album* (New York: Farrar, Straus and Giroux, 1979), 37–41. On the youth rebellion in California in general, see Joan Didion, *Slouching Towards Bethlehem* (New York: Farrar, Straus and Giroux, 1968).

26. RR to Dr. Samuel I. Hayakawa, circa 1968 or 1969; RR to Dr. Sam Hayakawa, after Jan. 4, 1971, *RLIL*, 188–89.

27. Leon Trotsky, *The Russian Revolution*, trans. Max Eastman (Garden City, NY: Doubleday, 1959), 114.

28. Cannon, *Governor Reagan*, 278.

29. Ibid., 271–96.

30. Rorabaugh, *Berkeley at War*, 121.

31. RR to "Pete," after spring of 1969, *RLIL*, 190–91.

32. RR to Jack [the Honorable Jack Williams], Mar. 17, 1969, ibid., 190; "The People's Park: A Report on the Confrontation at Berkeley, California, submitted to Governor Reagan," n.d., Reagan Papers, Box 24, HIA.

33. Cannon, *Governor Reagan*, 297–321.

34. Ibid., 313.

35. James Q. Wilson, "A Guide to Reagan Country: The Political Culture of Southern California," *Commentary* 43 (May 1967): 37–45.

36. Compare, to mention only one instance, the careers of François Furet and Eric Foner. The eminent French historian had been a member of the Communist Party and

broke with it after the Soviet Union's suppression of Hungary in 1956. He then discovered Tocqueville and began to rewrite the history of the French Revolution from a
liberal perspective. Foner, the Dewitt Clinton Professor of History at Columbia University, has been president of the American Historical Association and the Organization of American Historians and held the Harmsworth Chair at Oxford University. His
pro-Soviet, Marxist, communist affinities have undergone no change whatsoever in
forty years. Even after the fall of communism, he wrote articles wondering why the
Russian people had been unhappy with it. See John Patrick Diggins, "Fate and Freedom in History: The Two Worlds of Eric Foner," *The National Interest* 69 (Fall 2002):
71–90. The ultimate irony is that both Professor Foner and President Reagan are
admirers of Tom Paine. Only in America!

CHAPTER FIVE

1. Tip O'Neill (with William Novak), *Man of the House: The Life and Political Memoirs of Tip O'Neill* (New York: Random House, 1987) 330–75; RR to Rudolph Hines,
Aug. 22, 1984, *RLIL*, 791–92.
2. On Reagan and Vietnam, see Cannon, *President Reagan*, 289–301.
3. RR to Mr and Mrs. Elwood H. Wagner, June 22, 1973, *RLIL*, 777–78.
4. Quoted in Morris, *Dutch*, 403–4.
5. The debate is reprinted in William F. Buckley Jr., *Miles Gone By* (Washington, DC:
Regnery, 2004), 362–88.
6. Gary Sick, *October Surprise: American Hostages in Iran and the Election of Ronald
Reagan* (New York: Times Books, 1991).
7. Quoted in Michael Deaver, *A Different Drummer: My Thirty Years with Ronald Reagan* (New York: HarperCollins, 2001), 71.
8. Quoted in Cannon, *President Reagan*, 75.
9. Deaver, *A Different Drummer*, 84–85.
10. Morris, *Dutch*, 410; *The Role of a Lifetime* is the subtitle of Cannon's *President
Reagan*.
11. Martin Anderson, *Revolution* (New York: Harcourt, 1988), 213–14; Cannon, *President Reagan*, 503; Michael Schaller, *Reckoning with Reagan: America and Its President
in the 1980s* (New York: Oxford University Press, 1992), 39.
12. George P. Shultz, *Turmoil and Triumph: My Years as Secretary of State* (New York:
Scribner, 1993).
13. A valuable sketch of Casey is in Steve Coll's *Ghost Wars* (New York: Penguin,
2004), 89–105.
14. For a sketch of Darman, I am indebted to Laurence I. Barrett, *Gambling with History: Reagan in the White House* (New York: Penguin 1983), 388–400.
15. On Regan, see Cannon, *President Reagan*, 490–503; Anderson, *Revolution*, 231–36.
16. Reagan, *An American Life*, 228–29
17. Ibid., 229.
18. John W. Sloane, *The Reagan Effect: Economics and Presidential Leadership*
(Lawrence: University Press of Kansas, 1999), 117; Howard A. Winant, *Stalemate:
Political Economic Origins of Supply-Side Economics* (New York: Praeger, 1988); Drew
is quoted in Kevin McGruder, "Supply Side Economics: Success or Failure?" (paper
for my history seminar at the Graduate Center, City University of New York).
19. "Revenue Control and Tax Deduction, submitted to the California Legislature by
Governor Ronald Reagan," Mar. 12, 1973, Reagan mss. Box 41, HIA.

20. Anderson, *Revolution*, 151–53.

21. Sloane, *Reagan Effect*, 118.

22. Ibid., 194; Martha Derthick and Steven M. Teles, "Social Security Reform," in *TRP*, 182–208.

23. Daniel Patrick Moynihan, *Came the Revolution: Debate in the Reagan Era* (New York: Harcourt, 1988), 6.

24. David Stockman, *Triumph of Politics: Why the Reagan Revolution Failed* (New York: Harper & Row, 1986); Stockman is described by Regan as a "wunderkind" in the oral history collection, *RMHP*, 133.

25. Schaller, *Reckoning*, 48–49.

26. This quip was cited on television on June 5, 2004, during the week when the nation was in mourning over Reagan's death. As an example of Reagan's unscripted wisdom, I also recall when he was governor of California and a black journalist challenged his cutting back on welfare as a war against the poor. Reagan replied that he was trying to help the poor by making them more self-reliant. The woman at first remained skeptical, but as the exchange continued, with cameras going back and forth from the governor to the reporter, she ended up nodding in agreement.

27. Barrett, *Gambling with History*, 107.

28. Peter Biskind, *Easy Riders, Raging Bulls: How the Sex-Drugs-and-Rock 'n' Roll Generation Saved Hollywood* (New York: Simon & Schuster, 1998), 333.

29. Quoted in Barrett, *Gambling with History*, 118.

30. Quigley's remarks are in *RMHP*, 122.

31. Michael Reagan remarks, *RMHP*, 121.

CHAPTER SIX

1. Deaver's remark, *RMHP*, 116.

2. RR to Mr. and Mrs. Ronald D. Paton, July 16, 1984, *RLIL*, 379–80.

3. Quoted in *RLIL*, 373. Reagan slightly misquoted Winthrop, who said "a story and a byword *through* the world" (emphasis added).

4. RR to Mr. and Mrs. Peter D. Hammond, Feb. 10, 1983, RLIL, 278; criticisms of Reagan's religiosity is in Frances Fitzgerald, *Way Out There in the Blue: Reagan, Star Wars, and the End of the Cold War* (New York: Simon & Schuster, 2000), 15–41.

5. Friedrich von Hayek to RR, Feb. 11, 1981, Box 45, HIA.

6. Václav Havel, "Meeting Gorbachev," in *Open Letters: Selected Writings, 1965–1990* (New York: Vintage, 1992), 351–54.

7. RR to Mr. Armand S. Deutch, June 7, 1988, *RLIL*, 386.

8. Bertram D. Wolfe, *Strange Communists I Have Known* (New York: Stein & Day, 1965), 198.

9. Leonid I. Brezhnev, *Pages from His Life* (written under the auspices of the Academy of Sciences of the USSR; New York: Simon & Schuster, 1978).

10. Reagan, *An American Life*, 613.

11. RR to Leonid Brezhnev, Apr. 18, 1981, *RLIL*, 737–41.

12. Leonid Brezhnev to RR, May 21, May 25, 1981, Box 38, RRPL.

13. Richard V. Allen, "Memorandum for the President," May 28, 1981; Dennis C. Blair and Richard Pipes, "Press Background on President's Letter to Brezhnev," Sept. 22, 1981; "Memorandum for Richard V. Allen" from Richard Pipes, Jack Matlock's cable from Moscow, Mar. 27, 1981, RRPL.

14. Interview with George P. Shultz, Apr. 4, 2005; RR to Leonid Brezhnev, Feb. 4, 1982; Leonid Brezhnev to RR, Dec. 25, 1981, Box 38, RRPL.

15. Robert Scheer, *With Enough Shovels: Reagan, Bush, & Nuclear War* (New York: Random House, 1982).

16. The statistics and quotes cited, as well as Draper's illuminating debates with Caspar Weinberger, which first appeared in the *New York Review of Books*, are reprinted in Theodore Draper, *Present History* (New York: Vintage, 1984), 3–63.

17. Fitzgerald, *Way Out There in the Blue*, 460–99; Gary Dorrien, *Imperial Designs: Neoconservatism and the New Pax Americana* (New York: Routledge, 2004); Robert Tucker, "Reagan's Foreign Policy," *Foreign Affairs* 68 (1988–1989): 1–22; Fareed Zakaria, "Exaggerating the Threats," *Newsweek*, June 16, 2003, 33.

18. Quoted in Louis Menand, "Fat Man," *The New Yorker*, June 27, 2005, 92–98.

19. Richard Pipes, "Why the Soviet Union Thinks It Could Fight and Win a Nuclear War," *Commentary* 64 (July 1977): 21–34.

20. Leo Tolstoy, *War and Peace*, trans. Rosemary Edmonds (1869; New York: Penguin, 1982), 883.

21. Norman Podhoretz, *The Present Danger* (New York: Simon & Schuster, 1980), 11–12.

22. Christopher Andrew and Vasili Mitrokhin, *The World Was Going Our Way: The KGB and the Battle for the World* (New York: Basic Books, 2005), 115–36.

23. Jeane Kirkpatrick, "Dictatorships and Double Standards," *Commentary* 66 (Nov. 1979): 34–45.

24. Martin Malia, "Sur Lénine, Staline, et la Sovietology révisionniste," *Commentaire* 98 (Summer 2002): 453–70.

25. Jean-François Revel, "Is Commuism Reversible?," *Commentary* 95 (Jan. 1989), 17–24. This writer should acknowledge that he, too, subscribed to the theory of totalitarianism and at least was troubled by the thought that communism was irreversible. Then, as the regimes of Eastern Europe began to crumble, I couldn't wait to get back to the United States and rush to my campus office and revise my lecture notes. But as far as I know, neocon intellectuals feel no need to revise.

26. Anson Rabinbach, "Moments of Totalitariaism," *History & Theory* 45 (Feb. 2006): 1–29.

27. Diggins, *Mussolini and Fascism: The View from America* (Princeton: Princeton University Press, 1972), 20–22, 28.

CHAPTER SEVEN

1. Peggy Noonan, *When Character Was King*, 196–214.

2. John Lewis Gaddis, "Morality and the American Experience in the Cold War," in *Ethics and Statecraft: The Moral Dimension of International Affairs*, ed Cathal J. Nolan (London: Praeger, 1995), 171–94.

3. Reagan, *An American Life*, 373.

4. See Fareed Zakaria, *The Future of Freedom: Illiberal Democracy at Home and Abroad* (New York: Norton, 2003).

5. On this complex subject, I am much indebted to the valuable study by Coll, *Ghost Wars*.

6. Podhoretz, *Present Danger*, 12; Andrew and Mitrokhin, *The World Was Going Our Way*, 389.

7. The invasion of Afghanistan was clearly an attempt to shore up an unpopular Communist Party. What happened in Kabul in 1979 had happened in Budapest (1956) and Prague (1968) and would happen in Warsaw (1981). Soviet leaders could not bring themselves to talk about Afghanistan, so convinced were they so shortly after the invasion that it was a tragic mistake. Only when Gorbachev came to power could an exit strategy be discussed. The Afghan question is discussed in chapter 10.

8. Coll, *Ghost Wars*, 53–70.

9. Ibid., 99.

10. George Crile, *Charlie Wilson's War: The Extraordinary Story of the Largest Covert Operation in History* (New York: Atlantic Monthly Press, 2003).

11. Coll, *Ghost Wars*, 85–90.

12. Paul Berman, *Terror and Liberalism* (New York: Norton, 2003).

13. Phillips is quoted in Franklin Foer, "Are Foreign Rebel Leaders Duping the American Right, Again?" *The New Republic*, Aug. 18 and 25, 2003, 17–21.

14. Coll has an excellent account of the fate of Massoud, *Ghost Wars*, 505–35; on the questionable reasoning regarding America coming to the aid of Kuwait in the first Gulf War, see Theodore Draper, "American Hubris," in *A Present of Things Past: Selected Essays* (New York: Hill and Wang, 1990), 67–96.

15. Alan J. Kuperman, "The Stinger Missile and U.S. Intervention in Afghanistan," *Political Science Quarterly* 114 (1999): 219–64.

16. Mary Anne Weaver, *Pakistan: In the Shadow of Jihad and Afghanistan* (New York: Farrar, Straus and Giroux, 2002).

17. Mikhail Gorbachev, *Memoirs* (Garden City, NY: Doubleday, 1995), 138.

18. RR to William J. Buckley Jr., Jan. 5, 1984, *RLIL*, 448.

19. Kenneth Pollack, *The Threatening Storm* (New York: Random House, 2002); William R. Polk, *Understanding Iraq* (New York: HarperCollins, 2005).

20. Cannon, *President Reagan*, 580.

21. Begin is quoted in ibid., 350.

22. Ibid., 351.

23. The Reagan, Weinberger, and Shultz positions are thoughtfully dealt with in Cannon's chapter "Lost in Lebanon," ibid., 339–401.

24. Reagan, *An American Life*, 459–67.

25. Reagan and attaché quoted in Cannon, *President Reagan*, 394.

26. Quoted in Cannon, *President Reagan*, 394.

27. Congress's expression of stupidity in Cannon, *President Reagan*, 389.

28. Casey on the "axis" is quoted in Robert Gates, *From the Shadows: The Ultimate Insider's Story of Five Presidents and How They Won the Cold War* (New York: Simon & Schuster, 1996), 254.

29. RR to Leonid Brezhnev, Apr. 18, 1981, *RLIL*, 739–40.

30. Fred Bridgland, *Jonas Savimbi: A Key to Africa* (New York: Paragon Press, 1983); Michael McFaul, "Rethinking the Reagan Doctrine in Angola," *International Security* 14 (Winter 1989–1990): 99–135; Foer, "Are Foreign Rebel Leaders," 17–21.

31. Savimbi on taxes quoted in Foer, "Are Foreign Rebels Leaders," 19–21.

32. Carlos Moore, *Castro, The Blacks, and Africa* (Los Angeles: Center for Afro-American Studies, 1988); Gabriel García Márquez, "Cuba in Angola," in *Fidel Castro Speeches*, vol. 1, ed. Michael Taber (New York: Pathfinder Press, 1981), 356–57.

33. Gates, *From the Shadows*, 433–34.

34. Piero Gleijeses, *Conflicting Missions: Havana, Washington and Africa, 1959–1976* (Chapel Hill: University of North Carolinia Press, 2002), 254–62.

35. William R. Keylor, *A World of Nations: The International Order Since 1945* (New York: Oxford University Press, 2003), 296–97; Fidel Castro, "A Duty Fulfilled" and "Angola: African Giron," in *Fidel Castro Speeches; Cuban Internationalism in Sub-Saharan Africa*, ed. Sergio Diaz-Briquets (Pittsburgh: Duquense University Press, 1989).

36. Bernard-Henri Lévy, *Réflexions sur la Guerre, le Mal et la fin de l'Histoire* (Paris: Grasset, 2001), 31–53.

37. Castro quoted in Kai P. Schoenhals and Richard A. Melanson, *Revolution and Intervention in Grenada: The New Jewel Movement, the United States, and the Caribbean* (Boulder: Westview Press, 1985), 79.

38. RR, "Remarks on Central America and El Salvador, Annual Meeting of National Association of Manufacturers," Mar. 10, 1983; www.reagan.utexas.edu/resources/speeches/1983/31083ahtm.

39. Casualty figures vary in different accounts. A. Sutton Payne and P. T. Thorndike, *Grenada: Revolution and Invasion* (London: Croom Helm, 1984); Gregory Sandford and Richard Vigilante, *Grenada: The Untold Story* (Lanham, MD: Madison Books, 1984); Major Mark Adkins, *Urgent Fury: The Battle for Grenada* (Lexington, MA: Lexington Books, 1989); Schoenhals and Melanson, *Revolution and Intervention in Grenada*.

40. Comments on the Grenada invasion in Cannon, *President Reagan*, 392–93.

41. "Grenada: Media Liaison Official Records," Oct. 28, 1983, Box OA9636, RRPL.

42. RR, "Vietnam," Feb. 1978; "Joan Baez," June 29, 1979, in *RRSW*, 390–93, 456–59.

43. Cannon, *President Reagan*, 393.

44. Reagan, *An American Life*, 455.

45. The journalist is Claudia Dreifus, quoted in Andrew and Mitrokhin, *This World Was Going Our Way*, 31.

46. Quoted in Robert Kagan, *A Twilight Struggle: American Power and Nicaragua, 1977–1990* (New York: Free Press, 1996), 395; I am much indebted to Kagan's comprehensive book.

47. On Reagan's enthusiasm for the Contras, see Draper, *Present of Things Past*, 33–35; Reagan's reference to the Abraham Lincoln Brigade was made several times on television.

48. Quoted in Morris, *Dutch*, 483.

49. Andrew and Mitrokhin, *The World Was Going Our Way*, 124–26.

50. Gates, *From the Shadows*, 304–05; RR to Mr. Robert S. Lawrence, May 31, 1984, RLIL.

51. Kagan, *Twilight Struggle,* 203; Gates, *From the Shadows,* 308.

52. Kagan's description of the Sandinistas representing to the Soviets "a target of opportunity" is priceless; in the American academic world the same phrase is used to justify affirmative action.

53. Conor Cruise O'Brien, "God and Man in Nicaragua," in *Passion and Cunning and Other Essays* (London: Paladin, 1988), 157–58.

54. Castro quoted in Kagan, *Twilight Struggle,* 693, 726.

55. Gaddis, "Morality and the American Experience in the Cold War," 171–94.

CHAPTER EIGHT

1. Anatoly Dobrynin, *In Confidence: Moscow's Ambassador to America's Six Cold War Presidents* (New York: Random House, 1995), 477–98.

2. Donald A. Yerxa, "Armageddon: An Interview with Sir Max Hastings," *Historically Speaking* 6 (Mar.–Apr. 2005): 15–19. The idea that FDR had betrayed Europe at Yalta

was, Conrad Black has written, nothing more than the "lurid allegations by McCarthyite Republicans" (Conrad Black, *Franklin Delano Roosevelt: Champion of Freedom* [New York: Public Affairs, 2003], 1079.

3. Chambers, *Witness*, 361.

4. RR to Richard Nixon, July 15, 1960, *RLIL*, 704–5.

5. "Losing Freedom by Installment" is in the appendix of Edwards, *Early Reagan*, 547–60; RR to Professor Hayek, May 15, 1986, Hayek mss., HIA.

6. See Sidney Hook, *Political Power and Personal Freedom: Critical Studies in Communism, Democracy, and Civil Rights* (New York: Collier, 1962), 397–437.

7. François Furet and Ernest Nolte, *Fascisme et communisme* (Paris: Hachette, 2000), 35–44; Diggins, *Mussolini and Fascism*.

8. Reagan, *An American Life*, 239.

9. By the sheerest coincidence, I dealt with the accusation that fascism inspired the New Deal in a section of my doctoral dissertation, and when reporters investigated the story Reagan was spreading, they cited my book to refute it. See Lee Lescaze, "Reagan Still Sure Some in New Deal Espoused Fascism," *Washington Post*, Dec. 24, 1981; Melvyn B. Krauss, "Reagan's Comments on Fascism and the New Deal," *Wall Street Journal*, Sept. 9, 1980.

10. Richard Lowenthal, *World Communism: The Disintergration of a Secular Faith* (New York: Oxford, 1964), 176–77, 99–138; the "Finlandization" thesis is that of Norman Podhoretz and is discussed in chapter 6.

11. Andrew and Mitrokhin, *The World Was Going Our Way*, 27–138.

12. Marx, "The Eighteenth Brumaire of Louis Bonaparte," in *The Marx-Engels Reader*, 594–617.

13. Moynihan, *Came the Revolution*, 8–11.

14. Daniel Patrick Moynihan, *On the Law of Nations* (Cambridge: Harvard University Press, 1990), 126.

15. Ibid.

16. Quoted in Lawrence Freedman, "First Two Generations of Nuclear Strategists," in *Makers of Modern Strategy: From Machiavelli to the Nuclear Age* (Princeton: Princeton University Press, 1986), 774–75.

17. Moynihan, *Came the Revolution*, 186–91.

18. *Soviet Economy: Assessment of How Well the CIA Has Estimated the Size of the Economy*, Report to the Honorable Daniel Patrick Moynihan (Washington, DC: United States General Accounting Office, 1991).

19. Moynihan, *Law of Nations*, 124–25.

20. Ibid., 141.

21. Daniel Patrick Moynihan, *Secrecy: The American Experience* (New Haven: Yale University Press, 1998), 209.

22. Ibid., 208.

23. Ibid., 209.

24. Moynihan, *Law of Nations*, 125.

25. Ibid., 133, 174.

26. Adam Roberts, Foreword to Daniel Patrick Moynihan, *Pandaemonium: Ethnicity in International Politics* (New York: Oxford, 1993), x–xi; Hélène Carrère d'Encausse, *L'Empire Éclaté: La Revolte des Nations en U.R.S.S.* (Paris: Flammarion, 1978).

27. Nathan Glazer, "Daniel P. Moynihan on Ethnicity," in *Daniel Patrick Moynihan:*

The Intellectual in Public Life, ed. Robert A. Katzmann (Baltimore: Johns Hopkins University Press, 1998), 15–25.

28. Raymond Aron, *On War* (1957; New York: Norton, 1968), vi, 1.

29. Shultz, *Turmoil and Triumph*, 266–69.

30. Reagan, *An American Life*, 550.

31. James Mann, *Rise of the Vulcans: The History of Bush's War Cabinet* (New York: Viking, 2004); Anne Hessing Cahn, *Killing Détente: The Right Attacks the CIA* (College Station: Penn State University Press, 1998).

32. Anderson, *Revolution*, 61–99.

33. Ibid., 69–79.

34. Fitzgerald, *Way Out There in the Blue*, 19–41.

35. Ibid., 72–209; William J. Broad, *Teller's War: The Top-Secret Story Behind the Star Wars Deception* (New York: Simon & Schuster, 1992). Edward Teller to Irving Kristol, Mar. 30, 1982; Jay Keworth, "Recommendation That Edward Teller Receive an Appointment with the President," July 29, 1982, HIA.

36. Adam Michnik, *Letters from Prison and Other Essays*, trans. Maya Latynski (Berkeley: University of California Press, 1895), 94.

37. Fitzgerald, *Way Out There in the Blue*, 20–38.

38. Max Weber, "Politics as a Vocation," in *From Max Weber: Essays in Sociology*, ed. H. H. Gerth and C. W. Mills (New York: Oxford University Press, 1946), 77–128.

39. Unless otherwise specified, the quotes and following discussion come from a thorough work of scholarship to which I am greatly indebted, Theodore Draper, *A Very Thin Line: The Iran-Contra Affairs* (New York: Simon & Schuster, 1991).

40. Draper, *Very Thin Line*, 569.

41. Ibid., 219.

42. Ibid., 355; U. House & Senate, *Report on the Congressional Committee Investigating the Iran-Contra Affair* (Washington, DC: Government Printing Office, 1987), 21.

43. Peter Kornbluh and Malcolm Byrne, eds. *The Iran-Contra Scandal: The Declassified History* (New York: New Press, 1993), 190–91.

44. Richard Sobel, "Contra Aid Fundamentals: Exploring the Intricacies of the Issues," *Political Science Review* 110 (1995): 287–306 ; RR to Paul Trousdale, Nov. 14, *RLIL*, 467–68.

45. Draper, *Very Thin Line*, 569.

CHAPTER NINE

1. Barrett, *Gambling with History*, 438.

2. David Gergen, *Eyewitness to Power: The Essence of Leadership: Nixon to Clinton* (New York: Simon & Schuster, 2000), 171.

3. Barrett, *Gambling with History*, 441–54.

4. Quoted in Perlstein, *Before the Storm*, 500.

5. Arthur Schlesinger Jr., *A Thousand Days: John F. Kennedy in the White House* (Boston: Houghton Mifflin, 1965), 717; RR to Marion Foster, Feb. 24, 1987, in *RLIL*, 646–47; I am also indebted to Coleen Shogan, "Modern Presidential Leadership and Ideological Rhetoric: The Story of Silent Cal and the Great Communicator," paper read to the American Political Science Association, Chicago, Sept. 3, 2004.

6. Emerson, "Wealth," in Atkinson, *The Selected Writings of Ralph Waldo Emerson*, 621–41.

7. George P. Shultz, Foreword, *RRSW*, x.

8. Reagan, *An American Life*, 161.

9. Jeffrey Stine, "Natural Resources and Environmental Policy," in *TRP*, 233–58; RR to Laurence W. Beilenson, Sept. 5, 1985, in *RLIL*, 355–56.

10. Schaller, *Reckoning with Reagan*, 102.

11. The pioneer historian of the American West, the great Frederick Jackson Turner, partook of late nineteenth-century individualism when he insisted that the significance of the character of the frontier lay in barn raising, when farmers and cattlemen came together voluntarily to help neighbors erect structures without a government agent in sight. Later, in the twentieth century, the role of government was fully acknowledged, but the pendulum would swing again. See Patricia Nelson Limerick, *The Legacy of Conquest: The Unbroken Past of the American West* (New York: Norton, 1987) and *Under an Open Sky: Rethinking America's Western Past*, ed. William Cronon, George Miles, and Jay Gitlin (New York: Norton, 1992).

12. Cannon, *President Reagan*, 458–59; Hugh Davis Graham, "Civil Rights Policy," *TRP*, 383–92.

13. RR to Ben Hooks, Jan. 12, 1983, in *RLIL*, 337–38.

14. Anne Higgins, special assistant to the president, to Sidney Hook, Jan. 7, 1986, Box 24, HIA.

15. Transportation Secretary Elizabeth Dole was the resource person on affirmative action and the Equal Rights Amendment in the Reagan administration. While administration officials responded respectfully to the conservative antifeminist Phyllis Schlafly, they were impressed by Chester E. Finn's " 'Affirmative Action' Under Reagan," which appeared in April 1982 in *Commentary*. Finn was critical of the administration for backing away from taking clear stands and for allowing a policy of individual opportunity based on the principle of equality to become an identity politics based on group demands. Elizabeth Dole, White House Staff Office Files, Box 6388, RRPL.

16. Graham, "Civil Rights Policy," 385–90.

17. "Roberts Helped to Shape 80's Civil Rights Debates," *New York Times*, Aug. 4, 2005; the article deals with John G. Roberts Jr., George W. Bush's appointment as Chief Justice to the Supreme Court. Roberts had served under Reagan in the office of the attorney general.

18. Otis L. Graham Jr., "Failing the Test: Immigration Reform," *TRP*, 259–82

19. Ken Foskett, *Judging Thomas: The Life and Times of Clarence Thomas* (New York: Morrow, 2004).

20. Hamilton et al., *The Federalist Papers*, 500.

21. Kennedy's speech is quoted in Jeffrey Hart, *The Making of the American Conservative Mind* (Wilmington, DE: ISI Books, 2005), 307.

22. David M. O'Brien, "Federal Judgeships in Retrospect," in *TRP*, 327–54.

23. Quoted in Jane Mayer and Doyle McManus, *Landslide: The Unmaking of the President, 1984–1988* (Boston: Houghton Mifflin, 1988), 16.

24. RR to Mrs. William Loeb, Oct. 26, 1984, in *RLIL*, 562.

25. Morris, *Dutch*, 458.

26. RR to Florence Yerly, Dec. 17, 1951, in *RLIL*, 139–40.

27. RR, "Regulations," Mar. 12, 1975, *RIOH*, 294–95.

28. "Education," White House Staff Office Files, RRPL.

29. Joshua Green, "The Bookie of Virtues: William J. Bennett Made Millions Lectur-

ing People on Virtue—and Blows it on Gambling," *Washington Monthly*, June 2003; Michael Kinsley, "Bill Bennett's Bad Bet," *Slate*, May 4, 2003.

30. John Patrick Diggins, "The National History Standards," *The American Scholar* 65 (Autumn 1996): 495–523.

31. Daniel Patrick Moynihan, *Family and Nation* (New York: Harcourt, 1986), 66.

32. Bruce Bartlett, *Impostor: How George W. Bush Bankrupted America and Betrayed the Reagan Legacy* (New York: Doubleday, 2006).

33. John Patrick Diggins, ed., *The Liberal Persuasion: Essays in Honor of Arthur Schlesinger Jr.* (Princeton: Princeton University Press, 1999); Kevin Mattson, *When America Was Great: The Fighting Faith of Postwar Liberalism* (New York: Routledge, 2004), 104–5.

34. The story of Taylor is recounted by the editors in *RRSW*, 75–76.

35. See the special issue "The Welfare State," *Critical Review* 4 (Fall 1990).

36. Moynihan, *Family and Nation*, 134–35.

37. Gareth Davies, "The Welfare State," *TRP*, 209–32.

38. Durenberger is quoted in ibid., 219; Murray Kempton, *Rebellions, Perversities, and Main Events* (New York: Random House, 1994), 501–22.

39 Deborah Silverman, *Selling Culture: Bloomingdale's, Diane Vreeland, and the New Aristocracy of Taste in Reagan's America* (New York: Pantheon, 1986).

40. RR, Inaugural Address, Jan. 21, 1985, in *PSRR*, 268–87.

41. For Wedtech and the other financial scandals of the era, I am indebted to Schaller, *Reckoning with Reagan*. The White House followed closely the indictments of Edwin Meese and the investigation of Lyn Nofziger. Wedtech Files, WH Staff Office Files, RRPL.

42. Schaller, *Reckoning with Reagan*, 115–17.

43. The quotes and the following statistical data are from Lowell Gallaway and Richard Vedder, "The Distributional Impact of the Eighties: Myth vs. Reality," *Critical Review* 7 (Winter 1993): 61–79.

44. Michael J. Boskin, *Reagan and the Economy: The Successes and Failures of an Unfinished Economy* (San Francisco: ICS Press, 1987).

45. RR, "George Meany and Economics," May 1975, in *RRSW*, 29–31.

46. Alexander Hamilton, "Report on Public Credit," *The Papers of Alexander Hamilton*, 27 vols., ed. Harold C. Syrett (New York: Columbia University Press, 1961–1987), vol. 6, 106.

CHAPTER TEN

1. Cannon, *President Reagan*, 639.

2. On the question of presidential incapacity, see Mayer and McManus, *Landslide*, v, xi.

3. On Gorbachev, Yeltsin, and the fall of communism, see Martin Malia, *The Soviet Tragedy: A History of Socialism in Russia, 1917–1991* (New York: Free Press, 1994); David Remnick, *Lenin's Tomb: The Last Days of the Soviet Empire* (New York: Random House, 1993); David Remnick, *Resurrection: The Struggle for a New Russia* (New York: Random House, 1997); Jack F. Matlock Jr., *Autopsy of an Empire: The American Ambassador's Account of the Collapse of the Soviet Union* (New York: Random House, 1995).

4. Reagan, *An American Life*, 585–86; Watson quoted in Dobrynin, *In Confidence*, 526; "The Day After: Media Relations," Box OA9631, RRPL.

5. The "Able Archer 83" episode and Reagan's reaction are recounted in the valuable article by Jeremi Suri, "Explaining the End of the Cold War: A New Historical Consenus?" *Journal of Cold War Studies* 4 (2002): 60–92; Reagan, *An American Life*, 585–89.

6. Dobrynin, *In Confidence*, 515–16.

7. Ibid., 498.

8. Reagan, *An American Life*, 11–16; "Presidential Address: Joint Session of Congress, Report on Geneva, Nov. 21, 1985; "Memorandum of Conversation: Reagan-Gorbachev Meetings in Geneva," n.d., RRPL.

9. Dobrynin, *In Confidence*, 478; Reagan, *An American Life*, 582–84.

10. William D. Jackson, "Soviet Reassessment of Ronald Reagan, *Political Science Quarterly* 113 (1998–1999): 617–32; Barbara Farnham, "Reagan and the Gorbachev Revolution: Perceiving the End of Threat," *Political Science Quarterly* 116 (2001): 225–52; Beth A. Fisher, "Toeing the Hardline? The Reagan Administration and the Ending of the Cold War," *Political Science Quarterly* 112 (1997), 477–95.

11. RR to President Brezhnev, Sept. 10, 1981; "Memorandum: Alexander Haig to the President, Sept. 18, 1981, RRPL; Farnham, "Reagan and the Gorbachev Revolution," 228–35.

12. Jackson, "Soviet Reassessment," 618–25.

13. Carl von Clausewitz, *On War* (New York: Penguin, 1973), 1; Schell and Talbott are discussed critically in Patrick Glynn's hard line treatment, *Closing Pandora's Box: Arms Race, Arms Control, and the History of the Cold War* (New York: Basic Books, 1992).

14. Reagan's shifting views are taken up in the thoughtful articles by Farnham, "Reagan and the Gorbachev Revolution," and Fischer, "Toeing the Hardline," cited above.

15. George J. Church, "Holding Their Ground," *Time*, Oct. 8, 1984, 12–19.

16. Quoted in Robert D. English, *Russia and the Idea of the West: Gorbachev, Intellectuals and the End of the Cold War* (New York: Columbia University Press, 2000), 205.

17. RR to Charles Burton Marshall, Apr. 8, 1980; RR to Mr. Bob Michael, "circa late Jan. 1980"; RR to the Honorable George Murphy, Dec. 19, 1995; RR to Mr. Roy Innis, June 20, 1983, in *RLIL*, 398–99, 400, 415–16, 424; the definition of power comes from the philosopher Bertrand Russell, *Power* (New York: Barnes & Noble, 1962), 25.

18. Jackson, "Soviet Reassessment," 619–22; Dobrynin, *In Confidence*, 568–69; Reagan, *An American Life*, 550.

19. Max M. Kampelman, "The Ronald Reagan I Knew," *The Weekly Standard*, Nov. 24, 2003, 26–29.

20. Cannon, *President Reagan*, 673; Warren Hoge, "Once Red, 'Mr. Green' [Gorbachev] Is a Hero Anywhere but at Home," *New York Times*, Oct. 23, 2004.

21. Archie Brown, *The Gorbachev Factor* (New York: Oxford University Press, 1996), 24–29.

22. Mikhail Gorbachev, *Memoirs* (New York: Bantam, 1997).

23. Brown, *Gorbachev Factor*, 29–43.

24. Andrew and Mitrokhin, *The World Was Going Our Way*, 414–19.

25. Gorbachev, *Memoirs*, 260–71; Cannon, *President Reagan*, 675–77.

26. Jack F. Matlock Jr., *Reagan and Gorbachev: How the Cold War Ended* (New York: Random House, 2004), 182–83.

27. Cannon, *President Reagan*, 675.

28. Matlock, *Reagan and Gorbachev*, 154; Cannon, *President Reagan*, 674.

29. Stephen Sestanovich mss., handwritten notes, n.d., Box 90917, RRPL.

30. Cannon, *President Reagan*, 677.

31. Matlock, *Reagan and Gorbachev*, 164.

32. Hugh Thomas, *Armed Truce: The Beginnings of the Cold War* (New York: Atheneum, 1987); "President Reagan's Summit Meeting: Briefing Book, The Heritage Foundation," RRPL; Diggins, *Mussolini and Fascism*.

33. "Presidential Address, Joint Session of the Congress Report on Geneva"; RR to Mikhail Gorbachev, Mar. 11, 1985; "Meeting with the New General Secretary: Suggested Talking Points, Mar. 11, 1985; "The President's People-to-People Initiatives," Nov. 21, 1985, RRPL.

34. Cannon, *President Reagan*, 506.

35. On the historical controversy, see Furet and Nolte, *Fascisme et communisme*; Charles S. Maier, *The Unmasterable: Past History, Holocaust, and German Nation Identity* (Cambridge. Harvard University Press, 1988); Martin Malia, "Judging Nazism and Communism," *The National Interest*, 69 (Fall 2002): 63–78; Nolte's observation that the Gulag was "more original" than Auschwitz is discussed in Paul Ricoeur, *La Mémoire, L'Histoire, L'Oubli* (Paris: Seuil, 2003), 427–32.

36. Cannon, *President Reagan*, 507.

37. RR to Jesse A. Zeeman, Apr. 23, 1985, in *RLIL*, 537–38.

38. Cannon, *President Reagan*, 507–20.

39. RR on "the evil war of Nazism," in *RLIL*, 537; RR to Jesse A. Zeeman, Apr. 23, 1985, *RLIL*, 537–38; Reagan, *An American Life*, 378; Cannon, *President Reagan*, 510.

40. The United States Information Service kept the White House informed of European press opinion. USIS, "Prelude to Bonn Summitt: Bitburg Controversy," Memorandum, John F. Kordek, RRPL.

41. Alain Finkielkraut, *L'humanité Perdue. Essai sur le XX Siècle* (Paris: Seuil, 1996), 77–78.

42. Senate resolution quoted in Shultz, *Turmoil and Triumph*, 631.

43. Ibid., 624.

44. Ibid., 611, 624.

45. Mikhail Gorbachev and Zdeněk Mlynář, *Conversations with Gorbachev* (New York: Columbia University Press, 2002), 151; speechwriter Dolan is quoted in Abbot Gleason, *Totalitarianism: The Inner History of the Cold War* (New York: Oxford University Press, 1995), 197.

46. Freedman, "First Two Generations of Nuclear Strategists," 735–78.

47. Alain Frachan and Daniel Vernet, "Albert Wohlstetter: Le Stratège du mont Olympe," *Commentaire* 27 (Fall 2004), 667–74.

48. Morris, *Dutch*, 586.

49. David Hoffman, "I Had a Funny Feeling in My Gut!," *Washington Post*, Feb. 10, 1999.

50. RR to Mikhail Gorbachev, May 23, 1986; "Soviet Note Delivered," June 1, 1986, RRPL; Morris, *Dutch*, 587; Brown, *Gorbachev Factor*, 189, 231.

51. Cannon, *President Reagan*, 686; Buchanan's attitude was described by Cannon in a television interview with Steve Wasserman, book review editor of the *Los Angeles Times*.

52. Morris, *Dutch*, 601; Shultz, *Turmoil and Triumph*, 751–80.

53. Shultz, *Turmoil and Triumph*, 589; Fitzgerald, *Way Out There in the Blue*, 500.

54. Cannon, *President Reagan*, 683; Shultz, *Turmoil and Triumph*, 761.

55. Cannon, *President Reagan*, 688–90; Shultz, *Turmoil and Triumph*, 773.

56. Matlock, *Reagan and Gorbachev*, 212.

57. Gorbachev quoted in English, *Russia and the Idea of the West*, 219.

58. Cannon, *President Reagan*, 694–703; Shultz, *Turmoil and Triumph*, 1008.

59. Cannon, *President Reagan*, 697; Shultz, *Turmoil and Triumph*, 1001–11.

60. Jussi Hanhimaki, *The Flawed Architect: Henry Kissinger and American Foreign Policy* (New York: Oxford University Press, 2004); Hedrick Smith, "The Right Against Reagan," *New York Times Magazine*, Jan. 17, 1988; Lars-Erik Nelson, "Fantasia," *New York Review of Books*, May 11, 2000, 4–7; Dorrien, *Imperial Designs*.

61. RR to Lt. General Victor H. Krulak, Mar. 3, 1987; RR to William F. Buckley Jr., May 5, 1987, in *RLIL*, 417–19.

62. RR to Dr. Gerald B. Broussard, Feb. 15, 1988, in *RLIL*, 421–22; Gorbachev and Mlynář, *Conversations with Gorbachev*, 138–39.

63. RR to Laurence W. Beilenson, Aug. 1, 1986, *RLIL*, 428; "Remarks to the National Chamber Foundation," Nov. 17, 1988, *TQRR*, 217.

64. Matlock, *Reagan and Gorbachev*, 156.

65. Matlock, *Autopsy of an Empire*, 620.

66. RR, Speech to the Republican National Convention, Aug. 17, 1992, in *PSRR*, 330–32.

67. Thomas Carlyle, *On Heroes, Hero-Worship, and the Heroic in History* (1841; Lincoln: University of Nebraska Press, 1966), 216–17.

68. Cannon, *President Reagan*, 694–95.

69. Matlock, *Reagan and Gorbachev*, 298–99.

70. Shultz, *Turmoil and Triumph*, 1104.

71. Henry Adams, *The Education of Henry Adams*, in *Henry Adams* (New York: Library of America, 1983), 1094.

72. Cannon, *President Reagan*, 706–7; Emerson, "Self-Reliance," in Atkinson, *Selected Writings of Ralph Waldo Emerson*, 132–53.

73. Canon, *President Reagan*, 707; Matlock, *Reagan and Gorbachev*, 302.

74. RR to the Honorable George Murphy, July 8, 1988, in *RLIL*, 387.

75. Adams, *Education*, 1096.

76. Brown, *Gorbachev Factor*, xiii–xv, 106–29.

77. RR, "Remarks to U.S. League of Savings Association, Nov. 14, 1974, *TQRR*, 139.

78. Edmund Burke, *Reflections on the Revolution in France* (New York: Penguin, 1983), 150–51.

79. Ibid., 355; Peter Reddaway and Dmitri Glinski, *The Tragedy of Russia's Reforms: Market Bolshevism Against Democracy* (Washington, DC: United States Institute of Peace Press, 2001).

CHAPTER ELEVEN

1. This astute observation is quoted in Morris, *Dutch*, 661.

2. George Kennan, *Russia and the West Under Lenin and Stalin* (New York: New American Library, 1960), 372.

3. Lee Edwards, *The Conservative Revolution: The Movement That Remade America* (New York: Free Press, 1999), 242.

4. Bush is quoted in Eric F. Petersen, "The End of the Cold War: A Review of Recent Literature," *History Teacher* 26 (Aug. 1993): 471–85.

5. Thomas Risse-Kappen, "Did 'Peace Through Strength' End the Cold War?," *Inter-*

national Security 16 (Summer 1991): 172–74; the literature on this subject is vast and controversial, as indicated in the essay by Petersen, cited above.

6. Reinhold Niebuhr, *Moral Man and Immoral Society* (New York: Scribner, 1932); Niebuhr, *Irony of American History*, 130–50.

7. Matthew 19:21.

8. Emerson, "Self-Reliance," in Atkinson, *Selected Writings of Ralph Waldo Emerson*, 132–53.

9. The debate over Emerson between Bloom and others is discussed in Stanley Cavell, *Conditions Handsome and Unhandsome: The Constitution of Emersonian Perfectionism* (Chicago: University of Chicago Press, 1990), 129–38.

10. William F. Buckley Jr., "A Hero of the Reagan Revolution," in *Let Us Talk of Many Things* (Roseville, CA: Forum Press, 2000), 337–38.

11. The advertisement for Bloom's book is quoted in F. Russel Hittinger, "Reason and Anti-Reason in the Academy," *The Intercollegiate Review* 23 (Fall 1987): 61–64.

12. Richard Rorty, *Objectivity, Relativism, and Truth: Philosophical Papers*, vol. 1 (New York: Cambridge University Press, 1991), 203.

13. Quoted in Gil Troy, *Morning in America: How Reagan Invented the 1980s* (Princeton: Princeton University Press, 2005), 229.

14. RR to Sidney Hook, Oct. 28, 1982, Hook Papers, Box 24, HIA.

15. RR to Sidney Hook (cited above); Sidney Hook, "The Making of a Best-Seller," *The American Scholar* 58 (Winter 1989): 123–35; William F. Buckley Jr. to Sidney Hook, Aug. 1, 1988; Daniel Bell to Sidney Hook, Oct. 20, 1988, Hook Papers, HIA.

16. M. I. Finley, Introduction to Thucydides, *History of the Peloponnesian War*, trans. Rex Warner (New York: Penguin, 1954), 25; Thucydides, *On Justice, Power, and Human Nature*, trans. Paul Woodruff (Indianapolis: Hackett, 1993), 108; Hannah Arendt, *The Promise of Politics*, ed. Jean Cohen (New York: Schocken, 2005), 23–45.

17. Henry Kissinger, *Diplomacy* (New York: Simon & Schuster, 1994), 762–803.

A CODA

1. Thucydides, *History of the Peloponnesian War*, trans. Warner, 81–82.

2. RR, "Republican National Convention," Aug. 17, 1992, *PSRR*, 330–35.

3. Quoted in Hook, *Marxism and Beyond*, 135.

4. Hugh Sidney, "We're Still Jefferson's Children," *Time*, July 13, 1987, 14.

5. A popular saying among the Russian people, quoted in Malia, *Soviet Tragedy*, 510.

6. Gorbachev quoted in Robert V. Daniels, *The End of the Communist Revolution* (New York: Routledge, 1993), 165.

7. *TQRR*, 61; Gorbachev and Mlynář, *Conversations with Gorbachev*, 160.

8. Gorbachev and Mlynář, *Conversations with Gorbachev*, 129.

9. RR to Leonid Brezhnev, Apr. 18, 1981; RR to Mikhail Gorbachev, Nov. 28, 1985, in *RLIL*, 741–46.

10. Gorbachev and Mlynář, *Conversations with Gorbachev*, 37; on the Soviet archives, see Vladislav Zubok and Constantine Pleshakov, *Inside the Kremlin's Cold War: From Stalin to Khrushchev* (Cambridge: Harvard University. Press, 1996); Andrew and Mitrokhin, *The World Was Going Our Way*.

11. Thorton Stringfellow, "A Scriptural View of Slavery," in *Slavery Defended: The Views of the Old South*, ed. Eric McKitrick (Englewood Cliffs, NJ: Prentice-Hall, 1963), 86–98.

12. Daniel Bell, *The End of Ideology* (New York: Free Press, 1960); an earlier critique of Marxism as a supernatural illusion offered up as naturalistic materialism is Max Eastman, *Marxism: Is It Science?* (New York: Norton, 1940).

13. Karl Marx, "Economic and Philosophical Manuscripts of 1844," in *The Marx-Engels Reader*, 84.

14. Abraham Lincoln to Albert G. Hodges, Apr. 4, 1864, in *Abraham Lincoln: Selected Speeches and Writings*, 2 vols. (New York: Library of America, 1989), II, 585–86.

15. "Presidential Remarks: Toast at Dinner hosted by the Soviets," Nov. 19, 1985, RRPL; "History," *TQRR*, 152.

Bibliographical Note

The literature on Ronald Reagan, on his personal life, his movie career, and his many significant political engagements, is substantial and growing. The most comprehensive and judicially balanced study is Lou Cannon, *President Reagan: The Role of a Lifetime* (New York: Public Affairs, 2000). Edmund Morris's *Dutch: A Memoir of Ronald Reagan* (New York: Random House, 1999), although filled with authorial impositions and digressions, contains important insights on Reagan's character. Richard Reeves's *President Reagan: The Triumph of Imagination* (New York: Simon & Schuster, 2005) is a vivid account of Reagan's presidential years by a journalist with an eye for telling detail. Garry Wills's *Reagan's America: Innocents at Home* (New York: Doubleday, 1987), while conveying an aversion to capitalist individualism and an impatience with cold war anticommunism, offers a witty narrative with uncanny perceptions. The way Reagan polarized those writing about him is apparent in Michael Rogin, *Ronald Reagan, The Movie: And Other Episodes of Political Demonology* (Berkeley: University of California Press, 1987), and Haynes Johnson, *Sleepwalking Through History: America in the Reagan Years* (New York: Anchor Books, 1992), both hostile to their subject; and Dinesh D'Souza, *Ronald Reagan: How an Ordinary Man Became an Extraordinary Leader* (New York: Free Press, 1997), and Peggy Noonan, *When Character Was King: A Story of Ronald Reagan* (New York: Viking, 2001), both laudatory; and Paul Kengor, *God and Ronald Reagan: A Spiritual Life* (New York: HarperCollins, 2004), worshipful.

For Reagan's pre-presidential political career, see Lou Cannon, *Governor Reagan: His Rise to Power* (New York: Public Affairs, 2003); Matthew Dallek, *The Right Moment: Ronald Reagan's First Victory and the Decisive Turning Point in American Politics* (New York: Free Press, 2000); W. J. Rorabaugh, *Berkeley at War: The 1960s* (Berkeley: University of California Press, 1989); Craig Shirley, *Reagan's Revolution: The Untold Story of the Campaign That Started It All* (Nashville, TN: Nelson Current, 2005); and Steven F. Hayward, *The Age of Reagan, 1964–1980: The Fall of the Old Liberal Order* (New York: Forum, 2001).

Valuable portraits of Reagan's family background and his early life in Hollywood, as well as his marriages and relationship to his wives and children, may be found in Anne Edwards, *Early Reagan: The Rise to Power* (New York: Morrow, 1987), and Bob Colacello, *Ronnie & Nancy: Their Path to the White House, 1911–1980* (New York: Warner Books, 2004); see also Patti Davis's sensitive memoir, *The Long Goodbye* (New York: Knopf, 2004).

At a recent conference on the Reagan years, hosted by the Rothermere American Institute at Oxford University (November 10–12, 2005), the old crack that Reagan was nothing more than "an amiable dunce" (Clark Clifford) was mumbled now and then from the audience, only to be challenged by many of the panelists and plenary speakers. Those who assume that Reagan was old and tired and walked in his sleep through his political years should read his personal letters, public speeches, and radio talk transcripts. They can be found in *Reagan: A Life in Letters*, edited by Kiron K. Skinner, Annelise Anderson, and Martin Anderson (New York: Free Press, 2003); *Reagan, In His Own Hand*, also edited by Skinner, Anderson, and Anderson (New York: Free Press, 2001); *Actor, Ideologue, Politician: The Public Speeches of Ronald Reagan*, edited by Davis W. Houck and Amos Kiewe (Westport CT: Greenwood, 1993); and *Reagan's Path to Victory: The Shaping of Ronald Reagan's Vision*, edited by Skinner, Anderson, and Anderson (New York: Free Press, 2004).

The memoirs by Reagan and those relating to his political life are invaluable. Ronald Reagan, *An American Life* (New York: Simon & Schuster, 1990) is familiar to readers of Reagan, but his first memoir, Ronald Reagan and Richard G. Hubler, *Where's the Rest of Me? The Ronald Reagan Story* (New York: Duell, Sloan and Pearce, 1965), is more detailed about Hollywood life and the communist controversy. Other memoirs that are worth consulting are Martin Anderson, *Revolution: The Reagan Legacy* (Stanford: Hoover Institute Press, 1990); Whittaker Chambers, *Witness* (New York: Random House, 1952); Michael K. Deaver, *A Different Drummer: My Thirty Years with Ronald Reagan* (New York: HarperCollins, 2001); Anatoly Dobrynin, *In Confidence: Moscow's Ambassador to America's Six Cold War Presidents, 1962–1986* (New York: Times Books, 1995); Robert M. Gates, *From the Shadows: The Ultimate Insider's Story of Five Presidents and How They Won the Cold War* (New York: Touchstone Books, 1997); Mikhail Gorbachev, *Memoirs* (New York: Doubleday, 1994); Richard Pipes, *Vixi: Memoirs of a Non-Belonger* (New Haven: Yale University Press, 2003); George P. Shultz, *Turmoil and Triumph: My Years as Secretary of State* (New York: Scribner, 1993); Margaret Thatcher, *The Downing Street Years* (New York: HarperCollins, 1993); Henry Kissinger, *Diplomacy* (New York: Simon & Schuster, 1994); and Caspar Weinberger, *Fighting for Peace: Seven Critical Years in the Pentagon* (London: Michael Joseph, 1990).

More than eighty percent of the materials in the Ronald Reagan Presidential Library, at Simi Valley, California, remains classified. Only documents that have been "FOIAed" are accessible, and it took me several minutes to figure out that the librarian meant those made available by requests through the Freedom of Information Act. Fortunately, the Soviet archives have been opening up in recent years, and the following texts reveal much about the cold war and secret spy activity: John Earl Haynes and Harvey Klehr, *Venona: Decoding Soviet Espionage in America* (New Haven: Yale University Press, 1999); Harvey Klehr, John Earl Haynes, and Fridrikh Igorevich Firsov, *The Secret World of American Communism* (New Haven: Yale University Press, 1995); Christopher Andrew and Oleg Gordievsky, *KGB: The Inside Story of Its Foreign Operations from Lenin to Gorbachev* (London; Hodder and Stoughton, 1990); Christopher Andrew and Vasili Mitrokhin, *The Sword and the Shield: The Mitrokhin Archive and the Secret History of the KGB* (New York: Basic Books, 1999); Christopher Andrew and Vasilini Mitrokhin, *The World Was Going Our Way: The KGB and the Battle for the Third World* (New York: Basic Books, 2005); and Vladislav Zubok and Constantine Pleshakov, *Inside the Kremlin's Cold War: From Stalin to Khrushchev* (Cambridge: Harvard University Press, 1996).

Scholarship on the cold war and the fall of communism is as rich as it is controversial, dividing those who believed that the Soviet Union was on the road to reform and those who believed its total collapse was inevitable. The former view is held by Jerry F. Hough, *Russia and the West: Gorbachev and the Politics of Reform* (New York: Simon & Schuster, 1988), and Moshe Lewin, *The Gorbachev Phenomenon: A Historical Interpretation* (Berkeley: University of California Press, 1988). It is challenged by Martin Malia, *The Soviet Tragedy: A History of Socialism in Russia, 1917–1991* (New York: Free Press, 1994). The conservative view that Reagan forced the Soviets to succumb by virtue of America's overwhelming economic and military strength is in Peter Schweizer, *Reagan's War: The Epic Story of His Forty-Year Struggle and Final Triumph Over Communism* (New York: Doubleday, 2002) and his *Victory: The Reagan's Administration's Secret Strategy That Hastened the Collapse of the Soviet Union* (New York: Atlantic Monthly Press, 1994). More balanced and discerning, because the authors see things from the point of view of America's antagonist, are Archie Brown, *The Gorbachev Factor* (New York: Oxford, 1996); Jack F. Matlock Jr., *Autopsy on an Empire: The American Ambassador's Account of the Collapse of the Soviet Union* (New York: Random House, 1995); David Remnick, *Lenin's Tomb: The Last Days of the Soviet Empire* (New York: Random House, 1993); Lawrence Freedman, *The Evolution of Nuclear Strategy* (London: Macmillan, 1989); and John Lewis Gaddis, *The United States and the End of the Cold War: Implications, Reconsiderations, Provocations* (New York: Oxford, 1992). A chronicle of Reagan's lifelong aversion to war is Paul Lettow, *Ronald Reagan and His Quest to Abolish Nuclear Weapons* (New York: Random House, 2005). Priceless is the latest book by Ambassador Jack F. Matlock Jr., *Reagan and Gorbachev: How the Cold War Ended* (New York: Random House, 2004).

Reagan's battle with the cold war in the third world is dealt with in two thoroughly researched texts; Steve Coll's *Ghost Wars: The Secret History of the CIA, Afghanistan, and Bin Laden, from the Soviet Invasion to September 10, 2001* (New York: Penguin, 2004); and Robert Kagan, *A Twilight Struggle: American Power and Nicaragua, 1977–1990* (New York: Free Press, 1996). On the complexities of Angola, see Bernard-Henri Lévy, *Réflexions sur la Guerre le mal et la de l'Histoire* (Paris: Grasset, 2001), and Piero Gleijeses, *Conflicting Missions: Havana, Washington, and Africa* (Chapel Hill: University of North Carolina Press, 2002).

Books written by journalists and academics deserve attention. The first two off the press were the Swiftian treatment by Robert Scheer, *With Enough Shovels: Reagan, Bush, and Nuclear War* (New York: Random House, 1982), and the astute account by Laurence I. Barrett, *Gambling With History: Ronald Reagan in the White House* (Garden City, NY: Doubleday, 1983). Also valuable are Robert Dallek, *Ronald Reagan: The Politics of Symbolism*, with its new preface (Cambridge: Harvard University Press, 1999); Frances Fitzgerald, *Way Out There in the Blue: Reagan, Star Wars, and the End of the Cold War* (New York: Simon & Schuster, 2000); Michael Schaller, *Reckoning with Reagan: America and Its President in the 1980s* (New York: Oxford, 1992); and John Ehrman, *The Eighties: America in the Age of Reagan* (New Haven: Yale University Press, 2005). A particularly important collection of scholarly essays is *The Reagan Presidency: Pragmatism, Conservatism, and Its Legacies*, edited by W. Elliot Brownlee and Hugh Davis Graham (Lawrence: University of Kansas Press, 2003).

Reagan's politics in his early film career is dealt with in Stephen Vaughn, *Ronald Reagan in Hollywood: Movies and Politics* (New York: Cambridge University Press, 1994). Valuable for the many interviews is Ronald Radosh and Allis Radosh, *Red Star Over Hollywood: The Film Colony's Long Romance with the Left* (New York: Encounter, 2005); for a judicious overview, see Larry Ceplair and Steven Englund, *The Inquisition in Hollywood: Politics in the Film Community, 1930–1960* (Berkeley: University of California Press, 1980). Reagan's testimony before HUAC can be found in *Thirty Years of Treason: Excerpts from Hearings before the House Committee on Un-American Activities, 1938–1968*, edited by Eric Bentley (1971; New York: Nation Books, 2002).

The alleged "false consciousness" of elegant wastefulness of the era is dealt with in Debora Silverman, *Selling Culture: Bloomingdale's, Diana Vreeland, and the New Aristocracy of Taste in Reagan's America* (New York: Pantheon, 1986). A biting, though discerning, cultural history of the decade is Gil Troy, *Morning in America: How Reagan Invented the 1980s* (Princeton: Princeton University Press, 2005).

On Reagonomics and other domestic issues, see David Stockman, *Triumph of Politics: Why the Reagan Revolution Failed* (New York: Harper & Row, 1986); John W. Sloane, *The Reagan Effect: Economics and Presidential Leadership* (Lawrence: University Press of Kansas, 1999); and

Michael J. Boskin, *Reagan and the Economy: The Successes, Failures and Unfinished Agenda* (San Francisco: ICS Press, 1987). The learned countervoice to the Reagan administration may be found in Daniel Patrick Moynihan, *Came the Revolution: Argument in the Reagan Era* (New York: Harcourt, 1988).

The literature on the neoconservatives as an intellectual phenomenon is vast. The best place to begin is the comprehensive survey by George Nash, *The Conservative Intellectual Movement in America* (1975; Washington DC: Intercollegiate Studies Institute, 1996); see also Jeffrey Hart, *The Making of the American Conservative Mind: National Review and Its Times* (Wilmington, DE: ISI Books, 2005). For antecedents to Reagan's cold war intellectual advisors, see John P. Diggins, *Up from Communism: Conservative Odysseys in American Intellectual History* (1975; New York: Columbia University Press, 1997). For the consequences, see Richard Gid Powers, *Not Without Honor: The History of American Anticommunism* (New Haven: Yale University Press, 1998); James Mann, *Rise of the Vulcans: The History of Bush's War Cabinet* (New York: Viking, 2004); and Stefan Halper and Jonathan Clarke, *America Alone: The Neo-Conservatives and the Global Order* (New York: Cambridge University Press, 2004).

Photograph Credits

Index